ON LOUIS SIMPSON

UNDER DISCUSSION
Donald Hall, General Editor

Elizabeth Bishop and Her Art
  edited by Lloyd Schwartz and Sybil P. Estess

Richard Wilbur's Creation
  edited and with an Introduction by Wendy Salinger

Reading Adrienne Rich
  edited by Jane Roberta Cooper

On the Poetry of Allen Ginsberg
  edited by Lewis Hyde

Robert Bly: When Sleepers Awake
  edited by Joyce Peseroff

Robert Creeley's Life and Work
  edited by John Wilson

On the Poetry of Galway Kinnell
  edited by Howard Nelson

On Louis Simpson
  edited by Hank Lazer

On Louis Simpson
Depths Beyond Happiness

Edited by Hank Lazer

Ann Arbor
THE UNIVERSITY OF MICHIGAN PRESS

For Jane, Julie, and Gus

Copyright © by the University of Michigan 1988
All rights reserved
Published in the United States of America by
The University of Michigan Press
Manufactured in the United States of America

1991   1990   1989   1988   4   3   2   1

Library of Congress Cataloging-in-Publication Data

On Louis Simpson : depths beyond happiness / edited by Hank Lazer.
    p.   cm.
  Includes bibliographies and index.
  ISBN 0-472-09382-7 (alk. paper)   ISBN 0-472-06382-0
  (pbk. : alk. paper)
  1. Simpson, Louis Aston Marantz, 1923–   —Criticism and
interpretation.   I. Lazer, Hank.
PS3537.I75Z85   1988
811'.54—dc19   88-5753
                                                            CIP
                                                            AC

Contents

Introduction   1

Part One   Reviews

Works Reviewed in This Section   24

From "A Sampling of Pound and Modern Man"   25
GERARD PREVIN MEYER

From "Poetry, Unlimited"   27
RANDALL JARRELL

Letter to Louis Simpson   28
RANDALL JARRELL

From "Three Lyric Voices"   30
JOHN CIARDI

From "Nine New Poets"   31
WILLIAM ARROWSMITH

Coming Up: The New Poets   34
PAUL ENGLE

Verse   36
LOUISE BOGAN

From "Excellence and Variety"   39
THOM GUNN

From "The Anguish of the Spirit and the Letter"   42
ANTHONY HECHT

From "New Poetry: Prizewinners and Apprentices"   45
PETER DAVISON

From "Between New Voice and Old Master"   47
DANIEL HOFFMAN

Riverside Drive   50
JOHN K. HUTCHENS

This Week in Fiction   52
DICK WICKENDEN

From "Modes of Control"   54
THOM GUNN

From "From the Dreamcoast"   57
THOMAS MCGRATH

From "Terminations, Revelations"   61
WILLIAM STAFFORD

New Directions in Poetry: The Work of Louis Simpson   63
DUANE LOCKE

From "Time of Heterogeneity: A Chronicle of Fifteen"   66
RONALD MORAN

From "Transatlantic Poetry"   68
MARTIN SEYMOUR-SMITH

From "New World Poetry"   69

From "Uncharted Waters"   73
DONALD HALL

From "Orientations"   75
JAMES DICKEY

Classicists All   77
KARL SHAPIRO

Blood Brothers   80
SEAMUS HEANEY

From "Origins and Ancestors"   83
IAN HAMILTON

From "Reviews and Comments"   85
GREVEL LINDOP

From "New Poetry"   87
TERRY EAGLETON

From "Losses in Ceremonial Light"   89
DAVE SMITH

From "Academe and Open Air"   91
CYRIL CONNOLLY

Wanderings of a Lazarus   94
WEBSTER SCHOTT

The Private I   97
JAMES BOATWRIGHT

One of Life's Foot-Soldiers   101
ANTHONY RUDOLF

Pillars of the Church   106
RICHARD D. LINGEMAN

Critical Biographies   110
    L. S. DEMBO

Poetry and Its Genesis in the Twentieth Century   112
    MARK NEPO

In the Second Voice   117
    PETER STITT

Showing a Story   120
    STANLEY PLUMLY

Editorial   124
    C. B. COX

American Poetry Restored   125
    PAUL ZWEIG

The Discovery of a Voice   131
    TOM PAULIN

From "Three Poets"   137
    PAUL BRESLIN

From "Seven Poets"   141
    G. E. MURRAY

Poetry of Inclusion   143
    DOUGLAS DUNN

Caviare   147
    PETER MAKUCK

From "Living in the World"   156
    WILLIAM SCAMMELL

The Poet of the 5:51   158
    RICHARD TILLINGHAST

We're All in the Same Boat   162
    ALAN WILLIAMSON

Innocence Betrayed   166
    M. L. ROSENTHAL

Facing the World   170
    RICHARD SILBERG

Part Two   Essays

The Poetry of Louis Simpson   173
    YOHMA GRAY

The Poetry of Louis Simpson   193
    C. B. COX

The Hunger in My Vitals Is for Some Credible
Extravaganza   209
    RICHARD HOWARD

The Image of "America" in the California/Whitman
Poems of Louis Simpson   233
    RONALD MORAN

The Work of Louis Simpson   245
    ROBERT BLY

A Child of the World   258
    DAVE SMITH

Louis Simpson and Walt Whitman: Destroying the
Teacher   275
    HANK LAZER

Child of This World   303
    R. W. FLINT

"I Might Live Here Myself": On Louis Simpson   320
    DAVID WOJAHN

Revising the Poetry Wars: Louis Simpson's Assault on
the Poetic   334
    T. R. HUMMER

Louis Simpson: In Search of the American Self   347
    PETER STITT

Conclusion

Louis Simpson, Poet   391
    MICHAEL MILBURN

Index   393

Introduction

What then do I want?
A life in which there are depths
beyond happiness.
                              —*"Why Do You Write About Russia?"*

This book is intended for readers who wish to see what others have said about Louis Simpson's poetry and for writers who may be about to make their own contribution to the criticism of Simpson's work. I believe that the chronological order has an added benefit: a reading of these reviews and essays may aid the reader, indirectly, in acquiring a sense of recent American literary history. Over the nearly forty years of reviews and essays included in this book, the reader can see shifts in critical assumptions, and major changes in poetics, aesthetics, and literary politics. But the main purpose is to present the unfolding of reactions to Simpson's poetry, so that we can understand how he has become "a writer who now has every reason to call himself an American classic."

Louis Simpson has published eight volumes of poetry, two collections of "selected poems," a novel, and autobiography, three books of criticism, and two collections of informal criticism (reviews, addresses, interviews, and essays); coedited an important anthology of English and American poetry; and recently completed a third edition of his textbook, *An Introduction to Poetry*. He has also published, though not in book form, short stories, plays, and translations of poetry. *On Louis Simpson* includes essays and reviews about all of Simpson's book publications except *James Hogg: A Critical Study* and *An Introduction to Poetry,* the former because it reveals very little about Simpson's own poetic practice, the latter, which I treat later in this introduction, because I have been unable to locate any substantial reviews of it.

In 1949 Simpson published *The Arrivistes: Poems 1940–1949*, his first book of poetry. Simpson had the book printed himself in Paris and distributed by Fine Editions Press in New York. *The Arrivistes* had eleven reviews, a remarkable response for a first book. There were reviews in the *Nation* (Rolfe Humphries), the *Saturday Review*, the *New York Times Book Review*, the *New York Herald Tribune Book Review*, the *Yale Review*, and the *Partisan Review* (Randall Jarrell). In his introduction to *Louis Simpson: A Reference Guide*, William Roberson observes that the response to *The Arrivistes* "was diverse, with reactions to the poetry ranging from 'among the best written by anyone under thirty,' to 'meretricious doggerel.'" It was evident then, Roberson observes, that "few would remain neutral to Simpson's work." Gerard Previn Meyer, writing in the *Saturday Review*, observed that Simpson's poems "are dramatic in essence" and that the poet writes about his experiences "with controlled irony." I call attention to these observations since form and tone, especially tone, will become matters of controversy in the reading of Simpson's work. Randall Jarrell gave Simpson's first book a mixed blessing, saying "There isn't a good poem in *The Arrivistes*, but Louis Simpson is as promising a new poet as I've read in some time." Publicly, Jarrell warned Simpson not to listen to critics, but in a subsequent letter he admitted that "in the long run you benefit from them." The most comical misreading of Simpson's first book came from Babette Deutsch, writing for the *Yale Review*, who assumed that since Simpson was born and raised in Jamaica, he must be black. She urged him to learn from Villon for, according to Deutsch, Simpson failed to distinguish between vulgarity and a "healthy coarseness." In these and other reviews of his early writing, Simpson was praised for his technical accomplishments and ironic tone.

Simpson's second book of poetry, *Good News of Death and Other Poems* (1955), was read by John Ciardi as "a mannered poetry, a poetry of control." Again, reviews tended to emphasize Simpson's technical skill. William Arrowsmith, writing in the *Hudson Review*, singled out Simpson's poems for praise as the most promising under review (books by John Ashbery and Donald Hall were also included in the review). Arrowsmith's review is the first substantial, perceptive assessment of Simpson's writing. His observations remain valuable thirty years later, and they are worth considering for all of Simpson's poems. Arrowsmith called Simpson "deeply traditionalist in his temptations" and "a near master of rhetoric." The review concentrates on several crucial observations about Simpson's poetic disposition. Nearly twenty years before the major characters of Simpson's poems became figures of the "common life," Arrowsmith acclaimed Simpson's "concern, pity, wit and passion for the common condition." Furthermore, his focus is clear and accurate: "The central word for Mr. Simpson's poetry seems to me 'dramatic.'" In remarks that are perhaps even more applicable to Simpson's work of the past twenty years, Arrowsmith praised Simpson for drama drawn from "his sure knowledge of juxtapositions" and "the remarkable impression of power diffused over a poem, not concentrated on a single line."

Good News of Death appeared with collections of poetry by Robert Pack and Norma Farber in the second volume of Scribner's Poets of Today series. Again the critical response was remarkable. Poets of Today II was reviewed in the *Nation* (Ciardi), *Harper's* (Jarrell), the *New Republic, Hudson Review* (Arrowsmith), *American Scholar* (Hazard Adams), *Partisan Review,* and *Poetry* (Mona Van Duyn).

In 1957, Simpson, with Donald Hall and Robert Pack, co-edited *The New Poets of England and America,* an important book in the anthology wars of the fifties and early sixties, when critical descriptions tended to polarize poetry around the axes of Beat and Academic. Paul Engle praised *The New Poets* as "a daring and useful venture." He also noted a tremendous shift in emphasis: "These poems are astonishingly unpolitical. Twenty years ago the young poets would have been immersed in the social issues of the day. But these poets are concerned with the individual almost apart from society." Engle identified an emphasis on craft among the poets of *The New Poets,* whose writing was in keeping with the standards advocated by Eliot, the New Critics, and others. According to Engle, these were poets concerned primarily "with making the poem well" and marked by "almost a complete return to solidity of stanza, rhyme, and meter." From Engle's perspective, the anthology reads as an almost complete repudiation of William Carlos Williams's free-verse direction in American poetry. Louise Bogan concurred: "The poets of the youngest generation have come to realize, it seems, that form must be experienced and understood before it can be eliminated or tampered with." In this anthology of forty-six men and six women, ranging in age from twenty-two to forty years in age, all of whom (with one or two exceptions) wrote in form, Bogan saw a revival of the lyric, "but of the renovated, enlarged, and dramatic kind that has risen, phoenix-like, from the ashes of exhausted nineteenth-century song." While Donald Allen's anthology, *The New American Poetry* (1960), would present another, equally vital strand of American poetry, *The New Poets of England and America* consolidated the apolitical, formally traditional verse of Simpson and his contemporaries.

With *A Dream of Governors* in 1959, published early in Wesleyan University Press's impressive poetry series, Simpson consolidated his achievement as a poet of carefully crafted, intelligent, ironic formal verse. While Thom Gunn called *A Dream of Governors* "a brilliant book," he also introduced an important shift in the reading of Simpson's poetry: the poet/critic begins to feel uncomfortable with Simpson's accomplished technique. Gunn saw Simpson's chief temptation as "decoration for its own sake." He identified the other main danger of Simpson's poetry as the lure of didacticism. Peter Davison pronounced Simpson's writing "some of the best traditional verse being written by a young American poet today," noting too Simpson's attention to narrative, a direction that will become increasingly important to his poetry. Anthony Hecht remarked upon the great range of Simpson's subject matter, saying that Simpson "covers more ground, geographically, historically, and mythically, than almost any young poet writing today, and without in any sense being a 'War Poet' he has written the best poems to come out of the Second World War." While Daniel Hoffman praised Simpson for modernizing myths "to ironic advantage," he and Thom Gunn had sharply critical words for "The Runner," a thirty-page narrative poem. Both suggested that this story would be better told as prose fiction.

With *Riverside Drive* in 1962, the poet tried his hand at prose fiction, a venture that received qualified praise. Reviewers found that the qualities of Simpson's poetry were present in his prose.

"*Riverside Drive,*" said Dick Wickenden, " is basically a somewhat wry and melancholy work. But it is completely honest and its total effect is exhilarating."

In 1963 Simpson published *At the End of the Open Road,* for which he received the Pulitzer Prize. In this book he moved away from traditional forms. As Thom Gunn observed, other poets—Robert Bly, James Wright, W. S. Merwin—were undergoing a similar change. Gunn also called attention to a powerful self-opposition in Simpson's poetry between ornate style and a vigorous restlessness. Thomas McGrath observed that it was "interesting that the main theme of this book, the 'ending' of a dream, should coincide with a break in style by the poet." McGrath, in a remark that has turned out to be prophetic for much American poetry of the sixties and seventies, said that Simpson's book dramatized "the need to come back to the self as a starting point for a new movement." Appreciating the craft of these "looser" poems, William Stafford saw Simpson as achieving "joint membership in the formal and informal traditions," as Simpson takes Whitman's and the nation's dream of endless expansion, Westward movement, and progress, but darkens that dream "toward disquieting terminations."

But it is Duane Locke, writing in *Dust,* who most clearly perceived and put in perspective the changes marked by *At the End of the Open Road.* In fact, Locke's review convinces me that we cannot understand American literary politics and the poetry of the sixties and seventies without paying close attention to Louis Simpson. Locke saw *At the End of the Open Road* as marking a new "inwardness, an outburst of inner life." More precisely, he focused on the pronoun "I," which had been much more distant, rarely present in Simpson's work prior to *At the End of the Open Road.* Locke labeled this new poetry "phenomenalism" (a label in many respects preferable to the more popular "deep image") and saw it as an alternative to the polarizations of Academic versus Beat.

The reader who had been most prescient regarding this change in Simpson's writing is the poet Robert Bly (I have included Bly's three reviews of Simpson's poetry in the essay section of this book). In reviewing *The Arrivistes,* Bly found Simpson's theme to be the end of one age and the possible beginning of another, a theme similar to one of Whitman's central themes. But from the very beginning, Bly criticized Simpson for an overreliance on traditional forms: "The content seems to say one thing, and the form another." Bly suggested that Simpson "should search for a form as fresh as his content." Writing about *A Dream of Governors*, Bly criticized Simpson's reliance on "the old line." Crucially, rather than locating Simpson's strength in rhythm, diction, form, or even tone, Bly praised Simpson's "visual imagination" and his skill in making oddly effective juxtapositions: "This sudden shift from one kind of reality to another seems to me one of the major qualities of his poems." Indeed, these two qualities figure prominently in the success of *At the End of the Open Road*.

Just as this book appeared in America, *Five American Poets,* an important anthology coedited by Thom Gunn and Ted Hughes, was published in London. Reviewers singled out Simpson's poetry in this collection, and even before he had published an individual volume of poems in England, this anthology and its reception began to make his reputation in England. Martin Seymour-Smith said, "the one indisputably good poet in this book is Mr. Louis Simpson," and the *Times Literary Supplement*'s reviewer praised Louis Simpson and William Stafford as "the better poets in this collection" and called attention to this "third stream of emergent American poetry" situated between the Beat and the Academic.

In 1965, Simpson published his first *Selected Poems* (an English edition appeared in 1966). The collection confirmed Stafford's conferral of dual citizenship in the lands of formal and informal verse. Donald Hall was pleased that "fortunately the new colloquialism has not excluded the old lyricism; now Simpson can do anything." Confirming Locke's observation of an increased inwardness in Simpson's poetry, Hall called Simpson "the Columbus of an inward continent." While Hall reported that "finally it is America which is Simpson's theme," James Dickey explained that Simpson's treatment of America forces us to rethink what an American poet is.

Seamus Heaney's review, praising the American poet for achieving not "a mastery over material but of commingling with it" brought Simpson's balancing of opposites into perspective. Heaney mapped out Simpson's poetry as a complex balancing of formalism and spontaneity: "If Henry James represented the so-called Paleface tradition, writing out of a sensibility formed in the European mould, while Whitman was the archetype of the Redskin, reacting directly to raw experience, Louis Simpson's position might be termed 'blood brother,' a complex and interesting position to maintain." Heaney concluded that Simpson's "book is a valuable one, a touchstone for real poetry."

After achieving this recognition, Simpson waited until 1971, a period of eight years after publication of *At the End of the Open Road,* to publish his next new volume of poetry, *Adventures of the Letter I.* In the intervening years, a number of important essays appeared—including those by Yohma Gray, C. B. Cox, and Richard Howard reprinted in this volume—which began to shape the reading of Simpson's poetry. Perhaps the most important of these was an essay that proposed a kind of group identity: Ronald Moran and George Lensing's "The Emotive Imagination: A New Departure in American Poetry," which appeared in 1967 in the *Southern Review.* (In 1976, Lensing and Moran published *Four Poets and the Emotive Imagination: Robert Bly, James Wright, Louis Simpson, and William Stafford.*) The irony is that critics were associating Simpson with Bly's camp of the deep image precisely at the time that Simpson was moving off, independently, in his own direction as a poet, increasingly exploring the possibilities of narrative and of a poetry more and more drawn to the "common life."

In fact, in reviewing *Adventures of the Letter I,* Ian Hamilton called attention to Simpson's independence, particularly from Bly's deep image school. Simpson's new poems, according to Hamilton, relied on anecdote, parable, and character sketches, mixing discipline with an attractive casualness. This change in direction in Simpson's poetry met with a changed climate of critical reaction. Reviews of his poetry became more contentious. Not until the eighties perhaps, when critics have become more attuned to the principles of Simpson's narrative poetry, has his poetry received the kind of enthusiastic response to which he had become accustomed. Grevel Lindop, writing in England for *Critical Quarterly,* complained of Simpson's "distrust of ideas," adding that Simpson's poems feel like observations of suburbia left "strangely purposeless and incoherent." Lindop concluded that "it is as if Simpson had consciously decided to be a minor poet, and had set out to fumble a few of the big themes (the War, mental illness, Nazism, the moon landings) to prove it." While Dave Smith praised Simpson for "moving toward a looser structure in which narrative has replaced the lonely suggestiveness of sequential images," Terry Eagleton attacked the lack of complexity in attitude and language in Simpson's new poems.

Eagleton's remarks in particular force us to reconsider a critical dilemma underlying the more general task of understanding and evaluating much of the American poetry of the sixties, seventies, and eighties, and to the more specific task of forming an assessment of Simpson's writing. That dilemma is the relationship between complexity and excellence, a dilemma that, in my opinion, continues to play out two competing versions of modernist poetics: Eliot's high modernism, with its valorization of complexity, allusion, and ironic distancing, versus Williams's aesthetic of immediacy and directness. As the surface of Simpson's poems appears less complex (and also less prosodically traditional), as he moves away from the comfortable grouping of the deep image school, and as he begins in earnest his study of "the actual world in which we live," his work is frequently subject to critical dismissal for what seems to be a lack of complexity. It took nearly fifteen years for the complexity of Simpson's voice, tone, identifications, and sympathies to become apparent to many of his reviewers.

In an interview published in the *Ohio Review* shortly after *Adventures of the Letter I,* Simpson explained that "when . . . I'm writing a new book of poems, what it really means is this: I am getting a new vantage point from which to write. . . . Now what happens with me—I think—is that every book of poems I've published has represented a really new stage of development." With *Adventures of the Letter I,* Simpson's newest stage of development was at odds with prevailing critical attitudes, whether they were confessional, deep image, Zen-California, or nostalgic for the academic ironies of the Eliot- and Auden-dominated fifties.

In 1972, Simpson published his prose autobiography, *North of Jamaica* (it appeared in England under the title *Air with Armed Men*). The book received mixed reviews. Cyril Connolly, repeating Babette Deutsch's erroneous assumption that Simpson was black, attacked the position of a poet working within the university and judged the tone of Simpson's autobiography to be one of "mild irony." In a remark that applies equally well to Simpson's poetry, Webster Schott concluded that "feeling is another form of knowledge, and through Simpson we learn about ourselves." Though nearly every reviewer of Simpson's poetry pointed out his vast difference from the confessional poets, Simpson's forms of self-expression always being somewhat indirect, James Boatwright concluded that *North of Jamaica* seemed "to have at its center the chill emptiness of a solipsistic mind." Anthony Rudolf, in a detailed treatment of the autobiography in *European Judaism,* praised Simpson's insistent ordinariness and pointed out the precariousness of Simpson's Jewish identity.

Three on the Tower: The Lives and Works of Ezra Pound, T. S. Eliot, and William Carlos Williams appeared in 1975 to mostly positive reviews. While L. S. Dembo claimed that "the book has no meaningful thesis" and reveals "no really new perspective on either the lives or minds of Pound, Eliot, and Williams," Mark Nepo's praise for Simpson's "impassioned and active objectivity" was more typical of the book's reception. For several reasons I think it is important, even in a book devoted principally to Simpson's poetry, to give careful attention to his critical writing too. Oddly enough, the usual reason—a study of influence—does not apply; with rare exceptions, we do not find echoes of Pound, Eliot, or Williams in Simpson's own poetry. But in his books of criticism Simpson explores and works out many of the same problems—of tone, sensibility, the relationship of personal experience to the making of a poem, the function of narrative, and the distrust of abstract or theoretical frameworks—that occur in his poems. (The connections between poetry and criticism become even clearer with *A Revolution in Taste* in 1978.) In remarks that echo Hamilton's description of *Adventures of the Letter I,* Richard Lingeman described *Three on the Tower* as a book in which "the tone is easy, almost conversational, occasionally aphoristic." Lingeman also praised Simpson for his detailed consideration of the anti-Semitism of Pound, Eliot, and Williams. Historically, perhaps the most

important quality of *Three on the Tower* is that, in its clear prefer-
ence for the writing (and poetics) of Williams over Pound and
Eliot, the book marked a turning point in American literary
history. Lingeman noted that Simpson's book acknowledged
Williams's emergence as the most influential poet for "the con-
temporary generation of American poets."

Simpson's book of poems *Searching for the Ox* (1976) extended
his exploration of the narrative possibilities of poetry. Peter Stitt
compared these poems to short stories by Singer or short novels
by Bellow. In addition to making some useful observations about
the overall structure of the book, Stitt read *Searching for the Ox* as a
spiritual autobiography, in which "the speaker realizes that unless
he can find spirituality in the world itself, it can be of no real value
to him." Stitt also praised the rich, profound humor of these
poems. While C. B. Cox, writing in the English journal *Critical
Quarterly,* called *Searching for the Ox* the "best book of poetry
published in 1976" and praised the book for its Chekhovian
resonances, at this point in Simpson's career his poetry suffered
from a degree of critical neglect. Although he continued to be
reviewed steadily abroad (in England), at home, with the excep-
tion of extended reviews by Stitt, Stanley Plumly, Dave Smith,
and Robert Bly, Simpson's poetry received diminished attention.
Often, the reviews tended to be cursory notices of a book's
publication or a brief description of the kinds of poems included
in the book.

What accounts for this shift? I would suggest three factors.
First, in the mid-seventies, many critics devoted themselves to a
championing of the work of John Ashbery, who presents a tone,
stylistic complexity, and allusiveness ideal for a critical climate
becoming increasingly involved in the realm of theory, particu-
larly deconstruction. This second factor, the increasingly the-
oretical orientation of criticism, left Simpson, an avowed anti-
theorist, out. For Harold Bloom, Charles Altieri, Marjorie
Perloff, and Helen Vendler, who were drawn to the complexities
of Ashbery's poetry, Simpson's narratives of the "common life"
remained outside their critical enthusiasms. Third, with the pub-
lication of Robert Pinsky's *The Situation of Poetry: Contemporary
Poetry and Its Traditions,* critical debate focused on the worth of the
deep image and confessional schools. In such discussions, Simp-

son's later poetry was beside the point. So Simpson worked quietly and without acclaim in the seventies, developing a complex but accessible narrative poetry that would not really receive proper attention for nearly a decade.

As for the narrative style Simpson developed in *Searching for the Ox,* Stanley Plumly described it as "poetry about to break into prose." In nearly every poem he noted a tension between "how much the line, the stanza, can include versus what it must edit." And Plumly called attention to the isolation of the book's protagonist, an isolation which that protagonist struggles against.

In 1978 Simpson published another work of literary criticism based in biography: *A Revolution in Taste: Studies of Dylan Thomas, Allen Ginsberg, Sylvia Plath, and Robert Lowell.* Sympathetic readings of this work by Paul Zweig and Tom Paulin provide insights that again have an important implied relationship to Simpson's poetry, particularly Zweig's observation (which can also be applied to *Searching for the Ox*) that in *A Revolution in Taste* Simpson is writing "a species of spiritual autobiography."

While Simpson often presents himself as a latter-day Grigoryev, that is, a critic unable and unwilling to stick to any theoretical method, Zweig's review of *A Revolution in Taste,* which he read as a counterstatement to David Kalstone's *Five Temperaments,* accurately identified Simpson's critical position and preoccupation: the tracing of "the elusive passage of experience into imagery, tone, and theme" and "the radical merging of poetry and personal experience." In terms of method, Zweig correctly saw Simpson as turning New Critical assumptions upside-down, for Simpson begins with the life of the poet and the circumstances of composition and shows how these form the writer's ideas, and how ideas form the poem.

Tom Paulin's review of *A Revolution in Taste* also emphasized "this complex connection between poetic voice and family background" as Simpson "explores the determining weirdness and peculiarity of family background." (Again, these observations by Zweig and Paulin would be equally appropriate to Simpson's poetry of the seventies and eighties.) Paulin concluded that *A Revolution in Taste* "deserves to become a classic work." He admired the limitations of Simpson's interpretations, especially because Simpson refused to substitute "paraphrasable content for the experience of the poem." Such a substitution would elevate the ideas or meanings of the poem, extractable and paraphrasable, over the particular way in which the poem gets made. Paulin described Simpson's critical (and narrative) voice as "very distinctive—it is generous, sympathetic, spontaneously free and wittily fatalistic."

With *Caviare at the Funeral,* the book of poems he published in 1980, Simpson achieved consistent mastery of his new narrative style. G. E. Murray praised Simpson's oddly profound humor, and Douglas Dunn admired Simpson's inclusiveness. Peter Makuck singled out Simpson's "ability to accommodate the humorous, the terrible and the lyrical almost simultaneously," while noting that Simpson's images and narrative devices "never upstage the poem as a whole." This latter observation, echoing William Arrowsmith's remark about *Good News of Death* (1955), hints at a difficulty facing reviewers of Simpson's narrative poems: it is almost impossible to extract beautiful snippets in any meaningful way. On the important issue of sympathy, Makuck insisted that "Simpson's satire is never pitiless." On the other hand, in a review mixing praise and criticism, Paul Breslin claimed that Simpson's "reduction of other people to their most stereotyped behavior soon wears thin" and that Simpson lacked the gift of Chekhov and Proust "for seeing into the grief of others."

With *Caviare at the Funeral* Simpson's poetry began to receive renewed critical attention, perhaps as critics began to catch up with the full accomplishment of his fifteen years of independent development, during which he had defined his own particular combination of the lyric and narrative. Even so, too many reviewers—and this raises the problem of how to approach Simpson's deceptively accessible poetry—are content merely to label Simpson's kind of poetry as narrative, or the poems of a storyteller. Douglas Dunn began to explore Simpson's unique kind of narration. "His story-telling," said Dunn, "reminds me of a remark made by one of Chekhov's characters—'Keep it short and skip the psychology.' Any fool can be brief, but to skip the psychology is an achievement for an American poet." Even so, readers of Simpson's poetry may wish to consider the kinds of narration he employs, to discuss the implied poetics of such a project, and to suggest what kinds of relationships Simpson's narratives have with the reader.*

In 1981, Simpson published *A Company of Poets,* a collection of essays, reviews, and interviews (including three essays that seem to me to constitute a poetics for his narrative poetry: "To Make Words Disappear," "Rolling Up," and "Reflections on Narrative Poetry"). In reviewing this collection, William Scammell praised Simpson's generosity and astringent wit. Robert McDowell points out** that Simpson's book, and indeed the entire Poets on Poetry series, goes a long way toward correcting the impression that this generation of poets lacks opinions and does not write criticism. McDowell is correct to call attention to the fact that "these poets have chosen to make their stands in unconventional ways," especially through informal kinds of criticism such as interviews and addresses.

With the publication in 1983 of a new collection of poems, *The Best Hour of the Night,* and a volume of selected poems, *People Live Here: Selected Poems 1949–1983,* the fullness of Simpson's accomplishment as the maker of a new kind of narrative poem has become evident. Richard Tillinghast, writing in the *Nation,* noted Simpson's singular dedication to the everyday aspects of American life: "Someone who knew nothing of present-day America would get little idea of our life from most contemporary poetry." But to write about American middle-class existence is not to applaud it, and Tillinghast pointed to a moral dimension in Simpson's poetry: "For him, as for Matthew Arnold, poetry has been a 'criticism of life.'" Alan Williamson, in the *New York Times Book Review,* said that Simpson's "bare, unadorned poems of the common life" reminded him of Randall Jarrell. Touching upon the complex question of sympathy and judgment, Williamson suggested that "what makes his suburbanites most sym-

---

*I attempted such a reading in "The Figure a Poem Makes," a review of *The Best Hour of the Night* and *People Live Here* in the Autumn 1984 issue of the *Virginia Quarterly Review.*

**In "The Mum Generation Was Always Talking," *Hudson Review* (Autumn 1985), a review that only makes brief comment on Simpson's book and hence is not included in this volume.

pathetic, one finds, is their discontent." M. L. Rosenthal, review-ing *People Live Here* for the *Times Literary Supplement,* acclaimed Simpson's "attractively modest virtuosity" and pointed out a major continuity in his poetry by linking his lament for lost innocents (in the World War II poems) with his more recent laments for suburbanites.

The Character of the Poet (1986) was Simpson's second collec-tion of essays, talks, reviews, and interviews. Richard Silberg admired Simpson's "demystifying concern for humanity and the courage of his straightforward judgments." Silberg summa-rized several of Simpson's chief concerns in this collection, ob-serving that Simpson is "against poetry that wallows in the self, as so much of American poetry does, and he is against poetry that concentrates on language, itself; Simpson champions a 'transparent' language in which the reader looks 'through' the words to the subject matter." This collection is extremely important for setting forth Simpson's views of a poetry of the common life, the desirability of a "transparent" poetic language, and the importance of William Carlos Williams, and for present-ing his own embattled critical position on contemporary Ameri-can poetry.

Simpson has recently published a third edition of *An Introduc-tion to Poetry,* a textbook but also a book that explains several principles essential to his poetic practice and theory. Throughout this work Simpson emphasizes the immediate experience of the poem and urges the reader toward emotional engagement. Even so, traces of New Critical approaches to the poem appear, as when Simpson asserts that "a poem has an organic unity. Each part—imagery, rhythm, structure, the choice and arrangement of language—contributes to the effect of the whole." Ever sus-picious of abstract or theoretical statements, Simpson insists that "there is more to be learned from reading poems and discovering what is in the individual poem than from any amount of gener-alization." In terms of a theory of language, Simpson takes up a position close to the "phenomenalism" that Duane Locke men-tioned in his review of *At the End of the Open Road.* Words represent things for Simpson and do so best when they make a strong appeal to the senses: "Poets embody their thoughts in images, words that appeal to the senses for, as John Locke said, 'There is nothing in the mind that was not first in the senses.'"

An Introduction to Poetry also demonstrates the vast amount of learning behind Simpson's own poetry, a knowledge he wears with deceptive lightness. Some critics might be surprised to see the extent of Simpson's exactness and thoroughness in prosody or to hear him explain the ambiguities in a speech by Milton's Satan. His new edition of this textbook deserves praise for its range. He includes the work of poets he has argued against, such as John Ashbery and Richard Wilbur, and substantial selections from women poets (including Sharon Olds, Katha Pollitt, Jane Kenyon, and Carolyn Forché) and black poets (including Etheridge Knight, Dudley Randall, Lucille Clifton, and Alice Walker). He assists in making better known the work of poets such as Hugh MacDiarmid, Patrick Kavanagh, Robert Hayden, Ruth Stone, Hilda Doolittle (H.D.), Seamus Heaney, and Mary Oliver, as well as introducing younger poets: Garrett Kaoru Hongo, Toi Derricotte, and Jimmy Santiago Baca. From his own work Simpson selects "The Battle," "Chocolates," "Why Do You Write About Russia?" and "Physical Universe" (the last three from his two most recent collections of poems).

The first of the essays in part two of this volume, Yohma Gray's "The Poetry of Louis Simpson," begins by confronting the difficulty of establishing a successful critical method for reading Simpson's poetry. Gray reacts against the "objective criticism" of the New Critics and attacks the traditional *explication de texte*. Gray, whose essay covers Simpson's poems prior to *At the End of the Open Road* but who also had access to the poems of *At the End of the Open Road* (1963) and *Selected Poems* (1965), focuses on sensation and feeling in the poems and on establishing a relationship between the poems and the poet's life—not all that different from the critical stance Simpson himself would take in *Three on the Tower* and *A Revolution in Taste*. Gray's opening remarks describe a situation that has persisted throughout Simpson's career: his poetry and the prevailing critical interests of the day have never been well synchronized, or at least such has been the case since Simpson's early books. By the mid-sixties, Simpson's work was out of step with New Critical readings of ironically voiced poems having competing layers of meaning and allusion, and his poetry of the seventies and eighties is equally at odds with theoretically inclined criticism. While Yohma Gray laments the mismatch of Simpson's poems and New Critical methods of reading, she is at a loss to come up with an alternative approach, and her essay tends to become a series of labels and impressionistic summaries of Simpson's poems. Gray praises Simpson's work, but in terms that are often abstract and, while enthusiastic, imprecise: "His tragic sense serves to intensify the quality of life, just as his imagination intensifies the quality of reality." Gray sees Simpson as organizing reality, offering us "meaning for life." But the precise nature of that meaning is never quite explored in Gray's essay.

C. B. Cox's "The Poetry of Louis Simpson," one of the best of the early essays, also discusses the poems through *Selected Poems*. Cox presents Simpson's essential themes and techniques, emphasizing the multiple associations and "hallucinatory" effect of the images, which he attributes to their strong subconscious content. Cox suggests that "a feeling of being involved in historical processes which we only partly understand is typical of Simpson's work." Anticipating Simpson's "Grigoryev" position (against theoretical perspectives), Cox explains, "No explanation of human behavior can ever be final. . . . Like Philip Larkin he mocks his own poses, refusing to settle in any one form of knowing."

Richard Howard's "The Hunger in My Vitals Is for Some Credible Extravaganza" offers an assessment of Simpson's development through *Selected Poems*. Howard calls Simpson's early career "a sad, successful story." From his perspective as a fellow student at Columbia, Howard tells us that *The Arrivistes* confirmed Simpson's status as a kind of poetic prodigy and that, while Simpson's early work was not different from what others were doing at the time, it was significantly better. He calls the early Simpson "a university wit, the archaizing elegist who has read everything and rearranged everything." Howard describes both the shifts and continuities in Simpson's work. For example, he notes the "dismissive" way in which Simpson treats old stories and myths in his second book, while at the same time unfolding a continuing story, "the drama of waste and spoliation which follows in the wake of invasions to come." Howard sees Simpson in the mid-fifties shifting to home truths and a movement inward, from an outer to an inner war, from stories of arriving to stories of home. With *A Dream of Governors,* Howard observes, Simpson firmly situated himself in America. With *At* the End of the Open Road and Selected Poems, he has become "a dangerous, a monitory presence among us." Howard believes that Simpson's pronouncements fifteen years earlier were just as severe, but his new openness of form—"Simpson's lyric had become one with his speaking voice"—makes his pronouncements now less avoidable.

Ronald Moran, who along with Robert Bly, C. B. Cox, and Peter Stitt has done the most to promote an understanding and an appreciation of Louis Simpson's poetry, has published a number of important essays and reviews of Simpson's work. His review of At the End of the Open Road, included in part one of this volume, is a careful study of Simpson's development, themes, and imagery. Moran has also published a book-length critical study of Simpson's work, Louis Simpson (New York: Twayne, 1972), as well as other essays and reviews.

Moran's essay in this volume, "The Image of 'America' in the California/Whitman Poems of Louis Simpson," with its clear focus on California and Walt Whitman as key organizing devices for Simpson's poetry, may rightly be called the first "scholarly" essay on Simpson's work. In addition to tracking down a number of important allusions, Moran offers a sympathetic reading of several poems. He also makes definite a growing critical awareness: "'Walt Whitman at Bear Mountain' is perhaps Simpson's finest poem and is one of the most significant statements about America to emerge from mid-twentieth-century American poetry."

Robert Bly early on identified a conflict between the form and content of Simpson's early poetry: "the form doubts the poet, and everything he has to say, and continually tries to render it innocuous." By attacking Simpson's traditional forms while showing great understanding of his subject matter, Bly was able to encourage Simpson's exploration of the deep image and his development of looser formal structures for his poetry.

In examining Searching for the Ox, Bly faces a fellow poet who has, after a period of considerable kinship, departed from Bly's deep image school and gone off in his own direction. Bly notes that Simpson has abandoned his great gift for "the image with unconscious ingredients." He praises "Baruch" as "a masterpiece" and is quick to pick up the advantages of Simpson's new narratives: "The advantages are clear: the poem ["Baruch"] is rooted well in this world, and by leaving the image, it adapts itself to the narrative; by leaving the private realm it opens itself to other characters besides the poet." (It seems to me that this is a virtue Bly is struggling to incorporate in his own poetry, though he is less willing than Simpson to abandon the advantages of an image-based poetry.) Bly is also astute in pointing out potential dangers: at times, the details and objects of Simpson's poems become static and the writing flat. But Bly's overall reading of Simpson's work is sympathetic. In fact, his three pieces of writing gathered together in this volume are models of a great rarity: criticism that actually helps and engages the poet being criticized.

With Dave Smith's essay a different phase of Simpson criticism begins, one that already assumes his status as a major American poet and begins to read his exploration of narrative sympathetically. Smith cites a group of poets—Robert Bly, Donald Hall, Louis Simpson, James Wright, and James Dickey—who have changed American poetry: "together they have created the poetry of a surfaced, examined, and revitalized inner life, a life not simply of the mind but of the personalized mind." Smith adds that "no one of that grouping seems to have so steadily and honestly gone on creating a credible and shareable vision of life in this world, in these times, more than Simpson has." In an essay full of sure judgments, Smith calls Simpson "a consistently moral and ethical poet" concerned with the human as social, responsible creature. In calling Simpson "neither a poet of the deep image nor of the personality," which I see as the two dominant trends in American poetry in the sixties and seventies, Smith explains that Simpson "has come to a certain unfashionable narrative base."

One strength of Smith's essay is that he clearly understands that this narrative base is the crowning accomplishment of Simpson's career. Smith presents an excellent reading of *Searching for the Ox* (including a careful study of the title poem), and then opens this more focused reading into a general analysis of Simpson's work. Finally, he states that "one of the great strengths of Simpson's poetry, to my way of thinking, has been his refusal to accept an unearned vision of transcendence."

My own essay focuses on the depth and dialectic of Simpson's relationship to Walt Whitman, developing an overview of Simpson's career through his encounters with Whitman. I claim that tone, style, and even characters change in Simpson's poetry by way of that relationship to Whitman. Oddly enough, although Harold Bloom is a critic Simpson thoroughly dislikes, I make extensive use of Bloom's theories of influence and misreading to offer a model for Simpson's interaction with Whitman. Through Whitman I locate as the key dilemma of Simpson's poetry "the observer's relationship to the world he describes." As in Whitman's "Song of Myself," (and in a line cited by Simpson in his "The Champion Single Sculls"), the poet's task is to be "both in and out of the game." This difficult balance must be achieved, since a position of absolute brotherhood or identification can be mere rhetoric (as in the con man aspects of Whitman that Simpson attacks), and a position of strict detachment and judgment may lead to an equally unacceptable scorn for the average man. Simpson seeks aspects of both positions, and thus my essay explores the issue of sympathy and irony that comes up again and again in reviews of Simpson's work.

In addition to its thematic observations—"what angers him [Simpson] is boredom; that and not pessimism is his real nemesis"— R. W. Flint's "Child of This World" offers several interesting suggestions about the reader's relationship to Simpson's poems. Flint is impressed by Simpson's trust of and goodwill toward the reader. He argues that Simpson "enjoys thinking and wants to make it contagious," and he analyzes Simpson's original balancing "between the leisurely and the laconic, the hard and the soft, the sweet and the sour."

David Wojahn, in "'I Might Live Here Myself': On Louis Simpson," says that "Louis Simpson is one of our most indispensable talents. . . . While many of his contemporaries—James Dickey, for example, or Galway Kinnell—have shown a marked decline in power during the past decade, Simpson keeps getting better and better." Wojahn cautions that "one must examine Simpson's work with care and patience before seeing that he is not, in fact, the cynic and misanthrope he may appear to be and that he has instead become (somewhat begrudgingly) one of our most moral and convincingly humanitarian writers." In fact, Wojahn's attention to the moral dimension of Simpson's poetry also allows him to explain Simpson's movement away from the deep image: "Suspicious of both the solipsism of surrealism and its romantic amorality, he tempered his use of surrealism with a tone both ironic and discursive." In abandoning both surrealism and a generalized quarrel with America, Simpson chose "to abandon one of the most hallowed tenets of modernist art—that the artist must, to a large degree, be alienated from the society in which he dwells. Instead of conceiving of himself as a solitary *poète maudit,* Simpson sought to share in the alienation felt by his peers in the suburban middle class." Wojahn cautions that Simpson's narrative style, "despite its apparent straightforwardness, is one of implication rather than directness." Finally, Wojahn sees Simpson's recent poetry developing toward a moving humility.

Like Wojahn, Flint, Stitt, and myself, T. R. Hummer is writing about Simpson's work at a time when the publication, in a relatively short period, of *A Company of Poets, The Best Hour of the Night,* and *People Live Here* has made it possible to consider the nature of Simpson's poetics, his new narrative form, and the development of his poetry from *The Arrivistes* to the present. In "Revising the Poetry Wars: Louis Simpson's Assault on the Poetic," Hummer reveals the best understanding of Simpson's principles of organization in *People Live Here.* While not completely rejecting Stitt's division of Simpson's work into three distinct phases, Hummer questions these divisions. He also points out a fundamental continuity in Simpson's work, claiming that "Simpson is, in a real sense, always writing about shell shock," whether in his earlier war poems or in the more "peaceful" social settings of "Quiet Desperation" and other more recent poems of suburban life. What changes in Simpson's poetry, according to Hummer, is its "understanding and compassion," particularly for the casualties of social life. Hummer sees Simpson's work developing through a rigorous process of self-questioning: "In his practice as poet, it is the idea of the poetic that Simpson assaults—other people's ideas about it, yes, but more importantly his own." And Hummer praises Simpson's recent poetry for being attuned to "the exotic potential of the 'ordinary.' "

Stitt's essay delineates three major phases in Simpson's work, tracing a movement from alienation and irony to compassion and empathy. Stitt identifies Simpson's main theme as the conflict between the individual and the community. He asserts that "perhaps the most astonishing thing about Simpson's recent work is just how different the people he writes about are—not from the sensibility that inhabits his work, but from the characters who appear in contemporary American poetry generally." Stitt sees Simpson as "actively following advice he gave indirectly to Robert Lowell in a review written in 1977: 'He ought to try getting inside the skin of a few people who aren't like himself.'" There are two other important features to Stitt's essay. First, he calls attention to Simpson's long narrative poem "The Previous Tenant." Second, he notes the importance of sensibility in Simpson's recent work, explaining that, as in a great deal of lyric poetry, much of Simpson's recent work "depends for its coherence less on its details than on the sensibility that perceives and reflects on these details."

On Louis Simpson concludes with Michael Milburn's assessment, which places Simpson's accomplishment alongside that of writers of fiction such as Cheever and Updike, Carver and Beattie. Milburn observes that "we are less able to say why they [Simpson's poems] mean so much than that they do and are impossible to improve." He hears the poems as "the songs playing inside their [Simpson's characters'] heads, as quiet and humble and unbearable as their lives." And Milburn points out a fundamentally ineluctable, ungraspable quality in the best of Simpson's poems, a quality that somehow eludes analysis.

As for what remains to be done in Simpson criticism, let me hazard a few guesses. Of course, while Simpson's recent work (including poems published after *The Best Hour of the Night*) continues his development of a new narrative poetry, one cannot predict the nature of the poetry he will write, especially given his career-long habits of innovation and independence. But based on his work to date and on the criticism written to date, I see several areas that merit attention. First, as I suggested earlier, no critic has satisfactorily analyzed the poetics of Simpson's new narrative. Second, a more thoroughly integrated reading of the entire body of Simpson's poetry is now possible. While various critics have noted continuities in his poetry, there has been little in-depth attention to his earlier work, and thus we may be missing the beginnings of Simpson's carefully developed sensibility.

A third area of importance has to do with assumptions about the nature of language. Such discussions are not confined to Simpson's poetry; indeed, this issue is at the heart of most debates about contemporary poetry. Simpson has repeatedly attempted to stake out a poetry of the common life written in a transparent language. In "To Make Words Disappear" (from *A Company of Poets*), Simpson writes, "I would like to write poems that made people laugh or made them want to cry, without their thinking that they were reading poetry. The poem would be an experience—not just talking about life, but life itself."

More recently, in *The Character of the Poet,* Simpson expounds the virtues of a poetry of common life: "Poets have come to think that they are different from the common man and woman, and to think that because the common man and woman do not read poetry, poetry can exclude the common man and woman. This is the fallacy that has made so much poetry in our time empty and unimportant." As a "cure" for what he calls far-fetched poetry written in a special language, Simpson says, "there is no cure but immersion in the common life and the language, as Wordsworth said, really used by men." He adds, "Not only urban scenes but the minds of the people need to be represented, and I don't mean some programmatic literature about the working man or woman such as Socialist Realism produced—I mean poetry about the people you actually meet and the ideas they have, including the banal, foolish ones."

Louis Simpson's ideas about the relationship between language and experience will have an important effect on the development of his poetry and will continue to generate critical controversy. As I have argued intermittently in this introduction, to study the reactions to his poetry and his ideas puts one in touch with many of the key elements of American literary history, at least in poetry, from the fifties to the present.

I wish to thank Louis Simpson for his assistance and generosity. Without his help and encouragement, this book would not have been possible. My gratitude also goes to Donald Hall for his patience and advice, to LeAnn Fields for her encouragement, to Miriam Simpson for her work on the index and her proofreading, to Linda Howe for her thorough copyediting, and to Claudia Johnson for giving me the time to complete this book. Finally, I wish to acknowledge the importance of William H. Roberson's *Louis Simpson: A Reference Guide,* an invaluable book for anyone interested in Louis Simpson's writing and in critical reactions to that body of writing.

PART ONE *Reviews*

Works Reviewed in This Section

The Arrivistes: Poems 1940–1949 (1949)

Good News of Death and Other Poems (1955)

The New Poets of England and America (edited by Donald Hall, Robert Pack, and Louis Simpson, 1957)

A Dream of Governors (1959)

Riverside Drive (novel, 1962)

At the End of the Open Road (1963)

Five American Poets (edited by Thom Gunn and Ted Hughes, 1963)

Selected Poems (1965)

Adventures of the Letter I (1971)

North of Jamaica (prose autobiography, 1972)

Three on the Tower: The Lives and Works of Ezra Pound, T. S. Eliot, and William Carlos Williams (critical prose, 1975)

Searching for the Ox (1976)

A Revolution in Taste: Studies of Dylan Thomas, Allen Ginsberg, Sylvia Plath, and Robert Lowell (critical prose, 1978)

Caviare at the Funeral (1981)

A Company of Poets (essays, reviews, interviews; 1981)

The Best Hour of the Night (1983)

People Live Here: Selected Poems 1949–1983 (1983)

The Character of the Poet (essays, reviews, interviews; 1986)

GERARD PREVIN MEYER

From "A Sampling of Pound and Modern Man"

The pleasure to be derived from a reading of the poems in *The Arrivistes,* three of which are couched in dramatic form but all of which are dramatic in essence, is as various as the "subject matter" which encompasses, as Theodore Hoffman's preface notes, "the condition of modern man." Though young enough (twenty-six) to have gone through the war years as a combatant, Mr. Simpson is sufficiently aged-in-the-world's-wood to write about his experiences with controlled irony, with respect and horror, but without either illusions or disillusions. He is gay enough to turn out *erotica,* sober enough to be humorous about it.

Possessing a "varied enough national ancestry" (he was born in Jamaica), he can evolve such valuable and disciplined lines as

> This got the start of my bestial, indolent race
> With coarse skin, crazy laugh, nostrils like swords through the
>   face

He also, and especially, can convey the effect of big-city life upon our erstwhile human race, sieving it through Marvell-ous style until it emerges in such wise:

> Since sin requires some expense
> Our income is our innocence

and

> So shall we manage till the day
> Death takes the furniture away.

Review of *The Arrivistes, Saturday Review,* 24 December 1949, 14. Copyright © Saturday Review magazine. Reprinted by permission.

Mr. Simpson has studied at the Sorbonne; evidences of Villon and Rimbaud (two good guides to harsh reality) and vignettes of Paris, "the capital of the heart," testify to his absorption in and of Parisian culture. He proves in this first book that he has the kind of imagination that can cope successfully with both Paris and New York, love and war, seventeenth-century wit and twentieth-century perplexity; in sum, "a usable talent" capable of taking over the world's old clothes and making something new of them.

RANDALL JARRELL

From "Poetry, Unlimited"

There isn't a good poem in *The Arrivistes,* but Louis Simpson is as promising a new poet as I've read in some time. His poems are gay, felt, mocking, rather inexperienced, thoroughly uneven, thoroughly unexpected poems; they are not organized or thought out into successful works of art, but a few of their lines or stanzas are good, and more than a few are beautifully funny (for instance, the pseudo-Jacobean sections of "The Vagrants"). The ordinary young poet is a part of all that he has read, a summation of standard influences, as tame as can be. Mr. Simpson seems genuinely wild: sometimes he sounds like himself, a surprising creature in a surprising world, and the rest of the time he manages to make (sometimes very funny) allusions out of all his influences, so that his rhetorical education is one public joke after another. His worst mistakes, awful mistakes, somehow don't alienate you; at his best he is witty and moving, a fine amateur who ought—with luck—to turn into a good professional. He is a surprisingly *live* poet: as you read him you forget for a moment that we are the ancients. A critic can hardly resist saying to this particular poet: Whatever you do, don't pay any attention to critics—and here is a quotation to use as an amulet: "Against criticism we can neither protect nor defend ourselves; we must act in despite of it, and gradually it resigns itself to this."

Review of *The Arrivistes, Partisan Review* 17 (February 1950): 189. Reprinted by permission of Mary Jarrell.

RANDALL JARRELL

Letter to Louis Simpson

Dear Mr. Simpson:

Thank you for your letter—getting it was a real pleasure! I much enjoyed reading your book; I don't know which I liked better, the very funny parts or the live, startling, poetic parts. There are enough things in the book to make a number of very good poems: the only trouble is—if you won't mind my being a critic and saying *Go Thou and do otherwise*—that they're not organized into a few good poems. "The Vagrants" certainly is good of its kind—what ever that is exactly—but it's a kind that nobody knows quite how to value: is a big pink elephant better than a small Ford? I think I like "Resistance," especially the end, best among the entirely serious poems: the only trouble with the first part is that it a little too much requires the reader to consent, to be plain and bare and serious and hushed—that's the way one when one's writing the poem feels about the subject matter, so it's hard not to be that way, and yet one can't quite afford to. (Here I'm just talking from personal experience.) But the end of "Resistance" is extremely moving.

The amulet's from Goethe, who's extremely good about critics; they bothered him all his life. In general critics—this is me, not Goethe—want you to do what they once did or what you once did; all they ask is "perfection ready made," which (in Goethe's rhyme) is "the pedant's stock-in-trade." And so forth. But in the long run you benefit from them: by the time you're old and grey a couple of good ones have written well about you, and the bad ones have looked up allusions in the *Britannica*, explained them, and ignorantly marvelled at you enough for

---

The letter, undated, but probably from 1950, makes reference to Jarrell's review of *The Arrivistes* in *Partisan Review*. Reprinted by permission of Mary Jarrell.

readers to accept you as one more mountain-range. Anyway, I trust this happy ending is so.

I'm looking forward to reading your new poems when they come out in the magazines. I won't bother to go through *The Arrivistes* telling the lines or stanzas I particularly enjoyed—but, believe me, there were a lot.

Yours,
Randall Jarrell

JOHN CIARDI

From "Three Lyric Voices"

Louis Simpson works in seeming simplicities, favoring the short formal stanza and the simple word while relying for richness on the flow of a tremendous imagery caught up in meticulously turned phrases. It is a mannered poetry, a poetry of control, and it could easily be another man's disaster, but Simpson has obviously lived into it and something from the man comes through the surface of technique and takes over and makes the miracle happen, the true gooseflesh. Some of these poems—try "John the Baptist," for example—will certainly be a good reader's reward through any number of rereadings:

> The pagan fires smouldered on the plain,
> The tiger swung his lantern through the night.
>
> And to the valley's winding ways he ran
> Crying "Prepare the straight path for the Lord!"
> And came to shallow Jordan, where began
> The matter of the platter and the sword.

Review of *Good News of Death and Other Poems, New York Times Book Review*, 14 August 1955, 4. Copyright © 1955 by The New York Times Company. Reprinted by permission.

WILLIAM ARROWSMITH

From "Nine New Poets"

Of the nine poets here under review, by far the most exciting,
the most mature, the most promising, is Mr. Louis Simpson,
whose *Good News of Death* deserved independent publication
and whose excellence sits uncomfortably beside the mere com-
petence of Mr. Pack and Miss Farber. Like both of those poets,
Mr. Simpson is also deeply traditionalist in his temptations, and
he is also a considerable rhetorician; but unlike them, he has a
depth of experience and an appetite for complexity which ex-
actly match the form he works in; and if he is a rhetorician, he is
also a near master of rhetoric, firmly forcing his language's
urgency and gesture into the controlling shape of his poem's
experience. And, most important, he is a mature poet with a
driving theme constantly thrown up in new developments and
newly involved with the experience of each new poem. The
lovely opening poem, "The True Weather for Women," for
instance, is a deeply traditional poem and especially in its strik-
ing dependence upon Wyatt's "They Flee from Me" (visible in
the hovering, limping rhymes, the imagery and the movement),
but not a merely traditionalizing poem; for look at the remark-
able poem "Islanders," or "Ulysses and the Sirens," and one can
see that what is traditional here is also deeply personal my-
thology, all of it coming to terms dramatically with the ancient
but unembarrassed theme of the tragic simultaneity of experi-
ence, the simultaneity made possible in the oldest poetic way:
perception under pressure, with concern, pity, wit and passion

Review of *Good News of Death and Other Poems, Hudson Review* 9 (Summer 1956):
291–93. Reprinted by permission.

for the common condition. If he begins with rhetoric, he begins
with good rhetoric, nothing usurping the destined motion of the
poem:

> Poetry has no place, still you must choose
> A starting point—say, with the displaced Jews
> Who come to this small park from the ends of earth:
> They weep with sorrow and expect a birth,
> Their gutturals disrupt the summer nights
> While darkness slowly laps the river lights.
> Their skins are wrinkled like fine handkerchiefs
> Of Brussels, intricately stitched with griefs.
> The wind that stirs their soft curls makes you cold
> Thinking of Belsen and of Buchenwald.
> Their tears obscure your Christ like candlegrease—
> A swinging acrobat, no Prince of Peace!
> Cry thief! Someone has stolen the true Cross!
> Go to these Jews, accuse them of your loss!

And so it goes, the next stanza beginning from what has been
gained,

> Poetry has no place, but life is kind.
> Revenge yourself on a girl—she will not mind

and on and on, the rhetoric turning first to easy irony, then
sinister, then personal, then to a fine general flourish with the
lines spun out long in five and six stresses and turning ironically
anticlimactic at the close in heroic couplets (tacked onto stress-
lines!), and closing on what all this rhetoric makes simple and
right:

> Enough of these images—they set the teeth on edge!
> Life, if you like, is a metaphor of death—
> The difference is you, a place for the passing of breath.
> That is what man is. He is the time between,
> The palpable glass through which all things are seen.
> Nothing. Silence. A syllable. A word.
> Everything.
> > After your death this poem occurred.

You were the honored fragments from the Greek.
After your death these stones would move and speak.

The central word for Mr. Simpson's poetry seems to me "dramatic"; what "dramatic" involves here in subject is the interplay of past and present in a context of particular doing or passion; it is dramatic because it is complex, because it moves unmistakably from the unknown to the known and then, confronting what is known with what cannot be known, ends where it should, on a tragic frontier. No *aperçu,* that is, is final; an *aperçu* may resolve the particular poem, tame it to rest, but the *aperçu* becomes dramatic because it is related to that part of experience where perception becomes choice and fate. So, in Mr. Simpson's lyrics, the resolution *par excellence* is death, but that resolution is made complex and ironic by the human claim to significant passion in the interim that is everything. Technically, the dramatic element lies chiefly in Mr. Simpson's rhetorical control: his sure knowledge of juxtapositions, the deeply, almost embarrassingly traditional *sententia* offset by a happy irony or gruffly familiar and deliberately contrived *contretemps;* the varied measured climb of his rhetoric to the peak where direct statement becomes simplicity and relief; the motion of statement, almost never with repetition, but with force increased by steady enlargement of perception; and the remarkable impression of power diffused over a poem, not concentrated in a single line, but in the sustaining of statement that line by line looks almost flat, but taken as a whole strikes hard and tellingly. The dangers are apposite to the skills—danger of understatement for effect, coming down too hard on the core, anticlimax, and occasionally an unnecessary spinning out of the obvious. His love lyrics are extraordinarily effective, but too many of them ("Love, That Wears the Moonlight Out," "Song," " As Birds Are Fitted to the Bough") are too close to their Elizabethan models to convince one's feeling of them as lyric poems in their own right: they are almost too good. But this is a remarkable talent, and one, unless I am mistaken, exactly suited by temperament and skill to show us how verse-drama might really be written, for Mr. Simpson's real ability is *dramatic* verse, and yet his lyric abilities are good enough that they promise to support, without usurping, his dramatic sense.

PAUL ENGLE

Coming Up
The New Poets

The most important thing to be said to anyone interested in the present cultural condition of the U.S.A. far beyond the audience usually thought of as buying books of verse, is: Buy this book. It is the cheapest access to the future of any art developed in this country.

It is, indeed, a fabulous example of joining mass production and distribution with the highest level of artistic achievement.

To bring thirty-six new American poets together with sixteen new English poets was a daring and useful venture. It is solid confirmation of a very important fact: The cause, the art, the practice of poetry are flourishing still.

Many of the English poets are available in the United States for the first time, and many of the American poets will be unknown to the general reader, who will benefit most from a careful reading of this book.

There is great brilliance in poem after poem by people such as Anthony Hecht, Robert Lowell, Howard Moss, and by the Englishmen John Heath-Stubbs, Kingsley Amis and Philip Larkin, as fine utterances as a literature could ask from its younger poets.

There is great skill, too, page after page of imaginative image and conception given a firm excellence of expression. It is doubtful whether any previous period of our national life could have put together as distinguished a collection of poets as this one.

A tremendous shift has come about in subject and attitude in American poetry. These poems are astonishingly unpolitical.

Review of *The New Poets of England and America, New York Post,* 29 December 1957. Reprinted by permission.

Twenty years ago the young poets would have been immersed in the social issues of the day. But these poets are concerned with the individual almost apart from society.

Even when poems deal with war (as surprisingly few of them do) they assert the stubborn, single person surviving the mass experience.

They protest little save the validity of the human condition as one man filters it through his porous imagination.

For most of the poets, there is great concern with making the poem well; the abundance of definite forms, as distinct from free verse or the slightly rhythmical lines of poets such as William Carlos Williams, represents almost a complete return to solidity of stanza, rhyme, and meter.

The poet makes the poem firm and shapely, as if he were determined to prove that, in an age of indecision and anxiety, one decisive object can actually be created.

The editors state that they examined the work of three hundred poets. This is an encouraging fact by itself. But the fine importance of the book is in these carefully selected people: Howard Nemerov noting that the vacuum cleaner sulks with "Its bag limp as a stopped lung, its mouth grinning into the floor"; Donald Hall saying of a hill called the Sleeping Giant, "And winter pulled a sheet over his head"; or Donald Finkel commenting that "What was true in flesh is merely beautiful in silver."

This book is a strength to all who want confirmation that a depth of literary culture exists today, a warm stay against the confusions and alarums of the time.

LOUISE BOGAN

Verse

The groves of Academe were once thought to lie in the vicinity of the Muses' laurel wood, and poets could move between these two secluded areas freely and with ease. Nowadays there is a widespread belief that close contact with academic life is dangerous for the creative artist; he is warned, on all sides, that any relationship with institutions of learning will cause his gifts to dwindle, if not totally to disappear. In spite of such warnings, poets of the younger generation have taken to the teaching profession in numbers, and some of the results of this association are coming to light. A recent anthology, *New Poets of England and America* (Meridian Books), is edited by three young men (Donald Hall, Robert Pack, and Louis Simpson) who have themselves received fellowships, grants, and other honors, and who now teach. The volume, which has a delightfully shrewd introduction by the nonacademic Robert Frost, contains the work of forty-six young men (two of them appear posthumously) and six young women, British and American, whose ages range from twenty-two to forty. (Their nationalities and dates are listed.) Although their work seems to have escaped excessive conventional pressures, academic or otherwise, they all—with one or two borderline exceptions—write in form.

Freedom of technique has, in the last forty years, been equated in most people's minds with true poetic originality. But as we look back over the list of major modern talents, writing in English, from Pound and Eliot through Auden, we find that form, although loosened and revised, has never been wholly abandoned. Meter, rhyme, and the stanza have withstood many blows and have been transformed, but they have survived. We

Review of *The New Poets of England and America*, New Yorker, 29 March 1958, 122–24. Also published in *A Poet's Alphabet* (New York: McGraw-Hill, 1970). Reprinted by permission of Ruth Limmer, trustee of the Estate of Louise Bogan.

can even trace pattern and design of one kind or another in Marianne Moore's syllabic verse and in the rhythms, based on the truest of ears, of Pound and William Carlos Williams. The poets of the youngest generation have come to realize, it seems, that form must be experienced and understood before it can be eliminated or tampered with; that the range of poetic effects is too valuable and varied to be treated with carelessness or inattention; that the virtuosity of an Eliot or an Auden is based on both knowledge and practice; that power and nuance partially depend upon the poet's knowledgeable approach to language. These poets, moreover, have moved away from many of the more chilling dicta of modern criticism. If some of them are imitative of their elders, it is at least an imitation of other poets, and not this or that critic's say-so, that they are pursuing.

Very nearly all of the poems in *New Poets* are lyrics, but of the renovated, enlarged, and dramatic kind that has risen, phoenix-like, from the ashes of exhausted nineteenth-century "song." And the intractable subject seems to have disappeared, or, rather, been absorbed; machines, for example, are treated with casual directness. The love song written in the first person singular shows up only once or twice, but there are many disguised love poems, written in every sort of tone and manner. And the idea of death is presented from both the secular and the religious points of view, sometimes in elegies (often addressed to the young). Myth seems to be going out, while actual history is coming in—another good sign, since it is much more difficult to be fancy about history. Nature comes through in all aspects, together with the night side of things—dreams, nightmares, and the fantasies in between. The percentage of ballads is high. One, W. S. Graham's "Baldy Bane," is as close to the shocking subject matter of folk as the "coarse" ballads of the later Yeats. The collection is notably free of the coldly elaborate, the foolishly excited, and the gloomily bardic, and there is little word-spinning or verbalism for its own sake. And if few rebellious notes are openly struck, many of these young men and women are capable of satiric poems that indicate the working of a sharp and critical eye. We can only guess at the futures of these writers, and all are not on a high level of talent, but to see so much liveliness and accomplishment should stir our imagination and our hope. And the notion that any involvement with the academic automatically results in the drying up of talent should be reexamined, since some, at least, of these contributors seem not only to have survived exposure to learned institutions but actually to have drawn nourishment from them.

THOM GUNN

From "Excellence and Variety"

A Dream of Governors is in many ways a brilliant book. What one first notices about Simpson is his power over the single line—it is harmoniously filled out in the manner of some such musical Elizabethan as Sir John Davies.

> The treasures of Cathay were never found.
> In this America, this wilderness
> Where the axe echoes with a lonely sound,
> The generations labor to possess
> And grave by grave we civilize the ground.

This power is symptomatic, however, of his chief temptation, which is toward decoration for its own sake—decoration which may finally take the strength of the poem away, as it does in the first poem, "The Green Shepherd." A converse danger, though it is less extreme, is toward the didactic, as in poems like "Tom Pringle." (And here I ought to mention a long poem, "The Runner," though it is neither decorative nor didactic. I cannot help thinking that such a narrative would be more effective in prose.)

His strength lies between these extremes, in poems where neither rhetoric nor intention takes force from the other. Some of these are remarkably successful. If one jots down a list of the best poems in the book—"Orpheus in the Underworld," "I Dreamed That in a City Dark as Paris," "Old Soldier," "Hot Night on Water Street," "Carentan O Carentan"—one is struck by the fact that they are almost all about either hallucination or

---

Review of *A Dream of Governors, Yale Review* 49 (December 1959): 298–99.

something pretty close to it. Description of hallucination can be mere fooling, but the way in which Simpson does it is serious and with a purpose. Behind the real situation a ghost situation suddenly appears, grows clearer, and, without obliterating it, becomes as vivid as the original situation: so that each acts not only as a contrast but as a kind of verification to the other. The possibilities of this kind of poem are shown most strikingly by the structure of "Orpheus in the Underworld." The first nine stanzas, about Orpheus, seem part of a very accomplished but slightly academic exercise; then suddenly the narrator uses the first person (Simpson is an old hand at springing the first person on the reader with good effect: he did it in "The Battle," in his earlier book), and the narrator merges with Orpheus. As a result, the coolness of the description that has gone before now becomes in retrospect the restraint of a man who has gone through the same sort of experience as Orpheus. The story continues about Orpheus and the narrator simultaneously, each acting as a metaphor to the other, but each stronger in itself than a mere metaphor. The advantage of such a structure is obvious: the author has set himself at a remove from his subject, but not at such a remove that he is tempted to use fanciful embellishments. "I Dreamed That in a City Dark as Paris" does the same sort of thing, but even more subtly: a modern man (one suspects a soldier) dreams that he is a French soldier in an earlier war.

> The helmet with its vestige of a crest,
> The rifle in my hands, long out of date,
> The belt I wore, the trailing overcoat
> And hobnail boots, were those of a *poilu*.

He watches two planes at a dogfight, "till one streamed down on fire to the earth," and at the end, returned to his modern self, comments:

> My confrere
> In whose thick boots I stood, were you amazed
> To wander through my brain four decades later
> As I have wandered in a dream through yours?

> The violence of waking life disrupts
> The order of our death. Strange dreams occur,
> For dreams are licensed as they never were.

In a sense, this is his justification for the dream and hallucination as subject matter. But the poems themselves, honest without being tame, are justification enough.

ANTHONY HECHT

From "The Anguish of the Spirit
and the Letter"

The readers of *Hudson Review* are already familiar with the
poetry of Louis Simpson, whose work has often appeared in
these pages. But it is hard to realize how consistently excellent
and various his work can be without reading carefully through
his book again and again. This is one of the best new books of
poetry in years. He commands a style capable of great emotional
range, at once witty and dramatic, sometimes spare and ironic,
sometimes frighteningly phantasmagoric, always inventive and
not infrequently beautiful. His subject matter covers more
ground, geographically, historically, and mythically, than al-
most any young poet writing today, and without in any sense
being a "War Poet" he has written the best poems to come out
of the Second World War. His image of America is real and
complex, urban and rural, tawdry and powerful, and he is able
to make us feel both our connection with the Old World of
Europe and our independence of it. I hardly know what to quote
to show Mr. Simpson's versatility, but these snippets, even out
of context, ought to indicate something.

> Venice, the city built on speculation,
> Still stands on it. Love sails from India
> And Sweden—every hanging cloud pours out
>   A treasure-chest.
> It's love on the Rialto, news of love,
> That gives Antonio his golden life,

Review of *A Dream of Governors*. Reprinted by permission from *The Hudson
Review*, Vol. XII, No. 4 (Winter 1959–60). Copyright © 1959 by The Hudson
Review, Inc.

Even to Envy, sharpening a knife,
    His interest. . . .

The barns like scarlet lungs are breathing in
Pneumonia. The North wind smells of iron.
It's winter on the farm. The Hupmobile
That broke its back is dying at the fence. . . .

"Did you not call?" she said,
"Goodbye, then! For I go
Where I am wanted."
Till dawn I tossed in bed
Wishing that I could know
Who else she haunted.

But this is not very satisfactory. It does not show, for instance, how Mr. Simpson can take a particularly unprepossessing petit bourgeois French family, and by setting them upon the beach in "Côte d'Azur" amid foreign tourists laved in wealth and fame and ambition and self-love, make of them in their vulgar simplicity the loveliest things in the scene. Neither does it show Mr. Simpson's awful skill in rendering a clear picture of perverse Nazi insanity in "The Bird." Nor does it show the light and piercing wit of poems like "The Green Shepherd" or "The Custom of the World." He is a poet from whom it is hard to excerpt anything, for his design and tone depend upon the whole. His worst fault, I think, is to succumb to a kind of lyric neatness, a too pat arrangement of lines and words. For example:

There are designs in curtains that can kill,
Insidious intentions in a chair;
In conversation, silence, sitting still,
The demon of decorum and despair.

You would not guess, from the somewhat trivial artificiality of this first stanza, with its careful alliterations and precise rhetorical balances, how genuine, imaginative and free the rest of the poem is. This is a small fault, and Mr. Simpson doesn't let it happen very often. His publishers, who have had the good sense to publish him, have had the poor sense to remark in their advertising zeal that he has "a simplicity of form and phrase that has been compared to William Blake's. . . ." I cannot imagine by whom, but the comparison is misleading and unfair. Simpson is neither a mystic nor a symbolist. He has wonderfully assimilated his sources, which were more visible in earlier work, and Blake was not one of them. He is thoroughly American in style and attitude, and he is a man the Pulitzer Committee should regard with a thoughtful and appraising eye.

PETER DAVISON

From "New Poetry: Prizewinners and Apprentices"

Louis Simpson is a little older than [George] Starbuck, and one step further up the ladder of recognition, having held several fellowships and grants. *A Dream of Governors* (Wesleyan University Press) is his second book, and you will find in it some of the best traditional verse being written by a young American poet today. American poetry needs more than anything else a reinfusion of the narrative element, and Simpson is devoted to narrative. His book contains a long poem about World War II and the feelings of men in battle. It is, unfortunately, less a narrative poem than a short story told in well-written blank verse; its story gains little from having been told in poetic form. When it deals with a dramatic confrontation, as in the final battle when the Germans attack at Bastogne, it succeeds admirably; but it fails in conveying the passage of time, which is one of the hardest things for a narrative in verse to do.

Some of Simpson's shorter narratives do succeed: he retells myths (St. George, Orpheus, and others) in a rich aura of mysticism and moonlight. One day he will have achieved the full flavor of what he is striving for in his narratives; but this collection is uneven, and that time has not yet come. The final group of love poems, however, has things in it as whole and true as in any recent love poems I can remember. Poems like "The Custom of the World," "Rough Winds Do Shake," and "Summer Storm," a touching and humorous sonnet, are humane entities, full of feeling and vitally expressed. Listen to another kind of love from "The Goodnight," a poem to a small daughter:

> The lives of children are
> Dangerous to their parents

Review of *A Dream of Governors*, *Atlantic Monthly*, September 1960, 92.

With fire, water, air,
And other accidents;
And some, for a child's sake,
Anticipating doom,
Empty the world to make
The world safe as a room.

This is memorable writing.

DANIEL HOFFMAN

From "Between New Voice
and Old Master"

A couple of years ago Louis Simpson anthologized in *New World Writing* some poems by his contemporaries, heading his selection "The Silent Generation." That title appears again above one of his own poems— "It was my generation / That put the Devil down / With great enthusiasm. / But now our occupation / Is gone. Our education / Is wasted on the town. // We lack enthusiasm." Among the results of the situation Mr. Simpson so deftly epitomizes has been an impoverishment of sensibility for poetry, as for other areas of life. A set of difficulties, doubtless long present, becomes intensified for the individual who would discover fecund relations with history, place, myth, time. Mr. Simpson's third book, *A Dream of Governors,* goes an impressively long way toward articulating such themes with an authoritative command of both subject and technique that seems to transcend these contemporary dilemmas. Something of his range is indicated by the division of his book into five sections. He modernizes myths to ironic advantage, and contrasts "My America" with "The Old World." A fourth group includes some of the best poems to have come out of the Second World War, and the fifth presents love poems effective alike in their delicacy and wry strength. From this catalogue of subjects one would scarcely guess the complexity with which he realizes each, nor the variety of modes and tones his verse commands. Even his exorcisms, his phantasmagoria, his ballad of a lunatic Nazi, are lucid in organization and language, while his rationally developed poems, such as the neo-neoclassical "The Green Shepherd" and "The Flight to Cytherea," are alive with surprises of perception and diction. I've space to quote but a stanza

Review of *A Dream of Governors, Sewanee Review* 68 (Autumn 1960): 677–79.

from two other poems, to suggest still further the ranges in Mr. Simpson's unified book. From "An American in the Thieves' Market":

> But I am American, and bargain
> In the Thieves' Market, where the junk of culture
> Lies in the dust—clay shards, perhaps Etruscan,
>   And wedding rings . . .
> My father's ghost is ticking in a watch,
> My mother's, weeping in the antique bed,
> And, in a pile of swords, my cousins shed
>   The tears of things.

And "The Lover's Ghost":

> "Did you not call?" she said,
> "Goodbye, then! For I go
> Where I am wanted."
> Till dawn I tossed in bed
> Wishing that I could know
> Who else she haunted.

Mr. Simpson is skillful beyond fluency, and seldom does he allow himself the too easy versification mere fluency invites, nor expose his influences. (Yeats seems vestigially present in a couple of poems—"And what's the aftermath? A murdered man, / A crying woman, and an empty dish. . . .") In "The Runner" he turns from the short lyric to attempt a blank-verse redaction of the materials of *The Red Badge of Courage*. This thirty-page narrative poem is full of realistic observations that might have figured more potently in fiction; as it is, the texture of the verse is usually on its surface. There are fine touches of characterization and an unequivocal honesty in presentation but these virtues seem unassimilated into the verse. Perhaps the best part of the poem comes as the soldier, bivouacked in a rear area, stumbles into a trench dug in the first War. But Mr. Simpson makes more telling use of this conceit (or experience) in a short nightmare, "I Dreamed That in a City Dark as Paris," where he discovers that he *is* the alive statue of a World War I *poilu*:

                                        My confrere,
In whose thick boots I stood, were you amazed
To wander through my brain four decades later
As I have wandered in a dream through yours?

The violence of waking life disrupts
The order of our death. Strange dreams occur,
For dreams are licensed as they never were.

A Dream of Governors belongs among the handful of durable books by younger poets in the past decade.

JOHN K. HUTCHENS

Riverside Drive

"The improper study of mankind is woman," the much-beset narrator of *Riverside Drive* reflects toward the end of this rather melancholy, romantic first novel by Louis Simpson, the poet. It is one of those shiny phrases that can signify something or, on the other hand, nothing whatever, but in the context of the narrator's problem it does have a certain meaning.

Young Duncan Bell, sometime upper-class Jamaican self-removed to New York, aspiring writer, World War II paratrooper, obsessively loves a woman who for the most part rewards him with agony. By the time this has been going on for ten years, Duncan has had it.

Does the shade of Proust's poor Swann, yearning for his heartless Odette, lurk offstage in *Riverside Drive?* It does. Mr. Simpson even mentions Swann, along with other sorry lovers, and, indeed, has his narrator say in conclusion that "what I have told is the commonest story." He's as right about that as Ecclesiastes on the absence of novelty under the sun, but still it potentially is a new story each time it is told: sometimes for better and sometimes not.

Riverside Drive falls somewhere in between, a finishing position not calculated to make for immortality. And this is too bad, because Mr. Simpson brings to his first sortie into fiction a good many of the virtues of his poetry (*The Arrivistes, A Dream of Governors,* etc.): a firm intelligence, a spare, intense way with words, a gift for images used with a difference.

Young Duncan, a student at Columbia University, sees the even younger Mona Jocelyn one day along Riverside Drive, and is entranced. There is that about her precocious maturity which catches and holds the eye of any male of any age, though Dun-

---

Review of *Riverside Drive, New York Herald Tribune,* 9 May 1962, 27.

can would have held off for a while had he known that she was merely fourteen. (By so close a margin does a character in one book keep from wandering over into another one—*Lolita,* say.) He suspects her of carrying on with someone else. They part, and he goes off to the war.

It is those chapters on one young American's wartime experience for which, I suspect, you will best remember *Riverside Drive.* They are not less than brilliant, the war as seen by a man who believes in it but never is bemused by glory or glamour— who, coming upon a shallow trench of an earlier war near Rheims, is moved to ponder on the men of 1914 who were there:

> Rain had fallen, and snow; the stubble on their jaws had been caked with mud and covered with frost. They stamped their boots and wrapped their long overcoats around them and propped their long rifles against the parapet and stared into the east. It was too much for flesh to endure—so they murmured. Nevertheless, they had remained. . . .

But Duncan's war is little more than an interlude. Presently there is the civilian life again, a marriage entered into out of sheer apathy, and, always in the background and all too soon in the foreground, the promiscuous, irresistible, selfish and not very bright Mona, inducing jealousy from every pore. Thus was it ever with Fata Morgana's victims, and very sad too, but not, alas, inevitably fascinating in the telling, even when a writer as serious and well-meaning as Mr. Simpson has brought all his talent to bear upon it.

DICK WICKENDEN

This Week in Fiction

Like Duncan Bell, the narrator and central character of *Riverside Drive*, Louis Simpson was born in Jamaica, B.W.I., attended Columbia University, served during the war with an airborne division of the United States Army, and worked for a time as a publisher's editor. But if there are aspects of this first novel that are literally autobiographical, there is at least one important difference between its author and its hero: by the time Duncan Bell stops telling us about what he had to go through (his youth, in short) before settling down to lead his real life, he appears to have abandoned any literary ambitions, whereas Louis Simpson at not quite forty has won an impressive reputation as a poet.

Poets tend to write notably good prose, and an admirable style helps to make *Riverside Drive* enjoyable. Throughout the peacetime prelude with which the book begins, there is a perhaps too-conscious attempt at fine writing, which robs the scenes of vitality; but in subsequent vivid and somber sections about Duncan's experiences in the Army as Germany was collapsing, and later in a state mental hospital, there is a marked increase in vigor. Thereafter, as the book turns into an ironic comedy, the writing becomes consistently witty as well.

Duncan drifts through a series of preposterous jobs, and has some occasionally preposterous adventures as an expatriate in France. After his return to New York and a disastrous marriage, he enters upon a passionate affair with Mona, the girl who has kept reappearing ever since his first meeting with her, a decade earlier. Except for a brief postlude in California, the final stages of the book, which possess an almost Proustian subtlety and

---

Review of *Riverside Drive, New York Herald Tribune Books*, 13 May 1962, 8.

penetration, concern the incandescent life and inevitable death of this affair.

Riverside Drive is basically a somewhat wry and melancholy work. But it is completely honest and its total effect is exhilarating.

THOM GUNN

From "Modes of Control"

Louis Simpson's latest book shows change as well, and change in a direction that at least superficially shows some resemblance to [James] Wright's. Most of his new poems are in free verse, for example, and the uncanny image is doing far more work in them than formerly. However, poems like "The Morning Light" or even "Birch" are still traditional enough in structure to be understood in the same terms as his earlier poems:

> Birch tree, you remind me
> Of a room filled with breathing,
> The sway and whisper of love.
>
> She slips off her shoes;
> Unzips her skirt; arms raised,
> Unclasps an earring, and the other.
>
> Just so the sallow trunk
> Divides, and the branches
> Are pale and smooth.

The two images are presented in relation to one another, just as they would be in Herrick or Keats, and if the poem looks "modern" it is partly because it is in free verse (but a free verse that is very close to meter with substitutions, like most of Simpson's) and even more because the perception is expressed with accuracy and freshness and thus does not remind us of other poems.

Simpson, from his earliest work, has been attracted by the

Review of *At the End of the Open Road*, *Yale Review* 53 (March 1964): 457–58. Copyright © 1964 by Yale University.

ornate style—and if the word ornate sounds Elizabethan, the association is appropriate. At times, as in "John the Baptist" (from *Good News of Death*), he has been in danger of succumbing to its sweet seduction; but the peculiar strength of much of his best work has arisen from his awareness of the seduction, and the copresence of a hard resistance to it: a kind of vigorous restlessness, of a most exciting sort, has been brought about by his ability to be simultaneously inside and outside of the Bower of Bliss. At best the restlessness acts as a check to the sensuousness, and the sensuousness acts as a check to the restlessness. The quality resulting from such lack of repose is found at its most developed in "My Father in the Night Commanding No" in this collection, a lovely and at the same time sinister and uneasy poem, in which we are continually being put at momentary ease, in familiar surroundings as it were, and continually being made to realize immediately afterwards that we weren't where we thought we were at all. I find this possibly Simpson's best poem, but it is too long to quote in full and too tightly made to quote in part. Similarly excellent poems are "A Dream in the Woods of Virginia," which is the final section of a group ["The Marriage of Pocahontas"] that is otherwise lacking in energy, and "The Riders Held Back." (One English reviewer has damned this last as an "academic poem." It would probably be more accurate to call it an "unacademic poem," but whatever it is classed as, it is very good.)

There is also in this book an attempt—a development from a section of his last book—to define America, or the feeling of being in America, or the feeling of writing poems in America. Some of the results of the attempt seem to me a bit dated. The poem "American Poetry" looks almost as if it were written without knowledge of Williams or Hart Crane. Much of the time, however, Simpson's conclusions are exploratory and individual: "there is something unsettled in the air," he says, and "at the end of the open road we come to ourselves." He is most successful when he is defining a quality that turns out not to be particularly American:

> For we are the colonists of Death—
> Not, as some think, of the English.

And we are preparing thrones for him to sit,
Poems to read, and beds
In which it may please him to rest.

This is the land
The pioneers looked for, shading their eyes
Against the sun—a murmur of serious life.

["Lines Written near San Francisco"]

In such fine lines he seems to be denying the relevance of nationality as a primary quality, in poetry or in life. Certainly, it is something his best work has always transcended and continues to transcend.

THOMAS MCGRATH

From "From the Dreamcoast"

America in the form of a wagon train is crossing the continent. Somewhere in the Badlands we are jumped by Crazy Horse and the Ogalalla Sioux. We make a run for it, but the pesky redskins still keep gaining. Nothing to do but lighten load! Overboard goes Grandma Tradition, the European clock, the music box which played that song of Lawes, an ornamental chamber pot artfully inscribed "Into thy hands," family albums, tables of genealogy, preserved nail clippings. . . . Careening madly our caravan falls down the western slope of the Rockies, leaps the Grand Canyon, lunges through the Oregon deserts, swims the Potomac. At last, somewhat the worse for wear but still thanking God and Manifest Destiny we reach the Ultimate Coast. Canvas is ripped on the wagons; the wolves of Omaha have eaten Little Sister; felloes have dried up so that the rims have fallen from the wheels; a reach is broken. . . . Still, we have what is necessary: the tools (an atomic can opener, a fully transistorized computer) and the Bible. For it will be necessary to reinvent language, not only to praise the Absolute Gadget which our tools will help us create in the forms of a culture but to describe the fabulous coast itself: here Nature, in the form of a Redwood, appears to exist like the Word on the morning after creation. . . .

Everyone *knows* this scenario—our fathers all helped to write it. And we've all spent time on the Dream Coast with its litter of half-drowned wagons, half-buried shipwrecks, submerged streetcars seeking a further destination contra naturam. This littoral is anywhere outside the window. But it is one thing to *know* that something has stopped in America; it is an-

Review of *At the End of the Open Road, Carleton Miscellany* 5 (Spring 1964): 86–90.

other thing to *feel* that condition as a limit of Being. Moreover this condition cannot be changed in the "American Way." The West was the Earthly Paradise. In the American Way we charged into it hell-bent for Election. But, west of Eden, Paradise was only a mirage. We could enter it only in a fallen state, create it only through a Fall. And now there are only two possible ways to deal with the State of Its Hellship: Apocalypse (revolution) or Transfiguration—being born again. It is with some of these problems and possibilities that our two books deal.

Here is Louis Simpson come into California, "troubling the dream coast / With my New York face." The "epical clatter" of the westward movement is over:

> Lie back, Walt Whitman,
> There, on the fabulous raft with the King and the Duke!
> For the white row of the Marina
> Faces the Rock. Turn round the wagons here.

What we have come to is a view of Alcatraz, the new subdivisions built by "the same old city planner, death."

> We cannot turn or stay
> For though we sleep, and let the reins fall slack,
> The great cloud-wagons move
> Outward still, dreaming of a Pacific.
>
> ("In California")

This doesn't happen without irony:

> When they had won the war
> And for the first time in history
> Americans were the most important people—

Just then, or *because* just then, perhaps:

> Priests, examining the entrails of birds,
> Found the heart misplaced, and seeds
> As black as death, emitting a strange odor.
>
> ("The Inner Part")

58

Now, having had *in himself* the experience that is "history," the poet can go back to speak of it with Whitman. (I say "go back." I have no idea in what order these poems were written, but, as all good books are likely to be—and as the work of a great poet *always* is—the present volume is essentially a single poem.) He has not much to report: "The Open Road goes to the used-car lot." And Whitman is not surprised: "did I not warn you that it was Myself / I advertised?" Except for "pickpockets, salesmen" who had "contracted / American dreams," this revelation opens toward new possibilities:

> All that grave weight of America
> Cancelled! Like Greece and Rome.
> The future in ruins . . .
>
> The clouds are lifting from the high Sierras,
> The Bay mists clearing. . . .
>   ("Walt Whitman at Bear Mountain")

But if we are not condemned to the American dream, what *is* there and what must we do? On the coast the redwoods are speaking:

> O if there is a poet
>
> let him come now! We stand at the Pacific
> like great unmarried girls,
>
> turning in our heads the stars and clouds,
> considering whom to please.
>   ("The Redwoods")

The question is: how to please *them?* Is there any way to change the unpleasant condition we have come to?

In "Moving the Walls" one way is suggested. In this fine and fantastic poem the Prince of Monaco goes out on a sea voyage and finds in the deep many marvels including Leviathan. Later, part of the yacht and the whole collection is turned into a museum, but they have been transformed: "A walking stick made from the backbone of a shark."

And the sea is no mystery.
For a shark is a walking stick.

And this we call the life of reason.

Still, there were men of a different order:

When men wanted the golden fleece
It was not wool they wanted.
They were the trophies that they sailed toward.

When the sea takes them, they are transfigured and appear as
"new constellations."

They left no wreckage.
Nothing is floating on the surface.
For they yielded themselves
To the currents that moved from within.

Our hope is in a "sea-change" through a reentry into nature
and the depths of our own being. "At the end of the open road
we come to ourselves." To begin there, and to speak to the
redwoods, we need a new language. (It is interesting that the
main theme of this book, the "ending" of a dream, should coin-
cide with a break in style by the poet.) What kind of language?
Here is "American Poetry":

Whatever it is, it must have
A stomach that can digest
Rubber, coal, uranium, moons, poems.

Like the shark, it contains a shoe.
It must swim for miles through the desert
Uttering cries that are almost human.

This is more than a language for the redwoods. It would be
understood by those who appear to have a claim on the poet,
who want him "to live in the tragic world forever."

Simpson's book dramatizes the "return," the need to come
back to the self as starting point for a new movement.

WILLIAM STAFFORD

From "Terminations, Revelations"

Our continent, tilted west for long, begins to level itself; the
nation that journeyed with Walt Whitman, afoot and light-
hearted, finds that it too has become established, perhaps by
now itself an overpaid account. In California the westering
Americans—with money, with success, with power, with red-
woods, with San Francisco, with a sky like a perpetual Gug-
genheim—come to the end of the open road, which, Louis
Simpson finds, "goes to the used-car lot."

At the End of the Open Road plays against this pattern of West-
ward movement, tagging it with Whitman references but
darkening it toward disquieting terminations. For instance, even
on from California, in passage toward India, America is seen as
on the move, but with its power represented by such front men
as Realtors and Marines. Again and again the poems confront
new, grim aspects of America's formative traditions. It is as if
treasured documents like the Declaration of Independence
should glow under a certain light and reveal odd skeletons.

This is a wonderfully sustained and consistent book—even an
insistent book, with excitements and discoveries. In addition,
the book exemplifies throughout a quality intermittently or
variably present, at their best, in the other books under consid-
eration. The poems in *At the End of the Open Road* lead again and
again to an implied big story; the reader has a sense of living in a
sustained pattern which works along behind the poems and
makes of them a succession of glimpses into something ever
larger. Maybe all I mean is that some poems today—and among
them most of these in this book—carry a reader close to par-
ticipation in a drama continually implied by the circumstances of

Review of *At the End of the Open Road, Poetry* 104 (May 1964): 104–5. Copyright
© 1964 by The Modern Poetry Association. Reprinted by permission of the
Editor of *Poetry*.

our lives but never fully realized in the actual world. In our time, this implied story is never embodied in a complete work—a *Paradise Lost* or a *Divine Comedy*—and apparently such an established story cannot be at this time convincingly delivered to us. But some writers do entertain hints that back of the shifting present there impends a meaning. *At the End of the Open Road* bears that kind of extra effect; the thread of the poems recurrently demonstrates the power to be derived from working near the potential of an imminent revelation.

Tentatively, a further characteristic of this book is that the poems avail themselves frequently of two forms hitherto opposed but now more and more blended—or marbled—together. Where Mr. Simpson finds himself following a pattern of sound and stress he rides with it; but where he finds it an advantage to break the pattern, he does so. The result is that for varying intervals he enjoys formal reinforcements, but he retains a readiness to modulate at will from restraint. Ordinarily, we assume that writers take on a pattern, or they write freely, or make some regular adjustment. I see no net disadvantage in Mr. Simpson's kind of having and eating; in fact, I believe that what he does is much done, and that for some time we have been enjoying joint membership in the formal and the informal traditions. The success of this book gives occasion to take explicit note.

Though these poems are here collected for the first time, a number of them have been so effective in periodicals or so aptly used for touchstones that they are already more than magazine pieces; such poems are "Walt Whitman at Bear Mountain," "The Marriage of Pocahontas," "My Father in the Night. . . ." The authority of such poems helps to make this a resounding book, a solid achievement.

DUANE LOCKE

New Directions in Poetry
The Work of Louis Simpson

So much of modern art is concerned with the reaction or depiction of an endowed and cultivated sensibility in a civilization dedicated to a shallow hedonism: the worship of cigarettes, TV sets, bowling, beer, and real estate. Many of Louis Simpson's finest poems, in a distinctive and unique way, are centered on this concern. His work prior to *At the End of the Open Road* (Wesleyan) approaches the situation somewhat objectively and critically; but his *Open Road* poems display more of a sense of direct personal involvement and a subjective transcension.

In the pre–*Open Road* poems, he presents through indirections such as emblematic shepherds and the pastoral tradition the tragic folly of those who have disavowed the inner life to pursue an existence sold by the movie and advertising men. The earlier poetic organization is often traditionally formal, making use of stanzas and rhymes; but the formal patterns function as essential parts of the communication. The metrically controlled movement establishes an ironic undertone to a surface depicting the brutality of innocence, as in "The Green Shepherd":

> The vessel they ignored still sails away
> So bravely on the water, Westward Ho!
> And murdering, in a religious way,
> Brings Jesus to the Gulf of Mexico.

Simpson's enameled aspersions toward these innocents, who in their gay lightness and in their pursuit of superficial sensuality

Review of *At the End of the Open Road, dust* 1, no. 3 (Fall 1964): 67–69.

become oblivious of human misery and the cruelties of progressive civilization, never is reduced to a monovoiced howl, or a lifeless editorial; but is achieved with an insight that perceives the situation in its totality, sensing both the amusing and tragic implications. Always present among the dispassionate and conventionalized flirtations is the greatest destroyer of pleasure, death. Perfect nakedness cannot entice death to forget its mission, and inevitably death will take the furniture away. "And grave by grave we civilize the ground." Death is omnipresent, and often the earlier poems resemble rococo roses painted on a white skull.

Although basically objective, a subjective element, in the form of an "I," does appear in some of the pre–*Open Road* poems. This "I" is usually a stranger, or someone apart, so much apart from the ordinary amusements of humanity that he can make the perspicacious observation, "And nothing is more melancholy / than to watch people enjoying themselves / as much as they can," ("Côte d'Azur"). In "Hot Night on Water Street," the stranger is confronted by a cigar-smoking innocent who is completely unaware of the brutal casualness of his remarks, "Since I've been in this town / I've seen one likely woman, and a car / As she was crossing Main Street, knocked her down." Throughout the poems, the "I" is passive and never a real part of a situation. He goes to his room and reads the *New York Times;* but in *Open Road* there is often a transcendence of the scene through an inwardness, an outburst of inner life.

In *Open Road* the style loosens, the lines become uneven, and the movement of the natural voice and phrasal breaks replaces preconceived measurement. The imagery tends toward inwardness, and the result is a more phenomenal poetry, one in which the subjective imagination transforms by its own operations the objective into what constitutes genuine reality. Whether or not Simpson is developing toward a "deep image," Spanish Surrealism, or some use of poetic language similar to Rene Char cannot be determined at this time, although I doubt if Simpson will ever become automatic, autotelic, or hermetic. One of Simpson's recent poems, published in Robert Bly's *Sixties,* is a brilliant satire on the current influence of Pablo Neruda; and demonstrates the clarity and aloofness of a perception that will never allow itself to be swallowed up by the mere fashionableness of a movement.

Simpson's poetry, in going beyond the mere literal, is becoming more inward, and is developing toward phenomenalism. This phenomenalism, found in Jerome Rothenberg, Robert Bly, James Wright, George Hitchcock, and W. S. Merwin, is one of the most exciting developments in American poetry since the ascendancy of the Williams-Olson-Zukofsky tradition and the vernacular experiments, but phenomenalism has been largely overlooked by the well-paid commentators who seek to please the public mind by dividing American poetry into two hostile and warring camps, the Academics and the Beats (or Wild Men, as they have recently been termed by Chad Walsh), as if poets were big businessmen trying to outsmart one another in order to gain a monopoly.

This new inwardness in *Open Road* is seen primarily in the imagery, as in the strange poem "The Cradle Trap," when the reader is suddenly confronted with such exciting lines as "The light is telling / terrible stories," and as in "The Troika" with "I have lost my father's horses" and "I held the bird." Also, in the metaliteral scene in "On the Lawn at the Villa":

We were all sitting there paralyzed
In the hot Tuscan afternoon,
And the bodies of the machine-gun crew were draped over the
    balcony.
So we sat there all afternoon.

The imagery still has the clarity, keeps something of the literal, but it is more inward and less logical than much of the earlier Simpson. It foretells a new direction. The new looseness of style allows the drift into inwardness, and the charm and urbanity that is diminished with the discarding of the formal style is replaced by a new excitement and new significance.

RONALD MORAN

From "Time of Heterogeneity
A Chronicle of Fifteen"

Whatever else he did, the inexorable Walt Whitman started the
tradition in American poetry obsessed with defining what
America is. Whitman's job, though, was decidedly easier than
that of those now compelled to define in verse the nation that has
nowhere to go. At least in the middle of the nineteenth century,
there were frontiers—economic, social, and political, all of
which were made possible by a physical frontier that still had
somewhere to go. Now, however, America has to turn on the
inward spotlight to find a frontier; and introspection, especially
when the past made or suggested many promises, inevitably
lights up and focuses brightly on disappointments. A hundred
years later with frontiers exhausted, Louis Simpson emerges
with too much candlepower to let the products of the American
Story find any dark recesses in which to hide. There is little
doubt that the American Walt Whitman envisioned, at least up
to his later years, is the dominant image in Mr. Simpson's Pulit-
zer Prize collection *At the End of the Open Road.* The speaker of
"Lines Written near San Francisco" claims this of America:

> the banks thrive and the realtors
> Rejoice—they have their America.

So for those who measure the accomplishment of a nation by the
size of their billfolds, the American Story is paying off. From
"Walt Whitman at Bear Mountain," already an anthology piece
and something of an event poem, comes this indictment: "The
Open Road goes to the used-car lot." It is unpleasant to think of

---

Review of *At the End of the Open Road, Southern Review* 1 (Spring 1965): 475–77.

our land as a "used-car lot" with its landscapes of substitutes and second bests; this figure is particularly telling since the automobile has become more than mere transportation to many American families. Other poems, such as "Pacific Ideas—a Letter to Walt Whitman," "On the Lawn at the Villa," and "The Inner Part," stress *America-now, a definition,* but Mr. Simpson's work is not so besieged by this idea that his book is disproportionately balanced.

Although statements conventionally have been (and belong to) the domain of prose, some American poets, including William Stafford, Robert Bly, and Louis Simpson, use the statement method with surprising effectiveness. The best poems of this new movement (at least a new direction) rely on a quiet power generated through restrained diction, loose rhythms, and an imaginative interplay between subject and attitude. In order to make a statement poem work, the writer must have an extraordinary sense of timing, and this Mr. Simpson most certainly has. Couple it with an appropriate analogy, and the poem works better than the reader thinks it has any right to. I suspect that Mr. Simpson deliberately begins his short poems with flat statements so that the connections he makes will lift the reader high. Take, for example, "In the Suburbs":

> There's no way out.
> You were born to waste your life.
> You were born to this middleclass life
>
> As others before you
> Were born to walk in procession
> To the temple, singing.

I am not happy with Mr. Simpson's longer efforts, such as "Moving the Walls" and "The Marriage of Pocahontas." The former is prose with little justification or reward; the latter is weakly conceived, even though the narrative is handled satisfactorily.

MARTIN SEYMOUR-SMITH

From "Transatlantic Poetry"

This book contains a small collection of poems by each of five poets whose work has not yet appeared in this country in volume form: Edgar Bowers, Howard Nemerov, Hyam Plutzik, Louis Simpson, and William Stafford.

Some poets, the editors tell us in a brief note, "have written poems the editors like as much as many of the pieces included here." But they were omitted because they could not supply enough of them: "The aim was to make not a general anthology but five substantial collections." This approach has unfortunately led to an emphasis on quantity at the expense of quality; a general anthology of good poems would have been of more interest and value to the British reader.

The one indisputably good poet in this book is Mr. Louis Simpson. "The Flight to Cytherea," "The Lover's Ghost," "My Father in the Night Commanding No" and "In California," these are good poems by any standards, and I shall go back to them—not for their cleverness or their ideas, but for their deeply felt and disturbing revelation of situations lying deeper than material concerns such as what a decent procultural chap Mr. Simpson is, or what kind of stuff the magazines want this year. Mr. Simpson's poems have conviction, bite; they are occasioned by experiences other than ambition or vanity or abstractions. I hope someone will soon publish them on this side of the Atlantic.

Review of *Five American Poets*, *Scotsman* (U.K.), 27 July 1963, 2.

From "New World Poetry"

American poetic style in mid-century varies at its extremities like contemporary styles in music. The tonal composers are either deadly imitators or struggling to conceal a worn-out idiom, or have managed to freshen their convention through personality strong enough to enliven an essentially Romantic, eighteenth- and nineteenth-century method. The atonalists range between academic mathematicians of the row and the extraordinary speculations of advanced pointilliste serialists and beyond. John Ashbery's "Europe" might be put beside Jean Barraqué's "Séquence" to suggest an extreme point reached in the two arts. Atonality is a convention: the imitators of Webern are as dull as the severe American imitators of Ezra Pound and William Carlos Williams. The invention of a personal language and structure which are not stupidly original or stultifyingly traditional has never been easy in modern cultures. For their *Five American Poets* Thom Gunn and Ted Hughes have selected, safely, poets who use a basically conventional medium with varying degrees of freshness and lyrical invention, ranging from the iambic boredoms of Edgar Bowers to the occasional imagic releases in Louis Simpson and William Stafford. There is nothing particularly experimental here. All the poems are drawn from books and journals published between 1949 and 1962 and the choice is the editors', no more: it is not representative of new American poetry and is not meant to be, although the scene is strongly illuminated by the book.

The better poets in this collection are Louis Simpson and William Stafford.

In "What God Used for Eyes Before We Came" Mr. Stafford

Review of *Five American Poets*, *Times Literary Supplement*, 1 November 1963, 886.

tries to translate his western scene—here it is fog, pueblo, mountains, men in cars among the canyons—into a religious insight, but it falters into abstractions like "irrelevant history." But it is clear that he will be able to make this more ambitious poem some time through sheer dramatic presentation. Perhaps he needs the releasing deep image that Louis Simpson finds in his recent poems here: the image which strikes before its components are grasped. This would mean risking more than craftsmanship can discover. Mr. Simpson's poems are usually properly made, working in a variety of formal skills within his general lyric field. He can focus a conclusion to a lyric action without pedantry when it is about the times we live in:

> The violence of waking life disrupts
> The order of our death. Strange dreams occur,
> For dreams are licensed as they never were.

This neatness takes another turn in "To the Western World," a poem possibly better than Robert Frost's similar "The Gift Outright":

> . . . this wilderness
> Where the axe echoes with a lonely sound,
> The generations labour to possess.
> And grave by grave we civilize the ground.

Some of Mr. Simpson's American poems are too self-consciously public—historical exercises on a national theme. He is sometimes betrayed by highness into imitations of Auden and Baudelaire, reaching for abstraction before the initiating experience has been fully presented. A number of war poems seem too locked in the past for the necessary detachment, but "Carentan O Carentan" is a fine achievement; a combat poem which is clear, understated in a ballad technique and humanely ironic. Perhaps it does read sometimes like an exercise, in a type of poem, but as a whole it sticks. The patrol moves through the June sunshine, seriously parodying local farmers in the countryside; then—

> The watchers in their leopard suits
> Waited till it was time.

And aimed between the belt and boot
And let the barrel climb.

The remainder of the poem completes one of the nearest things to Wilfrid Owen to come out of the last war. Mr. Simpson's poems make a stand with persistence of life, the regaining of vision, against barbarian violence, whether it is sexual selfishness or war combat or the confused wisdom of an ascetic. How his sensibility could allow admissions like "the night was trembling with a violet / Expectancy," "cold hands, as cold as stone," and "I see through the illusions of the year," is hard to explain. But two of his recent poems evidence a new exploration of line and image which places him in the third stream of emergent American poetry today, poetry between the Beat and the Academic, which inherits Pound and Williams but respects the possible renewal of more formal poetic shapes and searches for the deep image—a term which rightly belongs to the theory and practice of Jerome Rothenberg and Robert Kelly, and Robert Bly.

Louis Simpson's "Walt Whitman at Bear Mountain" and "In California" are about freedom from the past and they are written in opening images rather than closed metaphors, in linear forms, which, like the overt statements in both poems, pay homage to Whitman and, by implication, his descendants in American poetry. Mr. Simpson's earlier poems usually had a strong sense of purpose; now the purpose is freer and more deeply felt. He does not employ the broken syntax and ideogrammatic layout of Olson's followers or the short-measure intensities of Creeley. Rather, the structures of these two poems hold their private events in a public focus in the manner of Robert Lowell's recent poems, works like "For the Union Dead." In the Whitman poem the old poet answers the new: "I gave no prescriptions, / And those who have taken my moods for prophecies / Mistake the matter. . . . I freely confess I am wholly disreputable." Official, commercializing society disregards him—"for they had contracted American dreams." Mr. Simpson moves his poem then toward a larger vision:

> But the man, who keeps a store on a lonely road,
> And the housewife who knows she's dumb,
> And the earth, are relieved.

All that grave weight of America
Cancelled! Like Greece and Rome.
The future in ruins!
The castles, the prisons, the cathedrals
Unbuilding, and roses
Blossoming from the stones that are not there. . . .

The clouds are lifting from the high Sierras,
The Bay mists clearing.
And the angel in the gate, the flowering plum,
Dances like Italy, imagining red.

It is the images in the ninth and last lines, rather than the ironic criticism of Goethe and Henry James, which show Mr. Simpson's progress in risking rhythms and images. "In California" is another complex action on the American city-country tensions, in which the poet's sense of old American nineteenth-century dreams of freedom and movement west, even westward from California, have become a "dark preoccupation" among the optimisms and greedy planning of capitalist democracy. But Mr. Simpson's individual thematic approaches are not yet matched by an inimitable voice. His rhythms tend to monotony, for one thing. Certainly, though, he and William Stafford are good signs of poetic health in the United States. Their poems respect more the individual perception than big iambic formalisms, the image or scene which reveals the private revelation rather than the large social, religious or philosophical scheme. They do not, at their best, argue or play the know-all internationalist, but prefer to present that nearly anarchic personalism which includes so much that is good in American poetry since the 1940s.

DONALD HALL

From "Uncharted Waters"

Ten or more years ago Louis Simpson wrote: "As birds are fitted to the boughs / That blossom on the tree / And whisper when the south wind blows— / So was my love to me." Here are some of the newest lines in these *Selected Poems:* "And yet there is also happiness. / Happiness . . . // If I can stand it, I can stand anything." Fortunately the new colloquialism has not excluded the old lyricism; now Simpson can do *anything*: in "Walt Whitman at Bear Mountain" he combines types of diction in a small compass with an extraordinary intricacy. His flexibility lets him move his tone with a sure inventiveness, by turns funny, descriptive, songlike, and fantastic to the point of surrealism.

Simpson has become primarily a poet of the imagination, but for him the imagination in no way necessitates suppressing the critical intelligence, or limiting the possibilities of language. Some of the new poems here, notably "The Laurel Tree" and "Things," look at his surroundings with new eyes. "In the clear light that confuses everything"—he begins "The Laurel Tree" with a typical paradox—"Only you, dark laurel, / Shadow my house." With the help of "a man in China" who suddenly appears in the back yard, the poet is able to look under the shiny surfaces of objects normally impenetrable: "I must be patient with the shapes / Of automobile fenders and ketchup bottles."

These shapes are American, and finally it is America which is Simpson's theme—his main entry into poetry. In his early work he wrote some of the best modern love poems, and certainly he has written the best American poems about World War II. (It is good to have all these old poems together in one volume; some of them were hard to get at.) But America was always there,

Review of *Selected Poems, New York Herald Tribune Book Week,* 5 December 1964, 44.

bothering him, needing to be considered from another angle, another kind of approach. At the start the country was largely historic and geographic; increasingly, as Simpson's imagination has become more daring and powerful, he has dealt with the spirit. He has a way of illuminating the domestic by setting it beside something apparently incomparable (the world of Asia and a ketchup bottle), but never merely to *prefer* the old or the exotic to the local. There is the little poem, "In the Suburbs":

> There's no way out.
> You were born to waste your life.
> You were born to this middleclass life
>
> As others before you
> Were born to walk in procession
> To the temple, singing.

This poem shows what is suburban about ritualism as much as it shows what is ritual about suburbia. But that is not the point: the clash of the enormous difference of the worlds makes an explosion of light. So does the Oriental in "Things" who says, "Machines are the animals of the Americans." With the aid of spiritual visitors from Asia, and the advice of Walt Whitman, Simpson is exploring a new America: "The clouds are lifting from the high Sierras, / The Bay mists clearing. / And the angel in the gate, the flowering plum, / Dances like Italy, imagining red."

He is the Columbus of an inward continent.

JAMES DICKEY

From "Orientations"

His *Selected Poems* shows Louis Simpson working, at first tenta-
tively and then with increasing conviction, toward his own ver-
sion of a national, an American poetry: as one reads, it becomes
easier and easier to think of him as a specifically American poet,
and one finds oneself more than a little surprised that this is so.
For after all, what *is* an American poet? Particularly *now?* At the
words, at the *thought* of an American poet, one thinks of several
alternative possibilities. The first is of a poet (or nonpoet) like
Russell Davenport, twenty-odd years ago, and his much-pub-
licized-in-slick-magazines-but-quickly-and-mercifully-forgotten
poem "My Country," and of writers like Stephen Vincent Ben-
ét at his worst. One also thinks of Whitman not only at his worst
but at his best, and of Hart Crane. One thinks of lesser "epical"
writers like Sandburg, Norman Rosten, Norman Corwin,
Harry Brown, Winfield Townley Scott. And one also remem-
bers chroniclers of the American *scene,* like Karl Shapiro and
John Ciardi, including the finest of them all, John Hollander.
Simpson is closer to this last group than to any of the others. He
demonstrates that the best service an American poet can do his
country is to see it all: not just the promise, not just the loss and
the "betrayal of the American ideal," the Whitmanian ideal—
although nobody sees this last more penetratingly than Simpson
does—but the whole "complex fate," the difficult and agonizing
meaning of being an American, of living as an American at the
time in which one chances to live. If it comes out sad, as it does
with Simpson despite all his wit and compassion, it is a whole
and not a deliberately partial sadness, and this gives the per-

---

Review of *Selected Poems, American Scholar* 34 (Autumn 1965): 650. Also pub-
lished as "Louis Simpson" in *Babel to Byzantium* by James Dickey. Copyright ©
1961, 1968 by James Dickey. Reprinted by permission of Farrar, Straus and
Giroux.

vasive desperate sadness of this book a terrific weight of honesty and truth. Nothing can be done, although at one time perhaps something might have been. But now the individual has only what he has, only what history has allowed him to be born to.

> There's no way out.
> You were born to waste your life.
> You were born to this middleclass life
>
> As others before you
> Were born to walk in procession
> To the temple, singing.

Through the used-car lots, through the suburbs, through the wars that are only the intensification and temporary catharsis of the life we lead now, Simpson moves in this book, and moves memorably and skillfully. Principally there is the feeling of the great occasions of a man's life being veiled, being kept from him by the soft insulations of his civilization, he being all his life comfortable and miserable, taken care of and baffled. Since there is no primitive singleness of response anywhere, since one cannot hope for spontaneity, one takes it out in wit. Simpson's tone is often much like Randall Jarrell's, although more nervous, irritable, and biting. Jarrell's poems deal with the slow wonder of loss; Simpson's less resigned ones are more bewilderedly angry. If I had any objections to Simpson's work they would tend to group around a knowledgeable glibness, an easy literary propensity to knock off certain obvious sitting ducks. But this is a very good book, a good spread of Simpson's work, and the intensity of his intelligent despair throughout it is harrowing. Although at times a little flip, Simpson is in reality no man for facile answers, and if he is self-consciously more American than most of our other writers, that is our gain, and, whether it wants it or not, our country's as well.

KARL SHAPIRO

Classicists All

Must one remonstrate with the editor? Four volumes of poems (five really) to be assessed in one brief notice—the editorial assessment has obviously been made for the reviewer. Or is the reviewer supposed to try for the upset of the week?

The collections can be reviewed one at a time or all together. Togetherness seems called for here. Someone is certain to write a book about Faulkner's poems, if he hasn't already. With Faulkner, the incredible mediocrity of the poetry becomes a major question, for not all great writers of fiction have been such miserable poets, and some have been marvelous. Well, Hardy anyway. Maybe even Melville. When we consider the poems of Joyce, Hemingway, Faulkner, Malcolm Lowry, the question arises: Where does poetry fail the great myth-makers of our time?

Three of the works [under review] are works of excellence (Humphries, Davidson and Simpson) in ways of excellence that have little to do with each other—and the lousy book is by a genius.

The youngest of the three excellent poets (Simpson) once wrote an exciting essay in which he complained or confessed that he wanted to write "bad" poetry (poetry that would not please) and was trying to find out how to do it. The statement showed a spark of genius. Unfortunately, Simpson later won the Pulitzer Prize and may never learn how to write Bad Poetry.

Faulkner in his chats with the University of Virginia students hit the nail on the head. Someone confronted him with his poems and demanded an explanation. He charmed his way out of the question by saying that he wrote "The Marble Faun" and

Review of *Selected Poems, New York Times Book Review*, 9 January 1966, 12, 14. Copyright © 1966 by The New York Times Company. Reprinted by permission.

"A Green Bough" at an age when people write poetry, seventeen, eighteen, nineteen; and then doubled back and said that when he knew he couldn't write poetry he did "the next best thing."

The next best thing! A quip that can explain away whole Oxford Books of English Verse, or French or German or Italian or Esperanto. One is not a duchess a hundred yards from a carriage—or an anthology.

These four poets are all ironists, of course. The trade name is classicist, though palladian might be a more suitable term. Humphries is a true classicist (namely, a man who knows and loves and is influenced by the ancient classics). His poetry is sure and beautiful, with no flicker of doubt about standards and principles.

Davidson is Neo, below-the-Mason-and-Dixon classical, influenced more by Robert Frost and Confederate corn than the real thing. Yet he writes what he must and how he must, and well.

Simpson is neo-neoclassical, Oscar Williams modern, sometimes termed baroque. He would not translate Edna St. Vincent Millay sonnets into Latin, as Humphries has the gumption to do, nor does he have any goods such as Davidson's Robert E. Lee. His nostalgia for mores turned to bitterness in his mother's milk; he is modern, angry, saturnine champing at the bit and biting his fingernails. He is interesting.

Modern poetry has long been an educational device, a "teaching aid" because poetry (as Faulkner learned early) somewhere turned into a hickory stick. It is punishment, maybe the only form of intellectual punishment we have left. Is it this that makes our poets the higher schoolteachers, and makes them the critics who carry the heaviest hickory sticks? This is a six-line poem by Simpson, called "American Poetry":

> Whatever it is, it must have
> A stomach that can digest
> Rubber, coal, uranium, moons, poems.
>
> Like the shark, it contains a shoe.
> It must swim for miles through the desert
> Uttering cries that are almost human.

One wants to cry: Stop hitting me, Simpson! Or to yell: Faulkner is a lousy poet, Simpson!

All of these books deserve preservation and attention. All in different ways are life-works. And all in different ways point to the failure of poetry in our time, the failure of the forms and, more crucial, the failure of the great art to utter cries that are a bit more than "almost human."

SEAMUS HEANEY

Blood Brothers

One can posit two poles between which the poetic imagination
veers continually: there is that which draws the consciousness
towards surrender to phenomena and that which subjugates
phenomena to an internal vision. Most poets are constantly
crossing the line and changing their latitudes in this imaginative
cosmos. Louis Simpson, for example, navigates the full distance
from the Antarctica of narrative ("The Runner") to the Arctic of
symbolism ("The Riders Held Back"), although most of the
time is spent in the temperate, tempered region between. After
all he is an American and he himself writes of American poetry:

> Whatever it is, it must have
> A stomach that can digest
> Rubber, coal, uranium, moons, poems.

Mr. Simpson has an extremely delicate sense of the traditional
singing line of the English lyric but manages in his work to
transform his notes to locks that hold the actual stuff of experi-
ence: he can digest the coal and the poems, in fact.

"Carentan O Carentan" is an early war poem that gradually
accumulates menace yet proceeds with all the grace of a minuet:

> The sky was blue, but there a smoke
> Hung still above the sea
> Where the ships together spoke
> To towns we could not see.

The mode involves the directness and simplicity of ballad
structure and a cavalier fastidiousness about diction:

Review of *Selected Poems, Times Literary Supplement,* 9 June 1966, 512. Also
published in *Phoenix* (U.K.) 5 (Summer 1969): 30–31.

Lieutenant, what's my duty,
My place in the platoon?
He too's a sleeping beauty.
Charmed by that strange tune.

In his best works Mr. Simpson has the capacity to internalize experience and then to objectify it in such a way that the poem seems independent of the processes of living that preceded it. The imaginative process is not one of mastery over material but of commingling with it. "The Redwoods" ask:

O if there is a poet

let him come now! We stand at the Pacific
like great unmarried girls,

turning in our heads the stars and clouds,
considering whom to please.

America is one of the poet's central subjects: the search for an American identity is the search for his poetic character. At first this produces the wide, idealized vistas of "American Preludes" and "To the Western World," placed above the landscape and the condition of being American; consequently this poetry has something of the generalized, orchestrated emotion of a national anthem. But as the poet finds himself, he touches down with more intimacy and confidence and begins a dialogue with the inhabitants that elicits the more personal emotions of love, anger and disillusion. This fulfilment is achieved in such poems as "Walt Whitman at Bear Mountain" and "After Midnight."

Characteristically also, as Mr. Simpson achieves an American identity, the cadences and patterns of his music depend less on the traditional iambic metre and begin to explore the possibilities of stress and sparseness:

I live by begging.
And it's not just for myself,
But the head and ears of the burro
Nodding against the stars.

If Henry James represented the so-called Paleface tradition, writing out of a sensibility formed in the European mould, while Whitman was the archetype of the Redskin, reacting directly to raw experience, Louis Simpson's position might be termed "blood brother." His poetic loyalties incline both ways, his ear responds to both musics. He gives the natural world its due, but remakes it compulsively and confidently. His book is a valuable one, a touchstone for real poetry.

IAN HAMILTON

From "Origins and Ancestors"

This new book by Louis Simpson is his best yet. Simpson is a skilful, intelligent poet who has shifted from style to style without really finding one that he could call his own; too adventurous to be a campus dandy, he was yet too clever and self-conscious to embrace, with any true conviction, the mysteries of Robert Bly's "deep image" school. In *Adventures of the Letter I* there are a few wisps of Blyish wistfulness ("In dreams my life came toward me, / my loves that were slender as gazelles") but by and large Simpson has moved well beyond all that into a manner which, although predominantly relaxed, ironic and coolly regretful, never quite becomes so smart or rigid that it can't admit the odd heave of lyric power.

It's a suitable style for what the book's about. Simpson is preoccupied with origins and ancestors, with his own ambivalent Americanism, and he approaches these concerns by way of anecdote, parable and character sketch, most of these being delivered by the voice he calls, rather cutely, "the letter I." A thin enough device, this, for getting at one remove from his material; if we find something a bit leisured and complacent in the tone of many of these poems, we are not supposed to blame it wholly on the poet. The letter "I," we gather, is an American of Russian origin ("I feel I am part of a race / that has not yet arrived in America") so he can excusably lay claim to poised detachment both in his reminiscences of childhood in the Russian province of Volhynia and in his meditations on America's past, present and unpleasant future.

Although few of the poems here achieve the intensity and resonance they are aiming for (Simpson relies too much on the power of a tremulous conclusion to transmute an essentially

Review of *Adventures of the Letter I, Observer Review* (U.K.), 11 July 1971, 28.

light poem into something strange and weighty), none of them slackens into flat colloquialese; though attractively casual, almost throw-away, at a first encounter, Simpson's conversational manner is in fact disciplined both by a fairly strict intelligence and by a responsible regard for the line by line shaping of each poem.

GREVEL LINDOP

From "Reviews and Comments"

The title of Louis Simpson's volume might well serve as a collective title for a great deal of recent American writing. Increasingly, the place and function of the writer, the questions of who he is and what he is supposed to be doing, have become central themes of American poetry and fiction.

Yet it would be a mistake to place Simpson alongside Mailer or even Lowell, for despite its unpromising title his collection of poems forms a reticent and almost Horatian body of work. The poet is in retreat, defining his own position by reference to his forebears (both Russian and American), his favourite writers, and the contemporary political crises of America. The poet's ego acts as focus, but is not paraded with ostentation.

The best poems in *Adventures of the Letter I* tend towards narrative: "A Son of the Romanovs," "Isidor" and "A Night in Odessa" are finely told anecdotes, given lyrical movement and satirical bite by Simpson's splendid use of rhythm, which continually approaches an epic swing, only to modulate into self-doubt or bathos:

> Let Yevtushenko celebrate the construction
> of a hydroelectric dam.
> For Russians a dam that works is a miracle.
>> ("A Friend of the Family")

The directly political poems are less successful. Simpson seems uncertain about his own feelings towards the United States as a political entity, but too often tries to appear convinced, so that the political satires and antiwar poems have a

Review of *Adventures of the Letter I, Critical Quarterly* (U.K.) 14 (Winter 1972): 379–80.

hollow ring. Those poems, however, which present the poet's perplexity in full contain some fine insights:

> . . . so much has changed;
> as though Washington, Jefferson, Lincoln
> were only money and we didn't have it.
>
> As though the terrible saying of Tocqueville
> were true: "There is nothing so sordid . . .
> as the life of a man in the States."
>
> ("Doubting")

With his usual ironic honesty, Simpson points to what may be the flaws in his own work:

> I am taking part in a great experiment—
> whether writers can live peacefully in the suburbs
> and not be bored to death.
>
> ("Sacred Objects")

> Like a peasant I trust in silence.
> And I don't believe in ideas
> unless they are unavoidable.
>
> ("An American Peasant")

To live, literally, in the suburbs, should be no particular disadvantage; but too many of these poems seem to come from a mental suburb. There does seem a genuine distrust of ideas, and in consequence an often myopic vision which presents the minutiae of life in a way that brings many of the poems close to Imagism, leaving them strangely purposeless and incoherent. It is as if Simpson had consciously decided to be a minor poet, and had set out to fumble a few of the big themes (the War, mental illness, Nazism, the moon landings) to prove it.

But the honesty of the poems, and Simpson's enormous technical skill, carry us through, for the most part. And the book does add up to a fairly clear, even sympathetic picture of how the world looks to one man with no particular commitments except to poetry and common sense. One suspects, in fact, that this restrained, humorous book may be read when the latest crew of Great American Writers have followed one another into obscurity.

TERRY EAGLETON

From "New Poetry"

The collections by Louis Simpson and J. V. Cunningham repre-
sent directly antithetical responses to the problem of American
materialism. Simpson is an important American poet, and has
been often enough praised; but I found this latest volume
slightly disappointing. Most of the poems are concerned with a
kind of amiable, ironic criticism of American society, enlivened
with a wry, defeatist, Jewish humour; but what comes through
as Simpson's most admirable quality—his simple, almost pas-
toral directness and lyricism—results at the same time in an
occasional lack of energy and complexity in the language itself.
The simplicity, with its air of composed but alert wisdom, is
itself a kind of social attitude, related as it is to a withdrawal
from civilized ideologies to what Simpson sees as more funda-
mental realities:

> . . . I came here with a radical
> who said that everything is corrupt;
> he wanted to live in a pure world.
>
> And a man from an insurance company,
> who said that I needed 'more protection'.
>
> Walking in the foggy lane
> I try to keep my attention fixed
> on the uneven, muddy surface . . .
> the pools made by the rain,
> and wheel-ruts, and wet leaves,
> and the rustling of small animals.
>
> ("The Foggy Lane")

Review of *Adventures of the Letter I, Stand* (U.K.) 13, no. 1 (1971): 78.

The nature/culture opposition here is delicate and oblique, free from the posturing affectation of the free-wheeling latter-day Whitmanites: those three "ands" in the last two lines easily escape a charge of self-consciously breathless naïveté. Yet given this, the opposition is still predictably conventional, in a way which robs Simpson's poetry of the possibility of a complexity of attitude equivalent to its verbal subtlety.

DAVE SMITH

From "Losses in Ceremonial Light"

In Louis Simpson's new collection of poems, *Adventures of the Letter I,* the adventurer turns out to be the self on the move through the logic of dreams, a lyrical narrator who journeys into and out of experience, time, history, myth, and fantasy on a heroic quest for an idealized America. Along the way the "Letter I" leads us to what we have come to expect from Simpson: the destructive forces of the cities, the seductiveness of "things," the perversion of the psyche, California as contemporary Sodom. But, in this, his most consistently impressive book, he also seems to be moving toward a looser structure in which narrative has replaced the lonely suggestiveness of sequential images. There is also less of the old caustic satire, less rage. But what is most unexpected is the self's urge to harmony through an intensified awareness of the "individual," a concern not for Life, but lives, a remarkable conciliation with the jangling machine of America.

From the first section of the book, it becomes clear in poems about a mythical Russian province named Volhynia that the "Letter I" is trying to establish roots. In the poem called "Adam Yankev," a title which fuses the First Man and the Proto-Yankee in a Russian-Jewish-immigrant context, the "Letter I" speaks of Jews in Brooklyn:

> Talking about their lives in the Old Country. . . .
> The passing headlights hurl
> their shadows against the wall.

It is not only Plato's Cave and the search for meaning which is evoked here, but also the loneliness of men in strange, often

Review of *Adventures of the Letter I, Shenandoah* 25 (Winter 1974): 92–93.

violent places. It is a paradigm of the illusory promise of America which the "Letter I" returns to in poems like "Indian Country" and "The Climate of Paradise" where the contemplative spirit is brutalized and perverted by invaders, barbarians who become, as in "On the Eve," titillated businessmen in San Francisco watching:

> The women stand up in cages
> and do it, their breasts in yellow light.

Against this betrayed country of the soul, the "Letter I" sets the strength of the individual self who learns to be silent, to pray, to travel through the dream image beyond life, death, history, or place in order to know, as the voice of "Doubting" knows, that

> Every day the soul arrives,
> and the light on the mental shore
> is still as clear, and still it is mysterious.

And it is only when the self resists the impingement of possessions, obsessions, and attitudes which mean imprisonment in an outer world, that individuals may emerge and become "people with their arms round each other // forever," as they are described in "A Friend of the Family," a long and central poem in the fourth section. Here, the self seeks Chekhov's house as an emblem of sanity in the maelstrom. In the last section Chekhov is exchanged for Whitman, for the Poet who sifts illusion and meaning and turns the self inward to the silent music of the dream which yokes everything, transcends everything; and in the poem called "Sacred Objects" the last stanza returns us to the self Simpson names the "Letter I":

> And at night when the passing headlights hurl
> shadows flitting across the wall,
> I sit in a window, combing my hair
> day in day out.

In an old vision and yet a glad one, in the poet's oblique light, this adventurer has everything to gain and to teach, as one of "a few of the last of the old religion."

CYRIL CONNOLLY

From "Academe and Open Air"

I first came across Louis Simpson in Donald Hall's *Contemporary American Poetry* (Penguin, 1962). In the course of reviewing it I noted that of these poets of the fifties nearly two-thirds were teachers. "To the journalistic mind," comments Mr. Simpson in his autobiography, "with its fear of schoolmasters, the fact that some of the 'New Poets of England and America' taught for a living was a handy peg on which to hang the label 'academic.'" But journalists are not afraid of schoolmasters: they are sorry for them—and some journalists are even sorry for themselves.

> A man lives close companion to disease and tears
> losing his love, working for other men.

In case anyone wants this poem for yet another anthology it is by Bhartrihari (Sanskrit, 6th c. A.D.). "Working for other men . . ." but Mr. Simpson makes the point that it is better to teach young hopefuls, who later may change the world, than to entertain a jaded public. Nevertheless teaching takes it out of people; the matter goes and only the didactic manner is left behind. This is, of course, a slow and insidious process and much less harmful to a poet with some of his writing life behind him.

Let us take Mr. Simpson: he is now a typical left-wing campus colleague, taking part in demonstrations against the Vietnam War and filling the latter section of his book with lectures on modern poetry, with the reaction against Eliot, Pound, Yeats and Auden which gave birth to the "new poetry" of Simpson, Snodgrass, Creeley, Bly.

The early chapters of this autobiography describe the poet growing up in Jamaica. His mother was a Russian Jewess, his father coloured, and the marriage unhappy. But Mr. Simpson's

---

Review of *North of Jamaica*, London *Sunday Times*, 9 July 1972, 31.

literary talent won him freedom from this oppressive atmosphere and he became an American citizen, continuing his studies in New York and fighting in the Ardennes offensive (frostbitten at Bastogne). After an unsuccessful attempt to study at the Sorbonne he returned to America and worked in a publisher's, publishing his own poetry in the *New Yorker,* about whose editorial paternalism he has some caustic things to say. Then follows California, teaching and protests, and the essays on modern poetry with which the book concludes.

There is nothing exotic about his Jamaica; Mr. Simpson is totally urban and the chief characteristic of his poetry is a mild irony, satires of poetry readings, parodies of Ginsberg:

> What was it Walt said? Go west!
> But the important thing is the return ticket
> The road to publicity runs by Monterey.
> I saw the best minds of my generation
> Reading their poems to Vassar girls,
> Being interviewed by 'Mademoiselle'
> Having their publicity handled by professionals.

Yet Mr. Simpson is himself a believer in poetry readings, and in the writing of poems which are meant to be read, and which have political implications: Neruda seems his hero. If he had stayed in Jamaica and become a lawyer he would have been one of the Founding Fathers of the new community like his friend Manley. "Of course, he will never be able to argue a case in court because of his teeth," wrote his father to his mother. "It was a pity you sent him the skates."

As a war writer Mr. Simpson has quality: he is without self-pity and not too savage about the American war machine which pitchforked him from meaningless fatigues and servitudes at home into the Ardennes offensive which the Allies so nearly lost:

> Our battle passed into print and history and the movies. There could come a day when we would not be able to distinguish between true and false; we would not remember what war was like. That would be for another generation to discover . . .

Most clearly of that battle I remember
The tiredness in eyes, how hands looked thin
Around a cigarette, and the bright ember
Would pulse with all the life there was within.

A breakdown on his return and the breakup of a marriage are somehow seen through the wrong end of a telescope, like his parents' earlier difficulties. "It seems I heard voices." . . .

I was beginning to see the paradox, the fundamental contradiction that made it impossible for the Empire to continue. The English were always educating people beyond their place in the class system. Then the young people came up against class barriers and were frustrated. So they became rebels.

But this happens in America, too; education everywhere is equipping youth for opportunities which have yet to be created. Mr. Simpson defends America.

The confusion of American democracy is its strength. Europeans have never been able to understand this. . . . Americans believe in the common man. Europeans have never been able to. America reminds them of what it would be like to be free, without a ruling class. More than once America has dragged Europe back from dying. No wonder they resent America.

WEBSTER SCHOTT

Wanderings of a Lazarus

We must call Louis Simpson comrade. For, although transplanted to Manhattan and then California from his native Jamaica, he is a contemporary annealed in American fires. To read his autobiography is to feel the flames and celebrate Simpson's survival. Now we understand why the persona of his poems travels under the name of Lazarus. Simpson has resurrected himself.

His father was Aston Simpson, one of the great advocates of the British West Indies and defender of Mrs. Lowry in a murder case made famous during the 1930s by American tabloids. But Aston Simpson was also a deficient human being who never learned, says Simpson, that "the secret of living well is to treat other people decently." While Louis Simpson was in prep school, his father divorced his mother and remarried a girl with good legs and fewer years. When he died (apparently she exhausted him quickly), he left her his fortune. Simpson got fifteen hundred pounds, half of his father's gun collection, and was thrown out of the family mansion. End of innocence and a promised life as colonial gentleman to be educated at Oxford or Cambridge. Simpson came to the United States, lived with his actress/cosmetics-saleslady mother, entered Columbia to study English, took possession of his heritage as a half-Jew, and was drafted into the Army.

A rifleman in the 101st Airborne Division, Simpson landed with the first wave at Normandy. As company runner, he carried messages through fields of dead to command posts in the rear. With thousands of others he was surrounded at Bastogne. His feet froze. And so did his heart. Simpson finally received his American citizenship at Berchtesgaden.

Review of *North of Jamaica, Washington Post Book World*, 17 December 1972, 5.

When the war ended Simpson returned to New York and Columbia. He published poems and stories while still a student. And he asked a girl to marry him. She said no. Simpson suffered a severe nervous breakdown. War backlash, perhaps. He was institutionalized after a violent episode, described in *North of Jamaica* as if seen in a trance. In a Long Island hospital he witnessed the murder of another patient by guards and was threatened himself. Slowly Simpson found solid ground. Then he held himself to it with literature—study abroad and a Prix de Rome, publication of a first book of poems and a novel, five years as an editor in New York, return to Columbia for a doctorate, more books of poetry, teaching at Berkeley, the Pulitzer Prize for poetry in 1964.

At the age of forty-nine Simpson has clearly made it in what Karl Shapiro used to call the poetry sweepstakes, which Simpson refuses to view competitively: "There is no way to prove that one good poem is better than another. In the republic of poetry all are equal. Yet some men have a historical importance that can be seen; they influence other people; they change the opinions of the age."

Poetry and the mountains you have to climb to keep perspective on a life's experience—these are Simpson's ultimate concerns. Along with the crushing Jamaican childhood, intense recollections of military regimentation and terrifying combat, commentaries and speculations about the relationship of teaching and writing, Simpson tells us a lot about poets (Donald Hall, Robert Bly, Allen Ginsberg) and the finding of poems, especially his kind.

Simpson is with Wallace Stevens: " 'Poetry is a process of the personality of the poet.' " Essentially a mystic, working in a vaguely defined medium, "The poet is reaching out to the person that he would be, and this is the poet's style—a sense of reaching, that can never be satisfied." Right now Simpson seems to be finding it tough to write. He says his "new kind of poem" composed of "images and reverberations" issues from the subconscious and requires not changes in technique but "work . . . at improving my character."

I'm not sure what all this means and doubt that Simpson has better words to express it. Contemporary poetry is an occult art and will remain so to most of our population for at least a century, or until the next revolution in education or sensibility. To say that writing poetry is "assisting at the birth of truth in beauty" doesn't help much unless that truth can be defined in recognizable terms.

But Louis Simpson knows exactly what it means to be a human being and he tells us in *North of Jamaica*. It's to struggle to find one's work, recognize the deepest emotions, seek values that sustain us under stress and, at times of failure, to continue the engagement anyway.

It seems to me it's at this level—not as a venture into the processes of art—that Louis Simpson's book makes serious claim for respect. He grants us entry to his self—his doubts, fears, aspirations, discovery of limitations. We never have difficulty knowing Simpson's feelings. Details and circumstances are less than transparent. Reality never comes easy. But we know his emotions. Indeed, he recreates them in the writing itself. It has the immediacy of experience.

I suppose *North of Jamaica* is such a good book, so moving in all kinds of ways, because Simpson is a good man. Sensitive. Compassionate. Strongly independent and suspicious of the glib and fashionable.

But this can only be a partial explanation of Simpson's power to draw us to him. A full explanation would bring us closer to the source of poetry and the truth of art. Simpson gives voice through language to what we would say had we the words. Feeling is another form of knowledge, and through Simpson we learn about ourselves.

JAMES BOATWRIGHT

The Private I

The oddest thing about Louis Simpson's autobiography is the tone. This isn't apparent at first, since the book begins, somewhat as Joyce's *A Portrait of the Artist as a Young Man* does, with a kind of baby talk which successfully reflects the child's perceptions and language. Simpson recounts his rather exotic boyhood: the son of a Scottish father and Russian mother, half-Jewish (although he doesn't know that until later) being brought up in Jamaica to be a typical English boy among other typical English boys in spite of mangoes, palm trees, and sharks.

The reader's awareness of a peculiar tone develops gradually, as Simpson tells of his parents' divorce, his father's remarriage, the schooling he and his brother received. Simpson discovers his vocation when he sees his first essay published; he falls in love; his father dies; he leaves for New York, at his mother's invitation.

By the end of this first section of the book I had decided that the voice was odd in some vaguely recognizable way, as if it recalled another kind of narrative. Only at the end of the narrative did I have this suspicion confirmed and clarified. Apparently Simpson has chosen (consciously or unconsciously) a theatrical strategy: to write an autobiography in a voice not his own, or at least a voice strongly influenced by a voice from the past. I haven't read the mid-nineteenth-century Russian poet and critic Apollon Grigoryev, but Simpson has, and in his next-to-last chapter (the most engaging passage in the book; the most *finished* in a novelistic way) he allies himself with Grigoryev. They are "unnecessary men": skeptical and uncertain, unable to sustain for long a thought or a story, their heads "full of seemingly significant scenes, gestures, faces, words spoken, that have

Review of *North of Jamaica, New Republic*, 23 & 30 December 1972, 30–31. Reprinted by permission of *The New Republic*, © 1972, The New Republic, Inc.

no significance because they are not connected and serve no purpose." Simpson and Grigoryev are not what the latter called *hommes fort,* who "have strong appetites for fame, money, women. In order to serve their appetites they seize life with both hands." Instead these two poets "inhabit the penumbra." Without convictions, they stand amazed before the *hommes fort,* those writers with certainty, with "their ability to generalize, the clarity of their ideas, their lack of sense-perception." (Note the bland irony in that last attribute.) Simpson and Grigoryev "could never write like that. We are obsessed with a handful of words, the way a branch keeps tapping against the window."

If my hunch about the book's voice is right, a good many mysteries are cleared up. The artifice of such a voice accounts for the narrator's *faux naif* diffidence, his dry, laconic manner of dealing with subjects usually described with more feeling. It also explains the flatness and disconnectedness of much of the prose. The narrator often sounds like a character who has wandered in from an obscure Chekhov play. It's not an easy voice to maintain, since it can slip rather easily into self-righteousness, its gesture the wide-eyed shrug of the truly simple man. It's a descent Simpson doesn't altogether avoid, but more on that shortly.

The obsession with a handful of words is, not surprisingly, the book's chief subject. Poetry, the life of the poet, the growth of the poet's mind, the state of poetry nowadays, poetry and politics: solid matter, handled with wit and brevity (too much brevity at times: Simpson's history of American poetry in the forties and fifties has a somewhat potted flavor. Is the reader drawn to this autobiography going to *need* this kind of lesson?) Simpson's war experiences and his observations of Whitman and the American landscape have fathered poems that are already ours: we can only be grateful to have him recite in another form those poems' origins.

The most moving chapter in this life describes Simpson's nervous breakdown some time after he had returned from the war. Understated and undramatized, the story barely rises to the surface *as* story, and the conclusions, the lessons learned have a stern austerity:

> My experiences in the hospital left me with a lack of sympathy for the everyday "problems" of human beings. I cannot

take people's troubles in love too seriously, and am unable to sympathize as I ought with a man who has difficulties finishing a job. As for people who think there is something romantic about mental disorder, I must confess I have contempt for them.

The narrative ends with a mysterious and troubling vision: "Around me were other patients—the one who lay face down on a bench, contracting, the four who were always playing cards. Then I heard, as distinctly as I have ever heard anything, a voice say 'Praise God! They resist, they resist.' Who resisted? What were they resisting? I wish that I knew."

The second half of the autobiography—the career: return to Columbia after the war, a year in Paris, five years working for a publisher, to Columbia again for the Ph.D., publication of poems and books of poems, a stint at Berkeley, putting together an anthology—is generally much less ingratiating than the first half, with the exception of the penultimate chapter I've already mentioned. Despite Simpson's gay assertion that he and Grigoryev "inhabit the penumbra," that they are free of the rigid certainties of their contemporaries, I come away from these later chapters with the exactly opposite impression. Is Simpson disingenuous or am I missing the irony? Is it an "unnecessary man" or an ordinary censorious man who is dead certain about the great many things he doesn't like: New York literary life, California ("O God, O California!"), "creative writing" courses, audiences at readings, McLuhan and Leary, flower children, the poetry of Lowell and Wilbur, the West Coast poets, Ginsberg's *Howl,* New Criticism, the *New York Review of Books, Hudson Review,* the *New Yorker* and its editorial policies, the Sorbonne, French educational bureaucracy, *Time,* the publishing industry, suburbia, Lionel Trilling, American foreign policy, the war in Vietnam, etc. A long plague list, and not an exhaustive one.

At the risk of appearing censorious myself, I suggest that there's something else even more seriously wrong with Simpson's autobiography, wrong, that is, if the autobiography moves within the borders of the novel, as it often does, I think, at its best. The poet's lyric meditation, the inward vision of the private I, might be expected to accede to the demands of prose narrative, to a recreation of the otherness of lives surrounding the poet-narrator's life. But such is hardly the case in *North of*

Jamaica. Others barely exist: names, blurred figures, a complimentary epithet here and there, more often characters dismissed with contempt, stereotypes who clearly deserve, in the narrator's eyes, little more. One passage is particularly suggestive: Simpson recalls his days at training camp and remembers no remarkable "characters" of the kind found in other, similar accounts. He doesn't say so outright, but there are no remarkable characters, any solid and vivid lives, anywhere in his book, except himself, his own. It's clear that such exclusions are a conscious choice—his first marriage and divorce each receives a sentence or so—but that fact doesn't save this autobiography from seeming to have at its center the chill emptiness of a solipsistic mind.

ANTHONY RUDOLF

One of Life's Foot-Soldiers

In this book [*North of Jamaica*] Louis Simpson says he would rather write extraordinary poems about being ordinary than ordinary poems about being extraordinary. His best poems are indeed out-of-the-ordinary and so is this autobiography. It is the book of a poet, one of life's "foot-soldiers" in his own phrase. The metaphor is appropriate, for one of the crucial experiences of his life was fighting in the Second World War. The first part of the book leads up to the war and is more emotionally involving for the reader than the high-spirited and more intellectual second half. The second half is engagingly and endearingly polemical, even bitchy at times, and the reader has a strong sense that some old scores are being settled in several anecdotes that take the lid off the stewpots of well-known people. For example, Lionel Trilling comes over as a petty-minded careerist, completely unfit to teach. Simpson, a former rifleman, alumnus of one of the toughest schools of recent times, does not mince his words. And if on occasion he seems to be an ordinary man, sometimes bearing grudges, sometimes intolerant and naive, sometimes quixotic and intemperate, sometimes holier-than-thou, sometimes a shit-or-get-off-the-pot man, well that is the point. He is an ordinary man retailing mundane events. So are most of us. But he admits it.

An ordinary man . . . who happens to be an out-of-the-ordinary poet. Sure he wants to learn how to live decently, to treat women properly (a subject on which he is explicitly reticent). Sure he comes across as a well-meaning, warm-hearted man; intelligent, thoughtful and concerned about the obligations of a university teacher (he teaches in the university because he finds it congenial) towards his students both as students and human

Review of *North of Jamaica*, *European Judaism*, June 1973, 52–54.

beings. As he rightly says, "No one can stand the man who feels teaching is keeping him from writing," but one keeps returning to the inevitable and poignant corollary of his being a poet, and all the more so because he rightly and sensibly includes a few poems at strategic points. The poems are more involving and interesting than even his excellent and serviceable prose, more involving and interesting than the life he describes and comments on. And that is surely as it should be and as he would want it, whose concern is to write extraordinary poems.

The rhythm of the prose is the rhythm of speech, his speech, his temperament, a prose that does not suffer fools or sentimentality gladly and whose tone makes a remarkable contrast with the Hardyesque loveliness of his early lyrics. It is the prose of a witty man. "This was real margarine, not one of your substitutes for butter. It was white and rancid, straight from the locomotive shed, and it had one advantage—it killed the weevils in the slice of bread and if it failed to kill them, bogged them down so that they could not be seen moving," or, "if turnips and cabbages had a voice they would speak Yiddish." The prose reveals a perceptive man, a man as single-minded as a good poet must be, a simple man with a Ph.D., a naturalised American with a Shmoedipus complex. But what will survive above all are his poems. And they will survive because of their art, made as usual out of very hard work and inspiration, i.e., seizing the right moment for the psychic exploration and implosion that will make "the inner and outer worlds . . . come together." The only way to get the full value from this book is to read his books of poems too, for his prose is overshadowed and knows it is overshadowed by the poems: the recent introduction to the second edition of his schools anthology (New York: Macmillan, 1972) has faults of structure and argument that he would never allow himself in his poems.

What turned him (or turns anyone) into a poet is a mystery. One might say, deriving from Simpson's own words, that when consciousness of a disturbed unconscious meets an inclination for rhythmic utterance in speech you get poems and a poet, given willpower and a certain ruthlessness. Certainly an "interesting life" is not even a necessary condition, and the war can reduce you to silence. Poetry is, he would agree, a divine game. Between the life and the poem, indeed between the prose and the poem—after all the psychology and sociology have been applied—falls the shadow, lies the mystery, "the mystery of as" in Michel Deguy's words, the undetermined freedom of humankind, the unprogrammeable margin of error, the angelic joy unamenable to a certain school of criticism. In the end, to trace the alchemy of a poet's mind is a fruitless exercise. If a poem changes you, then it *does,* and if it *does,* it is. All the rest is footnotes.

Simpson was born in Jamaica of a negro or half-caste father and a Russian Jewish mother. He does not discover he is Jewish until his divorced mother summons him to New York. He was raised by a stern father and an often absent mother—a shadowy figure who never fully comes alive though her presence clearly haunts the poet's imaginings (his first wife remains offstage and his second wife—to whom the book is dedicated—is not mentioned in the book). He was educated in a parody of a minor public school—vicious, cruel, snobbish, serving up the margarine described earlier. The remembered intensities of childhood—when his father dies he writes, "This was the fear of death, to have known my life in the death of another. Until this day there was someone else who would die, but from this day I began to die myself"—inform and energise the prose in a way lacking in the second half of the book. Furthermore, he gives valuable descriptions of various aspects of colonialist mentality in the Jamaican episodes.

Soon after reaching America he is drafted, and lives through an unpleasant and traumatic war. "Sometimes in speaking to older men I have sensed there is a veil between us; and to a man of twenty-five there are things I cannot explain." But was his war worse than say, Owen's or Rosenberg's? Still, out of it have come writings—poems and some of the descriptive pages of this book unequalled in the literature of the Second World War. On return, a nervous breakdown, a Ph.D., a trip to Europe that reveals a blatant prejudice: "France has no poets of the first rank." Then work as a publisher, marriage, divorce, and gradual fame.

The Jewish problem is the same for him as it is for many nonreligious and/or non-Zionist Jews not living in Israel, only more so in his case as a Jewish consciousness was not present in childhood when rituals, prayer, a certain warmth and sentimentality and perhaps a concern for social justice (for "we were slaves to Pharoah in Egypt") are permanently imprinted on future Jewish atheists who define themselves negatively, in respect of their Jewishness at least. Actually seeing the concentration camps when they were liberated profoundly affected Simpson's Jewish consciousness, indeed was the major factor in its birth, though one knows this from poems and statements he has made at poetry readings, not from this book. He makes Jewish jokes. Maybe, emotionally, "you were a Jew because other people thought you were" (and because fellow Jews had been destroyed) but this is very negative, the same approach as Sartre's—well-meaning but ill thought out—in *Portrait of an Anti-Semite*. Whether he realises it or not, Simpson's book is in part yet another case study in the problematic of Jewish existence for those Jews who can no longer find sustenance and roots in Zionism, revolution, the religious tradition or Yiddish culture. After Bashevis Singer, Bellow, after Bellow, Roth, after Roth? A deluge it won't be.

Simpson says that he was middle-aged before he was young and indeed, youthful sometimes malicious high spirits and humour come through in the anecdotes about the *New Yorker,* Dylan Thomas, Eliot and Ginsberg and other aspects of the politics of the literary world, as well as in the poems in his latest volume. The whole tone of this book is an implied snub to academic prose, as the loyalty to sense perceptions is an implied snub to scholarly hindsight, and the deep insights into the poetic process to critical apparatus and apparatchiki. Professor Simpson is rocking the boat. As he says, having a real live poet around is or was an embarrassment to university English faculties. I wish he had devoted more space to the radical change that has come over America in the last few years—no more for example could you say that *Commentary* and the *New York Review of Books* could publish the same articles. But despite interesting remarks on drugs, freedom and passive resistance, etc. Simpson is not a political animal in the way Bly is, and knows he is not. And he might have told us more about his adult relationships instead of shuffling off coiled mortals with the statement that women would form the subject of another book he will never write (to protect the innocent?). Is his reticence due to his education and subsequent poetic flowering? Are relationships—personal and group (i.e., political)—somehow less important than the Hitler war? And yet he says "Ideas depend so much on personal relationships." How that wants developing! But his ideas on poetry provide plenty of food for thought, not least the statement that to write better poems he would have to improve his character not his technique. He is not the only one.

I have to insist that beyond all this fiddle, beyond the anecdotes, the wit, the intelligence, the decency, the "normality," stand "a body" of poems. This is plenty. This is more than enough. In our time, perhaps the amazing thing, the amazing grace, is that he is not in the only place you can go beyond California: (as he says) out of your mind. But *this* book has its place in our view of this poet.

He quotes Apollinaire: "If you love home you must make a journey." Surely Louis Simpson is haunted by the other man he would have been had he followed his other star, the road he did not take. But roads not taken in life often end up as poems, where, briefly, roots are at one with routes.

RICHARD D. LINGEMAN

Pillars of the Church

When someone said that dead writers were remote from us because we know so much more than they did, T. S. Eliot responded, "Precisely, and they are what we know." The three twentieth-century American poets Louis Simpson writes about in *Three on the Tower*—Eliot, Ezra Pound, William Carlos Williams—have become, by now, sturdy pilings sunk in the river of the past, on which current poets can build. Although critical contention still swirls about them—and where can you find a more factious lot than poets?—they are a part of what we know.

There are, of course, other poets in our country who could be championed as being of equal stature and import, but the three Mr. Simpson has chosen seem most emblematic of the modernist movement that began changing poetry at the turn of the century (when Pound exiled himself to London), in revolt against romanticism and fin de siècle decadence. The house of modernism has many mansions, one of its strongest impulses being classicism—the recharging of old poetic batteries—but it was undoubtedly a response to the unwritten, secret psychology of the times by men of uncompromising individualism who wrote for the few and ended up as spokesmen for their age.

Compare the poetry movements of the first part of this century to one of those glass balls with a blizzard inside—swirling, all in flux. Now it has settled, and the obliterated structures have emerged in clear outline. Mr. Simpson figuratively holds the glass ball in his hand, shaking it from time to time to set the ideas swirling, then letting the flakes settle a bit in order to contemplate the standing structures.

Review of *Three on the Tower, New York Times,* 15 July 1975, 31. Copyright © 1975 by the New York Times Company. Reprinted by permission.

He has compacted a lot into this book—the lives of three poets, their ideas and theories and those that influenced them, and above all their poems. A poet, critic and teacher himself, Mr. Simpson brings all those backgrounds into play with fine effect. As a poet he can empathize with the process of creation and the technical choices made. As a critic and teacher he interprets and communicates lucidly the meaning of their work. By the end of the book the three seem as alive as people we had met and got to know well—if not intimately—on, say, a week's cruise.

The book is more a series of seamlessly linked essays than an in-depth critical study. The tone is easy, almost conversational, occasionally aphoristic. As in an essay, we have a sense of the free play of the writer's personality about a subject. Mr. Simpson, is, however, impeccably unobtrusive in the proceedings and his occasional personal asides almost slip by unnoticed. Yet *Three on the Tower* is not a partisan or idiosyncratic study, by any means. When discussing the poetry, Mr. Simpson walks respectfully with the most sound judgments of other critics (though occasionally deliberately falling out of step with the academics where his own poet's experience belies what they say), quoting them to effect, then proceeding to state his own view. He has a talent for cutting to the meaning of each man's life with brief strokes. He pokes fun at pomposity when need be.

On T. S. Eliot's later tergiversating critical essays: "It was hard to tell the difference between one of T. S. Eliot's definitions, arrived at after a struggle, and anybody's platitude."

Yet he is not lacking in moral insight. He stresses the anti-Semitism of all three of these poets and insists that it not be swept under the rug. Pound's anti-Semitism was the most notorious, but Eliot and Williams both used Jews as objects of aesthetic disgust. None, except arguably Pound in his broadcasts for Mussolini, ever lifted a finger against Jews, but all the same, as Mr. Simpson says about Eliot, "There are enough anti-Semitic remarks . . . to place him among those who in the nineteen-twenties and thirties encouraged anti-Semitism and made it possible for Jew-baiters to survive."

At the same time, all these men had a number of other equally crank ideas, of lesser impact, notably (again) Pound, and their lives were hardly exemplary—except as artists. And here, at the crux of their beings, is where Mr. Simpson plumbs for their greatness. He explicates their ideas about poetry with balance and insight (though some of the more programmatic movements, such as Vorticism, can induce mental numbness). The theories came as naturally to poets as they did not to painters (and Mr. Simpson often fruitfully relates the movements in the arts with those in poetry)—flags they flaunted to signal poetic ground occupied. Poets need public relations too, they must educate as they go along. Or even—poetry being as Eliot said, "a mug's game"—to waylay rivals. Imagism, objectivism, classicism—the most complex perceptual nexuses between the poet and nature, "reality," the world, whatever—are explored exhaustively—at times, exhaustingly.

Thus I felt a leap of sympathy when Mr. Simpson remarks at one point, in effect, that whatever the worth of the ideas just discussed, they enabled the poet to write. The payoff is the poetry; further, as Pound said, "In the first place it is necessary to be a poet." That seems so little, but it is so much; as Eliot put it, it meant total immolation of personality—that *renunciation* Joseph Conrad spoke of. All three sought to *present,* not to explain or incant—they reached beyond themselves for the images that expressed the deepest truths of their beings.

Ultimately, though, as Mr. Simpson writes, "The question of what poetry is always seems to return to the character of the poet." Pound and Eliot were elitists who despised the masses and thought that strong institutions guaranteeing social stability—the church in Eliot's case, Mussolini to Pound's downfall—provided the most propitious climate for the arts. Williams, the poet of experience, of locality, stayed in Rutherford, New Jersey, practicing medicine, writing his poetry in obscurity while the others were blazing the skies. But he was more attuned, Mr. Simpson says, to the age of the common man; he was tentative, pragmatic, grounded in experience, finding truth in ugliness rather than beauty.

Williams felt defeated when *The Waste Land* came out; it seemed to return poetry to the academy and deny all he was working toward. Yet he continued to pan the creekbeds of plain American speech, and now it is he who is the most influential poet with the contemporary generation of American poets. Williams, as Mr. Simpson's brilliant reading of *The Waste Land* demonstrates, was wrong to call the poem academic; it perhaps most successfully of all poems evoked the inner experience of twentieth-century man. Yet it is a mountain, while Williams's work is a pass to the territory ahead.

L. S. DEMBO

Critical Biographies

Professor Simpson has written a book of critical biographies—
neither the lives nor the works are glossed over. He has used a
special blend of literary criticism and literary gossip which will
satisfy both the scholar and layman. Remarkably readable
and thoroughly researched, this book, as no other before it, illuminates
the lives and the works of the founding fathers of twentieth-century
poetry.

Authors, of course, should not be held to the clichés of the dust
jackets that herald their books, but this particular statement
would have to be no exaggeration if *Three on the Tower* can be
regarded as worth the effort that apparently went into it. To
write at this time a "life and works" study of any one of these
poets, no less all three in a single volume, suggests a great deal of
something—energy and nerve, perhaps. That much can be con-
ceded at the outset, and, as it turns out, Simpson does, inde-
fatigably, put his reader in possession of the known facts, signif-
icant and trivial, about the poets' lives, and he does go into all
the important questions associated with their work. Moreover,
if one is not put off by the mannered simplicity of its style, the
book is in fact quite, if not "remarkably," readable.

What more can be said for this work I am not sure. The
scholar mentioned in the blurb might discover some things he
hadn't seen or noticed before, but he will find no really new
perspective on either the lives or minds of Pound, Eliot, and
Williams, separately or as a group. The sources Mr. Simpson
has used for his information are accessible to all and the insights
offered as literary criticism, while comprehensive, rarely go far
or deep. The title, which should be a clue to the unifying prin-
ciple of the book, is explained this way:

Review of *Three on the Tower: The Lives and Works of Ezra Pound, T. S. Eliot, and
William Carlos Williams. American Literature* 47 (January 1976): 646–47.
Copyright © 1976 Duke University Press.

Ezra Pound, T. S. Eliot and William Carlos Williams made their reputations with short intense, imagistic poems. There was, however, the question of how to continue—we live by the senses but at the same time we must have an aim that is not dependent on the senses. "Life itself" in incoherent, as a Great War plainly shows. "Our Spirit," says William James, "shut within this courtyard of sense-experience, is always saying to the intellect upon the tower: 'Watchman, tell us of the night, if it aught of promise bear.'"

We are still looking for ways to continue.

If this is the underlying philosophic connection that Mr. Simpson perceives, then he has given us three monographs in a single volume. This is not to say there isn't ample justification for treating these poets together; I am simply asserting that the book has no meaningful thesis and therefore no conceptual reason for existence. Since there are other reasons for existence, the lack probably will not prove fatal, and *Three on the Tower* will duly be added to the bibliographies of Pound, Eliot, and Williams scholarship, which seem to be destined for infinite accretion.

MARK NEPO

Poetry and Its Genesis in the Twentieth Century

> *The little seed of the Imagist movement made a great tree with twigs and leaves spreading over the world.*
>
> —Three on the Tower

Simpson seems to view literary history as a chemist's funnel with a long plastic stem. The point at which the funnel fans out marks the beginning of the twentieth century. The rising legacy of that stem till 1912 is characterized as a narrow and tidy corridor from Classicism to Romanticism, which he earmarks with Rousseau. Simpson's definition of literature is implicit and non-dissectible from his real interest; namely, the history and flux of ideas and how it shapes the men's lives who happen by it. The flux of ideas is the blood of the vein en route to the heart for Simpson, and literature is the indiscernible residue, part of the sheath formed and left behind to guide more stiffly the new blood which follows. And equally a credit to his dexterity of point of view is the emphasized truism that as inevitable as the rigor of old art must be, so too is it refreshingly sacred that life depends on the stumbling force of the new to break down the stiffness, to resist coagulation.

Though Simpson traces many divergent theories of causation with regard to poetry and its genesis in the twentieth century, his essential view is chemical; that is, literature, and particularly poetry, tends to progress by the chemical reactions and amalgamations of artistic circumstance in solution with the ideas that govern and dominate their lives. The variables are endless and the ideas serve as catalysts, unaltered and undiminished. And literary history, within the chemist's funnel, appears to form and move in clusters. Imagism, for Simpson, is the cata-

Review of *Three on the Tower, New Mexico Humanities Review* 3 (Fall 1980): 89–91.

lyst, the vapor which makes the stem spread to a funnel. It serves as the all important mode which thrusts literature and especially poetry into modernism, and beyond, into an unprecedented proliferation of art forms and messiahs, a volatile pyrrhonism—ever changing and uncertain. The book, therefore, concentrates on what Simpson declares as the most affected and effecting prophets of the Imagist solution, namely, the lives and works of Pound, Eliot, and Williams.

Four aspects of this endeavor mark Simpson as courageous and diligent in his scholarship. First is his eclectic and coherent use of biography, social context, and political relevance, solidified by a cogent dialogue which informs the reader of the constantly changing philosophical climate which seems inherent to this era of art. The book circles the embryo of modernism: Pound's struggle with the scope of history, language, and art and his exploration of dramatic personae; Eliot's turning to an allusive Classicism in order to exorcise the numbness prevailing in a hollow postwar world; and Williams with his adherence to experience and his endless pursuit of the American verse. Simpson uses the lives of these poets as vehicles, as telescopes which attempt to focus for the reader three divergent perspectives, the roots of a modern literary trinity, three stalks which like milkweed have since dispersed, invisible in the air we still breathe.

I have attempted to enter into the process. To do this I have had to understand each man's life—his connections with other people, his attitudes and beliefs. My rule has been to give these matters as much importance as he himself gave them. Williams wrote continually about his life, therefore I have talked about it in detail. Eliot hardly ever writes about his, but when he does it seems confessional. Pound, for all his volubility, gives little away; he writes about himself in the CANTOS, but nothing personal, this is the way I have dealt with him. (Preface, p. viii)

The success of this approach is that the book yields a steady course around the evolution of twentieth-century poetry as inadvertently shaped in these men's hands. And only when the enormity of events, personal or international, permeates the poet's artistic consciousness, only then are we privy to how

Douglas's theory of social credit coupled with Pound's being shut off from the London coterie might have been part of the silent fuse which later set off his war in the *Cantos* against usury. Only when Eliot writes to Richard Aldington while convalescing at Margate of "an aboulia and emotional derangement which has been a lifelong affliction," only then is biography given precedence over poetry in an attempt to illuminate the gestation of the poet's mind and soul and work. Simpson rotates his subject with dexterity so as to leave the important issue of the moment in full view of light.

Secondly, the work rests on a taut fabric of documentation. Simpson's own narrative throughout the book is minimal and integrating. His language is constantly and effectively interspersed with ripe selections of the poets' work as well as peppered with a precise framework indicative of the surrounding eras, be they comments from Keats or curios of the Italian Futurist poet of 1910, Marinetti. It is through this documentation that Simpson uncovers a convincing argument which posits T. E. Hulme and Ford Madox Ford as the timely flints around which Pound warmed his mind to the brewing doctrine of Imagism. But the value of Simpson's paradigm is again its chemical and clustered nature. He accurately displays the artifacts leading to Imagism (intuition, sensory images, use of objective language, the need for the "direct treatment of the thing") in references to Aristotle, Longinus, Conrad, Henry James, Whistler for his tapping into Japanese art, and then to Hemingway, and Henri Bergson, and Remy de Gourmont. But the strength of his chemical view of literary history persists, not as a confidence in fate, but as a powerful observation of the endless possibilities of currents, of ideas in flux:

> The truth is, no one invented Imagism, or everyone did. When an invention is needed and the time is right for it, people come upon it independently. Who invented radio? Ideas that were seized on by Pound and directed as the Imagist movement were discovered elsewhere by others and given other names. Pound, however, put the ideas to work. His way of taking an idea that had been neglected or not understood—at least not in English—stating it clearly, and showing how it can be applied, practically amounted to saying it for the first time. Pound was, like Thomas Alva Edison, a

genius at practical mechanics. It is hard to draw a line between this and invention. (P. 32)

Thirdly, Simpson maintains an impassioned objectivity throughout the book. He ascribes his feelings to the poet in question, to the mood which prevails in the moment of his text. This is what provides the book with its authenticity of immediacy; so that when Pound during one of his famous broadcasts in July of 1941 makes note of: "As my friend Doc Williams of New Jersey would say . . ." we are allowed to feel both Pound's desperate need for company in his crusade while feeling Williams's anguish and chagrin at such a public notice with "two sons in the navy." Again, the personal-political context serves as invaluable background to the work produced—in this case, the article Williams wrote in response, "Ezra Pound: Lord Ga-Ga!" But serious admiration must be given Simpson for his ability to address and deal with the varying degrees of anti-Semitism found in each of these men without jeopardizing his credibility as a literary historian. With the same investment of emotion, he enables us to feel Eliot's subtle and casual indifference to his anti-Semitism, comparable to a wealthy slave owner in the pre–Civil War South:

In later years Eliot denied that he was an anti-Semite and seemed not to understand why people thought him one. "It is a terrible slander on a man," he told William Turner Levy. "And they do not know, as you and I do, that in the eyes of the Church, to be an anti-Semite is a sin." (P. 134)

And Simpson responds with a deliberately felt point of view which avoids the overindulgence readily available to the author who finds himself reviewing material to which he is a victim:

Those who fail to see anti-Semitism in Eliot's writings—as with Pound, some of Eliot's admirers are wonderfully unobservant on this point—must themselves live where anti-Semitism is so much a part of the normal order of things as to be taken for granted. (P. 134)

To avoid the investment of one's humanity as a scholar is to record a sterile literary history. To let the dam break is to leave a map of distortion. I believe Simpson's treatment here to be a powerful example of impassioned and active objectivity, adhering to the idiosyncracies of his subject, responding when the issues point his way, as he must, but like a good friend who fights well, the fight is forgotten when we turn the page.

Finally, what makes this account of twentieth-century poetry unique and valuable is that Simpson himself is a poet who has a firm understanding of the confusions and exultations inherent in working in pursuit of a Muse. There is a drive for understanding, a motivation for a synthesis of ideas which will prove useful. From the onset, Simpson declares, "I had to write this book to clarify my ideas." Simpson's function in the book can be found in a passage he cites from Williams: "If your interest is in theory . . . and your mind is alive and you're trying to improve your poems technically you will produce the work, and will never cease to produce it." The work is vital because the everpresent tone is one of—how can I make use of this?

The modern poet has the ageless dilemmas to face: Romanticism versus Classicism, Technique versus Content, Experimentation versus Tradition. These decisions are made even more illusory by the mushroomed and chaotic field of choice now available to a poet of the seventies. This book, by an alert and thorough poet-scholar, is a fresh and valuable tool, useful as a catalyst in the chemical world of a developing poet.

PETER STITT

In the Second Voice

Louis Simpson's seventh volume of poetry is a tremendously refreshing book, as entertaining and enlightening to read as a collection of short stories by Isaac Bashevis Singer or a short novel by Saul Bellow. So many modern poets, even some of the best, seem to want nothing more than to write in what Eliot called the first voice of poetry—"the voice of the poet talking to himself—or to nobody." Simpson, by contrast, prefers Eliot's second voice, that of "the poet addressing an audience." His poems are meant to be read; indeed, the reader is welcomed with a warm embrace. The style in which they are written presents us with no barriers—it is plain, direct and relaxed. Moreover, the poems tell a story, or several stories, in which we can take a real interest.

Searching for the Ox is an autobiographical work loosely organized into four sections. The protagonist of the poems—whom Simpson prefers to call a "man with a background similar to my own"—feels the lure of two distinct, even contradictory ways of life. He is both sensual and intellectual, drawn alike to the life of the mind and the life of the body. The problem is that neither position alone is satisfying. Thus he searches for a way to unite the two.

In the opening section, he encounters characters who represent the two extremes at their worst. Marie Shulman, with whom he has a date, turns out to be interested only in possessions. When he romantically wishes they could "hire a taxi / and just keep going," Marie replies: "I'd rather have my own car." Professor Wilson, on the other hand, is an abstractionist for whom "the visible world [is] a dream." Simpson charac-

Review of *Searching for the Ox, New York Times Book Review,* 9 May 1976, 4, 32. Copyright © 1976 The New York Times Company. Reprinted by permission.

terizes him by describing the apartment building in which he lives. At one time, the lobby contained statues of Psyche (soul or mind)—made into a lamp—and Eros. Now, Psyche sheds "no light, / for the globe and the bulb were smashed," while "The couch in the opposite wall where Eros used to lie [is] empty." The professor's intellectuality, no longer actuated by a love for the physical world, offers neither light nor heat, but only empty phrases.

In the second section of the book, Simpson's persona tells how he worked in publishing for five years before giving it up. He had wanted to unite vocation, the necessity of earning a living, and avocation, his love of writing, but ended up instead pushing a heavy millstone around in a circle. The rest of the section is composed of poems in which Simpson describes various New Yorkers he has known. Some are trying to live the playboy life, while others are simply themselves—newspapermen addicted to poker, for example, or doctors devoted to poetry. These people are as grotesque and appealing as those who populate Jimmy Breslin's columns, and they are as lovingly described as E. A. Robinson's Tilbury Town characters.

The heart of this book resides in its third section. One of the best poems, "Baruch," begins with this amusing stanza:

> There is an old folk saying:
> "He wishes to study the Torah
> but he has a wife and family."
> Baruch had a sincere love of learning
> but he owned a dress-hat factory.

When the factory burns down, Baruch gives himself "to the Word"—but the change is too extreme, and he dies. At the end of the poem, the speaker recognizes that his dilemma is the same as Baruch's—though a man of the world, he also longs "to study the Torah."

The solution comes in the book's title poem, where Simpson gives himself entirely to a search for a Zen symbol of spirituality, the ox. As soon as this elusive creature is caught, however, it vanishes, and the speaker realizes that unless he can find spirituality in the world itself, it can be of no real value to him. He concludes:

There is only earth:
in winter laden with snow,
in summer covered with leaves.

Searching for the Ox is a book of celebration. The poems have much to offer—vividly drawn characters, a strong sense of place—chiefly New York City and Long Island—and a sense of humor that is both rich and profound. In recent years, Louis Simpson has taken the excellent advice offered by one of his characters: "If you want to be a writer, / write! . . . / Write reviews. Write articles. Write anything. / And don't think you're a genius." Simpson has published an autobiographical memoir, a critical study, and two excellent volumes of poetry in just the last five years. In *Searching for the Ox,* he is writing with the supple assurance of a poet superbly in control of his craft.

STANLEY PLUMLY

Showing a Story

Louis Simpson's preface to his seventh volume of poetry is in-
structive—less for the commentary that draws the parallel be-
tween Simpson's island life as a child on Jamaica ("I still have
dreams in which I am walking on a beach of white sand") and
his island life as an adult on the north shore of Long Island
("Walking along the shore I am aware that nothing much has
changed"). On the first island: "Isolation turned me to reading
stories and poems. It was stories I was after in either case; I
didn't want fine emotions as much as I wanted something to
happen to break the silence of the island." The two obvious
points here: one, the early interest in narrative as a preferred
means; two, "the silence of the island," the implicit sense of
isolation and search that is so ongoing in Simpson's recent work.
As if the poems themselves were not evidence enough, the
nature of this author's achievements in prose would indicate a
fair bias toward narrative: two critical studies, which use biogra-
phy as a guide to continuity; one novel, *Riverside Drive;* and one
autobiography, *North of Jamaica.* The present volume, *Searching
for the Ox,* distinguishes Simpson's pursuit of the narrative line
within the vertical dimensions of the poem and helps further set
him apart from the mode—once referred to as "the emotive
imagination"—with which he and William Stafford and James
Wright were once associated. To one extent or another, what-
ever its various lengths, poetry depends on getting the most out
of the "least" amount of language. And in any poetry that either
implicates or explicates through telling—no, showing a story, a
necessary selection and juxtaposition of image and information
will take place.

Review of *Searching for the Ox, American Poetry Review* 5 (July/August 1976): 42–
43.

One morning when I went over to Bournemouth
it was crowded with American sailors—
chubby faces like Jack Oakie
chewing gum and cracking wise.

Pushing each other into the pool,
bellyflopping from the diving boards,
piling on the raft to sink it,
hanging from the rings, then letting go.

Later, when I went into Kingston
to exchange some library books,
they were everywhere, buying souvenirs,
calabash gourds and necklaces made of seeds.

On Saturday night at the Gaiety
they kept talking and making a noise.
When the management asked them to stop
they told it to get wise, to fly a kite, to scram.

Simpson's best poems are all too long to be given full play, so
this is just the first part of "Venus in the Tropics." There is
selection and juxtaposition here, of course; but, to generalize
from this one example, there is a characteristic tone of voice, a
voice almost alien to the lyric, the most popular sound in poetry.
In its no-nonsense, frank, simple-because-it-was posture; in its
pacing, each line in full phrase or clause, each stanza laconic and
closed; in its emblematic use of detail ("chubby faces like Jack
Oakie"); in its colloquial diction ("bellyflopping," "scram") and
twelve-year-old sense of reality, its point of view—in short, in
its essential rhythm, from "one morning" to "Saturday night,"
it reads like poetry about to break into prose. This is its auditory
power, not its burden. It is an example of a tension that arbi-
trates nearly every poem in this new book: how much the line,
the stanza can include versus what it must edit. It is as flat-out as
the so-called singing voice can afford to be—and "singing" may
be beside the point. The voice in this excerpt, and in the main, is
closer to the declarative of drama, the voice of the actor over that
of a speaker. "The idea should be felt, seeming to rise out of an
event rather than being imposed," says Simpson. Which is why,

for all their autobiographical, north-of-Jamaica facts and figures, these poems never feel indulgent or self-reflexive. The raw materials of the narrative *include* Simpson; they are not extensions or assumptions of his person. He becomes an actor, among other voices, in his own stories—among the causes and effects in the "company of flesh and blood." But narrative technique, however handled, could never be enough, by itself, to make important, albeit different, poetry. Simpson once said in an interview:

> When you tell a narrative in poetry you must get beyond the particular into some general human element. . . . My own poetry has to be based very much in life, that is, in the recognizable world. But at the same time, it carries the recognizable world into the infinite or into something magical or mysterious.

Something magical, something more. Simpson does not always achieve such a "mysterious" quality in these poems, particularly in the final, satiric section, in which the concerns of the writer preoccupy those of the man. The book at its best, however, is about the man, and is magical, does search—through and through the first three sections. Jamaica and Long Island are the two haunts, the two sources. The isolation, the island of each becomes the isolation of the book's central "character," sometimes named as Peter. Whatever the protagonist is called, the story is autobiography, childhood and manhood. "Father, I too have my cases: / hands, eyes, voices, ephemera." This from the title poem, "Searching for the Ox." This poem is not only the centerpiece of Simpson's book—it is, as reviewers like to say, a text for the times. Its movement is in five parts, each in successive but nondirective search for something outside, beyond the seductions of happiness. The search started on the first island and has come to this—

> At dusk when the lamps go on
> I have stayed outside and watched
> the shadow-life of the interior,
> feeling myself apart from it.
> A feeling of—as though I were made of glass.

Or the balloon I once saw in Florida
in a swimming pool, with a string
trailing in loops on the surface.
Suddenly the balloon went swivelling
on the water, trying to lift.
Then drifted steadily, being driven
from one side of the pool to the other.

The poem is beautiful in its ambivalence, its philosophical peripeteia, its play. It arrives where it started, knowing the place, as always, for the first time: "There is only earth: / in winter laden with snow, / in summer covered with leaves." The ox does, near the end of the poem, leave a single hoofprint. By such signs are we led and by such signs disappear.

C. B. COX

Editorial

Nowadays an enormous amount of talk goes on about poetry. The reviews pour out in the *Times Literary Supplement*, the *New Review*, the Sunday newspapers; and there are all those discussions and readings on Radio 3. Amid all this chatter many of our best poets are still neglected. An obvious example is R. S. Thomas, whose latest book is likely to be dismissed in a few patronising sentences in the *Observer* and not to be mentioned anywhere else; yet he continues to write poems of great imaginative force.

Another example is the American poet Louis Simpson. His new book *Searching for the Ox* (Oxford University Press) was the best book of poetry published in 1976, but he too receives little attention. In an epigraph in this new collection he quotes Wordsworth: "I have wished to keep the reader in the company of flesh and blood." Many poems deal with a Chekhovian group of lonely people caught in the drifting, apparently futile confusion that is modern America. The narrator looks at his own life with a sense of bewilderment and wonder, as from the darkness through a window into a lighted room. Simpson's tragi-comic characters are described with a mixture of pathos and irony and it is sometimes as if we have walked into the world of *Uncle Vanya*.

Review of *Searching for the Ox*, *Critical Quarterly* (U.K.) 19 (Spring 1977): 3.

PAUL ZWEIG

American Poetry Restored

When did we start to tick off our cultural life by tens? First came the 1920s of scabrous high living, followed by the thirties of hard-bitten social responsibility. After an interlude for world war came the fifties with their backyard irony, the sixties of hair and revolt, the seventies of exhausted privacy. What began as a rough rule of thumb seems, by Whitehead's principle of the "misplaced concreteness," to have become a law of cultural time, and the resultant oversimplification has turned struggles of taste and values into a marching order for textbooks.

Louis Simpson's "revolution in taste" refers to an abrupt, almost right-angle change in the sensibility of American poetry, which is usually connected to the cultural expansiveness of the sixties. Actually, it was not so much a change, according to Simpson, as a return to the experimental tradition that had ruled American poetry since Pound and the Imagists but had been derailed during the fifties, largely through the influence of W. H. Auden, an ex-thirties radical who, with beguiling charm and wit, had turned his cultural coat and carried a generation of American poets with him.

Auden ruled with wit and a knowledge of verse forms; in comparison, the American poets who looked to W. C. Williams, or to a poet thought to be even more rudimentary, Walt Whitman, appeared to be bumbling provincials—certainly not worth the attention of readers who had been trained by the New Criticism to look for shades or irony and multiple, ambiguous meanings.

Review of *A Revolution in Taste, New York Times Book Review*, 17 December 1978, 9, 32. Reprinted by permission of The Estate of Paul Zweig and Georges Borchardt, Inc. Copyright © 1978 by Paul Zweig.

Auden is a convenient symbol for the witty formalism of American poetry during the fifties. But, according to Simpson, this "Audenesque facade" could not withstand for long the flow of the American mind, which soon burst it apart at the instigation, paradoxically, of another Englishman, Dylan Thomas, whose booming voice performing his poems in college auditoriums around the country, supplied, in copious draughts, what Auden had neglected: the "passion" of a man freely drawing on the internal matter of his life.

Simpson is not a cultural historian. This scheme, as it is set forth in his brief foreword, leans too heavily on the influence of two migrant Englishmen and is set to the tune of the marching decades. Yet it provides a convenient setting for the main work of Simpson's book, which is to look sympathetically at the radical merging of poetry and personal experience in the work of Dylan Thomas, Allen Ginsberg, Sylvia Plath and Robert Lowell: the poets who, he feels, were most instrumental in accomplishing the "revolution in taste" of his title.

Why these poets, the reader may ask, and not also Roethke, O'Hara, Berryman or, say, Elizabeth Bishop? In truth, Simpson's title is somewhat misleading, for it promises a theoretical and historical approach to this subject when, in fact, he has provided a series of engaging portraits of poets whom he presents less as cultural exemplars than as individuals struggling, as Baudelaire wrote, to absolve the pain of their lives with the grace of an enduring poem.

It is the life narrowing intensely and heatedly into the act of writing that interests Simpson, the life pared to the poem. And this has enabled him to write a series of compact literary biographies that have the pithiness of a seventeenth-century "character" and a literary good sense that reminds me of Johnson's *Lives of the Poets*.

Simpson uses known biographical sources to highlight the elusive passage of experience into imagery, tone and theme. In doing so, he reverses the wisdom of recent decades, which has preferred to approach poetry in a critical parenthesis and leave the life to the novelistic clutches of biographers, who were free to load their narrative with facts while the poem levitated beyond the uncertainties of merely living.

Except for a few pages of his essay on Plath and much of the essay on Lowell, Simpson approaches the poems by side glances and digressive commentaries. His eye is focused on that wavering permeable line between experience and artistic language and not, for the most part, on the poems themselves. In this sense, his book is a counterstatement to David Kalstone's recent *Five Temperaments,* which also treats the enigma of experiential poetry in the work of a number of contemporary poets, the only overlap between them being Lowell. Kalstone takes as his text the poems themselves, reading them adeptly as the record of a struggle between the impulse to revealing statement and the counterpull of art with its diversions, its displaced emotions, its formal play of language, enlarging and heightening what is "merely" personal.

A Revolution in Taste might almost be an answer to Kalstone's attack in the opening pages of his book, when he quotes, with "sinking heart," the following opinion of Simpson's:

> There are two kinds of poets. The first believe that poetry is a language-skill, that poems are constructed with words, not emotions. Auden was of this opinion and said so more than once. . . . The other kind of poet believes that poetry is a product of feeling rather than wit. He believes that words are not chosen by the poet's mind but, to the contrary, may be forced upon him, and the best writing is done this way.

I don't see why Kalstone's heart should sink at this perception of life's untidiness intruding into the artistic process. It is, in any case, Simpson's premise in *A Revolution in Taste* and explains his biographical approach to problems of "taste" and "revolution."

He is excellent, for example, in suggesting the boyhood roots of Dylan Thomas's obsession with body imagery and his consuming passion for the speaking voice, which, he suggests, was intensified by the discovery of a cancer in his father's mouth when Thomas was nineteen: "He identified himself with his father, especially his father's voice. The ulcer was located in the mouth, at the base of the tongue—it was poetry, his identity, that was threatened. Therefore he began to write in earnest, drawing images from the physical body."

Simpson connects Thomas's incandescent focus on himself to the oppressive physicalness of his mother, which was oddly reinforced by his father's skewed attitude toward his only son. D. J. Thomas was a lover of poetry, but he was also a stiff, authoritarian, disappointed man. He taught school, and Dylan grew up as his student. Yet, in the case of his son, he reversed his uncompromising nature, indulged him shamelessly, left him desperately free. Dylan grew up in a fragile climate of freedom, environed by grim disciplines that only he could avoid. This disjunction severed his reach into the larger world and left him spinning wildly in a personal space from which he could never emerge: "D. J. Thomas, a tyrant to every other boy, was the most permissive of masters where his son was concerned, and the result—Dylan locked into the narrow round of his own immediate consciousness, his poetry restricted to a view of the world as an extension of himself, literally, his flesh and blood and bones—was disastrous." The disaster, according to Simpson, fused into a unique poetry for a few incredible years of Thomas's youth and then began to spread hopelessly, eating up Thomas's genius and miring his life in self-destructive compulsions.

The portrait of Ginsberg is broader and more personal, probably because Simpson and Ginsberg were students at Columbia College around the same time. One suspects that Simpson is writing obliquely about himself when he describes Ginsberg's puzzled admiration for Mark Van Doren, whose emphasis on personal spontaneity and the mysteries of friendship was so inadequate a basis for Van Doren's own remote poetry and yet was so explosive in the churning minds of a younger generation. Simpson writes sympathetically about Ginsberg's troubled passage through Columbia, his off-key friendships, his need to find a connection between passionate beliefs and lived acts. He traces Ginsberg's various styles: the archaic romantic, the bleak William Carlos Williams economy of line, and finally, the visionary expansiveness of his mature poetry, derived from the Bible, from Whitman, but also from the lived act, i.e., from his mind-journeys under LSD and other drugs.

Here, as in the sections on Plath and Thomas, Simpson is not trying to cover new factual ground. He is recomposing what is known into a species of spiritual biography, focusing on the lived act of poetry. He is often at his best digressively, as when he quotes John Tytell on the experimental texture of sixties poetry: "As the mind does not perceive in the orderly arrangement of expository prose, it becomes almost a pretentious fiction to write a poem or story as if it did." This view of art, according to Simpson, "assumes that the aim of writing is to represent the working of the writer's mind, and the phrase 'pretentious fiction' suggests that only a literal account of the writer's life is admissible. . . . Thus Puritanism, the spirit that suspects that any kind of imagining is evil, that banned plays and made it wicked to read anything but the Bible, comes full circle in America as the voice of the avant-garde." This is astute, for it identifies the homogenized language common to much sixties poetry as a Puritanical distrust of language itself, surely a deadly belief for a poet.

In his chapter on Sylvia Plath, too, Simpson traces a suggestive line between the poems, with their oblique rhythms, their self-corroding imagery, their bursts of pain which become luminous, and the life of steely normalcy, with its drive to succeed, its puzzled swerves toward self-destruction. Here, as throughout the first three sections of his book, Simpson occupies the interspace between life and art with a fine instinct for psychological detail and a gift for narrative.

As good as Simpson's chapters are on Thomas, Ginsberg and Plath, that, unfortunately, is how bad his essay on Robert Lowell is. Here all of Simpson's intelligent sympathy, his ability to enter into another poet's experience and to render it tersely and sensitively, deserts him. Simpson finds Lowell an alien temperament. He seems to resent Lowell's struggle between art and authenticity, because he feels that, in Lowell's case, art won a cheap victory; above all, a loudly overpraised and overinfluential victory. According to Simpson, Lowell was Auden's accomplice in the counterrevolution of the fifties: He wrote in rhyme, he packed his poems with the sort of symbols explicators love; he dragged in history and classical references. His formidable gift for compacted language was set to perverse, "literary" ends. To be sure, Simpson agrees, Lowell broke free to his one triumph, *Life Studies,* but then he began a long declining curve back to his starting point as an iced, classical poet, which to Simpson means a dishonest "literary" poet surrounded by a chorus of "Eastern establishment" critics who, Simpson contends, diverted Lowell from his best impulse. Compared to Kalstone's careful probing of Lowell's poems in *Five Temperaments* this reads like a smear, and one can only wonder why Simpson so resents Lowell's achievement, which, for all its flaws and peculiarities, is one of the most impressive of recent decades.

Despite the failure of Simpson's chapter on Lowell, *A Revolution in Taste* is an engaging book. It is gracefully written; and it is original in its focus on the "lives" of poets who, in such different ways, tested the limits of art with the probing thrust of their personal experience.

TOM PAULIN

The Discovery of a Voice

There is a particular kind of literary critic whom Mandelstam classes among "the enemies of the word." This critic believes that a poem is primarily the vehicle of meaning and that his task is to explain this meaning through the use of what are sometimes called "critical tools." Wielding these implements, he leads search and destroy missions over the territory of the poem and he always returns with a band of captured opinions. Under interrogation these opinions inevitably appear feeble and disappointing, and they are soon forgotten. They are forgotten because, as any child knows, a poem is above all a chant, a rhythm, a cadence, not a heavy vehicle loaded with definite statements. If literary criticism is motivated by a wish to discover what some critical theorists would term "the actual meaning of a poem," then art is conscripted into the service of an idea or an ideology, and criticism is reduced to a brisk and coarse naming of parts. That vocal "relish" of which George Herbert sings is banished and there is little or no appreciation of what Louis Simpson finely calls "the joy in itself that distinguishes verse from prose."

Simpson's four essays are profoundly wise and wryly subtle in their approach to the life and work of Thomas, Plath, Ginsberg and Lowell. His vision is reminiscent of the account he gives of his own life and writing in *Air with Armed Men,* a remarkable autobiography which is impelled by a unique sense of the deterministic forces of culture, family and historical circumstance. Simpson does not believe in free will and he denies that anyone chooses to be a writer. A poet, he says, is "moved by the rhythms of speech":

Certain people have a physical, visceral way of feeling that expresses itself in rhythm. Some people play music, others

Review of *A Revolution in Taste, Times Literary Supplement,* 4 January 1980, 3–4.

dance, and others—who are attracted to words—utter lines of verse. These are the poets.

The rhythms of poetry rise from the unconscious. This is not generally understood, even by critics who write about poetry. Before a poet writes a poem, he hears it. He knows how the lines will move before he knows what the words are.

This is one of those rare moments when a writer reveals the essential reality of art and it is similar to Robert Frost's statement:

> *The ear does it.* The ear is the only true writer and the only true reader. I have known people who could read without hearing the sentence sounds and they were the fastest readers. Eye readers we call them. They can get the meaning by glances. But they are bad readers because they miss the best part of what a good writer puts into his work.

And like Frost, Simpson dismisses those critics who read only with the eye and so fail to relish the vocal fragrance of a poem.

That fragrance is beautifully present in Simpson's poetry, and the intonations of the direct speech in this stanza from "The Boarder" are to be savoured for their confident, strangely poignant ordinariness:

> The moon is brimming like a glass of beer
> Above the town,
> And love keeps her appointments—"Harry's here!"
> "I'll be right down."

The answer hovers between a glad ersatz merriness—like a chiming door-bell—and a quality that Hopkins termed "the first poised purport of reply." For all the banality of the call and the reply, they are an instressed recognition, a moment of grace in Oxidia.

Simpson is fascinated by such recognitions and he shows how as a child Dylan Thomas was enthralled by the poems which his bitter father read aloud, and how Thomas ended "the Age of Auden" by reminding his American audiences "that poetry can be passionate speech, and that this proceeds from the life of an individual." Simpson is not at all intimidated by the intentional fallacy and he demonstrates how Thomas insisted

> that sound, "the colour of saying," was of the first importance in his poetry, and that the meaning of words, and what the symbols might be said to stand for, had little importance. If Thomas's view of his poetry is correct, then much of the criticism of it has been mistaken. Critics have chosen to ignore his statements—perhaps on the assumption that what a writer thinks he is doing is not to be taken seriously—and have proceeded to show, line by line and symbol by symbol, the logic in his verse.

It's not that Simpson believes that the act of interpretation is wrong, only that it is "wrong to interpret too much" and so substitute paraphrasable content for the experience of the poem.

In his discussion of individual poems Simpson always remains faithful to that experience, and the main emphasis of his critical and biographical explorations is on the essentially vocal nature of poetry. He describes how William Carlos Williams helped Allen Ginsberg to arrive at this decisive understanding:

> They discussed meter and rhythm. Williams was taking the rhythms of his poems directly from his own speech or from speech overheard. He showed Ginsberg a phrase he had heard some workmen use, "I'll kick yuh eye," and pointed out that there was a little syncopation in "yuh eye" that would be very difficult to reproduce in regular meter. He was arriving at "little refrains, little rhythmic squiggles" unheard in poetry until now, taking them from the life around him, "right into his own ear from the streets."

There is nothing sterile about this acoustic aestheticism because it depends on living human speech, on all the quirks and tonal shifts and cadences of individual voices. Here, it is important to notice how Williams's delight in the vernacular is echoed in Frost's vocal aesthetic (my one slight quibble is that Simpson does not refer to his definition of it in a letter to John Bartlett). Frost offered a classic and provocative definition of a sentence as "a sound in itself on which other sounds called words may be strung" and he argued that these sounds-in-themselves or "sentence sounds"

> are apprehended by the ear. They are gathered by the ear from the vernacular and brought into books. Many of them are already familiar to us in books. I think no writer invents them. The most original writer only catches them fresh from talk, where they grow spontaneously.

This is what Mandelstam is saying in his essay, "About the Nature of the Word," where he questions the "bondage" of the word to its denotative significance and concludes: "the word is not a thing. Its significance is not the equivalent of a translation of itself."

Although Simpson admits that he dislikes poetry which is "a slippery, meaningless surface of words," his many brilliant remarks about the nature of the word issue from a bemused frustration with ruthlessly interpretative criticism. He mentions Flaubert's wish to write "a book about nothing, a book dependent on nothing external, which would be held together by the strength of its style," and this echoes Simpson's impatience with critics like Elder Olson who believe that poems have numerous levels of meaning, like high-rise apartments. Perhaps the purest kind of poetry is nonsense poetry, and certainly many critics ignore that sheer verbal playfulness which refuses to be guilty of a meaning.

Simpson's highly sensitive respect for the poem itself is accompanied by a deep respect for the mysteries of the individual life. As a biographer he is never crude, assertive or glumly factual—he is always deft and tactful, and this is partly because he makes a Yeatsian distinction between the private personality and the poetic character. The personal voice of a poem, he remarks, is "an expression of character. And character is something made."

Part of the charm of Simpson's method lies in his ability to transform various ordinary details into moments of imaginative recognition. He mentions that Sylvia Plath's mother moved the family to a small white frame house, and then he wonderingly suggests:

The small white frame house makes one think. It was a strange place for a poet to grow up in—perhaps all places are, but a white frame house is particularly dispiriting, antiseptic and antipoetic. Wallace Stevens has said that the people in such houses are haunted by white nightgowns, not green nightgowns, or purple nightgowns with green rings, or any other exotic combination.

And then he quotes the lines about the old sailor catching tigers in "red weather." This is ideal biography for it makes no distinction between fact and imagination, and Simpson's accounts of Thomas, Ginsberg and Lowell are similarly favoured with a warm, sometimes pungent imagining. As in *Air with Armed Men* and his great poem "My Father in the Night Commanding No," Simpson explores the determining weirdness and peculiarity of family background: Sylvia Plath's father was called "the Bee King" when he was a boy in Poland; Lowell remarked that his life "may have been determined in every respect by his relations with his parents"; and the melodious voice of Thomas's sour father led a posthumous life in "this monumental / Argument of the hewn voice."

Simpson's account of Ginsberg's student days is a curiously Zen-like narrative—chaotic events move within a dreamy stillness—and this enacts his perception of what is most original in Ginsberg's writing. At his best, he suggests, Ginsberg communicates a sense of everything being perceived both physically and as a "metaphysical presence." He argues that in order to write "America" Ginsberg "had to admit to being the son of Louis and Naomi Ginsberg," and this complex connection between poetic voice and family background is Simpson's central interest. He believes that it is a writer's difficult discovery of voice which frees him from the conditioning forces of his history (whatever the determining causes the result must appear like the operation of free will). Ginsberg made that discovery when he began to contemplate what he called "a world of pure intuitive sound," and this represented a decisive break with his previous style which was an odd and clumsy synthesis of Byron, Hopkins and Marvell.

For Simpson, the writer's true self is "manifested in style" and it therefore follows that an artist's identity has nothing to do with modish notions of self-discovery. In a close analysis of the shifts and changes in Lowell's style he remarks that the narrator's appearance of "thinking aloud" in *Life Studies* "is not 'confession,' it is a way of writing." And he demonstrates that M. L. Rosenthal was deeply mistaken when he said that Lowell's poetry "has been a long struggle to remove the mask, to make his speaker unequivocally himself." Every true writer therefore wears the mask of style, and here Simpson implies and applies Yeats's distinction between the "accidence" of the personal life and the transforming permanence of rhythm.

Aestheticism is often ridiculed nowadays as "insincere," and yet art and the life of manners share a fundamental distrust of facile sincerity. As Simpson insists, the personal and the artistic self are very different:

> The self that appears in the novel or poem has been constructed according to certain aesthetic principles. This version of the self is not intended to direct attention upon the author but to serve the work of art. The purpose is to create a symbolic life, a portrait of the artist that will have meaning for others and so create a feeling of community, if only among a few thousand.

In that last phrase, "if only among a few thousand," there is a resigned loneliness and an elegiac sense of the consolations of art. Simpson's critical and narrative voice is very distinctive—it is generous, sympathetic, spontaneously free and wittily fatalistic. Most originally, perhaps, this voice marries criticism, biography, literary and cultural history in an imaginative atmosphere of sheer wonder and discovery. Simpson speaks always as a wise, tender and relaxed authority, and this contemporary *Lives of the Poets* deserves to become a classic work.

PAUL BRESLIN

From "Three Poets"

To move from *Being Here* to Louis Simpson's *Caviare at the Funeral* is to enter a different world, literally as well as stylistically. Mr. Simpson's recent poetry is essentially urban and Jewish, as Mr. Warren's is rural and Southern. Mr. Simpson works in a plain style, so close to prose as to risk becoming prose altogether. But by concision, exactness of detail and a subtle heightening of language at the moments of greatest intensity, he achieves poems no less effective, though less immediately exciting, than Mr. Warren's. The opening poem, "Working Late," makes an excellent example. Here is the first stanza:

> A light is on in my father's study.
> "Still up?" he says, and we are silent,
> looking at the harbor lights,
> listening to the surf
> and the creak of coconut boughs.

The first line could just as easily be prose. The first three lines just might be heard as loose tetrameter, but the next two make it clear that this is free verse. That Mr. Simpson has echoed the sounds of *l* and *s,* and has modulated to low vowel sounds in the last line, one might notice only subliminally. But such patterns contribute to one's sense of hearing poetry rather than prose. At the end of the second stanza, there is a slight intensification:

> He is working late on cases.
> No impassioned speech! He argues from evidence,

Review of *Caviare at the Funeral, New York Times Book Review,* 2 November 1980, 12, 28, 29. Copyright © 1980 by The New York Times Company. Reprinted by permission.

actually pacing out and measuring,
while the fans revolving on the ceiling
winnow the true from the false.

Mr. Simpson, like his lawyer father, "argues from evidence"
rather than "impassioned speech," but nonetheless he introduces
metaphor into the poem for the first time with his lines about the
fans. By the fourth stanza, we can accept a personification of the
moon, and by the end of the fifth, two lines that are "poetic" in
the usual sense, with their projection of the poet's mood into
nature:

I can see the drifting offshore lights,
black posts where the pelicans brood.

In this stanza, the view from the poet's window reminds him
that nature, at least, has not changed since the days when his
father paced the study late at night. This affirmation of con-
tinuity is the climax of the poem; the last stanza reverts to the
plain style of the opening, and to the image of the lighted room:

And the light that used to shine
at night in my father's study
now shines as late in mine.

So casual is the diction that one might miss, on first reading,
the rhyme of "shine" and "mine."
When I claimed that Mr. Simpson's poetry is "urban," I did
not mean to imply that he simply adores contemporary urban
life; the celebration of the city is a theme for James Schuyler, not
Louis Simpson. Throughout *Caviare at the Funeral,* there is a
tension between the Old Country and the New World. The
poems are divided into four groups, the third of which is about
the poet's Russian Jewish heritage. Russia means suffering and
persecution, but it is also the "far place the soul comes from,"
more richly human than America. Mr. Simpson thinks of it as

a sound, such as you hear
in a sea breaking along a shore.

138

My people came from Russia,
bringing with them nothing
but that sound.

But this sound is muffled in the material comforts and spiritual impoverishment of American life. The American Jews Mr. Simpson writes about live

As though when they left the Old Country
and the streets knee-deep in mud
they swore an oath: Never again!
It would be nothing but steam heat from now on
and carpeting, wall to wall.
They would take ship to the highest city
and cling there, looking down.

Mr. Simpson's poetry of the prosaic makes a perfect satirical instrument for depicting the American impoverishment of spirit, as in the savagely banal language of "The Beaded Pear":

She has seen enough television
for one night. She gets out the beaded pear
she bought today in the Mall.

A "Special $1.88 do-it-yourself Beaded Pear.
No glueing or sewing required.
Beautiful beaded fruit is easily assembled
using enclosed pins, beads, and decorative material."

She says, "It's not going to be so easy."

"No," he says, "it never is."

And yet, the complaint that Americans are zombies milling about in shopping malls has long been a cliché. Mr. Simpson's reduction of other people to their most stereotyped behavior soon wears thin; he sees them from the outside only. Granted, his point is that they haven't any "inside" to see, but he assumes this judgment too readily. He has learned, from his heroes

Chekhov and Proust, the significance of the seemingly trivial detail and the importance of memory. But he lacks their gift for seeing into the grief of others. Nonetheless, in the poems about the Old Country and about his childhood in Jamaica, also in such poems as "New Lots" and "Little Colored Flags," where the critique of American life is tempered with sympathy for the individuals trapped inside it, Mr. Simpson transforms the language of the ordinary into an austere music.

G. E. MURRAY

From "Seven Poets"

Contemporary life may be stranger than fiction, but not poetry. Even in this time tranquilized to sullen indifference and outrage, the truth-loving misdirections of our poets can still amaze, if not always commandeer faith, in ways at once dazzling, practical, and enduring. At a minimum, incisive poets may serve the era by suggesting some levels of personal good sense relative to certain senseless, impersonal realities. Further to the point, the right poet's eye can fire mysteries in both extreme and ordinary events. Such aspects of the art connect with the modern poet's secret goal to establish a private foothold of authority, what John Berryman called "imperial sway," or that which Wallace Stevens understood as "a sensible ecstasy." It would seem that this is the potential edge poetry makes available to any number of its most capable and intimate handlers.

Louis Simpson, of course, knows where and how this authoritative edge cuts. Indeed, just when it seems that Simpson has reached the comfortable height of his powers, as evidenced by six formidable earlier collections, including the Pulitzer Prize–winning *At the End of the Open Road,* he penetrates forward with *Caviare at the Funeral.*

All of his best ruling qualities are displayed in this work: the introspective and observant eye, expressive detail, an easy mastery of line and stanza, the storyteller's craft and unassailable wisdom, a spirit of slightly cryptic conversation, his way of rendering anew the tactile world, usually in lamentable decline or disrepair. All this we have come to expect from Simpson.

But now there is more: this poet's ability to transmute elements of his poems into something even richer and more profound than before, to invest the poem with an unmistakable

Review of *Caviare at the Funeral.* Reprinted by permission from *The Hudson Review,* Vol. XXXIV, No. 1 (Spring 1981). Copyright © 1981 by The Hudson Review, Inc.

radiance that inspires the lines yet somehow remains outside them, like a nimbus around the head of a saint. One begins to suspect that he sanctions this effect, in part, through an extensive range of delivery systems—descriptive, lyrical, funny, somber, fantastic. So much of Simpson's maturity comes, ironically, from his ability to heed the challenges of experiment, to stay verbally energetic.

The longer storytelling poems remain his most compelling, in this instance particularly the title work, "Chocolates," "The Man She Loved," "Sway," "Typhus," and "Why Do You Write About Russia?" Sometimes it is as if Simpson is the most cunning of sleuths, able to reconstruct the far-fetched story of a life from "the contents of your purse . . . / among Kleenex, aspirin, / chewing gum wrappers, combs, et cetera." Then other times the story merely emerges from air, the narrator staring out the kitchen door on a hot, bug-ridden night.

There is humor here, too, but what to call it? Not black humor, and not white humor either. Poetic humor, then, in the most delicate of circumstances. And the wisdom of the humor comes from the association created between the body of the poem's stated experience and Simpson's imposition of a conclusion, his valued judgment at the end, which understands that the "words you thought were a joke, / and applied to someone else, / were real, and applied to you."

As usual, Simpson also examines the underbelly of American landscape, our urban shams and sorrows, especially in the excellent three-part movement "The Beaded Pear." But he confronts more than the bitter shortcomings inherent in our roadside junkyards, shopping malls and real estate agencies. American life—in its abundance and flux—is his projected subject. Since he does encompass so much, in unpredictable patterns, unconcerned with climaxes (the usual poetical devices are unnecessary here), the lines at last just move. Then the pointillist's dots of individual images begin to shape into surprisingly complex yet familiar configurations. Once onto this mode, one is forced to conclude that it's the real world that is arbitrary, while these poems seem inevitable.

Such is the final authority Simpson commands in this edition of thirty-four new titles, most of which provide conclusive evidence of remarkable advances in suppleness, clarity, balance, scope of feeling and thought amid the strangeness of contemporary passions.

DOUGLAS DUNN

Poetry of Inclusion

In the late 1950s, Louis Simpson—like the late James Wright—
dismantled the masterly verse technique of his previous writing
to follow a more self-consciously American mode, one in which
metre seems to have been abhorred as wicked. Readers who had
been impressed by Simpson's (and Wright's) metrical accomp-
lishments must have thought their new methodology a bit dis-
obliging, a poet's peevish ploy—no sooner do you get to like
their work than they change it. In retrospect, it looks as if a fresh
and critical experience of the impact of American materialism
was the most important factor in forming the important literary
group that was to be seen then in Robert Bly's magazine(s) the
Fifties and the *Sixties*.

This is Simpson's "American Poetry" (from his *Selected
Poems*):

> Whatever it is, it must have
> A stomach that can digest
> Rubber, coal, uranium, moons, poems.
>
> Like the shark, it contains a shoe.
> It must swim for miles through the desert
> Uttering cries that are almost human.

A poetry capable of leaving nothing out, a digestive poetry, it
despised abstract language at the same time as it gave the impres-
sion of looking, in a state of strenuous happenstance, for named
and concrete things to include. In his enjoyable new collection,
Caviare at the Funeral, Simpson writes in "The Man She Loved"
of a young writer in a family that is a little strange to him,
"talking Yiddish." "To their simple, affectionate questions,"
Simpson writes,

Review of *Caviare at the Funeral, Times Literary Supplement,* 5 June 1981, 645.

he returned simple answers.
For how could he explain what it meant to be a writer . . .
a world that was entirely different,
and yet it would include the sofa
and the smell of chicken cooking.

An idea of "including" has been apparent in Simpson's poetry for some time. But although the range of experience from which he draws is a wide one—a Jamaican childhood, a reimagined Russia that was his mother's birthplace, Jewish families in Brooklyn, military service, postwar Paris, travels, living in California (and now Australia, which gets a sequence in the new book)—these sources are reiterated as often as his idea of inclusiveness is suggested. "The smell of chicken cooking" returns the reader to a poem of two decades ago, "A Story about Chicken Soup," as surely as the taste of the madeleine, that hint in the senses which can be anything and can come from anywhere.

"The Man She Loved" is like most of the poems in *Caviare at the Funeral* in that it is a story and proud of it. Most of the poems are shaped, it seems to me, by the notional form of stories. Chekhov appears to be Simpson's persistent standard of storytelling, which is as it should be. The book's title and the title poem come from Chekhov's story "In the Ravine"—"This was the village where the deacon ate all the caviare at the funeral." What we get in the poem, though, has little to do with Chekhov's gloomily evoked industrial village, but another story.

"Chocolates" is an amusing account of an incident from Chekhov's life. But the Chekhovian atmosphere on which Simpson's imagination seems to thrive is peculiarly adaptable to American settings. His storytelling also reminded me of a remark made by one of Chekhov's characters—"Keep it short and skip the psychology." Any fool can be brief, but to skip the psychology is an achievement for an American poet. In poems like "Sway," for example, or "Basic Blues" and "A Bower of Roses" (both about the 1940s), or "American Classic" (a Hopperesque roadside scene), Simpson effortlessly avoids psychological intrusions: he simply tells us what it was like, what happened or didn't happen, and who said what. Significances are evoked rather than moralized into grand finales. "A Bower of

Roses" ends with an American soldier visiting an affectionate French whore. He lies beside her thinking about the young women he knew in America and "who would not let you do anything." He thinks about a song of the Great War, "How Are You Going to Keep Them Down on the Farm? (After They've Seen Paree)." The poem ends:

> He supposed that this was what life taught you,
> that words you thought were a joke,
> and applied to someone else,
> were real, and applied to you.

The potency of cheap music, as it was said elsewhere, in another story. In several of Simpson's poems the titles of popular songs crop up as if to prove that they are implicated in how we live and feel. And they are; or in Simpson's poems they are.

A possible problem with storytelling in free verse is that it makes for a quiet poetry, one in which language is disturbingly close to prose in both rhythm and the distribution of images and figures of speech. Simpson seems to have forbidden himself cadences which would not be permitted to a narrator in a prose short story. Personally, I don't think it matters: interesting stories solicit my gratitude, and the questions one is at first tempted to ask—"Is this verse? Is this poetry, or is it prose?"—are about as important as "Is this a true story?"

In his overtly American stories, Simpson is predisposed towards a sad, gentle satire. He evokes unhappy couples trapped in materialism and the conventions of society. "The Beaded Pear," "The Ice Cube Maker" (both reminiscent of John Cheever's stories) and "A River Running By" express that banal loneliness which is frequently the subject of short stories. Names of products, titles of movies and TV shows, tunes, sights, sounds and smells, those bits of everything which Simpson in that earlier manifesto-poem said American poetry ought to annex: all are drawn in to evoke people in their time and place. It makes his poems tangible and effective, though there is also a touch of arrogant stand-offishness in describing lives palpably not one's own so largely in terms of surrounding paraphernalia. It is not exactly a technique of caricature, or of outline; but something does seem left out.

Even so, Simpson is a gently accepting observer and partici-
pant. If he shakes his head with sadness at what his characters get
up to, the result is bewilderment, the dawning of wisdom and
not finger wagging: no one ever learned anything without first
being confused. As for the effect on memory of people, places,
things, overheard events and people hardly known—that
vagueness, and interest, outside the circle of one's own inti-
macy—Simpson has the last and memorable word:

> These things make an unforgettable impression,
> as though there were a reason for being here,
> in one place rather than another.

PETER MAKUCK

Caviare

Cette vie est un hôpital où chaque malade est possédé du désir de changer de lit. Celui-ci voudrait souffrir en face du poêle, et celui-là croit qu'il guérirait a côté de la fenêtre.

—*Baudelaire*

Since the Pulitzer Prize–winning volume *At the End of the Open Road* (1963) through *Adventures of the Letter I* (1971) and *Searching for the Ox* (1976), Louis Simpson has been quarreling with America and questioning the possibility of happiness, or looking for, as he says in this latest book, a "life in which there are depths / beyond happiness." Simpson's poetry has been characterized by a strong narrative impulse, open form, a fine mix of the dramatic and the discursive, literary and colloquial diction, dream imagery, a mastery of the working line, and, with increasing frequency, personal subjects such as ancestral Russia, childhood in Jamaica, soldiering in World War II. His new book, perhaps his richest yet, is vintage Simpson and provides the reading we have come to relish: freshness of sensation, telling detail, an ability to accommodate the humorous, the terrible and the lyrical almost simultaneously. Simpson implicitly describes his own work in "Why Do You Write About Russia?": "So it is with poetry: whatever numbing horrors / it may speak of, the voice itself / tells of love and infinite wonder." Voice, an incredibly natural voice, is part of the triumph of *Caviare at the Funeral*.

There are thirty-three poems in this volume of four sections, and at least two-thirds are more than a page in length. Subject matter varies: the Australian outback, Chekhov, an icemaker, a Magritte, an old graveyard, a car stalled on the highway, New York suburbia, malls, trade publishing, Russia, guests at an out-of-season hotel, soldiers on furlough. Boredom and one of its other faces, restlessness, are major themes and from poem to

Review of *Caviare at the Funeral, Tar River Poetry* 21, no. 1 (Fall 1981): 48–53.

147

poem we see people change houses, cars, wives; they vacation in Bermuda, shop for the sake of shopping; they watch TV while their children cruise about in the family car. These are human poems, seldom self-centered; they exhibit a strong interest in the lives of others and the vital signs of the nation generally.

Continuing the personal inquiry of the Russian poems appearing in his last two books, Simpson begins *Caviare at the Funeral* with a poem about Jamaica and his childhood there. "Working Late" is positive yet elegiac like the book's wonderful title (taken from Chekhov's "In the Ravine"); it also announces the themes of longing and restlessness. The recollected Jamaica of this poem is variously illuminated, first by light in the study where Simpson's father, a lawyer, worked late preparing cases. But we also see harbor lights, a lighthouse, "drifting offshore lights," and the terrible longing light of the moon that has "come all the way from Russia," his mother's homeland, "to gaze for a while in a mango tree / and light the wall of a veranda / before resuming her interrupted journey. . . ." Once the father and son sat silently and listened to the surf and the pleasant creak of coconut boughs. But there is also a darker memory, one of his father using a plaster head and brass curtain rod to show a jury "the angle of fire— / where the murderer must have stood." Subsequently the son has recurring visions of a "dead man's head / with a black hole in the forehead." But this poem is a luminous one and Simpson's act of recovery glows with acceptance. "Working Late" ends as it began—with light—and the whole memory is haloed:

> And the light that used to shine
> at night in my father's study
> now shines as late in mine.

Typical of Simpson's less personal, more socially critical poetry is "The Beaded Pear," a triptych of American boredom wherein middle-class comfort and soullessness (not simply shallow consciousness) is detailed with such subtle accuracy that a reader hesitates between laughter and tears. The first part, "Shopping," is about a suburban family's excursion to a mall where "by actual count / there are twenty-two stores selling shoes"; Simpson provides an unholy Whitmanesque litany to underscore the absurdity and obscenity of such abundance. The family splits up to shop in different directions after agreeing to meet later at the "fountain":

> The Mall is laid out like a cathedral
> with two arcades that cross—
> Macy's at one end of the main arcade,
> Abraham and Straus at the other.
> At the junction of transept and nave
> there is a circular, sunken area
> with stairs where people sit,
> mostly teenagers, smoking
> and making dates to meet later.
> This is what is meant by "at the fountain."

The middle part, "Why don't you get transferred, Dad?" finds the American family at home, momentarily, for teenage Jimmy and Darlene are about to go out with friends, Darlene pausing long enough to ask Dad why he, like her friend Marion's father, doesn't get the company to transfer him. His answer is appropriate for an American Dreamer: "I'd like to . . . / I'd also like a million dollars." As he has previously, Simpson ponders the mad and bewildering movement that America has become. Here, answers to the family's frequent where-else-would-you-like-to-live game partially explain this disturbing movement.

> Darlene likes California—
> "It has beautiful scenery
> and you get to meet all the stars."
> Mom prefers Arizona, because of a picture
> she saw once, in *Good Housekeeping*.
> Jimmy doesn't care,
> and Dad likes it here. "You can find anything
> you want right where you are."
> He reminds them of *The Wizard of Oz*,
> about happiness, how it is found
> right in your own backyard.

In the third part, "The Beaded Pear," after dinner, after the children do the dishes and go out again, after Mom and Dad watch "Hollywood Star Time" and Dad is faced with the serious decision of whether to watch a horse race film or "an excellent melodrama of the Mafia," Mom decides she has had "enough television for one night" and will work on

> A "Special $1.88 do-it-yourself Beaded Pear.
> No glueing or sewing required.
> Beautiful beaded fruit is easily assembled
> using enclosed pins, beads, and decorative material."

> She says, "It's not going to be so easy."

> "No," he says, "it never is."

> She speaks again. "There is a complete series.
> Apple, Pear, Banana, Lemon, Orange,
> Grapes, Strawberry, Plum, and Lime."

The situation and dialogue stir memories of absurdist drama. There is little authorial control over reader reaction. Malicious laughter or sympathetic moans are both possible. It is hard to say what texts are behind this poem or many other Simpson poems where people are distracted from distraction by distraction but one might think of Dostoyevsky's Zossima and his fiery denunciation of materialism, or of Pascal's dread-producing *pensée: "La seule chose qui nous console de nos misères est le divertissement, et cependant c'est la plus grande de nos misères."* Malls that may be twentieth-century man's only cathedrals, Mom/Dad clichés posing as thought, decisions that do not dignify the word, the mindless dream of California, wisdom in *The Wizard of Oz*— surely there is an existential dirty joke in all of this. In *A Dream of Governors,* when still working with meter and rhyme, Simpson wrote:

> Some day, when this uncertain continent
> Is marble, and men ask what was the good
> We lived by, dust may whisper "Hollywood."
>   ("Hot Night on Water Street")

Though his vision of contemporary society is sharply critical, Simpson's satire is never pitiless. If we laugh at the situation and behavior of the family described above, we had best beware. The closure of another poem, "A Bower of Roses," I think, easily applies to the reader of "The Beaded Pear":

> He supposed this was what life taught you,
> that words you thought were a joke,
> and applied to someone else,
> were real, and applied to you.

In a finely unified volume such as *Caviare,* one expects poems to comment on each other, and they do. "A River Running By," for example, deals with a possibly adulterous situation in which the speaker contemplates marriage, fading passion, inevitable loneliness. His thoughts sharpen our perception of the couple in "The Beaded Pear":

> The trouble with love
> is that you have to believe in it.
> Like swimming . . . you have to keep it up.

> And those who didn't, who remained
> on the sofa watching television,
> would live to wish that they had.

Hemingway, in a letter to Edward J. O'Brien, said that he was trying "to do country so you don't remember the words after you read it but actually have the Country." Simpson, too, would like the words to disappear and one never finds in his work images or similes that are suspiciously stunning. What we have instead are wonderfully natural figures that never upstage the poem as a whole. Consider:

> There stands my wife, in the garden
> gathering lilacs . . . reaching up,
> pulling a branch toward her,
> severing the flower with a knife
> decisively, like a surgeon.
>
> ("Unfinished Life")

Or:

> The air was aglimmer, thousands of snowflakes
> falling the length of the street.
>
> Five to eight inches, said the radio.
> But in the car it was warm;
> she had left the engine running
> and sat with both hands on the wheel,
> her breast and throat like marble
> rising from the pool of the dark.
>
> ("A River Running By")

Even the discursive moments of these poems have something pleasantly unforced about them, but are richly suggestive and resist the intelligence almost successfully:

> Poetry, says Baudelaire, is melancholy:
> the more we desire, the more we shall have to grieve.
> Devour a corpse with your eyes; art consists
> in the cultivation of pain.
> . . . .
> Restlessness is a sign of intelligence;
> revulsion, the flight of a soul.
>
> ("Peter")

Although restlessness is a sign of intelligence, the often aimless movement Simpson describes in a number of these poems is more a sign of ennui, especially when the movement involves automobiles. "American Classic," a bitingly humorous poem, begins the second section of the book and is about a couple who are ashamed and embarrassed because their car has broken down on the highway for all to see, making them outsiders to the automotive part of the American Dream that goes whizzing past.

> In the fume of carbon monoxide and dust
> they are not such good Americans
> as they thought they were.

The feeling of being left out
through no fault of your own, is common.
That's why I say, an American classic.

Cars appear frequently throughout the rest of this section. The last poem, "Unfinished Life," is about writing and publishing but it is not without screeching tires and the diminishing ring of a wobbling, postcrash hub cap. For Simpson, cars are most often emblems of boredom, and in and through them drivers are brought no nearer to the happiness they are seeking.

In "Lines Written near San Francisco," last poem in *At the End of the Open Road,* Simpson wrote, "The land is within. / At the end of the open road we come to ourselves." In our time few take the road of inwardness, and travel is often simply another form of distraction, of delivery from the empty self. But travel is desirable if one knows how to—as the epigraph to the last section of *Caviare* indicates—*"voyager loin en aimant sa maison."* Travel, in this instance, is a sign of persistence at the highest human endeavors. Simpson has traveled to Australia and has given us a number of fine place poems, and a lyrical essay entitled "Armidale" which tries to understand why we often turn both from ourselves and from nature:

In America from the beginning when people were dissatisfied they were able to move to a better place. But there is no better place in Australia—the first was best, around the edge, where colonies were planted. Outback is desert and rocks. The Australian psyche answers to this geography. People don't want to venture inland—they don't want to explore the Unconscious, they know it will be a desert. They cling to the coastal rims and towns. They stand elbow to elbow in the public bar and stupefy their senses with beer. They are satisfied with betting on horses or watching football on TV. . . .

I am not accusing the Australian—he is the white man everywhere, flourishing on the outside and empty within. This continent is like a projection of our inner state. We are all clinging to the edge and asking for distractions. Australia is like a screen on which we see the deserts of the psyche in an age of mass-production.

153

Simpson points out, of course, that the Outback was not a desert to the aborigine who knew quite well how to live there, who was in touch with the spirits of his ancestors there, who knew where the water was and could harvest the growing things. But the fate of the aborigine is similar to that of the American Indian. In reading "Armidale," one naturally thinks of D. H. Lawrence's Australian and American writings in which he strongly identifies with primitive peoples and urges a resurrection of the body and the reawakening of a fierce rapport with earth and stars. For Simpson, it is too late for that.

> I don't want to live "against nature" like a Symbolist or a Surrealist. But as bureaucracy triumphs over every foot of the earth's surface, and men go to their labor like ants, and huddle in multi-level buildings above ground or in tunnels beneath it, they have to find their happiness in illusions. There will be generations that have never touched a leaf. Millions of people in the United States are already living this way.
>
> But whereas the Symbolists and Surrealists created their illusions, in the future illusions will be provided. The masses will sit gazing at pictures of green hills and breaking waves, with appropriate sounds. They won't even have to applaud— they will hear the sound of applause. Access to the real thing will be prohibited to all but a few thousand members of the ruling political party.

No caviare at this funeral, only popcorn perhaps.

But Simpson's book does not end here. He is less interested in the future than the present, as in the beautiful "Maria Roberts":

> In the kingdom of heaven
> there is neither past nor future,
> but thinking, which is always present . . .

And after closing the book, we remember the scope, unity, wit, humor, and complexity of these poems. In this land of the devalued word and of so many "unreal occupations" ("New Lots"), we remember how important is a commitment to words, we remember that what often produces happiness, or the depths beyond it, is perception, imagination, language:

The things we see and the things we imagine,
afterwards, when you think about them,
are equally composed of words.

It is the words we use, finally,
that matter, if anything does.

("Unfinished Life")

WILLIAM SCAMMELL

From "Living in the World"

"When people worry about the state of poetry in Britain, especially in comparison with the States, I think that what they are worried about is literary movement and excitement. Good poets are nice to have, but movements are more fun, and these days the Americans seem to be having all the fun." Thus Louis Simpson, in 1971, in a wise and witty essay called "Advice to the English." *A Company of Poets* brings together a wide variety of Simpson's autobiographical pieces and talks, reviews of contemporary poetry, and interviews. It contains a great many good things, especially in the reviews section. Here he is on Allen Ginsberg, for example: "He was perfectly capable of writing advertising copy and paying his analyst, but the voice of William Blake kept breaking in." Of the same writer's *Journals* he observes ". . . dreams do not make good reading—no wonder psychologists are paid large fees for listening to them!" But he is too good a critic to settle for the settling of scores. Admitting that he was one of the people who did not pay sufficient attention to Ginsberg's poems when they first came out he says "I am happy to have this opportunity to say I was wrong—not merely wrong, obtuse. I still don't care for 'Howl'—Lucien Carr and Neal Cassady were not my idea of 'the best minds in America'—but other poems in the volume are superb, and 'Kaddish' is a masterpiece. Anything the author of these poems wrote deserves to be read. . . ."

That sort of generosity permeates the book, together with an astringent wit. On some aspects of Pound: "This is the typewriter trying to do the work of the imagination." On shoddy verse: "Without an involvement in technique, the practice of

Review of *A Company of Poets*, *Times Literary Supplement*, 11 September 1981, 1043.

any art must degenerate into a desperate exertion of mere personality." On Robert Duncan: "Duncan reminds me of the French Revolution: he is both the best of times and the worst of times. I know that it is useless to wish that a poet of this kind would try to be clearer, for his poems are the result of his confusions. Nevertheless, it is a fact that William Blake, by persisting in his follies, did not become wise; he merely became tedious." On Gary Snyder: "This may be the peace of the Orient, but I doubt it. I think it is just monotony."

The Interview With a Famous Writer is a dubious genre—quiddity, someone must hope, emerging from the *quid pro quo* of prompter and vatic mouthpiece; but Simpson triumphantly withstands his various grillings. Of his recent work, which reaches, in very American fashion, after a new honesty and simplicity, he says

> Writers have all sorts of ideas, but what counts is the created work. I believe that my attachment to the surface of things will create in the reader a greater affection for life. In American writing we have had a number of weird creations: a woman who wears a scarlet letter, a white whale, a hero who cannot make love, and so on. But it seems to me that we are short of people who love their lives. Do you know the saying by Goethe? "Prophets to the right, prophets to the left . . . the child of the world in the middle." Well, I'm a child of the world. I want to write poetry for people who live in the world.

It is a heartwarming book, confirming one's intuition that the man—it is not always so—is as fine as the poems.

RICHARD TILLINGHAST

The Poet of the 5:51

"It has come true," reads the first Louis Simpson poem that I encountered some twenty years ago,

> The journey and the danger of the world,
>   All that there is
> To bear and to enjoy, endure and do.
>   ("My Father in the Night Commanding No")

A fitting summary of Simpson's poetry. After reading his new book, *The Best Hour of the Night,* I want to add—sticking to the rhyme scheme—"suburbia too."

Having been from the beginning an admirably "impure" poet (to borrow Czeslaw Milosz's sly term for Whitman, Shakespeare, Homer, Dante, et al., as opposed to those modern poets who aspire to an art of "pure" imagination), Simpson has taken on the challenge of trying to make sense of contemporary life, from his soldiering experiences in World War II to American historical myths and realities—wherein "The Open Road goes to the used-car lot." Increasingly, he writes about ordinary characters and their everyday experiences. Simpson stoutly refuses the pressure from "purists" to force poetry into a limited and marginal role. The title of his selected poems, *People Live Here,* is an indication of this writer's determination to engage his imagination with characterization and plot. For him, as for Matthew Arnold, poetry has been a "criticism of life." Simpson has consistently chosen a large canvas, and this selection displays thirty-four years of work that is various, compassionate, committed and often astonishingly beautiful. He is adept enough—

Review of *The Best Hour of the Night* and *People Live Here, Nation,* 11 February 1984, 166–67.

and I would say, humane enough (I take the will to communicate as a gauge of an artist's humanity)—to be clear and readable. If the rhetorical intensity of his poems slackens in the process, it should also be noted that their plainness of diction contributes to their directness.

Reading the more than two hundred pages of *People Live Here,* one is struck both by the range of subject and treatment and by the unifying effect of Louis Simpson's voice and attitude on heterogeneous material. While capable of lyric rapture, the poet typically holds himself at some distance from his subjects and is by turns satirical, bemused, sorrowing, disdainful, sympathetic, wry. Yet to say that he *holds* himself at some distance is less accurate than to note that while sympathetic, Simpson seems by his very nature to be an outsider. He grew up in Jamaica, West Indies, with parents of Scottish and Russian descent; he was seventeen before he moved to the United States. While he engages himself passionately with American life, at times it is as if the poet were an anthropologist from an alien culture observing American ways. Simpson was the alien Easterner in California, for instance, two decades before *Annie Hall:*

> Here I am, troubling the dream coast
> With my New York face,
> Bearing among the realtors
> And tennis-players my dark preoccupation.
>
> ("In California")

And here is his account of certain Long Island folkways:

> There aren't too many alternatives.
> The couple sitting in the car
> will either decide to go home
> or to a motel.
> Afterwards, they may continue
> to see each other, in which case
> there will probably be a divorce,
> or else they may decide
> to stop seeing each other.
>
> ("Little Colored Flags")

The poet's attitude is deadpan, insistently noncommittal. In "American Classic" he addresses the issue of alienation:

> The feeling of being left out
> through no fault of your own, is common.
> That's why I say, an American classic.

The Best Hour of the Night reflects Simpson's increasing focus on life in the suburbs. "Suburbia" is a word that one rarely pronounces without sneering, but to dismiss or ignore it is to eliminate from consideration a significant slice of the American pie. As Robert Lowell put it, "History has to live with what was here." Someone who knew nothing of present-day America would get little idea of our life from most contemporary poetry. I often think of a student of mine some years ago who said, "I never feel completely at ease outside of Great Neck," and I can almost imagine her in a Simpson poem. His view of these brief-case-carriers, deal-strikers, Saturday-night poker players and village-meeting-goers combines detachment with a self-effacing sense of identification.

In his examination of *Homo suburbanus,* Simpson does not avoid the iffy area of morality. "Do you know the eleventh commandment?" Harry, one of his characters, asks. (The eleventh commandment is "Don't get caught.") After Harry makes this remark, the poet, almost but not quite a straight man, notes coolly: "Then, as I recall, everyone laughs." Harry is later sent to prison for

> kickbacks, misapplication of funds,
> conspiracy, fraud, concealment, wire fraud,
> falsified books and records, and
> interstate transportation of stolen property.
> > ("The Eleventh Commandment")

The poem concludes with the poet's dry comment on greeting Harry's young son after the father's removal: " 'Hi there,' I say to him. / What else do you say to a six-year-old?"

In staking out fresh material for his poetry, it is not surprising that Louis Simpson should feel the necessity of creating new or at least hybrid forms. This he has done notably in "The Previous

Tenant," which is something like a short story in free verse. The form allows the writer to highlight certain details without being bound to the three-dimensional realism and continuity of traditional fiction. (While "postmodernist" fiction writers take the same kinds of formal liberties, of course, Simpson is not attracted by their interest in fantasy and "meta-realism.") The speaker rents a cottage where the previous tenant has left some of his belongings, and through conversations with the landlord and others, pieces together the story of an affair his predecessor had that caused him all sorts of trouble including the divorce that necessitated his moving into the cottage in the first place. It's a fascinating, skillfully spun tale in which we learn all sorts of different things about the characters involved, the speaker, the little suburban town in which the story is set and, finally, about American values.

If you cling to the impression that poetry is by nature obscure, forbidding and otherworldly, buy one of these books by Louis Simpson. You may be the only passenger on the 5:51 reading it, but you will feel a shock of recognition at poems that dare to come to terms with this country we live in—even though, as Simpson says in "Walt Whitman at Bear Mountain":

> . . . all the realtors,
> Pickpockets, salesmen, and the actors performing
> Official scenarios,
> Turned a deaf ear, for they had contracted
> American dreams.

ALAN WILLIAMSON

We're All in the Same Boat

Over the years, one has often been tempted to ask, "Will the real Louis Simpson please stand up?" For there have been several. There was the correct but amazingly precocious young Briton from Jamaica, the coeditor of *The New Poets of England and America,* a few of whose poems are preserved in the opening sections of *People Live Here.* There was the brief but shrill convert to the school of Robert Bly. There was the author of critical books like *A Revolution in Taste,* which seems to me all too English in its breezy mixture of gossip and snap judgments. Finally, there is the wonderful poet of the last ten years, whose bare, unadorned poems of the common life remind me of Randall Jarrell.

That Mr. Simpson knows where his best work is to be found is indicated by both the title of *People Live Here,* a selection of poems written in the past twenty-four years, and its organization. He has arranged the poems chronologically within thematic sections, so each early poem, whether on war, Jewish life in Russia or modern lives, seems a kind of preliminary draft for a recent masterpiece, such as "On the Ledge," "Typhus" or "Sway," placed at or near the end.

"I am the man, I suffered, I was there," Walt Whitman wrote. Mr. Simpson, who has given us a very lovable, if deconstructive, portrait of our national bard in the poem "Walt Whitman at Bear Mountain," suffers and benefits from the same inability to distance himself from the pathos of other lives. In the middle of the night, he has a vision of a bachelor acquaintance with home-repaired glasses:

Review of *The Best Hour of the Night* and *People Live Here, New York Times Book Review,* 29 January 1984, 26. Copyright © 1984 by The New York Times Company. Reprinted by permission.

He is reading a novel by Morley Callaghan.
Whenever I wake he is still there . . .
with his glasses. I wish he would get them fixed.
I cannot sleep as long as there is wire
running from his eye to his ear.

In another poem, "The Mexican Woman," the poet relives an old beggar's tales of war and infidelity:

I know what it's like to serve
in Mexico with Black Jack Pershing.

And to walk in the dust and heat . . .
for I can see her hurrying

to the clay wall where they meet,
and I shall be wise to her and the lieutenant.

Here "wise," the old beggar's word, expands marvelously to its full meaning, as if to participate in the pain and the victory of other lives were the essence of wisdom.

But wisdom has a less ecstatic dimension—the need to face up to hard moral facts and unresolvable contradictions in our lives. Mr. Simpson has been adamant about the place of such facts and contradictions in poetry and about the need to emphasize them by breaking rules at times. The ending of the first section of "A Story about Chicken Soup" has become famous:

But the Germans killed them.
I know it's in bad taste to say it,
But it's true. The Germans killed them all.

The continuation of the poem is perhaps even more remarkable. As a young soldier in the ruins of Hitler's retreat, Berchtesgaden, the poet encounters "A German girl-child— / Cuckoo, all skin and bones." The juxtaposition in itself could be sentimental, but the poem continues:

Then as we splashed in the sun
She laughed at us.

We had killed her mechanical brothers,
So we forgave her.

This, one feels, tells the whole truth about the mean emotional bargains people strike with themselves. We may not be as bad as Hitler, but as Freud observed in *Civilization and Its Discontents,* we do not achieve disinterested love without some propitiatory offering to aggression and hatred. The quality the lines have of being "not poetry," rather something like a proof in logic, is part of their power.

But Mr. Simpson did not arrive at this difficult, equalizing wisdom easily. The one group of displeasing poems in *People Live Here* is in a section called "A Discovery of America" that gathers together poems from the 1960s. In them Surrealism is used to distance and dehumanize Americans, particularly Californians: "The businessmen of San Francisco / . . . rise from the ooze of the ocean floor." The compassion is merely condescending, and the contrasting praise of traditional societies is peculiarly simple-minded, even allowing for the general simple-mindedness of modern poets on this subject:

> You were born to waste your life.
> You were born to this middleclass life
>
> As others before you
> Were born to walk in procession
> To the temple, singing.

Even Mr. Simpson's best previous book, *Caviare at the Funeral,* did not allow quite the same degree of humanity to his Long Island neighbors as to soldiers, prostitutes, immigrant Jews, sad young proletarian girls and sad, corrupt editors. He does extend his compassion to those neighbors in his new book, *The Best Hour of the Night.* But what makes his suburbanites most sympathetic, one finds, is their discontent. They know dimly that something is lost when life ceases to be raw and cruel, although they also know that rawness can brutalize. On a fishing trip to Alaska, one Jim Bandy (Simpson's comic names can be wonderful) has a brush with the uncompromisingness of life:

A bear came out of the forest.
Jim had two salmon . . . he threw one
but the bear kept coming.
He threw the other . . . it stopped.

On his return, Bandy reflects:

They do a lot of drinking in Alaska.
He saw thirty or forty lying drunk
in the street. And on the plane . . .

They cannot stand living in Alaska,
and he cannot stand Long Island
without flying to Alaska.

This poem says what most of Mr. Simpson's best poems seem to say—that, finally, no life is satisfactory but there is the paradoxically healing corollary that all lives are somehow the same life. Perhaps that is a kinder way of reading the unsuccessful early poem mentioned before—"You were born to this middleclass life." But the healing insight is expressed much more charmingly in "Physical Universe," the first poem in *The Best Hour of the Night*. As the poet is ranting late at night about metaphysics—"Or should we stick to the Bible?"—his wife mutters in her sleep, "Did you take out the garbage?" The poet "thought about it," and her words become an answer, the only possible answer:

Like a *koan* . . . the kind of irrelevance
a Zen master says to the disciple
who is asking riddles of the universe.

M. L. ROSENTHAL

Innocence Betrayed

> *Carentan O Carentan*
> *Before we met with you*
> *We never yet had lost a man*
> *Or known what death could do.*

Ever since Louis Simpson's ballad "Carentan O Carentan" appeared in his first volume, *The Arrivistes* (1949), it has been one of a very few American touchstone poems of the Second World War. Its ritualized near-doggerel rehearses the pastoral hell of fledgling soldiers cut down by enemy fire in the Normandy countryside. In its stunned lament for innocents betrayed into death, it is also a key to Simpson's work generally. The same fresh horror persists, for instance, in a more recent poem, "On the Ledge," which recalls yet another ambush like that at Carentan. This time the German unit was destroyed just in time by artillery rockets, but inwardly the poet has remained frozen on the edge of annihilation:

> There is a page in Dostoevsky
> about a man being given the choice
> to die, or stand on a ledge
> through all eternity

and:

> . . . like the man on the ledge
> I still haven't moved . . .
> watching an ant
> climb a blade of grass and climb back down.

Review of *People Live Here, Times Literary Supplement*, 4 July 1986. Copyright © 1986 by M. L. Rosenthal.

Simpson shares with the psychologically war-wounded everywhere a particular sort of alienation, based on the lesson that the powers that be, on whatever side, care nothing for the traumatized "man on the ledge." In this respect he is closer to British poets of Wilfred Owen's and David Jones's generation than to his American contemporaries. Perhaps the fact that he was born and grew up in Jamaica, the son of a "native" (his word) father of partly Scottish background, has something to do with this affinity. On the other hand, his mother was a Russian-Jewish immigrant and a naturalized American, and he has a natural family feeling for her childhood world and the life destroyed by the Holocaust. Also, he has lived in the United States since university days and identifies with his adopted country's exhausting struggle against self-corruption. Two wry passages will illustrate these Jewish and American preoccupations. The first is from "A Story about Chicken Soup":

> In my grandmother's house there was always chicken soup
> And talk of the old country—mud and boards,
> Poverty,
> The snow falling down the necks of lovers.
>
> Now and then, out of her savings
> She sent them a dowry. Imagine
> The rice-powdered faces!
> And the smell of the bride, like chicken soup.
>
> But the Germans killed them.
> I know it's bad taste to say it,
> But it's true. The Germans killed them all.

The second passage, from "Walt Whitman at Bear Mountain," is part of an imagined exchange with Whitman's statue:

> "Where are you, Walt?
> The Open Road goes to the used-car lot.
>
> "Where is the nation you promised?
> Those houses built of wood sustain

Colossal snows,
And the light above the street is sick to death."

As in the war poems, extreme alienation is implied in both
these instances. Other poems show that an important influence
on Simpson's bleak vision has been what Hart Crane once called
"the curse of sundered parentage." One of Simpson's most tell-
ing pieces, "Working Late," refers obliquely—but with that
dazzling emotional clarity an "obscure" poem can sometimes
have—to his parents' separation and his mother's occasional
trips to Jamaica to see him. The atmosphere of the house is
charged with loneliness. The father, a lawyer of coldly logical
temperament, had once constructed a plaster head to show a
murderer's angle of fire:

> For years, all through my childhood,
> if I opened a closet . . . bang!
> There would be a dead man's head
> with a black hole in the forehead.

The half-joke hardly conceals the unresolved memory of
fright. Meanwhile, the disappearing mother, in the image of the
inconstant moon, is presented richly and longingly. His phrasing
for her shows Simpson's ability to shift tones rapidly between the
jarring or prosaic and the lyrically evocative:

> All the arguing in the world
> will not stay the moon.
> She has come all the way from Russia
> to gaze for a while in a mango tree
> and light the wall of a veranda,
> before resuming her interrupted journey
> beyond the harbor and the lighthouse
> at Port Royal, turning away
> from land to open sea.

Somehow, these compelling sources of depression allow
room for warmth and humour as well, especially in the poems
devoted to the mother's childhood world in Russia. Here Simp-
son takes on the homely role of a Yiddish storyteller, a sort of

English-speaking Sholem Aleichem freely deploying Chekhovian and Symbolist flourishes with an attractively modest virtuosity. These poems combine fantasy, pathos, nostalgia and gaiety and leaven the whole collection. They stand in sharp contrast to bitter poems like "American Classic" and "Quiet Desperation," which see the United States drifting into bourgeois emptiness; and to poems of revulsion like "The Inner Part," "Lines Written near San Francisco," and "Indian Country," which speak of modern Americans as "colonists of Death" and dwellers near "the Lethe of asphalt and dust." The blackest mood of all, perhaps, is found in the short, slightly mysterious "Back in the States," a poem that *seems* to be about a war prisoner just back from the miseries of Vietnam and "already becoming like the rest of us."

Many of the poems are complex mixtures of style and tonality. In particular, this is true of poems having to do with memories of women—most notably "Sway," about a wartime friendship with a waitress to whom the young poet read Rilke and whose intense though pointless life continues to haunt his imagination. Some of Simpson's purest pieces focus on remembered scenes or moments of relationship felt to hold important, yet elusive, ultimately lost meaning: "Maria Roberts," "The Hour of Feeling," "A River Running By"—each centred on a woman's remembered words or perplexing companionship.

People Live Here provides the fullest view thus far of Louis Simpson's technical and emotional range. In an admirable sense, he is a representative American poet of this century: intimate with that realm of "lost connections" of which Robert Lowell wrote and in which Kenneth Fearing lived, but quickened nevertheless by whatever life and language have brought his way.

RICHARD SILBERG

Facing the World

The tone of Louis Simpson's writing in this collection of reviews and essays is frankly polemic. He is against poetry that wallows in the self, as so much of American poetry does, and he is against poetry that concentrates on language, itself; Simpson champions a "transparent" language in which the reader looks "through" the words to the subject matter, and he believes that subject matter should be the common experience of our twentieth-century lives in factories and streets, on assembly lines. He favors drama, the narrative, because he believes narrative turns the writer away from the self, compels him to "face the world." His final goal is poetry that energizes our human community in technology and cities.

I have some problems with Simpson's position. Wallace Stevens, one of the great poets of our century, becomes a bad guy in Simpson's argument as does John Ashbery, another pretty fair writer. Also, although Simpson explicitly disavows it, there is a social realism implied in or consequent on Simpson's poetic. On the other hand, I admire his demystifying concern for humanity and the courage of his straightforward judgments.

Polemicism excepted, though, this is an intelligent, enjoyable book. He has much to say about Wordsworth, Whitman, Williams (the W's), about line breaks, i.e., prose versus poetry, closed form versus free verse, among other things, and he is himself an important American poet so that his discussion of his own writing process, his genesis as a writer, his coming to terms with the inevitably tiny audience for poetry, his aspirations for poetry, glows with achievement and sensibility.

Review of *The Character of the Poet, Poetry Flash* 159 (June 1986): 13–14.

PART TWO *Essays*

YOHMA GRAY

The Poetry of Louis Simpson

The paradox inherent in objective criticism of lyric poetry is nowhere more apparent than in an analysis of Louis Simpson's poetry. Lyric poetry seeks to describe intense but transient sensations and emotions which prose cannot, seeks to suspend primary experience for a moment in time so that it may be savored and relished. Many primary experiences are basically incommunicable on *any* level. Consider the difficulty of describing, to someone totally ignorant of the experience, how a cello sounds, or how sandpaper feels, or how a puppy's mouth smells. So-called objective or judicial criticism, therefore, which is mere *explication de texte,* is obviously self-defeating because the subject of a lyric poem is, by definition, beyond the ordinary domain of prose. It does not gain its effect through the information it contains but through the feeling it evokes, and the poem exists because poetry is the only medium through which the experience can be shared.

Louis Simpson published his first book of poems, *The Arrivistes,* in 1949, *Good News of Death* in 1955, and *A Dream of Governors* in 1959. Shortly he will publish a fourth volume of verse, *At the End of the Open Road,* and he plans an edition of *Selected Poems* in 1964. Many of his poems have been published separately in the *New Yorker, Hudson Review, American Scholar, Paris Review, Partisan Review* and in other journals and anthologies. In addition to his poems he has published one novel,

Tri-Quarterly 5 (Spring 1963): 33–39. Reprinted in *Poets in Progress* (Evanston: Northwestern University Press, 1967), 227–50. Copyright © 1967 by Northwestern University.

Throughout this essay, Yohma Gray often makes use of Simpson's poems as they appeared in magazines prior to their publication in *At the End of the Open Road* (1963) and *Selected Poems* (1965). In cases where versions of a particular poem differ, I have retained the earlier version as quoted by Gray.—ED.

Riverside Drive, in 1962, one record in the *Yale Series of Recorded Poets,* one critical study, *James Hogg,* in 1963. He edited *The New Poets of England and America,* together with Donald Hall and Robert Pack, in 1957, and he has published critical articles in leading magazines. He is married, has three children, and is currently an associate professor of English at the University of California at Berkeley.

Although any one of his poems is self-sufficient and self-contained, the relationship between the poems, and between his life and the poems, perhaps deserves some mention. With first-person authority he writes primarily about war, love, urbanism, the American dream, and human mortality. He was born in 1923 in Jamaica, British West Indies, of varied national ancestry. He came to New York to study at Columbia College in 1940 but his studies were interrupted by World War II, during which he served in the 101st Airborne Division of the U.S. Army, through the invasion of Europe from Normandy to Berchtesgaden. He emerged from the war with a Bronze Star, a Purple Heart, and United States citizenship, not to mention frozen feet and delayed shock. He returned to Columbia to receive bachelor's, master's, and doctor's degrees. He was an associate editor with the Bobbs-Merrill publishing company until 1955, and since then has been teaching. The obvious use he has made, therefore, of all this experience invites the so-called intentional fallacy, or the use of biographical material and explicit intention, and the so-called affective fallacy, or the use of emotion and association through "objective correlatives."

Formally his poems fall into three general types: short lyrics; longer poems which depend on topical and historical allusions but which are nevertheless more lyrical than academic in tone; and long dramatic poems. His point of view is more subjective than objective; the reader is aware of the intrusion of the poet's private, inner life in the poems rather than the insertion of an invented character from whom the poet is detached. He does not demonstrate what Keats called "negative capability," or what has been more recently called aesthetic distance. Although he sometimes writes in the third person, the reader senses a subjective "I" in the poem, just as Browning often writes in the first person but conveys the sense of an objective "he." (His dramatic poems are no exception; however, the focus of this essay is on the lyrical poems.) In "The Battle," for example, he delays and thereby intensifies the meaning of the experience to the subjective "I":

> Helmet and rifle, pack and overcoat
> Marched through a forest. Somewhere up ahead
> Guns thudded. Like the circle of a throat
> The night on every side was turning red.
>
> They halted and they dug. They sank like moles
> Into the clammy earth between the trees.
> And soon the sentries, standing in their holes,
> Felt the first snow. Their feet began to freeze.
>
> At dawn the first shell landed with a crack.
> Then shells and bullets swept the icy woods.
> This lasted many days. The snow was black.
> The corpses stiffened in their scarlet hoods.
>
> Most clearly of that battle I remember
> The tiredness in eyes, how hands looked thin
> Around a cigarette, and the bright ember
> Would pulse with all the life there was within.

In the midst of all that death, the meaning of life becomes momentarily clear in the ordinary act of smoking a cigarette; and in the midst of all those extraordinarily dramatic images, the mundane image becomes extraordinarily intense.

I am not suggesting that the poems are more concerned with literal than artistic truth or that Louis Simpson is masquerading as all the characters he creates; rather, I mean to call attention to the repersonalization which these poems represent in the direct relationship between reader and writer. They seek to create a rapport which has not been generally characteristic of poetry in the first half of the twentieth century. They appeal not to some past, lost, and eternal truth as a means of salvation, but rather to some present, hidden, and internal relationship which can become an effective conspiracy against the dehumanizing forces in the modern world. His intention becomes explicit in "Room and Board":

> The curtained windows of New York
> Conceal her secrets. Walls of stone
> Muffle the clatter of the fork.
> Tomorrow we shall see the bone.
>
> In silence we construct a sect . . .
> Each of us, comrades, has his own.
> Poems that will not take effect,
> Pictures that never will be known.
>
> The landlord wipes his mouth of pork,
> Pauses to eavesdrop, disconnect
> The water and the telephone;
>
> And Death's unmarried daughter crawls
> Along the thin lath of the walls
> And knocks, because we live alone.

Despite the tone, however, there is never a sense of the narrowly parochial nor the embarrassingly intimate. This is not merely self-introspection nor self-analysis. Theodore Hoffman says of the poetry, " . . . nor is it the victim of either of the affable poetic vices of the day, for it neither attempts to buckle its matter into a self-designed system nor is it engaged in a capricious quest for conceits." That, I think, is one of its major achievements as mid-twentieth-century American poetry.

Louis Simpson never departs from traditional form and structure and yet he never departs from contemporary themes and concerns. In "The Lady Sings," for example, he handles a modern psychological situation in the delicate cadence of seventeenth-century verse:

> The lady sings her child
> Will be such a one
> As the world has not known:
> Jesus without tears.

And as her heart goes wild
Between gates of bone
He comes into his own,
Having his own ideas.

The days her lover smiled
Are as a summer gone.
Over a telephone
We talk across the years.

Now she may be beguiled
By apricocks, and groan
Her secret to the sun.
Shake her and she bears.

The central feeling of the defeat of a possessive mother through
the independence of her son begins with a reference to the Vir-
gin, ends with an oblique reference to the *Duchess of Malfi,* and
contains diction as diverse as "apricocks" and "telephone," yet
synthesizes the elements gracefully.

In the last stanza of "Invitation to a Quiet Life" Simpson
demonstrates the precision of his ear as well as of his eye as he
imitates a traditional pastoral form:

Since, Amaryllis, you and I
Adore an advertising sky
And find happiness to stare
At the enchantments of thin air,
Let us go in, and not regret
The endings that we never met,
But in security applaud
The ecstasies we can't afford.
So shall we manage till the day
Death takes the furniture away.

The pastoral form and the urban theme combine ironically and
the irony intensifies and clarifies the metropolitan anxieties
which are the subject of the poem. Simpson uses a similar device
in "Arm in Arm," a war poem:

Beside a Church we dug our holes,
By tombstone and by cross.
They were too shallow for our souls
When the ground began to toss.

Which were the new, which the old dead
It was a sight to ask.
One private found a polished head
And took the skull to task

For spying on us. . . . Till along
Driving the clouds like sheep,
Our bombers came in a great throng:
And so we fell asleep.

The tumultuous chaos of the bombing of a churchyard and the
grisly mingling of old corpses and new is the subject of the
poem, but the fragmentary senselessness of the experience is
enhanced by the deliberately measured and regular meter, and
the strife of the battle is heightened by the suggestion of sleep
and of the calm of the pastoral scene. There is a kind of literary
dialectic in these poems . . . thesis, antithesis, synthesis . . .
which forms the dynamic process of an "internal colloquy."

In examining the plight of modern man, Louis Simpson finds
all the contemporary tensions between imagination and reality,
between fragmentation and continuity, between city and coun-
try, between Old World and New World, between military and
human values, between the American dream and the American
actuality; but he neither moralizes nor wails. To him poetry is
not the only suitable subject for poetry, nor expressionism the
only suitable mode for it. He does indeed juxtapose images
which are abstracted from their normal context, creating an
apocalyptic quality, but the final effect is to clarify rather than to
cloud. If his poems do not always follow an obviously logical
progression, the total insight is rational and conscious and the
associative progression makes ultimate sense. Throughout his
"Jamaica," for example, he relies on metaphors of the body until
the final stanza when he shifts to prestige symbols of modern
culture:

Life is a winter liner, here history passes
Like tourists on top-decks, seeing the shore through sun-
    glasses:
And death, a delightful life-long disease,
Sighs in sideways languor of twisted trees.

The shift from organic to mechanistic images is significant in itself and provides an insight into the values of modern life. The form and theme are skillfully unified by the unexpected break at the end of the second line, where the word "sun" (the natural light which makes all sight possible) is sharply juxtaposed to the word "glasses" (artificial devices which alter vision) at the beginning of the third line, with the hyphen intensifying the cleavage. Thus the very abruptness of the shift in associations has a logic of its own to modern man. Simpson is not courting madness in this "multiverse," nor is he insisting that modern man is forever "caught between two worlds, the one dead, the other powerless to be born." In the Romantic tradition he is relying on sensibility as a basis for orientation and movement in a chaotic world, but his reliance on human viscera and cerebra is neither frightening nor agonizing to him. He is quite explicit in a stanza from "Islanders":

Enough of these images—they set the teeth on edge!
Life, if you like, is a metaphor of death—
The difference is you, a place for the passing of breath.
That is what man is. He is the time between,
The palpable glass through which all things are seen.
Nothing. Silence. A syllable. A word.
Everything.

Sensational perception and individual identity are his broad concerns. His rhetoric is often ironic; that is, a subtle reversal takes place between the literally expressed and the implied values, through naive narration, understatement, and romantic illusion and disintegration. His presentation of these generalities, however, is always through the animation of particulars. "He who wishes to see a Vision, a perfect Whole, must see it in its Minute Particulars," according to William Blake, and Louis

Simpson adheres to that dictum. He sees reality through particulars; he is a kind of "responsible vagrant" who finds meaning in any situation. He has the talent, however, to generalize his experience without diminishing its concreteness. That is why he can be personal but universal in his tone. "Hot Night on Water Street" is little more than a series of particulars but it conveys the whole of an American small town, universally recognizable:

> Three hardware stores, a barbershop, a bar,
> A movie playing Westerns—where I went
> To see a dream of horses called *The Star,* . . .
> Some day, when this uncertain continent
> Is marble, and men ask what was the good
> We lived by, dust may whisper "Hollywood."
> . . . .
> At the newsstand in the lobby, a cigar
> Was talkative: "Since I've been in this town
> I've seen one likely woman, and a car
> As she was crossing Main Street knocked her down."
> I was a stranger here myself, I said,
> And bought the *New York Times,* and went to bed.

"Music in Venice" demonstrates a similar capacity to evoke wholeness through particulars:

> It's night in the Piazza. Lighted space
> Burns like your brandy. Violins and brass
> Play waltzes, fox-trots. On a cloud, St. Mark's
>   Winged lion perches;
> High palaces go sailing to the moon,
> Which, as advertised, is perfectly clear.
> The lovers rise, moon-struck, and whisper their
>   *Arrivedercis.*
> . . . .
> Venice, the city built on speculation,
> Still stands on it. Love sails from India
> And Sweden—every hanging cloud pours out
>   A treasure-chest.
> It's love on the Rialto, news of love,
> That gives Antonio his golden life,

> Even to Envy, sharpening a knife,
> His interest.

In "The Inner Part"[1] a few trivial particulars serve to characterize American mentality before her emergence as a world power into the twentieth century, and American maturity and deep disillusionment after the war to make the "world safe for democracy":

> When they had won the war.
> And for the first time in history
> Americans were the most important people—
>
> When the leading citizens no longer lived in their shirt sleeves,
> And their wives did not scratch in public;
> Just when they'd stopped saying "Gosh!"—
>
> When their daughters seemed as sensitive
> As the tip of a fly rod,
> And their sons were as smooth as a V-8 engine—
>
> Priests, examining the entrails of birds,
> Found the heart misplaced, and seeds
> As black as death, emitting a strange odor.

In this poem the shift from the naive buoyancy of pre–World War I America to the sophisticated despair of post–World War I America conveys, as a prose paraphrase cannot, a sense of the exchange of innocence for the knowledge of good and evil. The oblique reference to classical civilization ominously suggests the inevitable consequence of that knowledge, death. Ironically it prophesies World War II.

The value of such a talent is inestimable. Every society has areas of gross insensitivity, some of them positively necessary for carrying on the life processes and some of them merely destructive of the subtle nuances of primary experience which comprise human fulfillment, realization, and delight. There are primitive tribes, for example, which have only three words to denote color: one term for white, one term for black, and one term for all others. Assuming that language and perception are inextricably linked, the level of color awareness in these societies is extremely primitive. Reading the poetry of Louis Simpson makes it obvious that some of our perceptions are equally primitive and undeveloped. We are daily bombarded with sensations from which the conscious mind extracts only a few functional impressions, leaving a vast aggregate of experience to be dismissed or buried in the inner recesses of awareness, below the conscious level. The economy of concentration is often practical but it deprives us of our full power and the responsibilities of that power; it makes us "emotional illiterates," often totally out of touch with our own feelings. Even in the most mundane experience there is a vast area of unperceived reality and it is Louis Simpson's kind of poetry which brings it to our notice. It enables us to see things which are ordinarily all about us and which we do not ordinarily see; it adds a new dimension to our sensational perception, making us hear with our eyes and see with our ears. His poem "Frogs,"[2] for example, seems to be a recollection of details of ordinary experience and yet subtly becomes an implied metaphor so that in the resolution, both the particular and the general are sharply impressed on the consciousness:

> The storm broke, and it rained,
> And water rose in the pool,
> And frogs hopped into the gutter,
>
> With their skins of yellow and green,
> And just their eyes shining above the surface
> Of the warm solution of slime.
>
> At night, when fireflies trace
> Light-lines between the trees and flowers
> Exhaling perfume,
>
> The frogs speak to each other
> In rhythm. The sound is monstrous,
> But their voices are filled with satisfaction.
>
> In the city I pine for the country;
> In the country I long for conversation—
> Our happy croaking.

The "shock of recognition" in the final stanza is all the more powerful because of the reader's obtuseness and complacency in the first four stanzas and because the subject of the poem is finally an implied obtuseness and complacency.

"Birch"[3] is another poem which depends ultimately on a metaphor which is really obvious, but only after the reading of the poem:

> Birch tree, you remind me
> Of a room filled with breathing,
> The sway and whisper of love.
>
> She slips off her shoes;
> Unzips her skirt; arms raised,
> Unclasps an earring, and the other.
>
> Just so the sallow trunk
> Divides, and the branches
> Are straight and smooth.

In "The Boarder," Simpson once again selects the most mundane particulars of a situation to convey the most profound of human feelings:

> The time is after dinner. Cigarettes
>   Glow on the lawn:
> Glasses begin to tinkle; TV sets
>   Have been turned on
>
> The moon is brimming like a glass of beer
>   Above the town,
> And love keeps her appointments—"Harry's here!"
>   "I'll be right down."
>
> But the pale stranger in the furnished room
>   Lies on his back
> Looking at paper roses, how they bloom,
>   And ceilings crack.

The images of the first two stanzas convey the feeling of conviviality and community, and the images of the last stanza convey the feeling of alienation and separation so powerfully because of the contrast between the dynamic processes implied in the former and the static situation implied in the latter. The contrast depends primarily on the jarring tension between the adjective "paper" and the noun "roses," and the implication of disintegration. Simpson is creating meaning from the raw material of experience and is bringing the reader to a deeper level of awareness.

In the same manner but on a different level of matter, Simpson vivifies experience which is not a part of everyone's ordinary storehouse but which then becomes as real as frogs or birches or paper roses. In short, some of his subject matter is "raw" and some of it is "cooked"; some depends on common experience and some on special knowledge, but the meaning is always universal. "A Story about Chicken Soup,"[4] for example, depends on some general knowledge of World War II and on some general association of chicken soup with Jewish customs:

> In the ruins of Berchtesgaden
> A child with yellow hair
> Ran out of a doorway.
>
> A German girl-child—
> Cuckoo, all skin and bones—
> Not even enough to make chicken soup.
> She sat by the stream and smiled.
>
> Then as we splashed in the sun
> She laughed at us.
> We had killed her mechanical brothers,
> So we forgave her.

Similarly, familiarity with literary history intensifies appreciation of Simpson's ability to imitate faultlessly. "Invitation to a Quiet Life" reverberates through three centuries of poetry with its echoes of Marlowe:

> Come, Amaryllis, let us go
> To see the moving picture show

Where the small people, closely pressed,
Walk all together in their best.

"Ballad of the Beery Boys" humorously combines strains of
Browning and a familiar popular poem:

Up Flotsam, up Jetsam, up Donner and Blitzen!
I galloped, he galloped through barrels of Pilsen
To Maidenhead, Munich, Sversk and Vienna,
(A landscape of umber, a sky of sienna).

"Over at the Baroque Ryehouse" is reminiscent of the style of
Emily Dickinson:

I've had my cut of sin,
A passing glimpse of heaven,
And hope to meet Christ in
The city after seven.

"Room and Board" is suggestive of Auden's "Musée des Beaux
Arts" in the stanza

The landlord wipes his mouth of pork,
Pauses to eavesdrop, disconnect
The water and the telephone.

Finally "Song: 'Rough Winds Do Shake the Darling Buds of
May'" combines Renaissance conceits and modern form:

Rough winds do shake
                    do shake
                              the darling buds of May
The darling buds
            rose-buds
                    the winds do shake
That are her breasts.
Those darling buds, dew-tipped, her sighing moods do shake.

On several levels, then, Simpson's poetry has an incisive
quality which enables us simultaneously to see and to be sud-

denly aware that we are seeing, and thus to double the delight. Sometimes he gives the reader the relief of "what oft was thought, but ne'er so well expressed," but more often he intensifies particulars which have never been anything but amorphous, which have never taken on the discipline of form. Who does not remember the delight of seeing, on a cold, wintry day, snowflakes under a magnifying glass for the first time, and who has forgotten the awe at the illumination of the hitherto unsuspected and unperceived mystery, both as an external phenomenon of nature and as an internal phenomenon of perception? Perhaps Robert Louis Stevenson was aware of that kind of delight when he said, "The world is so full of a number of things, I'm sure we should all be as happy as kings." Reality, of course, has a dark as well as a light side, and reality in itself is not always delightful to human perception, is often more somber; perceiving and knowing, however, are always an enhancement of human values, whether their objects be beautiful or ugly. Louis Simpson's poetry imparts new sensibility; the heat of his imagination and the pressure of his experience fuse both the raw materials and organized systems of life into lyrical poems which reflect and refract human emotion with the same beauty and brilliance that diamonds do physical light.

Mid-twentieth-century society is generally unsympathetic to knowing for the sake of knowing. (Even in the realm of science, pure research has been defined as the name we give any project when we don't know what we're doing). Useless, that is, inapplicable knowledge is a term of opprobrium. The truth of the human heart is, however, that some things are worth knowing for the sake of knowing, that somehow awareness and perception are fundamental to the quality of being human. There is a value simply in knowing, and Louis Simpson's poetry reflects and refines that value. Descriptions of so-called objective reality, that is, reality irrelevant to human passion, are very recent developments in human evolution, but very powerful developments for all their newness. Man has always tried to resolve the mystery of his environment and himself, but only recently has he sought to do this by discounting and dismissing his own reaction to the world around him, by the so-called scientific method. In many ways, of course, science and art serve the same general function, the penetration and description of reality, but science elevates the fact and submerges the emotion, and art elevates the emotion and submerges the fact. The world within, however, is still as important as the world without, and the publication in the last decade and a half of lyric poetry of the quality of Simpson's is firm testimony to the fact that it is still a lively art whose concern is human feeling and whose instrument is human imagination.

I do not suggest, however, that his poetry inspires only isolated flashes of dissociated insights. Poetry in general and his poetry in particular can and does produce systematic and coherent organizations of reality which take us deeper into the mystery than we could ever go by ourselves. Simpson is an intellectually mature and responsible poet who is ultimately committed to making human sense of what *is,* although he is never unaware of the eternal paradoxes and possibilities of what *ought to be.* His war poems, for example, intensify particulars but ominously suggest also in a systematic way that war is a singularly ineffective behavior pattern if the human animal really wants to improve his condition. "I Dreamed That in a City Dark as Paris" links both world wars to suggest the futility:

> I dreamed that in a city dark as Paris
> I stood alone in a deserted square.
> The night was trembling with a violet
> Expectancy. At the far edge it moved
> And rumbled; on that flickering horizon
> The guns were pumping color in the sky.
> . . . .
> These wars have been so great, they are forgotten
> Like Egyptian dynasts. My confrere
> In whose thick boots I stood, were you amazed
> To wander through my brain four decades later
> As I have wandered in a dream through yours?
>
> The violence of waking life disrupts
> The order of our death. Strange dreams occur,
> For dreams are licensed as they never were.

Simpson also consistently suggests the futility of heroism through war, as in "The Heroes":

I dreamed of war-heroes, of wounded war-heroes
With just enough of their charms shot away
To make them more handsome. The women moved nearer
To touch their brave wounds and their hair streaked with gray.
. . . .
A fine dust has settled on all that scrap metal.
The heroes were packaged and sent home in parts
To pluck at a poppy and sew on a petal
And count the long night by the stroke of their hearts.

In the same manner, Simpson vitalizes the particular images of love but generalizes about its timeless quality in "The Green Shepherd":

Here sit a shepherd and a shepherdess,
He playing on his melancholy flute;
The sea wind ruffles up her simple dress
And shows the delicacy of her foot.

And there you see Constantinople's wall
With arrows and Greek fire, molten lead;
Down from a turret seven virgins fall,
Hands folded, each one praying on her head.
. . . .
But the green shepherd travels in her eye
And whispers nothings in his lady's ear,
And sings a little song, that roses die,
Carpe diem, which she seems pleased to hear.
. . . .
The groaning pole had gone more than a mile;
These shepherds did not feel it where they loved,
For time was sympathetic all the while
And on the magic mountain nothing moved.

"The Silent Lover"[5] is more fragmentary in its progression, but it equates love to concrete images which are in turn associated with eternity, and thus accomplishes the same end:

She sighs. What shall I say?
For beauty seems to grow
In silence, when the heart is faint and slow.

Sing, sing . . . How shall I sing?
In silent eyes, where clouds and islands gaze,
The waves bring Eros in.

I think the rustling of her clothes
Is like the sea, and she
A wild white bird,

And love is like the sighing of the sand.

Similarly, his poems on an urban theme illuminate the strange, historic dilemma of alienation from and integration with the great masses of people and materials that we call cities; thus in the poem "In California"[6] Simpson combines his urban concern with his feeling of the failure of the American dream as it was articulated by Walt Whitman:

Here I am, troubling the dream coast
With my New York face,
Bearing among the realtors
And tennis-players my dark preoccupation.

There once was an epical clatter—
Voices and banjos, Tennessee, Ohio,
Rising like incense in the sight of heaven.
Today, there is an angel in the gate.

Lie back, Walt Whitman,
There, on the fabulous raft with the King and the Duke!
For the white row of the Marina
Faces the Rock. Turn round the wagons here.

Lie back! We cannot bear
The stars any more, those infinite spaces.
Let the realtors divide the mountain,
For they have already subdivided the valley.

Rectangular city blocks astonished
Herodotus in Babylon,
Cortez in Tenochtitlan,
And here's the same old city-planner, death.

We cannot turn or stay.
For though we sleep, and let the reins fall slack,
The great cloud-wagons move
Outward still, dreaming of a Pacific.

Finally, while Simpson passionately and graphically describes the ugliness of death in particulars, he generalizes in a more restrained manner about the fact of human mortality in "Early in the Morning":

Early in the morning
The dark Queen said,
"The trumpets are warning
There's trouble ahead."
Spent with carousing
With wine-soaked wits,
Antony drowsing
Whispered, "It's
Too cold a morning
To get out of bed."

The army's retreating,
The fleet has fled,
Caesar is beating
His drums through the dead.
"Antony, horses!
We'll get away,
Gather our forces
For another day . . ."
"It's a cold morning,"
Antony said.

Caesar Augustus
Cleared his phlegm.
"Corpses disgust us.
Cover them."
Caesar Augustus
In his time lay
Dying, and just as
Cold as they,

On the cold morning
Of a cold day.

His tragic sense serves to intensify the quality of life just as his imagination intensifies the quality of reality.

Simpson's art imposes order from within on chaos without, gives meaning to the apparently meaningless, suggests fresh vantage points from which to probe experience. In "Lines Written near San Francisco"[7] he summarizes the current American condition with oblique references to our military and material madness, and he proffers a possible solution which suggests the process toward individual human realization and maturity as the defeat of death:

> Every night, at the end of America
> We taste our wine, looking at the Pacific.
> How sad it is, the end of America!
>
> While we were waiting for the land
> They'd finished it—with gas drums
> On the hilltops, cheap housing in the valleys
>
> Where lives are mean and wretched.
> But the banks thrive and the realtors
> Rejoice—they have their America.
>
> Still, there is something unsettled in the air.
> Out there on the Pacific
> There's no America but the Marines.
>
> Whitman was wrong about the People,
> But right about himself. The land is within.
> At the end of the open road we come to ourselves.
>
> Though mad Columbus follows the sun
> Into the sea, we cannot follow.
> We must remain, to serve the returning sun,
>
> And to set tables for death.
> For we are the colonists of Death—
> Not, as some think, of the English.

And we are preparing thrones for him to sit,
Poems to read, and beds
In which it may please him to rest.

This is the Land
The pioneers looked for, shading their eyes
Against the sun—the world of flowers and dreams.

Poetry rarely commands the intensity of religious belief, but it seeks the same end, that of using the materials of human life . . . senses, emotions, intelligence . . . to formulate a coherent and significant meaning for life. The poetry of Louis Simpson offers us that meaning.

NOTES

1. First published in the *Sixties*, 1963.
2. First published in *Prism*, 1963.
3. First published in *Generation*, 1963.
4. First published in 1963.
5. First published in the *New Yorker*, 1962.
6. First published in 1963.
7. First published in *Paris Review*, 1963.

C. B. COX

The Poetry of Louis Simpson

"Descriptions of poetry by men who are not poets are usually
ridiculous, for they describe rational thought-processes."
—Louis Simpson

I

For the soldier in the last war a common experience was to be
whisked off in a truck to an unknown destination, ordered to get
out, to get back in again, in an apparently meaningless series of
manoeuvres. This sequence is described in Louis Simpson's long
narrative poem, "The Runner" [in *Selected Poems*], as in 1944 the
101st Airborne Division of the U.S. Army moves into the Ar-
dennes to counter a German attack. For Dodd, the main char-
acter, the journey seems dreamlike, the occasional view of ra-
vine, forest or black-clothed villagers like a glimpse into some
fantasy world through which, against his will, he is forced to
travel.

A feeling of being involved in historical processes which we
only partly understand is typical of Simpson's work. His poems
often convey a sense of hallucination, as if our everyday percep-
tions on our journey through time hide a reality that reason
cannot fully comprehend. Dodd dreams that he hears voices of
men who fought in the wars of the past; in another poem, "I
Dreamed That in a City Dark as Paris" a modern soldier for a
few moments inhabits the mind of a *poilu* in the 1914–18 war,
watching with his eyes a dogfight in the sky. As Simpson's
imagination ranges over the history of the West, the many wars
and the thousands killed, his characters appear to touch upon
archetypal experiences which ordinarily we evade, but which are
revealed by proximity to death. This hallucinatory quality pro-
vides one reason why he has written some of the best poems
about World War II. Like Wilfred Owen, he presents the people
and events of war not fixed by their particular backgrounds, but

Critical Quarterly (U.K.) 8 (Spring 1966): 72–83.

like shadows in some cosmic drama that involves all humanity.

"Carentan O Carentan" is perhaps his best war poem. The particular scene, vividly created as by "the shining green canal" the soldiers walk towards ambush, merges into the experience of all men as they pass through life towards death:

> Could you have seen us through a glass
> You would have said a walk
> Of farmers out to turn the grass,
> Each with his own hay-fork.

This shift of perspective, imposing a ghostlike pastoral scene on the menacing images of war, draws the everyday routine of the farmers into the context of death. The poem moves backwards and forwards in time, linking together the ambushed soldiers with the lovers who "in the old days" wandered hand in hand from Carentan. This changing perspective is also presented by the simple ballad form, which at first links the narrative to universal folk experience and the romantic associations evoked by the name "Carentan"; but at the end a series of inappropriate images breaks down, almost with an excess of crudity, the illusions of magical romance:

> Lieutenant, what's my duty,
> My place in the platoon?
> He too's a sleeping beauty,
> Charmed by that strange tune.

2

"Carentan O Carentan" is typical of many Simpson poems in that it presents strikingly clear images which confuse and disturb. When his early work was reviewed in the American magazine the *Fifties,* he was accused of using the traditional forms of a previous age to assert modern revolutionary ideas, and the reviewer argued that the split between context and form was self-destructive. Simpson has often written in conventional rhythms and stanzas, and his name has been associated with the Academics in the battle against the Beats. Certainly his early books, *The Arrivistes* (1949), *Good News of Death and Other Poems* (1955) and *A Dream of*

Governors (1959) include a fair number of poems in pedestrian style where the need to maintain patterns of rhyme and rhythm leads to clumsiness. But the successful poems, and these increase from volume to volume, often use traditional forms in highly novel and arresting ways. There are poems such as "Song: 'Rough Winds Do Shake the Darling Buds of May,'" in which a parody of Elizabethan lyrical conventions associates them with an uncompromisingly physical account of sex. In "The Bird" a childlike narrative in simple four-line rhymed stanzas is used for a story about the German gaschambers. At the conclusion Heinrich, the simple-souled executioner, escapes from the Russians presumably by turning into a bird, still sadly singing his favourite song: "Ich wünscht', ich wäre ein Vöglein." The poem shifts in macabre and terrifying fashion from one area of experience to another—childish innocence, killing of Jews, nostalgia.

In Simpson's view,[1] the poets of fifth-century Athens or Elizabethan England were closely associated with aristocratic communities, and so could relate their experiences to the conventional literary forms of their society. The poet used common forms to express thoughts which were acceptable to his fellow men. Since the end of the eighteenth century the artist has been in recoil from the middle-class ethos of science and business and progress. Great modern poets are eccentrics, "and in my opinion this must be so, for the modern world, with its pervasive materialism and wars, is by no means a happy place." These attitudes to history explain the repeated ironic contrasts in his work between traditional form and modern experience.

In his poetry satire of middle-class materialism is linked to rejection of the belief that there is an external world of objects, existing independently of our forms of description, which we can describe, if we are careful enough, just as it is, from an absolute standpoint. In his view poetry touches upon a reality beyond the compass of any trust in rationalism and "hard facts"; it derives from the subconscious in a manner which must always remain incomprehensible: "Poetry is a mystery. No-one has ever been able to define it." In his poems the sudden shifts of tone and perspective reflect his belief that no single mode of apprehending reality can ever be fully satisfactory. In his later, more mature, work he introduces the "deep image," which in itself contains a multiplicity of meanings, and which resists rational interpretation. In contrast to the early Imagists, he does not forswear moral and intellectual comment, but weaves together imagery, irony and concept. His best poems refuse to limit themselves to obvious meanings, and in this way reflect the "modern" belief that systems of harmony and order which explain every feature of the universe are no longer possible. In "Tonight the Famous Psychiatrist" he mocks a successful American psychiatrist, enjoying his party of celebrities, but unable to cure his wife who thinks she still lives in Hungary. No explanation of human behaviour can ever be final. In his poems statement is followed by counterstatement, lyrical emotion by irony. Like Philip Larkin he mocks his own poses, refusing to settle in any one form of knowing:

> I have the poor man's nerve-tic, irony.
> I see through the illusions of the age!

Such conflicts between different ways of apprehension are strikingly illustrated in one of his best-known poems, "My Father in the Night Commanding No." This poem, as it examines parent-child relationships, proceeds by repeated reversals of tone, one form of knowing criticized implicitly by the next:

> My father in the night commanding No
> Has work to do. Smoke issues from his lips;
>   He reads in silence.
> The frogs are croaking and the streetlamps glow.

The first line, with its rhetorical flourish, recalls the child's response to absolute authority, to adult society with its strict positives and negatives; but the curious break at the end of the line disturbs its simple force. The father's command seems not to be an important moral pronouncement, for the verb "has work to do" deflates him to an ordinary mortal ordering his child not to interrupt. "Smoke issues from his lips" recreates the strangeness of the father's world for the child, and the stanza ends with an evocative, magical landscape. In his "Confessions of an American Poet," he contrasts his father, a lawyer with a passion for facts, with his exotic Russian mother, an emigrant who made a career in motion pictures. She had a passion for opera, and told him stories of Russia, in which snow was always falling and the wolves howling in the distance. In the second stanza of the poem his mother winds the gramophone, "The Bride of Lammermoor begins to shriek," or she reads a story of Thule, "at midnight when the mice are still." His father's life of practical reality is opposed by his mother's romanticism, but the word "shriek" tips the scene over towards comedy. The poem proceeds by describing the poet's own romantic journeys to the great cities of Europe; he has even visited Thule itself. Eventually he finds himself a father in his turn.

> Here is my house. Under a red rose tree
> A child is swinging; another gravely plays.
>   They are not surprised
> That I am here; they were expecting me.

These lines, affirmative in tone, evoke the wonder of love and children, yet even here the narrator remains slightly bewildered by the enigmatic situations through which he moves. "And yet . . . And yet . . ." he continues, still unable completely to fathom the archetypal relationships between father and child, realism and romance. The poem ends inconclusively, with a series of questions, as the wind whispers an answer the children cannot hear:

> Father, why did you work? Why did you weep,
> Mother? Was the story so important?
>   "*Listen!*" the wind
> Said to the children, and they fell asleep.

The simple pattern of the four-line stanza is strictly adhered to, so that the uncertainties of the narrator are balanced by the lucidity of the form. Simpson is a brilliant verse technician. Here the end-stopped stanzas, with the first and fourth lines usually linked by very simple rhymes, provide brief striking images; such momentary flashes of illumination offer no total scheme of thought, only conflicting impressions.

The description of Nature in Simpson's poems, like those in his mother's stories, often seems appropriate for a tale of high romance: "The stars were large with rain," "rainpools glimmered in the moonlit fields," "wild is the wind." In "The Troika" the narrator passes through archetypal romantic landscapes, as in a dream sequence: the greybeards playing chess, the moon looking down on the guardsmen in trenches "wind fluttering their rags," the nightmare when he loses his father's horses, the vision of the white bird which turns into a beautiful girl:

> Troika, troika! The snow moon
> whirls through the forest.

Such dreamlike images, contributing to the hallucinatory quality of many poems, have a double effect. Their magic creates a sense of mystery, of imminent revelation, but at the same time they are slightly exaggerated, so noticeably archetypal we can never lose ourselves completely in their romantic evocations. Like Marvell, Simpson places moments of lyrical splendour in an ironic context:

> Ranching in Bolinas, that's the life,
> If you call cattle life.
> To sit on a veranda with a glass
> And see the sprinklers watering your land
> And hear the peaches dropping from the trees
> And hear the ocean in the redwood trees . . .

Here the contrast between the excess of Nature and the rancher sitting on his veranda, glass in hand, makes him appear comic. Simpson's imagination responds to hugeness in Nature, to expanses of sky or the antiquity and size of redwood forests in California. He has a wonderful lyric gift and has written many beautiful short poems—"The Boarder," "Birch," "Luminous Night." But in the longer poems he usually retains a sense of ironic bewilderment, a refusal to delude himself that he has reached some final insight. Throughout his poems irony is in perpetual debate with romantic imagination. His poems move towards an understanding of man, but never underestimate his essential mystery:

> It seems that a man exists
> Only to say, Here I am in person.

These double attitudes are also reflected in the numerous poems he devotes to America, his adopted country. As epigraph to "Walt Whitman at Bear Mountain," he quotes Ortega y Gasset: " . . . life which does not give the preference to any other life, of any previous period, which therefore prefers its own existence. . . ." For him this is the life that America ought to represent, the dream of the pioneers who followed the open road to the West. In California, at the end of the trek, the cloud-wagons move on, "dreaming of a Pacific," but beneath the realtors have taken possession of the land; for the "Open Road goes to the used-car lot." In "Lines Written near San Francisco," he says:

> While we were waiting for the land
> They'd finished it—with gas drums
> On the hilltops, cheap housing in the valleys
>
> Where lives are mean and wretched.
> But the banks thrive and the realtors
> Rejoice—they have their America.

Always something of an alien, his criticisms reflect personal dissatisfaction because he can never completely associate his own cosmopolitan literary inheritance with the brash and expansive landscapes of America. For him the real search is not for new lands, but for one's true identity and the meaning of one's death:

> The land is within.
> At the end of the open road we come to ourselves.

Simpson's poems turn repeatedly to the significance of death. As poet he is like Orpheus, descending to the shades to bring back news of kingdoms beyond the range of normal understanding. In California, the "dream-coast," he troubles the realtors with his "dark preoccupation." His poem "Orpheus in the Underworld" includes an eight-stanza straightforward recreation of the story of Orpheus and Eurydice, but in other sections the figure of Orpheus merges with the poet himself, who by the Mediterranean once discovered in the dark night "the fearful sense / Of mortal love." The sudden shifts from Orpheus to poet and back again make it difficult for the reader to locate himself in the poem. The journey into the shadows seems both a legendary event, which we can observe with cool detachment, and a concern of the present moment involving strong personal emotions. The legend of Orpheus thus becomes an archetypal experience, always waiting for the individual poet who must make his own way, to quote Lawrence, "among the splendour of torches of darkness."

In "Good News of Death," a kind of mock pastoral, not very successful and not included in *Selected Poems,* Simpson contrasts Pagan and Christian attitudes to death. After the Agamemnon-Clytemnestra-Orestes cycle of murder and retribution comes Christ's good news of death. But one of the banished Furies insists that the turning wheel will eventually bring the Christian faith to its end:

> And the event will prove
> The truth is always so.

Truth is the fact of death, which men avoid by their "dreams," by their "yearning outwards," but acceptance of death releases a man to discover his true self. "Lines Written near San Francisco" ends:

> Though mad Columbus follows the sun
> Into the sea, we cannot follow.
> We must remain, to serve the returning sun,
>
> And to set tables for death.
> For we are the colonists of Death—
> Not, as some think, of the English.
>
> And we are preparing thrones for him to sit,
> Poems to read, and beds
> In which it may please him to rest.

This is the land
The pioneers looked for, shading their eyes
Against the sun—a murmur of serious life.

3

It has sometimes been said that Simpson has considerable technical skill, but that he lacks a distinctive voice. His poems on America, for example, have been criticized as a kind of superior journalism. This seems to me quite untrue. The distinctive mark of a good Simpson poem is that the formal clarity, the self-controlled manipulation of language, build up total effects which, in their mingling of different accounts of reality, can both surprise and disturb. This is best seen by examining a complete poem, and so I quote the whole of "Moving the Walls":

> The Prince of Monaco
> Was sick of English ladies.
>
> The Prince had a yacht
> And her name was *Hirondelle*.
> She was cousin to the yacht of the Kaiser
> And niece to the yacht of the Tsar.
>
> And the Prince was interested in the sea—
> That is, oceanography.
> So he furnished the yacht with instruments
> And with instruments of brass,
> Burners and sinks and instruments
> Of the most delicate glass.
>
> There was also a whaleboat
> And a whole crew of harpooners.
> There was a helmet and suit of armor
> For the wars of the ocean floor.
>
> The *Hirondelle* trembled like a fern,
> And the crew stood at attention,
> And they piped the Captain aboard.

Cloud-sailed, the *Hirondelle*
Pursued the horizon.
At night she skimmed
The phosphorescent surges.

And now they are on the Pacific,
The bottomless sea.
And out of the deep they have drawn
The whale, Leviathan, with a hook.
They have captured the giant squid
That has ten arms, claws like a cat's, a beak like a parrot's,
And a large malevolent eye.

They stepped from the whaleboat onto shoals,
The crests of sunken mountains.
In nets they gathered
Plankton and weeds and crabs that looked astonished.

And there were nights, O Prince,
When you stretched your hands and feet
In the leaves of the pomegranate tree!

And all went into the log.
The various sea trophies
Were written down in the log.
The darkening sky, the storm,
And tranquil days—
All, all went into the log.

3

The Prince returned—a hero of sorts.
He returned to his former life,
To the lights of the Grand Hotel
And the Russian ladies with their eternal cigarettes.

Then he built a museum.
The wheel of the *Hirondelle* is there,
And also the laboratory, the strange heart of the ship
Uprooted, leaving red holes
In the deck that vanished in smoke.

Here are the trophies:
A walking stick made from the backbone of a shark;
Tortoiseshell combs, and fans of mother-of-pearl;
Corals that faded,
Losing the changing hues of sea and sky;
Sea shells under glass
That are as dull as buttons
Sewn on garments by girls who have faded.

The Philippine Islands are a box
And the smile of a lady in a mantilla.
A walrus stuffed with straw
Faces the diving helmet.
They remember Verdun and Passchendaele,
The mud-clouded wars of the ocean floor.

So all that oceanography, after all,
Was only a pawnshop.
For they brought home the tooth of the whale
And said, "Look!
It is only a doorstop, after all."

For Leviathan does not exist,
And the sea is no mystery.
For a shark is a walking stick.

And this we call the life of reason.

4

Idiots!
We too are all for reducing
The universe to human dimensions.
As if we could know what is human!

Just a few dippers of sea water
And a fair wind home . . .
Then surely we won't be destroyed.

A strange idea, if you consider
The dust of those settlements—

The parlors where no one lives;
The splinter that wounds the foot sole
On its way to the double bed;
And Leviathan over all,
The cloud shaped like a weasel or a whale,
Leviathan rising above the roof tops.

5

When men wanted the golden fleece
It was not wool they wanted.
They were the trophies that they sailed toward.

They were the sea and the wind
That hurled them over
Into the sea. They were the fishes
That stripped their thin bones. And they rose
In the night in new constellations.

They left no wreckage.
Nothing is floating on the surface.
For they yielded themselves
To the currents that moved from within.

They are mightily changed
In the corollas, the branched sea-heaven.

And you, my country,
These days your walls are moving,
These nights we are branching among the stars.

I say, but my mind is doubtful.
Are there any at sea?
If so, they have not whispered lately.

Bored with aristocratic society, the Prince of Monaco decides
to amuse himself by exploring the unknown depths of the sea.
The whole of the first section is delightfully ironic. Like the
Hirondelle, the swallow, the Prince will only skim the surface. A

dilettante, he treats Nature as a plaything, and is untouched by the hidden power of the sea, the great flood of archetypal experience. The tone of the narrator mimics the kind of childish wonder typical in stories of magic and adventure:

> There was also a whaleboat
> And a whole crew of harpooners.

"A whole crew"—how colossal an enterprise! This satire of aristocrats, indulging their fancies just before the outbreak of European war and Communist Revolution, is linked with ironic treatment of the pretence that reason and science can control and finally comprehend the universe. In the middle group of lines, the repetition of "instruments" delicately mocks the Prince's determination to measure Nature scientifically. One line alone stands out from this slightly comic portrait—"the wars of the ocean floor." This hints at another form of reality whose importance will be revealed later in the poem.

In the second section the *Hirondelle* pursues the horizon, the unreachable limits of human apprehension, and skims over the phosphorescent magic of the seas. But soon the Prince's playing at exploration is contrasted with the mysteries of the bottomless sea; like the rationalist, he is trying to understand the unfathomable. Leviathan drawn with a "hook" suggests ironically the inadequacy of his instruments. Again, the tone of the narrative, as in a child's adventure story, seems incongruous with the horrors of the deep—Leviathan, the monster that represents Satan, and the malevolent squid; even the crabs look "astonished," perhaps at the presumption of the sailors. Yet, against this comic background, the depths invite the travellers into a magical seascape, and the poem breaks out into lyrical exuberance:

> They stepped from the whaleboat onto shoals,
> The crests of sunken mountains . . .
>
> And there were nights, O Prince,
> When you stretched your hands and feet
> In the leaves of the pomegranate tree!

It is as if they step out of human limitations to become, for a brief space, involved with the mysteries of Nature. "Onto" rather than "into" shoals is highly evocative. They step not onto land but onto the sea itself—almost like Christ walking on the water. "Shoals" suggest both low-lying waters and the abundance of fish, while "the crests of sunken mountains" associates them with magic undersea kingdoms. And so on some nights the Prince sensuously participates in the luxuriant beauty of Nature. These lines offer multiple suggestions, and are typical of Simpson's recent use of imagery. As in Marvell, moments of rich sensuousness and vision are presented in a tone of almost comic surprise. And so the section ends with irony, as everything is recorded precisely, superficially, in the log.

In section 3 the Prince, unchanged by his explorations, returns to his dull social round, and the wonders of the deep are translated into the knick-knackery of a museum. The life of reason reduces the underwater life to mundane, everyday articles. Yet the tearing out of "the strange heart of the ship" and the "red holes / In the deck that vanished in smoke" suggest that some explosive force has existed in the laboratory. Beneath the surface of pre-1914 aristocratic society waited the horror of Verdun and Passchendaele, the knowledge of evil and death which the Prince preferred to ignore.

In the fourth and fifth sections the narrator steps forward to provide a moral. Today we continue to evade the destructive element, to impose secure dimensions on the "mud-clouded wars of the ocean floor." The great epic heroes discovered themselves by their explorations, joined themselves to the hugeness of Nature. Perhaps America may repeat those epic journeys, moving the walls outwards, embracing the mysteries of the depths. But in the last stanza the poem turns round on itself:

> Are there any at sea?
> If so, they have not whispered lately.

The poem is set in a literary tradition, reminding us of the voyages of the *Nautilus* in Jules Verne's *Twenty Thousand Leagues under the Sea,* or of Captain Ahab's pursuit of Moby Dick.

Throughout Simpson's poems we find echoes of other poets—Marvell, as we have seen, Auden or Eliot. In "Moving the Walls" formal lucidity and the literary background provide a traditional means of control for the material. The experiences of the poem are set not in a rational framework but in this context of man's greatest imaginative responses to the enigma of the universe.

4

In the 1950s, the debates between Movement and Maverick, Academic and Beat, were dangerous because both extremes limited the resources of poetry. Simpson finds no absolute value in any one form of communication, but uses both rational statement and evocative image to convey his personal sense of reality. In his most recent work his rhythms have become more free, less tied to iambic norms, and he makes increasing use of mysterious imagery whose total effect is beyond rational appraisal. The process reflects his own multiple response to life, what a *Times Literary Supplement* reviewer called "an anarchic personalism" which offers private revelations rather than large social, philosophical or religious schemes. In a recent poem, "Things," an ironic "I" debates with a man who has seen a vision. The visionary tells him that even household articles hold a mystery, and the "I" replies:

> I said, "I have suspected
> The Mixmaster knows more than I do,
> The air conditioner is the better poet.
> My right front tire is as bald as Odysseus—
> How much it must have suffered!

The mock-epic tone, like that of Pope in *The Rape of the Lock,* works in two conflicting ways. It satirises the American worship of "things," yet also evokes the fantastic wonder of modern inventions. So the poem ends when the "I" acknowledges the mystery of objects, and asks for a kind of apprehension which unites the true functions of reason and imagination, irony and vision:

Then, as things have a third substance
Which is obscure to both our senses,
Let there be a perpetual coming and going
Between your house and mine."

NOTE

1. See his "Confessions of an American Poet," *New York Times Magazine,* 2 May 1965.

RICHARD HOWARD

The Hunger in My Vitals Is for
Some Credible Extravaganza

A legendary predecessor of mine, this poet, I can remember, was the object, almost the victim of my envious wonder as I regarded him, obliquely, in the halls of Columbia University, where his three years of wartime service had caused Simpson's classroom education to overlap with my own. I knew he had been raised in Jamaica—not the suburbs but the South, that West Indian island where "the sun was drawn bleeding across the hills," as he said of it in a poem written when he was nineteen, that Caribbean paradise where

> Death, a delightful life-long disease,
> Sighs in sideways languor of twisted trees . . .

—and that he had renounced this tropical nurture in some dissatisfaction, anyway some ambiguity of response. In his novel *Riverside Drive,* as a confirmed if adoptive New Yorker, he was to define the situation this way, with a characteristic insertion of self into surround, seeking a dozen years later the widest possible locus for perception:

> Only in the north is history made. In the north man has contended with nature and earned his right to a roof, a hearth and a book. But in the tropics how can you achieve anything? You can't even tell good from bad. There are no seasons; the sun shines equally on good and evil; there are neither punishments nor rewards. . . .

From *Alone with America: Essays on the Art of Poetry in the United States* (New York: Atheneum, 1969), 451–70. Copyright © 1969, 1980 Richard Howard. Reprinted with permission of Atheneum Publishers, Inc.

As I saw him, then, Louis Simpson was resuming an academic career interrupted by the war—though as he was often to put it later in his poems, he was also resuming a war, a war that *was* inward, according to Miss Moore's famous prescription, a war with these United States that had been merely intermitted by an overseas engagement, from Normandy through Holland and Bastogne to Berchtesgaden, which was surely the last of its kind: "to every man," Simpson remarks in one of his terrible aphorisms, "his war seems final, for *that* was the war in which he had exhausted himself." After winning the Bronze Star and the Purple Heart in all that fighting, Simpson was back in the arena of his own true hostilities, the national conflict having given him, like Yeats's spirits, metaphors for poetry; if in fact we consider Simpson's war poetry as a version of pastoral, and his poems about America and his life there as a collection of military tattoos, we shall come closer to the exasperated spirit of the man, who like any modern Odysseus returns from his wanderings to find the real battle on his own doorstep, in his own hall, at his own bedside. But I saw none of this as I spied on Simpson between classes. I had heard that he was finishing up his degree—weren't we all?—before leaving New York for the Sorbonne, and neither the exoticism nor the heroism of the poet's career inspired my envy: what made him legendary for me and for my friends was that in 1949, *while still in school,* Louis Simpson had published a collection of his poems, "more or less in the order of composition, the poems his friends like best," as Theodore Hoffman said in his preface to *The Arrivistes,* a privately printed book in very plain wrappers, dedicated to Mark Van Doren, and including work from the author's seventeenth to twenty-sixth years.

If Simpson's military career and the sense of his displaced biography afforded the nourishing terms for his poetic progress, which has steadily, even relentlessly, attached itself to the condition of his country, his academic career has fed upon itself, and as we look *back* on the honors list, it is difficult to discern the breach at all, so perfectly healed is the tissue of achievements and distinctions: corresponding to those military medals, a Ph.D. from Columbia and a Prix de Rome; a doctoral dissertation on James Hogg, the author of the *Memoirs of a Justified Sinner;* a clutch of fellowships even as the poet, along with two others, produced a first selection of the most effective anthology of the period, *The New Poets of England and America,* a compilation which required Simpson to read the work of some three hundred poets by his own count. The ineluctable current bore Simpson onward—a Pulitzer Prize for Poetry in 1964 and professorships in English at various universities, a wife and children. Simpson's own commentary on this trajectory can be, perhaps unfairly, elicited from the titles of his first four books in the order of their writing:

> *The Arrivistes* (1949)
> *Good News of Death* (1955)
> *A Dream of Governors* (1959)
> *At the End of the Open Road* (1963)

It is a sad, successful story.

What I think spurred my envy along with my admiration of *The Arrivistes* as it came to my hands in 1949 was that it seemed not so much different from what the rest of us wanted to do, even in school, but that it seemed, simply, better: wittier, more intelligent, and crowded with a sense of a various and complex experience unavailable to undergraduates whose careers were altogether unexposed to the illuminations that led Simpson to say, as a soldier on leave in Paris:

> . . . We, on the other side,
> Are still intruders to our atmosphere.
> Concrete and cactus are the real
> American tragedy.
> We should collect our souvenirs and leave.

What we lacked, and what we felt or rather heard in Simpson, was "syllables of other people's time," the sense that having seen something else, however awful or elegant, he could return to what we were seeing and see it more clearly than we. Of course, reading the book today, it is easy to discover and to smile—though surely more in appreciation of the successful apprenticeship than in any spirit of dismissal—at the variations on traditional themes:

> Love's funeral requires
> A lyrical instrument.
> A hollow heart with wires
> Will make the wind lament.
> The wreath I've sent
> Is roses wrapped with briars.

This conjugation of the wry with the sweet, the savage with the neat, is articulated further by the poet into a typical learned imagery, a trope of experience via erudition in his long poem "Laertes in Paris." Here the control of the quatrain-and-couplet stanzas sets off the illuminating action of the poet's intelligence, which has moved beyond imitation to metaphor, beyond assimilation to invention:

> Each man has his Hamlet, that dark other
> Self who is the conscience left behind,
> Who should be cherished clearly as a brother
> But is a sort of madness of the mind:
> A serious dark-dressed entire shape
> From which no slightest duty can escape.
>
> And every man his Denmark, that dark country,
> Familiar, incestuous, to which
> He must return, in his turn to stand sentry
> Until his blood has filled the Castle ditch,
> And clear his father's honor with his life,
> And take a perfect ignorance to wife.

From this point, Simpson is able to look in several directions at once—back to his easy exploits as a university wit, the archaizing elegist who has read everything and rearranged everything:

> Who sails into the seagirls' teeth
> A lifebuoy it shall be his wreath;
> Who stands admirant of such views
> His bones shall little boys amuse . . .

—and inward to a kind of Oedipal *acedie,* as disenchanted with promiscuity ("I think we have ruined our fathers") as he is with the domestic relations which leave "you and her nothing much to say / except the children," the muddle of middle-class marriage:

> O marriage, the one sail to catch a wind!
>
> Man comes from forests and from furnished rooms,
> Out of the Egypt Land of Eat-Your-Spinach.
> Love leads him like a river over booms
> Into a woman like an open beach . . .

—and ahead to the dominant, sullen vision of America, or of what America, that *given dream,* has come to, when "the earth, so often saturated by colors false as blood, takes on your American gray." The secret, Simpson determines,

> . . . is to overhear the world,
> Seeing at once all phases of the moon.

An ambitious project, even for the disabused poet who has shelved the suburban sanctities in a heartless couplet:

> So shall we manage, till the day
> Death takes the furniture away.

But even in this first book, that to me had seemed the epitome of what one could aspire to as court jester to the College Outline Series, the tonality in which Simpson is to deal with his ambiguous citizenship is established, perhaps so precociously because of the European confrontations. "The West," Simpson said with an early arrogance he was later to dispute with himself, to question as he had questioned the provincial pieties which generated it, "the West was never an original, but one of many copies." Having discovered what the copies were of:

> Back to Paris for a kindly refuge
> You come, demoralized and drenched again
> With your poetic soul like a black dog . . .

or again, in prose: "In Italy, where everything had already happened, and every kind of man had already existed, I could pick up the life that someone else a few years or centuries ago had discarded. There I could sink into oblivion or happiness"—having determined that "the sadness of the provinces is the thought of life vanishing without a mark," the poet sets out to anatomize the prospect before him, determined to spare himself nothing, and to spare the landscape and its attendant blank history nothing of himself:

> A night-sky like the passion of a saint
> That clears to let the sudden moon look through.
> It seems the very gods come here to paint
> And hang their pictures up for public view.
>
> Not like that sullen city in the West
> Blazing in a romantic solitude
> Where each American's a self-made artist
> Who knows his masterpiece will not be viewed.

The wit of Simpson's rhymes keep whatever is apocalyptic in his emblems of a national *manteia* from toppling into the sententious, and of course he also wields a kind of wild humor, a post-Dada wackiness which is exploited (read, diluted) in his later work but here has a kind of inspired ease to it, without strain or evasion:

> The sun is reversible and may be used
> As a moon when necessary.
>
> The poodles of spring
> are on winter's traces.

The book closes with something of all these notes mustered for two eclogues, very much influenced by the pastoral—in both senses—Auden (*For the Time Being* was published in 1944, and *The Age of Anxiety: A Baroque Eclogue* in 1948) and, at least in the title poem, suggesting the torment of the young poet still within my view: "In their confused state, Peter and Athridat cannot separate words from meaning." The *façon* of these poems was to be pursued by Simpson (to pursue him?) into his second book, but in their gleeful unpleasantries and elegiac wrenches—

> The barge Espoir
> Thumps upstream with wet laundry
> On her gay lines.
> Lend me your camera—

they suggest not so much concerted works as the advice Pound gave the old Yeats, to write plays for the sake of the songs that would occur in them, lyrical pieces, fragments and even figments which would retain something of the intensity of their dramatic function even when the matrix had fallen away. But these questions take Simpson into his second book, and out of my envying purview at Columbia.

When a poet has initially presented himself, revealed his intentions with all the stunning insolence of talent which Simpson displayed and even commanded in his first book, affording a variety of tone along with a persistence of temperament, it is surprising to come upon not so much a development in his production, with that word's implication of wraps being removed, the cerements trailing away like fussy clouds from the transfigured body inside the sarcophagus, not so much a growth as a gap, a silence just when, indeed, we had expected the echoes so featly raised to ring still louder. But the echoes, as Simpson says, increased the silences, and it was to be six years before the poet published his second book (1955). "My mind," as he accounted for it later, "was a negative on which colors and sensations were being photographed"—a registering process which, in its necessary elisions of the actual ("it is one thing to know, another to exist," the poet adds), permitted Simpson to articulate his themes: the erosion of selfhood as an analogue of the land's breakdown; the brutality of history which affords a tenderness only in combat, in warfare and in erotic engagements ("I never met a man who regretted making love"); the assumption of a position outside the battle but not above it, the poet as a kind of Lord of Misrule, the clown whose buffoon's mask suddenly falls off and we look straight into the face, as Northrop

Frye says about certain Shakespearean comedies, of a beaten and ridiculed slave:

> The city tilts and founders in a turbulence of gulls
> . . . .
> Enough of these images—they set the teeth on edge!
> Life, if you like, is a metaphor of death—
> The difference is you, a place for the passing of breath.
> That is what man is. He is the time between,
> The palpable glass through which all things are seen.
> Nothing. Silence. A syllable. A word.
> Everything.
>   After your death this poem occurred.
> You were the honored fragments from the Greek.
> After your death these stones would move and speak.

And not merely his themes but his music, the characteristic cadence of his sense-making, set down with a sharper relevance, the succinctness which is the illumination of a focused method. Apposite here is Simpson's own brash note at the start of the collection:

> I do not apologize in these poems for my own experience, nor do I feel these things have been said before. . . . I once thought of calling them Lyric and Dramatic Poems. They are lyric in manner, the sound is the form—the sound gives a dimension of feeling. Dramatic, because the poems deal more or less with a Dramatic or human situation, as opposed to metaphysics, literature or a transitory mood.

Songs from plays, in other words, as I suggested in other words about the eclogues which close *The Arrivistes,* a genre which applies *a fortiori* to the title poem of *Good News of Death.* Simpson is less successful, however, in enclosing the lyric impulse within his varsity-show pastoral than he is in letting the whole dramatic contour break through the order of lyric itself. In this sense, he is an apocalyptic or revelatory poet, rather than a dramatic or satiric one, and that is why the occasional poems, as one must see them to be, in *Good News of Death,* do so much more for Simpson than the affected structures which contain, and prop, and ultimately impede them:

> . . .The Furies, vexed,
> From Hades in their endless coils arise,
> I see them at the corners of my eyes,
> I run into the dark. . . . And from this day
> I run, I run, and can no longer stay
> Than sleep, but that's another kind of pain,
> And when I sleep I cry to wake again.

The neat reversal of Caliban in the last line reminds us of the exploitive gift of this cultivated man, and if we consider Simpson a moment from this point of view, what is as surprising as the intervening silence is the increased mastery he shows in the deployment of the purely lyric instance upon a derived or conventional theme. Take the new poem "Early in the Morning," a highly condensed, three-stanza witticism about Antony, Cleopatra and Caesar, which in the first book would have run—indeed, *did* run—to the Higher Sententiousness in the form of symbolic glamor. Here, the form itself does the judging, and Simpson is free to concentrate the "story" and its referents into just a few tart words, as in this final stanza:

> Caesar Augustus
> Cleared his phlegm.
> "Corpses disgust us.
> Cover them."
> Caesar Augustus
> In his time lay
> Dying, and just as
> Cold as they. . . .

There are a number of other poems still dedicated to the *conceded* mythologies in this second book, though Simpson is evidently less patient with the old stories than he was in his days of arrival, and more concerned to get on to the themes which will, from now on, seem unquestionably his if only because to no one else have they seemed even to be themes: the unpossessed yet ruined country whose promise was celebrated before its possibility. The briskness with which the poet deals with "The Man Who Married Magdalene" or gets on, in his poem "John the Baptist," with "the matter of the platter and the sword" has something dismissive about it. Even as the emptiness of "Aegean" has a certain relief in its gaiety:

> There's no one any more
> But Echo on the shore,
> And Echo only laughs and runs away.

so Simpson's old favorite, the theme of war's disasters, is considerably distanced by its formal precision and witty touristic allusions, as in "Memories of a Lost War":

> The scene jags like a strip of celluloid,
> A mortar fires,
> Cinzano falls, Michelin is destroyed,
> The man of tires.

Significantly, the one mythological subject lingered over is "Ulysses and the Sirens," for what concerns Simpson now is not the time away at the wars, but getting back to the home place. And in the first important poem of the book, "The Return," he transforms the Odyssean restoration into something very personal and strange—the characteristic discovery of this poet that in growing older we do not necessarily grow in any other way, but rather we are *outgrown* by what we thought we had been and owned:

> The entrance of the liner to the city
> Was pure confusion, as if whales should neigh,
> And you have lost your sea simplicity.[1]
> . . . .
> As we grow older everything comes true.
> . . . .
> We are the giants and we are the elves,
> And soon we are the only mystery
> And we must make the voyages ourselves,
> And learn a parlor trick, wear one false nose,

And act as uncles, and do not disclose
What is not there at all,
Until we turn into the scenery
And children swing upon us like a tree.

It is the sense of being possessed by his landscape, and dis-possessed by the terrible American emptiness which he sees so clearly, that gives Simpson his extraordinary poise and presence of mind—literally that allows his mind to be present in scenes ordinarily qualified by the absence of imagination: "the river glittered in moonlight. The dark Palisades loomed against the sky and the moon paced through heaven." That is the unmedi-ated locus, upon which the poems, the consequential poems in *Good News of Death,* get to work, for as Simpson says in perhaps the darkest and deepest of all his exergues to the American expe-rience, "whatever we imagine is real. The life we have not lived can never be finished."

Hence the studies in post-Columbian anecdote, beginning with the group called "American Preludes" which flashes before us the entire sweep of continental chaos, from the Elizabethans' view of us as Setebos:

This isle hath many goodly woods and deer,
Conies and fowl in incredible abundance;
The woods, not such as you find in Bohemia,
Barren and fruitless . . .

to the decline of the Wild West:

Vaquero, I have seen your ending days,
Looped in a lariat, dragged at the heels
Of the black horses.

and sets the scene for the drama of waste and spoliation which follows in the wake of the invasions to come; it is a *mise-en-scène* without allegory, and in its initial terms almost without affect:

Maple and berry dogwood, oak, are kings.
The axe is lively and your pale palm stings
While Echo claps her hands on the bare hill.
The scene is clear. The air is chill.

The swish of the scythes of judgment, though, is audible in a poem like "Mississippi," where the kind of neat lament Simpson had reserved for fallen myths and wars lost abroad is now brought to bear—quite coolly, with more facts than fuss—on the home truths, the outrage of the War Between the States and inevitability of regional decay:

> When we went down the river on a raft
> So smooth it was and easy it would seem
> Land moved but never we. Clouds faded aft
> In castles. Trees would hurry in the dream
> Of water, where we gazed, with this log craft
> America suspended on a gleam.
> . . . .
> And Brady photographs the men like flags
> Still tilted in the charges where they died.
>
> The river is too strong for bank or bar,
> The landmarks change, and nothing would remain
> But for the man who travels by a star,
> Whose careful eye adjusts the course again . . .
> Still shadow at the wheel, his rich cigar
> Glowed like a point of rectitude—Mark Twain.
>
> If ever there were Mississippi nights,
> If ever there was Dixie, as they sing,
> Cry, you may cry, for all your true delights
> Lost with the banjo and the Chicken Wing
> Where old St. Joe slid on the water lights
> And on into the dark, diminishing.

The wonder of it is that in this first apprehension of the native strain, Simpson's movement inward (in all literary structures, surely, the final direction of movement is inward) from Jamaica, that offshore island, to the other island, Manhattan, and penetrating ever deeper to that final dead center which is the end of the open road indeed, Simpson's grasp of the American transit is distributed with such equanimity that he can accommodate, in his vision, the buildings of New York, "dull pyramids, too large to be destroyed, / that even ruined could not be enjoyed," as well as the eroded pastoral of the redwoods that "held the eagles in their state / when Rome was still a rumor in the boughs." In the climactic poem in this book, a poem in which Simpson assigns himself his mission like a doom, it is the City which is hypostatized when "her father asks her where she's going—'Out!' And that means America. She may go far . . ." That mission is the burden of civilization itself, the enterprise of making a total human form out of a despised nature, and in "Islanders" the poet accepts in the person of his compatriots his tragic perspective:

> . . . Beyond the daily wage
> They're caught in their own lives, the outer cage,
> And cry for exits, hoping to be shown
> A way by others, who have lost their own.
>
> And yet, seen from a distance and a height,
> How haunting are the islands of the night,
> The shores on which we dream, with the deep tide
> Of darkness rushing in on every side . . .

Four years later, in 1959, Simpson's third book was published, *A Dream of Governors,* which included four pieces from *The Arrivistes* of a decade before though none from *Good News of Death,* and borrowed its title from an Orphic line by Mark Van Doren (who has never shied out of the harness that pairs poetry and politics): "The deepest dream is of mad governors." And it is America from which, as from a sign of the apocalypse, Simpson will henceforth speak, whatever his enterprise and however despairing his undertaking:

> It was my generation
> That put the Devil down
> With great enthusiasm.
> But now our occupation
> Is gone. Our education
> Is wasted on the town.

The reminiscence of Othello in the topiary, the vainglorious black mercenary ("our occupation is gone") peering through the carefully clipped verses, is a typical effect of Simpson's at this point. The book, in fact, is chambered like a heart, its five parts patiently receiving their energies as the poet chooses to administer his sentence, never communicating or overlapping, so that the metahistorical group of lyrics which opens the book is curiously—though deliberately—irrelevant to the war poems in the section called and containing "The Runner" or to the love poems, and so forth. The partitioning is a way the poet has of knowing what he is talking about, and the voice in which he addresses himself to his task—"an easy and natural lyric charm," as Randall Jarrell called it, veraciously if we take "charm" in its old sense as a magic, an incantation, a song—is certainly appropriate to the thirst for discretion, the kind of intellectual *apartheid* from which this poet draws his surest effects, being something of a mad governor himself, as I mean to show.

The indifference to History of personal history, the enclave nature of the private life which particularly in its erotic and ecstatic course, as the word implies, is linear in form, irreversible in temper, accumulating a one-way anthology of significant episodes—the severance of individual happiness from the endless round of the cosmic comedy which is the history of nations, constitutes the doom of these first five poems, along with a certain redeeming satisfaction that human life persists at all, for as Simpson has said, "the will of things is for man not to exist; whatever we are, we are in spite of things." In any case, the drama of selfhood has nothing to do with the pageant of the Eternal Return:

> Now Portugal is fading, and the state
> Of Castile rising purple on Peru;
> Now England, now America grows great—
> With which these lovers have nothing to do.
>
> What do they care if time, uncompassed, drift
> To China, and the crew is a baboon?
> But let him whisper always, and her lift
> The oceans in her eyelids to the moon.

"These lovers" are the green shepherds—green in fecundity, green in lack of experience—whom Simpson has apostrophized in all his books, people who are concerned to endure the pains of their largely unconscious existence in order to enjoy the pleasures:

The groaning pole had gone more than a mile;
These shepherds did not feel it where they loved,
For time was sympathetic all the while
And on the magic mountain nothing moved.

Appropriate to this acceptation of selfhood *against* history and
the promptings of mere reason is an imagery of fairy tales, hier-
atic and rich in tropes of dismissal. So in the title poem, which is
found in this section too, that double-barrelled notion—always
associated, never assimilated—of life as a dream and the world
as a stage, is inevitably invoked, *Märchen*-style:

> The chorus in a play
> Declaimed: "The soul does well
> Keeping the middle way."
> He thought, That city fell;
> Man's life is founded on
> Folly at the extreme;
> When all is said and done
> The City is a dream.

There is a towering irresponsibility, always, in metahistory, a
refusal to commit the self to more than a handful of cyclical
myths which for all their inclusive appeal ("everything is per-
fect, calm and clear") cannot save the poet, speaking in his own
person, from his anguish:

> In conversation, silence, sitting still,
> The demon of decorum and despair.

We start over in the section called "My America," which
offers an easy survey of the betrayed Cytherea, Simpson's beau-
tifully "civilized" verses running counter to the awful wilder-
ness that was here first and then so immediately converted into
an awful subculture without ever passing through a metro-
politan phase; consider these two pictures, the poet urges, on the
one hand:

> The treasures of Cathay were never found.
> In this America, this wilderness

> Where the axe echoes with a lonely sound,
> The generations labor to possess
> And grave by grave we civilize the ground.

and on the other,

> Some day, when this uncertain continent
> Is marble, and men ask what was the good
> We lived by, dust may whisper "Hollywood."

I have spoken of these poems as apocalyptic in their enterprise of converting the fallen nature which is the object of their vision into a total human form; the apocalyptic poet sees all of experience as part of his poem, assigning it a place in his vision, rather than (stoically) accepting his vision as one more fact in nature. There is an interesting parallel in the very construction of Simpson's verses to this terrorism of vision; it seems to me that his great lines, for instance the famous one I quoted earlier about the redwoods or the terrible "and grave by grave we civilize the ground," devour the poems in which they occur in precisely the way apocalyptic works devour nature; that is, refusing to occur *within* another structure, they attempt to *contain* everything they approach or touch—accounting in a sense for the exasperated or shrill or even frantic overtones in this poet's later work, "while beauty loses all her evidence." That is what I mean by Simpson as a mad governor—the intuition that he is always swallowing his substance by a judgment which *must* contain all the evidence, rather than letting the evidence reveal the judgment. Certainly, as Simpson says about women, "their selfishness will always entertain," and in the American poems he has been able to compass his prophetic rage within a language so physical, so *fitting* to the "country Columbus thought he found" that we *do* listen, we *are* entertained, understanding selfishness finally to be a conviction of identity, gained by governance:

> The country that Columbus thought he found
> Is called America. It looks unreal,
> Unreal in winter and unreal in summer.
> When movies spread their giants on the air

The boys drive to the next town, drunk on nothing.
Youth has the secret. Only death looks real.

We never die. When we are old we vanish
Into the basement where we have our hobbies.
. . . .
And life is always borrowing and lending
Like a good neighbor. How can we refuse?

It is no surprise that this poet announces, in another place in this
section, "the melancholy of the possible / unmeasures me"—
for it is precisely the impossible that calls forth measure from
him, permitting him and probably forcing him to assign the
kind of coherent "government" to his oracles that makes the
unreal so actual here. Simpson skips from his epiphanic America
to "The Old World" for five poems to remind himself that this
is not his matter; as before, he resents the metaphysical tourism
which would allow his countrymen the comforts of self-
acceptance:

Humankind, says the poet, cannot bear
Too much reality.
                        Nor pleasure.
And nothing is more melancholy
Than to watch people enjoying themselves
As much as they can.

The war and love poems which end the book, including the long
battle narrative "The Runner," which indeed Simpson rewrites
in his novel *Riverside Drive*—though I prefer the earlier verse
rendition for its speed and exhibited confidence in the me-
dium—are far less interesting—less interested—achievements,
and the sections are impatiently filled out by repeats from earlier
work. Having come down from the hills, the dark fanatic deliv-
ers his alarums in the marketplace and withdraws, mission ac-
complished, the warning spoken. *A Dream of Governors* ends,
then, on a characteristic note of removal. I have already spoken
of Simpson as a Lord of Misrule whose mask, when the revels

get beyond him, suddenly falls off—and that is what happens here. The fist is shaken one last time, in "Against the Age":

> . . . our lives
> Are lives of State, the slogans for today.
> That wind is carrying the world away.

and then abruptly, in "The Goodnight," a poem of astonishing tenderness when one notices how much it owes to those fierce old men Yeats and Frost, Simpson turns into his own green shepherd, saying good night to his sleeping daughter and dismissing the inevitable Armageddon he has just announced, abiding by his own humanity:

> Who said that tenderness
> Will turn the heart to stone?
> May I endure her weakness
> As I endure my own.
> Better to say goodnight
> To breathing flesh and blood
> Each night as though the night
> Were always only good.

Another pause of four years, and in 1963 appeared a book of Simpson's poems, his fourth, which won the Pulitzer Prize and brought him a certain wondering fame from the quarterlies, whose critics (I was one of them) marveled that a poet could speak so harshly of these States and still be prized by them. Further, *At the End of the Open Road* appeared to jettison all the scrimshaw-work which had been such a typical and such a reassuring aspect of Simpson's verse: as if, surely, anyone who had troubled to accommodate his vision so elegantly, so arbitrarily to the modes of convention could not be seriously troubled, or worse still, *troubling*. But the new book urged two conclusions upon us: first, that Simpson, determined as he was "to live in the tragic world forever," was a dangerous, a monitory presence among us:

> There's no way out.
> You were born to waste your life.
> You were born to this middleclass life

>   As others before you
>   Were born to walk in procession
>   To the temple, singing.

and second, that the poet, acknowledging the presence of "that same old city-planner death" as he went about his duties in California, deploying "among the realtors and tennis-players his dark preoccupation," had achieved a cadence when he merely *spoke,* barely raising his voice above the unquestioned prose of the quotidian:

>   In the morning light a line
>   Stretches forever. There my unlived life
>   Rises, and I resist,
>   Clinging to the steps of the throne
>   . . . .
>   And my life, pitilessly demanding
>   Rises forever in the morning light.

had found a measure which fell as strictly within the compass of his requirements:

>   Love, my machine,
>   We rise by this escape.
>   We travel by the shocks we make.
>   . . . .
>   I am going into the night to find a world of my own.

as any of his old lilt, yet with a new freedom that had the whole autonomy of the man's body under it; Simpson's lyric had become one with his speaking voice, a congruence which for any poet is the moment of release into himself, the moment when, no matter what is said, "the waves bring Eros in," as the Western Sea confirmed:

>   When men wanted the golden fleece
>   It was not wool they wanted.
>   *They* were the trophies that they sailed toward.
>
>   They were the sea and the wind
>   That hurled them over

Into the sea. They were the fishes
That stripped their thin bones. And they rose
In the night in new constellations.

Here, even when Simpson is not admonishing his country, his apocalyptic impulse to enclose the natural within the human until the elements themselves are encysted in man's form, to turn the heroic quest into an exploratory operation, is patent. Also, I think the poet relies more on *personality,* his own awareness of his voice ("I seek the word. The word is not forthcoming, O syllables of light . . . O dark cathedral . . ."), as a mortar to hold his lines together, dispensing him from certain evidences, certain cartilages in his text. There are still the devouring, oracular lines, of course—"The Open Road goes to the used-car lot," or again,

Then all the realtors,
Pickpockets, salesmen, and the actors performing
Official scenarios,
Turned a deaf ear, for they had contracted
American dreams.

—but they no longer blow up the rest of the poem in Simpson's new rhythmical dispensation, but rather dig where they stand, as Browning said of the lyric necessity. I believe Simpson has said things just as devastating before, but in their new accommodation the damages are apparent, are not to be avoided:

We cannot turn or stay.
For though we sleep, and let the reins fall slack,
The great cloud-wagons move
Outward still, dreaming of a Pacific.

Now that he has engorged his America, from the Atlantic cities where "when darkness falls on the enormous street the air is filled with Eros, whispering" and there are whole blocks "where no one lives," to that Hesperidean verge he cannot forgive himself for despising ("surely there is a secret which, if I knew it, would change everything"), Simpson speaks with the true might of apocalypse, finding everything within his own vision, nothing *outside* himself. That is what gives him the right to his ferocity: his refusal to dismiss anything that is not already encompassed by his own life. When he apostrophizes "the future in ruins!" and addresses himself to the rest of us:

> O businessmen like ruins,
> bankers who are Bastilles,
> widows, sadder than the shores of lakes,
> then you were happy, when you still could tremble!

his own fate is also in question, and his version of our future, the terrible prophecy of "The Inner Part," cannot be muffled or missed as we would miss the imprecations of someone who separates himself from our condition:

> When they had won the war
> And for the first time in history
> Americans were the most important people—
> . . . .
> When their daughters seemed as sensitive
> As the tip of a fly rod,
> And their sons were as smooth as a V-8 engine—
>
> Priests, examining the entrails of birds,
> Found the heart misplaced, and seeds
> As black as death, emitting a strange odor.

Simpson ends this brief, brilliant book with his finest poem so far, "Lines Written near San Francisco," an achievement that reaches so far outward largely because it reaches so far in, though the talent for the apocalyptic image, the oracular rhythm must not be discounted in the total effect, the gift for seeing the *telling* detail in a landscape otherwise determined to give away nothing, to repress its self-loathing even as it boasts of its prosperity:

> Every night, at the end of America
> We taste our wine, looking at the Pacific.
> How sad it is, the end of America!

While we were waiting for the land
They'd finished it—with gas drums
On the hilltops, cheap housing in the valleys

Where lives are mean and wretched.
But the banks thrive and the realtors
Rejoice—they have their America.

Still there is something unsettled in the air.
Out there on the Pacific
There's no America but the Marines.

Discovering the whole of his country to be held in an everlasting
and endless body, as Blake does, Simpson offers his revelations
with a strange detachment at the end—or now, not strange but
simply necessary in a poet who no longer finds the enemy out-
side or over the water, but in the vitals of a titanic self, that
"credible extravaganza":

Whitman was wrong about the People,
But right about himself. The land is within.
At the end of the open road we come to ourselves.

In 1965 was published that sober recognition of a poet's pres-
ence on the scene, a *Selected Poems* of Louis Simpson, who chose
to include only the three love lyrics from his first book which he
had reprinted in his third, a fair sampling from the second and
third books, and a very full series from *At the End of the Open
Road,* suggesting the perspective in which he wished to consider
his own work, and the direction he intended to take. This direc-
tion was confirmed, even rather insistently signposted by a
dozen new poems which continue, like Simpson's old classmate
at Columbia Allen Ginsberg, "to cry out against the cities," and
which initiate a more personal note in the loosened stanzas.
From the first, Simpson has known how to entertain, how to
underscore his effects with a shrewd application of clown white,
and doubtless the terrible shopping centers of California feed his
theatrics with a profound and deserving futility:

. . . I have suspected
The Mixmaster knows more than I do,

The air conditioner is the better poet.
My right front tire is as bald as Odysseus—
How much it must have suffered!

The tonality is different, but it is still the old paranoiac articulation of the adversity of *things*. The city, of course, is the largest thing of all, and though Simpson declares himself resigned to the likelihood that Salvation will be granted by some kind of electric pencil-sharpener—

I must be patient with shapes
Of automobile fenders and ketchup bottles.
These things are the beginning

Of things not visible to the naked eye

—he sees the urban matrix as a failure, a force *counter* to our lives: "the streets lead on in burning lines / and giants tremble in electric chains. . . . It seems that a man exists / only to say, Here I am in person." Of course the city is inside the self in Simpson's apocalyptic view, a sort of cancer to which the "young man" who is the poet's surrogate appeals:

Yet, over the roofs of the city
The moon hangs, faithful to the last,
Revealing her amorous craters.

Muse of the city, hope of the insane,
What would he do without you?

And as the poet explores this transformed landscape ("a country that cannot fail," his Columbus reports, "for there's no finding it") by the moonlight which is his hope, he finds that in the cellar of his habitation, shattering roots "had broken through the wall, / As though there was something in my rubbish / That life would have at last." It appears, then, that even the city can be forgiven, can be given life, at least, and that nature, now inside the mind and body of an infinite man, can be given the "lineaments of gratified desire." It is not reality, Simpson says at the end, but it is, in terms like Dante's, conceivable:

> . . . a vision
> Of mankind, like grass and flowers,
> The same over all the earth.
> We forgave each other; we gave ourselves
> Wholly over to words.
> And straightway I was released
> And sprang through an open gate.

NOTE

1. "The sea reminds us of our early loves," Simpson says in another poem in this book.

RONALD MORAN

The Image of "America" in the California/Whitman Poems of Louis Simpson

When in 1959 Louis Simpson moved from New York City to Berkeley, California, where he was to reside for the next eight years, his move had a significant influence on the direction his subject matter was to take; for along with stylistic innovations came an intense examination of America, especially the America of California. Simpson's poetic interest in America was not new; for a few of the poems from *The Arrivistes* (1949), notably "Invitation to a Quiet Life," more poems from *Good News of Death and Other Poems* (1955), and an entire section from *A Dream of Governors* (1959) treat material indigenous to America; but only in isolated instances, such as "West" from *Good News of Death and Other Poems,* and "The Boarder" and "Landscape with Barns" from *A Dream of Governors,* does he succeed measurably in coming to terms with what America and the American spirit mean. At the same time, "Mississippi" from the 1955 volume and "To the Western World" from the 1959 volume contain examples of the faults that mar Simpson's earlier efforts at working with America: reliance on stock associations and on surface perceptions. Curiously, the poem "West," with its Imagistic structure and colloquial base, is strikingly similar, though it was published nearly a decade before, to the America poems from *At the End of the Open Road* (1963), the collection that includes the poems under consideration in this essay.

From *Geschichte und Gesellschaft in der amerikanischen Literatur* (Heidelberg, West Germany: Quelle & Meyer, 1975), 211–19. Published in slightly different form in *Louis Simpson* (New York: Twayne, 1972), 108–20. Copyright © 1971, Twayne Publishers, a division of G. K. Hall & Co., Boston.

Simpson's preoccupation with America has received considerable attention by reviewers of *At The End of the Open Road* and *Selected Poems* (1965). In my 1965 review of *At the End of the Open Road,* I indicate Simpson's concern with America in the tradition of Walt Whitman:

> Whatever else he did, the inexorable Walt Whitman started the tradition in American poetry obsessed with defining what America is. Whitman's job, though, was decidedly easier than that of those now compelled to define in verse the nation that has nowhere to go. At least in the middle of the nineteenth century, there were frontiers—economic, social, and political, all of which were made possible by a physical frontier that still had somewhere to go. Now, however, America has to turn on the inward spotlight to find a frontier; and introspection, especially when the past made or suggested many promises, inevitably lights up and focuses brightly on disappointments. A hundred years later with frontiers exhausted, Louis Simpson emerges with too much candle power to let the products of the American Story find any dark recesses in which to hide.[1]

Both Thom Gunn and William Stafford are aware of Simpson's commitment to America. To Gunn, "There is also in this book [*At the End of the Open Road*] an attempt—a development from a section of his last book—to define America, or the feeling of being in America, or the feeling of writing poems in America."[2] Stafford, whose own poems are built on the American land, recognizes Simpson's belief that the foundations—the principles on which America was founded—are perhaps more illusion than substance: "Again and again the poems confront new, grim aspects of America's formative traditions. It is as if treasured documents like the Declaration of Independence should glow under a certain light and reveal odd skeletons."[3]

In the *San Francisco Examiner Book Week* for December 5, 1965, Donald Hall, whose interest in Simpson's career as a poet has been consistent, seems to touch directly on the poet's continuing and progressively complex treatment of America: "America was always there, bothering him, needing to be considered from another angle, another kind of approach. At the start the country was largely historic and geographic; increasingly, as Simpson's imagination has become more daring and powerful, he has dealt with the spirit." The London *Times Literary Supplement* reviewer echoes and expands upon Hall's analysis in a June 9, 1966, review of the Oxford University Press edition of *Selected Poems:*

America is one of the poet's central subjects: the search for an American identity is the search for his poetic character. At first this produces the wide, idealized vistas of "American Preludes" [from *Good News of Death and Other Poems*] and "To the Western World" [from *A Dream of Governors*], placed above the landscape and the condition of being American; consequently the poetry has something of the generalized, orchestrated emotion of a national anthem. But as the poet finds himself, he touches down with more intimacy and confidence and begins a dialogue with the inhabitants that elicits the more personal emotion of love, anger and disillusion. The fulfillment is achieved in such poems as "Walt Whitman at Bear Mountain" [from *At the End of the Open Road*] and "After Midnight" [from *Selected Poems*].

Simpson has found in the state of California an ordering device, notably absent from his earlier work, for several of his America poems. The figure of Walt Whitman appears as a second ordering device in these same poems, which include "In California," "Walt Whitman at Bear Mountain," "Pacific Ideas—a Letter to Walt Whitman," and "Lines Written near San Francisco." Whitman's image of the open road ("Song of the Open Road" and other poems) serves Simpson more than any other specific image from Whitman. Although we could argue that Whitman's stylistic abandon exerted a determining influence on Simpson's stylistic departure, which began around 1959, I think perhaps too much could be made of this. Certainly, Simpson's apparent discovery of Whitman as subject matter coincides with his new manner of writing; but other poets, including James Wright and Robert Bly, were also writing and continue to write in a manner similar to Simpson's. Of course, all of them probably acknowledge Whitman as the spiritual father of their poetry; but I prefer to think that Simpson's style is more individual than derivative.

The influence, rather the force, of Whitman on Simpson lies primarily in subject choice and attitude—and, more exactly, in providing Simpson with a way of looking at America, its spirit, character, philosophy, and direction. Nonetheless, the attitudes are entirely Simpson's; they are not extensions or refinements of those Whitman seems to hold. Since, more than any other American poet, Whitman tries to embrace and embody all of America, it is only reasonable that he provides a point of departure for Simpson, a set of attitudes about the country from which Simpson departs; for, assuredly, Simpson is not the optimistic celebrator of America that Whitman is; moreover, the poetry of Simpson is original in thought and in execution.

At the End of the Open Road begins with "In California," a poem that establishes Simpson's attitude toward the dream America has held and holds about itself. The opening lines not only set the tone, so to speak, but also document the poet's abandonment of meter and rhyme in favor of the inner-directed method of statement:

> Here I am, troubling the dream coast
> With my New York face,
> Bearing among the realtors
> And tennis-players my dark preoccupation.

In fact, the statement is so direct, so free from embellishment, that the speaker is clearly Simpson himself, a new thorn in the side of California. The "dark preoccupation" is a particularly apt appraisal of the attitude projected in the poems of this volume. Equally appropriate are the allusions to the California "dream coast" (the embodiment of and the end to the American Dream) and to the "tennis-players" who represent California's need, or rather propensity, for outdoor recreation. Indeed, this stanza is a most honest introduction of Simpson to readers of *At the End of the Open Road*.

The second stanza suggests American history and literature, as well as the American Dream, which is itself a significant ingredient in both the country's history and literature:

> There once was an epical clatter—
> Voices and banjos, Tennessee, Ohio,

Rising like incense in the sight of heaven.
Today, there is an angel in the gate.

The "angel in the gate," which reappears in "Walt Whitman at Bear Mountain," is explained later in the discussion of that poem. It suffices here to say that "heaven" implies a paradise in America, a Garden of Eden perhaps. The point to be made here is that America did seem to be a paradise, or at least to suggest a paradise, in its years of westward expansion. In a literary context, the "epical clatter" could allude to the writings of Whitman as well as to songs indigenous to the American pioneering spirit.

Walt Whitman and Mark Twain, the two nineteenth-century American authors whose work most approaches a sense of the American epic, are yoked in the opening lines of the third stanza by the speaker's enjoining Whitman to "Lie back . . . on the fabulous raft with the King and the Duke!" "For," as the poet continues bitterly, "the white row of the Marina / Faces the Rock. Turn round the wagons here." Both Whitman and Twain use the journey motif: the former, in "Song of the Open Road" and other poems; the latter, in Huck and Jim's Odyssey on the Mississippi River. And America itself is a journey, to which Simpson bears witness in the title of this collection of poems; but the journey ends at the Pacific Ocean, a figure Simpson employs again and quite appropriately in "Lines Written near San Francisco," the last poem of the volume. The "wagons" in the last line of the third stanza allude to the wagon trains that brought settlers to the West; and, with the settling of California, the frontier, in effect, ceased to be. What remains fronting San Francisco Bay is Alcatraz, the Rock. The speaker, then, is providing a second answer, in addition to the Pacific Ocean, to the question of what is at the end of the open road: a prison.

Whitman is enjoined to "Lie Back!" a second time in the opening line of the fourth stanza. The speaker then shifts point of view from "I" and the implied "you" to the collective "we" to emphasize that the conditions of which he talks have meaning to all Americans:

Lie back! We cannot bear
The stars any more, those infinite spaces.
Let the realtors divide the mountain,
For they have already subdivided the valley.

The speaker's irony is aimed not only at the realtors but also at the American penchant for moving forward—for progressing toward anything anywhere. However, since we cannot do anything about the "stars" (space exploration had not yet been a major American effort) and since "those infinite spaces" bother us by the fact of just *being* there, we must find somewhere to continue our pioneering efforts. So we cut into the mountain, after having already civilized the valley. But, again, where are we really going? What are we really accomplishing? These answers follow in a remarkably ironic stanza:

> Rectangular city blocks astonished
> Herodotus in Babylon,
> Cortez in Tenochtitlan,
> And here's the same old city-planner, death.

Just as Herodotus, "The Father of History," and Hernando de Cortez, the Spanish conquistador, must have been astonished when they saw the architecture of Babylon, the capital of Babylonia, and Tenochtitlan, the capital of the Aztec Empire, so must we be astonished when we realize that our own empire ends with the "rectangular city blocks" of Alcatraz. Great empires perish; the "same old city-planner, death," is working on the American empire as it did to the Mesopotamian and Aztec empires. The figure of "death" appears later in subsequent poems by Simpson.

"Walt Whitman at Bear Mountain" is perhaps Simpson's finest poem and is one of the most significant statements about America to emerge from mid-twentieth-century American poetry. Since I treat the poem elsewhere at some length,[4] a brief discussion of its thematic relevance will suffice for this essay. The poem is a serious indictment of the American condition and, at the same time, an exoneration of Whitman from the frequent charge that his poetry prophesies the fulfillment of promises held in the nineteenth century. Just as we, as readers, have been misreading Whitman to the extent that we have assigned prophetic powers to what were only his moods, so too has America been misinterpreting itself. Perhaps the promises ("American dreams") that we thought were integral to the nature of America were, in fact, nonexistent. Perhaps we have been misled into thinking our country was and is a Garden of Eden. At this point in the poem, the speaker, who is Simpson (as the case is with his California/Whitman poems), claims that some Americans, however, have been spared this false illusion: "But the man who keeps a store on a lonely road, / And the housewife who knows she's dumb, / And the earth, are relieved" [of the charge of having contracted the disease of "American dreams"]; for they have been conditioned to humility and thus do not expect to create microcosmic empires. Now that we understand the delusion under which we have been living, a great burden has been lifted, and America feels the relief:

> The clouds are lifting from the high Sierras,
> The Bay mists clearing.
> And the angel in the gate, the flowering plum,
> Dances like Italy, imagining red.

I wrote to Simpson, asking in particular about "the angel in the gate," which appears also in "In California." His reply, dated August 3, 1967, contains the following explanations:

> The image at the end of Walt Whitman ["Walt Whitman at Bear Mountain"] is a composite of: (1) The angel of Eden, (2) a plum tree, magentacolored, that I had at the time.

> Maybe (1) needs more explanation. The point of the argument is that Americans might try not being so expansive for a change; not being programmed for empire. If they waited, then, as Rilke suggests in the Duino elegies, "happiness" might fall. A Renaissance is graceful. Then the "angel in the gate"—here symbolized as a plum-tree, a color that is given, not created by an act of will—would rejoice. My angel is the dance of "the given" (though, as I've suggested above, it was suggested also by the old angel of Eden, driving man out to a life of will. Here, if you like, the angel's job is over.)

"Pacific Ideas—a Letter to Walt Whitman" again indicts an aspect of the American condition; then it curiously turns inward and concludes by focusing not too clearly on the speaker himself. The opening stanza calls to mind, as in "In California," the wagon trains moving westward; then images are effectively juxtaposed:

> When the schooners were drifting
> Over the hills—schooners like white skulls—
> The sun was the clock in that parlor
> And the piano was played by the wind.

The second stanza begins with the word *but,* a word in modern American poetry usually indicating that a sharp reversal or shock of some sort is to follow. In this case, it is suggested, but not explicitly stated, that the American spirit to move must eventually stop. The speaker continues that "things" (material possessions) "are necessary," after which Walt Whitman is addressed: "Those 'immensely overpaid accounts,' / Walt, it seems that we must pay them again." The quotation the speaker cites comes from Whitman's "Song of the Exposition" in the following context:

> Come Muse migrate from Greece and Ionia,
> Cross out please those immensely overpaid accounts,
> That matter of Troy and Achilles' wrath, and Aeneas',
>   Odysseus' wanderings,
> Placard "Removed" and "To Let" on the rocks of your snowy
>   Parnassus . . .
> For know a better, fresher, busier sphere, a wide, untried
>   domain awaits, demands you.

Whitman is invoking the Muse to make both himself as a poet and America as a country forget the Old World as far as, among other considerations, subject matter for poetry is concerned. The "immensely overpaid accounts" are debts paid over and over again to heritage and history, both real and imagined, that are exerting influences overwhelmingly out of proportion. Whitman wants new subjects for a New World.

Although Whitman's "immensely overpaid accounts" (at least in the context in which it appears above) relate primarily to the writing of poetry, this is not the one use to which Simpson puts the phrase in "Pacific Ideas—a Letter to Walt Whitman." Rather, Simpson is concerned with the way in which America is being civilized as a nation and society. In the third stanza, the speaker tells of the difficulties inherent in solidifying a society destined for greatness:

> It's hard to civilize, to change
> The usual order;
> And the young, who are always the same, endlessly
> Rehearse the fate of Achilles.

It is hard, he means, to alter the pattern by which a society grows into greatness. The young leaders of a young, emerging country have the identical ends in mind as the young leaders had of earlier civilizations; they are guilty of pride, "the fate of Achilles." It is interesting to note that Simpson cites Achilles just as Whitman does in "Song of the Exposition," but there is, of course, a contextual difference.

"Pacific Ideas—a Letter to Walt Whitman" closes with these lyrical and strange lines:

> But here is the sea and the mist,
> Gray Lethe of forgetfulness,
> And the moon, gliding from the mist,
> Love, with her garland of dreams.
>
> And I have quarrelled with my books
> For the moon is not in their fable,
> And say to darkness, Let your dragon come,
> O anything, to hold her in my arms!

The change in language and rhythm from the first four stanzas to the last two is one from colloquial statement to lyrical intensity. The new direction is from the external of Walt Whitman, business executives of the "upper floors," and English professors to the internal of the speaker's emotions. Facing the Pacific Ocean, the westward limit to physical expansion, the speaker is caught up in the romantic mood created by mist over the ocean. That he has "quarrelled" with his books serves to link him with Whitman, a professed anti-academician. The exotic setting exerts a Lethe-like influence over the speaker; he forgets the concerns that prompted the "Letter" to Whitman in the first place, and he seems to emerge with a plea for Love, personified as the moon "gliding from the mist," to come to him regardless of what perils she may bring. I am reminded here of Whitman's short lyric "When I Heard the Learn'd Astronomer," in which the poet says he has had enough of an astronomer's discourse on the scientific properties of stars, and so goes out into the night: "Till rising and gliding out I wander'd off by myself, / Into the mystical moist night air, and from time to time, / Look'd up in perfect silence at the stars." Something of the same seems to have happened to Simpson's speaker, who, like Whitman's, uses the word gliding and feels a touch of wetness in the night air.

Appropriately, the final poem of *At the End of the Open Road* and the final one in which Walt Whitman figures significantly is "Lines Written near San Francisco." Consisting of three nine-stanza parts, each stanza having three lines, it is one of the longer poems of the collection. Despite the stanza consistency, there is neither rhyming nor a metrical pattern; both diction and rhythms are based on the colloquial. Whitman does not appear in the poem until the final section and then only in terms of a single reference, but the reference is important. "Lines Written near San Francisco" assimilates Simpson's attitudes toward America found in the three previous California/Whitman poems.

The poem opens with a dramatization of the San Francisco earthquake and fire of 1906. The central figure is the great operatic tenor Enrico Caruso, who is presented as having been in the act of performing when the first tremors began. Then characters from operas—Otello, Don Giovanni, Figaro, and Lucia—imaginatively act out their roles during the live performance of the natural disaster. Part 1 concludes with Death, the central character of the poem, seen at rest after the "tremors / Passed under the waves."

Part 2 is involved with the efforts to rebuild San Francisco. A "bowler-hatted" engineer is writing down (there is a shift to the present tense in the poem) instructions; a boy takes them to the workmen, who are just in the act of giving their mules orders to start pulling the wagons. Then the speaker intercedes to question the wisdom of their actions and those of their ancestors: "Say, did your fathers cross the dry Sierras / To build another London? / Do Americans always have to be second-rate?" One of the workmen speaks, concluding the second part of the poem: "'San Francisco / Is a city second only to Paris.'" The speaker of "Lines Written near San Francisco" realizes, however, that his pleas will go unheeded; for "already they have nailed rough boards together" and "the mortar sets—banks are the first to stand." Thus San Francisco will be a new mirror to reflect the Old World and to reflect "banks," symbolic of American materialism.

Suitably, part 3 is a lament for the real and symbolical "end of America." The vigor of the language and the insistent rhythms of the first two parts give way to quiet and somber reflection and exposition, exemplified in this stanza (despite the exclamation mark): "Every night, at the end of America / We taste our wine, looking at the Pacific. / How sad it is, the end of America!" The speaker then brings in "cheap housing in the valleys," "banks [that] thrive," and the "realtors," who appear in both "In California" and "Walt Whitman at Bear Mountain." Nonetheless, the unsettling of the city by earth tremors still is "in the air," and "out there on the Pacific / There's no America but the Marines." It is difficult for a nation "programmed for empire" to relinquish its momentum.

With the loss of the frontier and with the retention of the American need to move forward, there is nowhere to go but inward. Still, the bankers and realtors have cause to rejoice; for they are able to subdivide the valleys and mountains, to partition the continent to suit their needs. Their inward continent is physical, not spiritual; but Simpson's is inward: "Whitman was wrong about the People, / But right about himself. The land is within. / At the end of the open road we come to ourselves." By coming "to ourselves," the speaker means that, since we no longer have land to pioneer—land which both uses and satisfies our physical needs—we must turn inward; we must examine our spiritual resources; we must, in effect, identify and analyze our values; for now we have no excuse (a physical entity) to delay doing so.

The image "colonists of Death" in part 3 sets the foreboding tone on which this poem and the volume end. Americans are "colonists of Death" because of several interrelated factors with which Simpson has been working in the four California/Whitman poems: (1) Materialistic forces, symbolized in the figures of realtors, bankers, and the like, are constructing the wrong temples and altars ("In California," "Walt Whitman at Bear Mountain," "Pacific Ideas—a Letter to Walt Whitman," and "Lines Written near San Francisco"). (2) We cannot adjust to our now nonexistent physical frontier and cannot come to terms with our own inward resources, if, indeed, we have the *right* resources ("In California" and "Lines Written near San Francisco"). (3) We have deceived ourselves into thinking that from the beginning of our country we held and could fulfill great promises ("Walt Whitman at Bear Mountain" and "Lines Written near San Francisco"). (4) We were so caught up in historical emulation of great societies that we are deaf to our own sounds ("Walt Whitman at Bear Mountain" and "Lines Written near San Francisco"). Thus our promise is Death, "the land / The pioneers looked for"; our "pioneers" shaded "their eyes / Against the sun—a murmur of serious life"; and we follow in their steps, believe the same lies, and are passing them on to our children, according to Simpson.

NOTES

1. Ronald Moran, "Time of Heterogeneity: A Chronicle of Fifteen," *Southern Review,* n.s. 1 (Spring 1965): 475–76.

2. Thom Gunn, "Modes of Control," *Yale Review* 53 (Spring 1964): 458.

3. William Stafford, "Terminations, Revelations," *Poetry* 104 (May 1964): 104.

4. Ronald Moran, "'Walt Whitman at Bear Mountain' and the American Illusion," *Concerning Poetry* 2(Spring 1969): 5–9.

The Work of Louis Simpson

I

Louis Simpson's poems are outstanding among those of the younger poets because of the experience that lies behind them. He has an advantage over other poets before he begins to write a poem because his experience seems strangely deeper: the poems suggest hopeless moods, profound voyages into water over his head, massive disappointments and failures. He is deeply aware, for instance, of living in one age and not in another. Everywhere in Louis Simpson's work there is the sense that an age of some sort has come to an end:

> O the ash and the oak and willow tree
> And that's an end of the infantry!
>
> Collect yourself. Observe,
> It's nearly day . . .
> Concrete and cactus are the real
> American tragedy.
> We should collect our souvenirs and leave.
>
> Though for a turn or two we had a king . . .
> The naked wickedness of his designs
> Brought on Democracy, a steady thing.
>
> No witnesses remain
> Of battles on the plain
> And the bright oar and the oar spray.

Part 1: "The Work of Louis Simpson," *Fifties* 1 (1958): 22–25; part 2: "Louis Simpson's New Book," *Sixties* 4 (Fall 1960): 58–61; part 3: "Fragrance of the Unknown," *Moons and Lion Tailes* 2, no. 2 (1976): 49–53.

We remember that Whitman, whose theme was somewhat the same, namely the end of one age, and the coming of another, made the content and form say the same thing. When he spoke of a new age, his form was also new. But in Mr. Simpson's case, this is not true: the forms he uses are traditional. The question then is, why use forms of a previous age if, within the poems, you continually suggest that that age has come to an end? The content seems to say one thing, and the form another, and opposite things. The contrast is particularly noticeable, and effective, in Mr. Simpson's new ballad, "The Bird," in the Autumn, 1957, *Hudson Review*. In this poem, a kind gentle German who always sings, "I wish I were a bird," takes up duties at a concentration camp for Jews.

> "You'll never be a beauty,"
> The doctor said, "You scamp!
> We'll give you special duty—
> A concentration camp."

But Heinrich learned:

> "*Ich wünscht', ich wäre ein Vöglein,*"
> Sang Heinrich, "I would fly . . ."
> They knew that when they heard him
> The next day they would die.

When the Russians arrive, and search for him, they find the Bird has flown the coop, and only a bird in a tree can be seen. The description of a modern German's vicious adventures written in a gay ballad meter emphasizes the viciousness and insanity of the whole thing, and suggests, more strongly than ever, that something has come to an end. Occasionally in Mr. Simpson's other poems this contrast works as well.

But we also remember Blackmur's comment on Robert Lowell, a very interesting comment to the effect that the content is hair-raisingly revolutionary, and the form fanatically conservative, so that there is a conflict between form and content within the poem, and a conflict that tends to be self-destructive. I feel that slightly in these poems also. In one sense, the form, by contrast, reinforces the content; but in another sense, the form doubts the poet, and everything he has to say, and continually tries to render it innocuous.

The people in his poems also interest me—John the Baptist, Antony, Mary Magdalene. Girls and women seem to take a larger part in his book than in many books of poems. Most of the poets of our generation are like Ulysses, tied to the mast to keep them from yielding too much to women, and they sail on to the Ithaca of their art, pure but somewhat stiff from being bound by ropes. Mr. Simpson is more at home in this world. He understands a man like Antony, who goes too deep. As Antony says to Cleopatra, when Caesar's armies near:

> It's
> Too cold a morning
> To get out of bed.
>   (*Good News of Death and Other Poems*)

His poetry has a wry and compassionate view of people, which does not exclude humor or tenderness. There is a magnificent poem in his first volume, *Arrivistes* (Fine Editions Press, New York, 1949), called "Song: 'Rough Winds Do Shake the Darling Buds of May.'" The second stanza reads:

> She is sixteen
>   sixteen
>   and her young lust
> Is like a thorn
>   hard thorn
>   among the pink
> Of her soft nest.
> Upon this thorn she turns, for love's incessant sake.

Later he describes a woman with one line:

> Noli me tangere was not her sign.

All through his work we are aware of two choices toward experience, and so of experience itself, deeper than these.

The third thing that interests me are his poems about the war. Surely "Carentan O Carentan" in *The Arrivistes* is the best poem written yet about World War II by any generation. It does not seem the poem of a spectator, but a participator. "Arm in Arm" and "Alain Alain" in that book are also extremely good, as well as "Memories of a Lost War" and the magnificent "The Ash and the Oak" in the later book. It is astonishing how aware one is whenever we read Louis Simpson of historical periods. The war described in his poems could never be any other war than the Second World War. It is not "war itself" but a specific battle, which in a mysterious way, seems already imagined in the long train of crusades, sieges, and battles over one thousand years, of which it is a part. As we read his poems, the events of the West appear, as if by Surrealist means, as a sort of mirage in our minds; we glimpse a battlefield here, a tower there, some crusaders, now a Roman legion, a fop of Louis XVI, now vast armies, now a man eating locust. In short, his subject matter is partially the history of the West.

It seems obvious that the most important event in Western History of the last three thousand years is the death of pagan religion and the acceptance of Christ, and all that implies. We are not surprised then to find that this is precisely the subject of the short play, "Good News of Death" at the end, which is the most brilliant single thing in the new book.

On stage, as you watch, the pagan religion dies, in the form of a sheep in which Orestes has taken his last habitation. The sheep, pursued, as he should be, by the Furies, expires on the stage; and all accept his death, and he is borne offstage.

Suddenly, in the next scene, Christ is mentioned, and the sheep, to everyone's astonishment, returns carrying his grave-clothes. He announces that after death, there was some singing, some talk, Christ was there, and he awoke. When the Furies become aware of this, they realize, of course, that they have been betrayed, and they know that the old order is over. Now for the first time in human history, the dead may awake. Death is conquered. As Peter says, "This is good news of death, if it is true."

The meaning is conveyed entirely by these "images" and the delicacy of making Orestes a sheep, who, nevertheless, passes after death into the new order in which, of course, Christ is a Sacrificial Lamb, continues its suggestiveness, and cannot be praised enough. He also uses the images for humor, as when the resurrected sheep reports that "the wool was pulled from my eyes." In the background are hurrying businessmen.

Strangely enough, this magnificence takes place in the midst of rather commonplace diction and very tired forms. The lines are mostly rather monotonous iambic pentameter. Again the specter appears of a war between content and form, with the form acting so as to render the content innocuous, or as a sort of protective camouflage to conceal exactly how revolutionary the content is.

This poet's strength is great love of humanity, elegance, openness to experience, great intelligence, and courage; but he should avoid his fault, which is a tendency in form to do well what has already been done. He should search for a form as fresh as his content.

2

Our intention is not only to publish essays on the work of some of the poets of the fifties and sixties, one essay in each issue, as we have already done with Louis Simpson, Robert Creeley, Donald Hall, and W. S. Merwin, but also to comment on the later work of these poets as it appears.

Mr. Simpson's new book, *A Dream of Governors,* is divided into five sections, one of which contains war poems. The longest of these is a narrative poem called "The Runner." "The Runner" gives the impression of an experience of great depth, brought up into very awkward poetry. The effect is of an unfinished work. The poetic line is modeled roughly on the Shakespearean or Wordsworthian five-beat line. Such a line does not fit the experience with which the poem is concerned.

The iambic line is often said to be a valid line for poetry in English. This is true. Mr. Simpson has rejected, however, the usual content associated with that line—the hoary castles, the girls, the wan faces are after all valid content! Rejecting these, he has substituted his own original content—but strangely enough, he retains the old line. As a result "The Runner" seems only half-conceived.

Despite its awkwardness, the writing in this poem has great power. Judson Jerome, in a review in the *Antioch Review,* suggested that we are never far from hallucination in Mr. Simpson's

poems—and it is true that his descriptions often have a halluci-
natory power. I will quote a passage from "The Runner" which
will perhaps show both its strength and its weaknesses. An
American infantry company is on the front near Bastogne in
1944. It is winter. The Americans are retreating. There have
been rumors all night that the company is being left to face the
Germans alone. Suddenly near dawn, the German tanks appear.

> At the foot of the slope
> The trees were shaking, parting. There emerged
> A cannon barrel with a muzzle-brake.
> It slid out like a snake's head, slowly swinging.
> It paused. A flash of light came from its head
> . . . .
> The tank was growing large.
> The cannon flashed. Machinegun tracers curved
> Toward it, and played sparkling on the steel.
> Still it came on, glittering in return
> From its machineguns. Then, a crashing flame
> Struck it, leaving a trail of smoke in air.
> The tank shuddered. It slewed broadside around.
> Inside the plates, as on an anvil, hammers
> Were laboring. It trembled with explosions,
> And smoke poured out of it.
>
> The slope was still,
> Sprawling with hooded figures—and the rest
> Gone back into the trees. Then there began
> The sound of the wounded.

The writing is very strong, but its power is in the decision of the
visual imagination, not in the rhythm or diction. It is as if one
were sitting in a sunlit room with clouded windowpanes. The
strength comes from the sun, but the light is dimmed. The
rhythm reminding one of Wordsworth clouds the pane, and the
diction, which is neither unusual nor inadequate, but more or
less what one would expect, also dims the light. The poet is
describing new experiences and inner sensations, for which there
is no extensive precedent in English poetry, with a rhythm and

diction developed in another century for totally different moods and events. Because the poem is divided against itself, a prosiness comes in. This division is a profound problem in American poetry: we have many new experiences and no real way to write about them. The older poetry of the sonnet, of the *Prelude,* is of very little help.

Embarking on a poem with such an intractable subject matter, a poet might decide not to do it at all—or to wait twenty years hoping he will have an appropriate line by then. Mr. Simpson chose to write it now, using whatever form seemed to him most appropriate. The poem fails, but this failure is worth many successes.

In Mr. Simpson's work generally one is surprised by the appearance of unpleasant public realities such as the Second World War, or the gas chambers, for instance. This is one reason I think so highly of *A Dream of Governors;* there is a great reluctance among poets recently to bring such subjects in poetry. Writers such as James Merrill, for example, would never think of it; his idea of poetry does not include long wars. The war or its concentration camps to not break the composure of W. D. Snodgrass's book, nor Robert Creeley's—and no sane man demands that they must. Still, to be able to hold in the mind these ghastly facts and poetry at the same time is a great achievement. I do not know another American writer who has attempted a serious poem on the Nazis, yet the Nazis are as clearly a part of our world as the old Italian campaigns were of Hemingway's, or the subways and bridges of Crane's.

In the fine poem called "The Bird," a Nazi kills Jews mournfully to the tune of his favorite song, "I wish I were a little bird." When the Russians liberate the camp, the Nazi is nowhere to be found. He has evidently turned into a bird, for the Russian colonel, writing his report, sees a small bird singing outside in a tree. I am very interested in these strange shifts of reality. In another poem, an American soldier dreams he is in Paris during the First World War. Looking up, he sees two old biplanes fighting, and realizes he is a French soldier, and that some long-dead French soldier fought through the Second World War in his uniform. Mr. Simpson's poetry at times is like a man who sits in a livingroom quietly talking, and gradually smoke begins to come out of his ears, and to gather over his head. This sudden shift from one kind of reality to another seems to me one of the major qualities of his poems.

I am also interested in the poetry about America. "America is old." "We were the first to enter on the modern age." "America begins antiquity." Mr. Simpson treats America somewhat as the Russian writers treat Russia—they talk about their country, and give what ideas they have. Mr. Simpson offers the metaphor of "Pure space" for America—where there is nothing but an infinite freedom to look. Lacking any monuments of grief or suffering, the land remains wild or inhuman.

> The country that Columbus thought he found
> Is called America. It looks unreal.

But man came:

> And murdering, in a religious way,
> Brings Jesus to the Gulf of Mexico.

His poetry is in one sense the opposite of the poetry of Jiménez, who wanted his poems to be "all present and no history." Mr. Simpson insists that the past be somehow in the poem.

The first poem in *A Dream of Governors* is a short history of the West from pastoral Greece to the present. The recent growth of the secular powers, such as America, greeted with such cries of joy from Hillyer, Ciardi, and the other poets of the Uplift, is described in this way:

> Old Aristotle, having seen this pass,
> From where he studied in the giant's cave,
> Went in and shut his book and locked the brass,
> And lay down with a shudder in his grave.

The reviews of the book were strange. In the *Saturday Review,* Winfield Townley Scott has an incredibly stupid review of *A Dream of Governors* in which he dismisses it as light verse. On the contrary, Louis Simpson's poetry, unlike the optimistic verse of the forties, has a darkness and a suffering, without any schemes to avoid them.

In the first article on Mr. Simpson's work, in the *Fifties,* no. 1, I criticized Mr. Simpson for disharmony between form and content. He sometimes gives the effect of being simply lazy, and choosing any form that will do, just as people going to the Front commandeer any old car. At other times, he gives the effect of tremendous vigor and strength, pushing a subject to its limits. In his tragic feeling he is alone in his generation.

3

Louis Simpson has a considerable gift for the image with unconscious ingredients, "the drugstore glows softly, like a sleeping body." In *Searching for the Ox,* he lets that gift lie. He's tired of that. He's going to let others do it; there are lots of imitators paddling on the waters of the unconscious in small kayaks. He's gone off on a tack this time, alone, and I'll try to describe that tack, as I understand it from this book.

Couldn't we say that images, when used by a genius, make up a kind of living face of the unknown? We are quietly watching that face as we read a poem; all at once the face opens an eye unexpectedly, and we shudder . . . for somewhere inside, our feelings respond to that. An eye in us opens. So a group of images can convey from one person to another the expression on the face of the unconscious as it turns.

How many other faces do we know for the unconscious? Well, the Sufis use funny stories as a face, and they work. By "work," I mean they bypass the blocks of the overcivilized mind and penetrate to our living intelligence instantly. Music is a sort of mask or face . . . sometimes so well fitted that we weep hearing it, probably at the same places the composer wept. The occult theories of alchemy make a face. And there is another face few people think of—the ordinary details of daily life. I mean the details that actually happen! Simpson decided to stake his book on these. After all, if the unconscious is truly powerful, why shouldn't its secret face be utterly visible in the banal details of what happened? Do we think the unconscious is so weak it can only influence the minds of Surrealist poets? It must also influence the choice of records a drunk puts on just before he falls asleep; it must influence the sounds you hear after coming back from a date with a woman attached to her parents; it must influence what the movers do when they come to cart away furniture from a house after a divorce. (In the last instance, Simpson says, the movers tore up the poster of Adlai Stevenson and burned it in the fireplace, put African drums on the stereo and went stomping around.)

Every detail in the poem "Baruch" is ordinary. I think "Baruch" is a masterpiece, so I'll concentrate on it as an example of the best poems in the book. One of the greatest qualities human beings have is longing—longing for spiritual labor. "He wishes to study the Torah." In the world of consciousness, a division so many humans have experienced is the conflict between the longing spirit and the banal details of working for a living, raising children, talking each day with a wife or a husband. "He wishes to study the Torah / But he has a wife and family." Apparently the unconscious wants human beings to experience more of the unknown, whether it is the undiscovered ocean and its terrors—as in Melville—or the weirdness of the edges of the mind-area, as in parapsychology. But for such discovery we need training, or the unknown can kill us.

All of this is said in the first section of "Baruch." Baruch could not give in to his longing to study the Torah because he owned a dress-hat factory. One night it burns down. That detail is right—as Melville and Hawthorne would say. An event in the physical world hides behind it a spiritual truth, namely, between heavy earth details and the intensity of spirit-air lies fire, the only way to move from one to the other. So, when fire takes his business, relieved, Baruch gives himself to the Word:

> And he did from that day on,
> reading Rashi and Maimonides.
> He was halfway over the *Four Mountains*
> when one day, in the midst of his studying,
> Lev Baruch fell sick and died.
> For in Israel it is also written,
> "Prophecy is too great a thing for Baruch."

In part 2 of "Baruch," Simpson goes over the ground again of the conflict between *logos* longing and this world, showing how it can influence a woman's life. Cousin Deborah had read too much. Literature was her ghostly lover, she was engaged to

Pushkin, the intellect was her ghostly husband. What chance did a man have competing with that?

> On her wedding day she wept,
> and at night when they locked her in
> she kicked and beat on the door.
> She screamed. So much for the wedding!
> As soon as it was daylight, Brodsky—
> that was his name—drove back to Kiev
> like a man pursued, with his horses.

What is left to say in part 3? Well, Simpson could talk about Americans. He does:

> Even here in this rich country
> Scripture enters and sits down
> and lives with us like a relative.
> Taking the best chair in the house . . .

He mentions that those who love literature often live among frayed carpets, walls with cracks in them. Then he restates the conflict again, brilliantly. This time we are on a train. Life on a train is banal. The wonderful banality of life that is so appealing, and makes such a genuine contrast to learning, is represented by a smoker car, with four or five men playing poker, happily, late at night. After the card playing, the male intelligence is alone, watching prairie lights; and the pale face from the unconscious appears, floating above the meadows and trees, reminding the man the love of the Torah is immortal. "He wishes to study the Torah." What has living in another country got to do with it? The love of learning never dies.

We notice there are no wild images. Every detail is tied into this stolid, hopelessly banal world, and yet these "flat" details make up a true and living mask for the face of the unconscious. The unconscious gives us its haunting look, which means, "Oh, God, are you going to be loyal to Ramon Lull's book or to your family?" And we see that look. The eyes alive, looking at us.

What can we say about that? I have to say, terrific. What else can I say? In art, I want to see the "unknown" looking at me. I have a great thirst for that. I drink it in Conrad, in Chekhov, in *The Sorrows of Young Werther,* in *Moby Dick,* in Russel Edson, in some Persian paintings, in a hundred works of art and psychological speculation. I don't have time to think, "It's better than so and so and worse than the generation of Pound." If a man or a woman in art slowly creates a face we do not expect, we know that if we look at it closely, we will see the face of the unknown looking back. The face of the unknown is capable of many expressions, some that are so ecstatic we close our eyes, others that make the chest thump, as when an ant looks at us, but I am learning to judge poetry by how many looks I get in a book. If I get one or two, I am grateful for years and keep the book near me.

My words are a clumsy description of Louis Simpson's venture in this book. The advantages are clear: the poem is rooted well in this world, and by leaving the image, it adapts itself to the narrative; by leaving the private realm, it opens itself to other characters besides the poet.

What are the disadvantages of it? Most of us are asleep, having absorbed some sleepiness from tables and chairs and stoplights. By sticking to our details, you are liable to describe people who are asleep. Secondly, objects get thick. We know the unconscious has elements in it that are eternal. When the poet concentrates on banal details, these details seem to take on something of the eternal. We get the sense that things are permanent. It seems as if things could not be otherwise than they are. Louis Simpson apparently has taken on this conviction. I'll quote his poem about Hannibal in its entirety:

> At times I am visited by a donkey
> who was once the great soldier Hannibal.
>
> The reason he didn't take Rome,
> he says, was a fear of success.
>
> Now that he has been psychoanalyzed
> he would, he is confident, rise to the occasion.
>
> But then he wouldn't be Hannibal.
> People would say, "It's a donkey."

> So, once more, Hannibal has decided. . .
> Moreover, if he succeeded it wouldn't be Rome.

The conclusion of the poem seems to be that the substructure of events is impenetrable to unconscious or conscious will. If Hannibal had not turned back, he wouldn't be Hannibal. So, in this brave attempt to give the hard objects of the world attention, he gives them too much attention, and the inner transformative energies are lost sight of. We then experience the poem as circular and suffocating, in much the same way daily life is experienced as circular and suffocating. The book has a number of poems with the last mood. Banal details seem to block every way out.

And yet, a number of poems, among them, "The Stevenson Poster," "The Middleaged Man," "The Sanctuaries," and "The Tree Seat" are rich and brilliant. They have the fragrance of the unknown in them, achieved by means of this difficult and unusual discipline.

DAVE SMITH

A Child of the World

In 1967, M. L. Rosenthal, in *The New Poets,* described a number of poets he found to have some tenuous connection with Robert Bly's the *Sixties* and said of them: "this group, which includes Robert Bly, Donald Hall, Louis Simpson, James Wright, and James Dickey, is seeking to affect the aims of American poetry." If that sounds like an ominous and card-carrying cartel, one can only say that Rosenthal deserves high marks for a half-correct prescience. Though I think it is arguable that American poetry had *aims,* clearly the poets have affected the nature and direction of the art. Whether it was the bottle and filler of traditional verse or the "I-like-Ike" hypocrisy of "all's right with the Republic" that stung such poets into a conviction that poetry was not what it ought to be is for scholars to sift and weigh as is their wont. We know the poets wanted something that wasn't coming up on the Wurlitzer. They wanted something personal though, with obviously differing opinions, they were inclined to refuse mere personality with its eccentricities: postures, fantasies, self-deceit, solipsisms, hermetic escapisms—all those soapboxes of assertion which publicly seemed to have no more real authority than the monkish sign-carriers of doom in so many cartoons.

More than two decades have passed since the first books of these poets appeared and while it is still unclear that any of their names will name the literary age to be described in anthologies years hence, no serious reader of poetry can be unaware that each has affected not only what American poetry is but also what it might be. If it is impossible to think of Bly, Hall, Simpson, Wright, and Dickey as conspirators of one mind, it is nevertheless true that together they have created the poetry of a

American Poetry Review 8 (January/February 1979): 11–15. Reprinted in *Local Assays: On Contemporary American Poetry* (Urbana: University of Illinois Press, 1985), 148–62, copyright © 1985 by the University of Illinois.

surfaced, examined, and revitalized inner life, a life not simply of the mind but of the personalized mind. They have been noisy, exuberant, truculent, testy, and necessary—like many children in a house too small. Of Rosenthal's appointed group, perhaps the quietest and least public and even least affective on younger poets has been Louis Simpson.

A practicing Christian would surely remind me here that the least shall enter Heaven first and a good case for that could be made on Simpson's behalf. In the end it is not going to be noise or influence that matters, but the durable quality and scope of achieved art. No one of that grouping seems to have so steadily and honestly gone on creating a credible and shareable vision of life in this world, in these times, more than Simpson has. It is, of course, not necessary to reduce the value and accomplishment of another poet to praise Simpson. I have no wish to do that. I only say that the poetry of Louis Simpson seems to me extraordinarily beautiful and complex, that it demonstrates an engagement with the vicissitudes and antinomies of American life in the 1960s and 1970s that is equal to the best we have, and that it may even possess a greater, quieter power of staying because it is extremely accessible. Accessible, yes, but scarcely without the deep resonance and luminosity of an imaginative intelligence whose reach is inward and outward, vertical and horizontal at the same time. Quoting Goethe, Simpson has called himself "the child of the world in the middle." In his seventh collection, *Searching for the Ox,* Simpson has extended that middle world beyond the prophets right and left, creating a remarkable vision of fundamentally human ground upon which, sooner or later, we all must stand.

Louis Simpson's poetry is marked by its steady development in two directions. From the beginning he has wanted a synthetic vision, hence his attraction to Whitman, which would discover and fix the true nature of human existence and which, moreover, would reaffirm traditional and timeless values of the human as social and responsible creature who might, nevertheless, intuit some binding, beyond-reason force. He has been, therefore, a consistently moral and ethical poet. Not, I insist quickly, a moralistic poet, one who writes a poetry that bends our ears with a prefabricated polemic. He has not been a ferocious preacher in the manner of Bly, but he has been a kind of conscience in the way of James Wright. And, like Wright, Simpson has always found himself equipped with an ironic voice, a disposition toward a poetry of steely intelligence which would play Mercutio to a poetry of romantic moaning in the dark bushes. It is this second strain in his poetry which accounts for his frequent humor, satire, social comment, good citizenry, and, ultimately, the evolution of his mature poetic style. Simpson has come far from that ideal music of the 1950s. His language now, as Randall Jarrell would say, is often clear enough even for cats and dogs. He has come to a certain unfashionable narrative base, to a poetry that unabashedly employs the devices of prose fiction. But not, it should be noted, to the fashionable prose-poem, for he appears to believe he can still detect a valuable difference between poetry and prose, a difference that is marked by the continued prominence of such tensions and ironies as are generated by the contending of mind and heart under equal pressure.

Louis Simpson has made a poetry out of ourselves who want mystical unity, harmony, and escape from the almost unendurable brutalities of the world; but he has also made it out of ourselves who are grinning realists, who know that escape from the difficulties of being human, especially in poetry whose function is to help us be more human, serves the forces of brutalization and division. Simpson has never forgotten, moralist and artist as he is, that a poem must have an audience before it is a true poem, that such a poem is a bridge to somewhere and to someone. His poems, therefore, are always testing their own authority and reality—they are always having to prove their right to exist—for he has wanted what he has increasingly created, an art which speaks in plain language about subjects experienced in a social world of ordinary people. He says, "I have a sort of Wordsworthian vision: a picture of a very ordinary human being who is also highly intelligent and likes to read poetry; he is the one I write for. This man knows what a garage looks like, this man knows what a milk-bottle sounds like on the back porch in the morning." Simpson does not aspire to mass pablum, however, but to a total and authentic communication through art, a speaking that is both deeply personal and broadly human. He says:

Total poetry, like the total human being, must include so-called rational as well as irrational states—the poem must be logical as well as unpredictable. Images that move us do so because they are connected to logical thought processes which we all share. They are connected to the psyche of the author and an understandable feeling, or idea if you prefer, underlying the poem. Poetry in which there are no dream states is trivial, but dream images may be trivial also when they are produced by automatic writing, without a necessary direction by the psyche of the poet.

More than his contemporaries, then, Simpson has searched for a poetry which would not be content with either a fabric of associational images and an esoteric mysticism or a poetry of received ideas and rational discourse. Though his early work demonstrated the traditional, literate, and neatly cadenced character of late Modernism, there was also a strain of fresh diction which was not decorative figuring but muscular nomination. He moved away from the poem *bien fait,* closer to that diction which James Wright called the "poetry of a grown man." Increasingly he has employed rhythms and organizational units which parallel actual human speech, knowing it was this speech which would allow the resonance of both personal and mythic, or psychic if you will, depths. This direction has meant a reliance on image juxtaposition that has seemed to some critics to keep him in lockstep with Robert Bly, but he has never been truly illogical or surreal. While others have gravitated toward hermetic languages of utter personality, toward European modes of the fabular, toward anecdotal journalism, Simpson, like Wordsworth, sought a dialect of the actually spoken. He has told stories in a parabolic speech of local roots. It is no accident that he has often praised William Carlos Williams. It is as if he had believed everything in the phenomenal world might speak if the right plain language could be wrestled to the purpose. The risk, and he has sometimes succumbed to it, has been a loss of tension, a flattened music, a prose. The gain has been that widened world of experience which is not *merely* personal, which is never gamesmanship or buffoonery, which is recognizably diverse, contradictory, mature, and immediate. He has come to a poetry that, as he says, "addresses itself to the human condition, a poetry of truth, not dreams . . . [that] depicts human actions and the way we live. Poetry must express the reality behind appearances . . . This poetry will frequently be in the form of a narrative. Not a mere relation of events, but a narrative of significant actions."

It is Simpson's insistence on "significant actions" which has led him to reject the poetries of tonal effects, assertion, dream fragments. Such poetries, apparently do not provide enough of the objective life. They do not, arguably, cause poetry to help provide designs for healthy living based on historical values such as love, pride, piety, responsibility, etc. The drive toward a literature (I do not think Simpson would find that word offensive) of moral and ethical service must employ but go beyond the eccentric collisions of image, just as art goes beyond anecdote. Simpson wants to look *through* the events and language of the common world to what he has intuited: a kind of changeless reality. He says, "The happening, or the mere field of events, is very little. . . . The real problem of fiction is what is the significance of these events?" That is, what good will these arrangements of word and action, these reflectors of reality, do for anyone? The evident answer is that appropriate actions appropriately arranged, and memorably, will allow a reasonable reader to experience the extrapersonal continuous world. Simpson is neither a poet of the deep image nor of the personality. Like Whitman he contains many selves who go adventuring within the letter *I*. Some of them see synthesis, some of them see division.

Searching for the Ox contains less than half-a-dozen poems which are not remarkable for motion, for this adventuring. Here someone is always walking, wandering, motoring—engaging in a ruminative movement which observes people, landscapes, circumstances, the thingness of community. The first poem, "Venus in the Tropics," begins "One morning when I went over to Bournemouth," and we are immediately placed by a gesture characteristic of the collection. There are no obscurities, no psychic or metaphoric flights, no elaborating descriptions, only an action that takes us from a closed world to an open one. In this event we hear the story of Peter, Simpson's name for a character created out of the memory of himself as a boy. It is an initiation story in which Peter discovers ugliness through American sailors, the gauds of city life, prostitutes, and the unknown humanity of his family. Protected from such worldly "truths" by his relatives and driven back to his Caribbean home, the boy remains isolated—but through his memories we learn what subtle changes come in the first growth of vision. The poem also provides certain vital images which recur in Simpson's poetry:

> I sat by the pool at Bournemouth
> reading *Typhoon*.
> I had the pool all to myself,
> the raft, the diving boards, and the rings.
> There wasn't a living soul.
>
> Not a voice—just rustling palm leaves
> and the tops of the coconuts
> moving around in circles.
>
> In the afternoon a wind sprang up,
> blowing from the sea to land,
> covering the harbor with whitecaps.
>
> It smelled of shells and seaweed,
> and something else—perfume.

The poem's invocation of Conrad does two things: it sets youth's early vision of simplistic hero-dreaming as a base against the book's drive toward maturity and it evokes a master of moral and ethical inquiry. The last two stanzas also invoke Ernest Hemingway's "Ten Indians"—whose concern is with sexual and ethical initiation. Simpson's poem, of course, generates greater compression as it works more in the direction of archetypal rather than rounded experience. His intention is to lead us to that "perfume" which may make the whole curvature and complexity of sexual knowledge, its joy and pain, suddenly visible.

Simpson's echoes of Hemingway and Conrad derive from his wish to create a language of precise nomination in which appearance and reality, with minimal intrusion by the author's personality, stand in subtle but bright opposition. Events in the world, after all, do not ordinarily come with a gloss, though they are not less meaningful for that. The poet's task in his arrangement of words is to release meaning.

Simpson's second poem, "Dinner at the Sea-View Inn," suggests Hemingway's "Hills like White Elephants" and is, essentially, a short story of dialect and scene. Peter, now a young adult, has had dinner with Marie and her parents. He and Marie go for a walk during which he wants to tell her something of his perceptions about how things are in the world:

> "When I was a child," said Peter,
> "I used to think that the waves were cavalry . . .
> the way they come in, curling over."
>
> She said, "Is that what you were in,
> the calvary?"
>
> He laughed, "Calvary? For Christ's sake . . ."

The literate and sensitive young man recognizes the irony of Marie's mistake. He is reaching for an image of vitality and motion and she has transposed it to an image of death. Marie is offended, yet Peter understands it has been, somehow, a moment of insight for him. Returned to his apartment, he begins to see how the moment and the event reveal the bittersweet flow of life:

> Lying in bed, hands clasped beneath his head,
> listening . . .
>
> to the stopping and starting of traffic
> in the street five floors below.
> And the opening of the elevator,
> and the sound of feet going down the corridor.

All of the poems in the first section of Searching for the Ox are such moments of maturation and recognition. As Simpson writes, "all the voyage would be inward" and in "The Psyche of Riverside Drive" Peter visits his old professor of literature who tells him that "the visible world was a dream." Once Peter would have believed that but now he knows that "there is a difference between dreaming and waking," though false art and weak intelligences may blur the difference. Confused now, and feeling betrayed, Peter abandons the counsel of his professor and seeks "the solidity / and resonance of the sidewalk under his feet." He has become the proto-American, dreamer and pragmatist, an exile in his native land. Now he falls back to the first language of perception: feeling.

> There is always some passionate race
> that has just arrived in America.
>
> And a fragrance, *pimienta,*
> the wind brings over the sea.

In "Lorenzo," Simpson's Peter has become a fledgling writer, another sort of exile, and the experience which initiates is that of visiting novelist Harry Ascham on *his* island, of entering the metier of D. H. Lawrence and "Tom Eliot"—all exemplars of the tradition into which he hopes to fit his individual talent. He moves from first awe to the sad recognition of what a pitiful and magnificent thing is the man who would write:

> Sitting among these stones
> I listened to the dry leaves rustling
> and thought of a poet's life.
> *Genus irritabile vatum.*
> Because he longs for Beauty
> with man he grows enraged.

Speaking in Eliot's tones Peter sees Eliot as the dry leaf no young man quite expects to become. He would be a susceptible prophet on whom nothing is lost, with sensitivity and glamor, a universal wayfarer among angels. Yet there is Ascham, an example of the plain, sad end most writers come to. But also there is Lawrence "bending his neck to the yoke / of local speech and custom . . . / whatever smells of the earth." Or is this Ascham that Simpson describes? Simpson has tried to be so clear in contrasting the failed and the worldly successful writer that one can't quite tell who is who. Perhaps the implication, for Peter, is that any writer is a little of both.

Simpson called the first section of this book "Venus in the Tropics" in order to indicate the tangled and initial confusion of love at its sources. He calls the second section "The Company of Flesh and Blood" to suggest a further movement into the social world. Peter is now "five years in publishing" but has discovered little of the inner life's intuited connection with the visibly shabby life around him. He must now learn, if his engagement is to be with art rather than publishing and commerce, to go beyond the surface. He encounters a manuscript which frames for him his feelings of both discontinuity and isolation as well as a sense of communal identity. He writes, "Words are realities. They have the power / to make us feel and see." Echoing the Romantic manifestos as well as Conrad, it is a bluntness which any aggressive young editor might bridle at, yet the manuscript, those words, changes Peter's life; it turns him from publishing to writing. Peter undertakes the writer's mission, a mission that is not entirely attractive since there must be nothing marginal about it. The true writer stands outside the superficially committed who are but people with the one story of their lives, just as he is most essentially outside the more ordinary society. In "The Stevenson Poster," Simpson reveals what Peter will give up for art: a lucrative job, comfortable circumstances, expensive possessions, various political stances, all the illusions of normal prosperity and happiness—for the educated and upwardly mobile young people. Instead, with luck, he must apprentice himself to the imaging and creation of character and truth. He must become a messenger of the true news. At best, he may feel he is not "missing out on life." With this choice, he begins to read "a deeper significance / into everything," not manipulating the world, but allowing the world to reveal its perpetual and significant speech. This starts with his reading of the manuscript written by a paranoid woman—which, as it reveals a distorted, divided reality, he rejects. Peter has begun to look both *at* things and *through* things in "The Hour of Feeling," a poem Simpson identifies as an advance in his art because it marks the discovery of love, the power through which inert phenomena achieve meaning. In consequence, Peter makes further discoveries. He had thought significant art required an excess of emotion to the point of illness ("You have to be mad, that's the catch") but learns it requires feeling tempted by labor, steady attention, intelligence, and self-argument:

I sit down to write . . .

An hour later the table is covered
                with words.
And then I start crossing them out.

The remaining poems of section 2 dramatize the refusal of glib and received public truths and show the artist asking of each thing and each event: "What is it to me?" By structuring his collection in the quasi-plot form of a fictional and spiritual auto-biography, Simpson brings his reader into the progress of his own mind, though without a single indeterminate *you* of address. Effectively, he forces us to look for ourselves, as Conrad has said he would make us *see*.

Perhaps because of his intention to create a poetry leavened with ideas, Simpson has provided a preface to his collection and in it he tells us, of his third section, "Poems in the third part are more meditative; they are about a way of life." These seven poems are dense narratives but their story lines seem less important than a substructure of imagery drawn from Zen Buddhist writing, an imagery which creates an architecture of knowing. In "Chimneys" a speaker walks to a cliff overlooking a harbor and describes the far shore. The posture of exile has become the posture of inbetweenness. In "Cliff Road" this posture is extended to a line of fishermen "surfcasting, in absolute silence" at the New York seashore. Exemplary figures, both Platonic and literal,

"Two fishermen, wearing straw hats
that conceal their faces. They look Chinese.
The boat in which they sit seems to be drifting
on images—of the shore, with trees
and a white cloud standing over."

These fishermen, described in "The Sanctuaries," are only images in the speaker's mind, not literal observations. They are reminiscent, too, of Yeats's Chinamen who stare at the "tragic scene" with their serene, gay eyes. What is important here is that Simpson has been building a single, vital pattern of imagery—of the sea, water's thoughtlike movement, shores, and that sifting, imagining observer who stands nowhere really, or stands midway between a human landscape and that yearned-for other shore. Because we most immediately know the physical, Simpson shows us the sea through acute sensory images: we see, we smell, we hear, and this leads into the untouched depth of memory where the self, or selves, resides. In a poem from his earlier collection, *Adventures of the Letter I,* Simpson shows his intention:

PORT JEFFERSON

My whole life coming to this place,
and understanding it better
maybe for having been born
offshore, and at an early age
left to my own support . . .

I have come where sea and wind,
wave and leaf, are one sighing,
where the house strains at an anchor
and the salt-rose clings and clambers
on the humorous grave.

This is the place, Camerado,
that hides the sea-bird's nest.
Listening to the distant voices
in summer, a murmur of the sea,
I seem to remember everything.

Simpson recalls love's promise in the tropics, that Eden, and recalls a time before division from place, people, and continuity. He seems indeed, in his assumption of Whitman's expanded personality, to contain all history, all human events, all emotion. Ironically he stands on the ground of promise which he had described in "Lines Written near San Francisco" and "the land / The pioneers looked for, shading their eyes / Against the sun— a murmur of serious life." Simpson's careful working of image patterns means to suggest the internal and the external life is one, and is always a journey. Consider what he is attempting in the light of this passage from the *Manual of Zen Buddhism* (D. T. Suzuki, Grove Press): "What is *Paramita?* This is a Sanskrit term of the Western country. In T'ang it means 'the other shore reached.' When the meaning (*artha* in Sanskrit) is understood, one is detached from birth and death. When the objective world (*visaya*) is clung to, there is the rise of birth and death; it is like waves rising from the water; this is called 'this shore.' When you are detached from the objective world, there is no birth and death for you; it is like the water constantly running its course: this is 'reaching the other shore.' " In Zen, the "other shore" symbolizes great wisdom. We are at liberty to examine the connection of Simpson's poetry with Zen vision since he has told us that the third section of the book defines a way of life and since the book's title is taken from Zen writing.

"Searching for the Ox," the title poem of the fourth section as well as of Simpson's collection, is obliquely related to a series of ten oxherding pictures by Kakuan Sji-en, a Zen master of the Sung dynasty. The pictures seem to be a visual parable of the process by which man moves from an ordinary unenlightened state of the spirit (the condition of dualism or division) to the state of Buddha in which he experiences and exists in what is called, variously, the Essence, Oneness, Suchness, etc. It is extremely difficult for me to discuss this mystical process, having no experience in Zen understanding. (Yet if the poem is successful it must have an accessibility to those who haven't Zen knowledge, though perhaps it will be richer for those who have it.) Zen writing says, however, that one reaches Buddhism only when one makes no assertive definition about it. For example, "When one attains this stage of realization, seeing is no-seeing, hearing is no-hearing, preaching is no-preaching." Or, again, "The Essence is neither in the world nor of the world, nor is it outside the world."

The idea is that a man is betrayed by the assertions of his mind so long as he is disconnected from the Essence. Discontinuous, he is said to be "astray" and thereby will be fooled by a false vision of dualism. The first portrait in the oxherding series, "Searching for the Ox," carries this gloss: "The beast has gone astray, and what is the use of searching for him? The reason why the oxherd is not on intimate terms with him is because the oxherd has violated his inmost nature. The beast is lost, for the oxherd has himself been led out of the way through his deluding senses. His home is receding farther away from him, and by-ways and crossways are ever confused. Desire for gain and fear of loss burn like fire; ideas of right and wrong shoot up like a phalanx" (D. T. Suzuki, *Manual of Zen Buddhism*).

Interestingly, this picture contains no ox while the cover portrait on Simpson's book contains no man and features the ox. In the Zen series the ox is the symbol of man's spirit-soul-connection with Buddha. The man in the parable has to track, find, tame, and ride the ox. When this has happened, both man and ox disappear into the "serenity of non-assertion." Inner and outer life are fused, continuous.

Simpson's "Searching for the Ox" is divided into five parts. In section 1 we hear the speaker has "the one face that will listen / to any incoherent aimless story." We are told "There is something in disorder that calls to me. / Out there beyond the harbor," and that caller is the far shore of great wisdom. But the speaker tells us of his discontinuity:

> I have stayed outside and watched
> the shadow-life of the interior,
> feeling myself apart from it.

Section 2 contrasts this intuited inner life with the public disciplines of "engineering, law" which dominate contemporary life and generate enormous but superficial power. These the speaker rejects, saying "They will send me off to Heaven / when all I want is to live in the world." Section 3 appears to suggest that all disciplines which take us out of this world are distortions; it says, "The search for the ox continues." Section 4, reinforcing the need to live by the inner discipline, says, quoting Cavafy, " 'As you have wasted your life here in this corner / you have ruined it all over the world.' " There follows a tableau of social life which is continuous in the things and the people of the world. In the fifth section Simpson directly approaches, for the first time, the Zen portrait:

> Following in the Way
> that "regards sensory experience as relatively unimportant,"
> and that aims to teach the follower

"to renounce what one is attached to"—
in spite of this dubious gift
that would end by negating poetry altogether,
in the practice of meditating
on the breath, I find my awareness
of the world—the cry of a bird,
susurrus of tires, the wheezing

of the man in the chair next to me—
has increased. That every sound
falls like a pebble into a well,
sending out ripples that seem to be continuing
through the universe. Sound has a tail
that whips around the corner;
I try not to follow. In any case,
I find I am far more aware
of the present, sensory life.

I seem to understand what the artist
was driving at; every leaf stands clear
and separate. The twig seems to quiver
with intellect. Searching for the ox
I come upon a single hoofprint.
I find the ox, and tame it,
and lead it home. In the next scene
the moon has risen, a cool light.
Both the ox and herdsman vanished.

There is only earth:
in winter laden with snow,
in summer covered with leaves.

Simpson now appears to have entered the parable in order to
express apprehension of a singular life, the inner and outer made
one. Choosing to live well within the vicissitudes of this world
but rejecting "desire for gain and fear of loss," he will not yearn
for another shore but attempt to turn more intensely the light of
the mind to the shore where he stands. Simpson has placed
himself in a Keatsian circumstance and he has realized that to
have crossed—even in the assertions of the imagination—to that
other shore would have been to lose the chance to become more

human. Extrapersonal visions are, he seems to feel, both escapist and without truth. His conclusion suggests that his poetry will be the act of knowing better the ordinary reality of life. Or does it?

I have said that Simpson's ironic second voice prevents him from the lyrical assertion which is not tested by felt experience. Why has he told us that the twig quivers with intellect rather than feeling? And why is it that "the ox and herdsman" have vanished rather than the "ox and I"? Is it possible there is a countermovement even to the Zen mysticism? One of the great strengths of Simpson's poetry, to my way of thinking, has been his refusal to accept an unearned vision of transcendence. In the final poem of *Adventures of the Letter I,* he wrote: "And now we talk of 'the inner life,' / and I ask myself, where is it?" Having been a geographical orphan who was compelled to argument with his adopted country, Simpson is, similarly, an orphan of belief. He argues with himself about what may be believed. He is not, I think, a Zen believer but is merely using an imagery which may help to make visible certain values which must be true, primarily that life is good and that art helps us to "prove" it so. It is not that the inner life is less beautiful or necessary than jacket copy says it is, but that the kind and quality of that life is as complex and hard to know as external life. In his poem "Big Dream, Little Dream," based on a Jungian description of the Elgonyi tribal belief, Simpson examines the power of the big (some would say racial, some would say archetypal) dream to produce images which might be translated into human action. All images are not wonderful; some may be dangerous. In his poem, the American president has a big dream "and before you know it there is war." Unless I am far off the mark, Simpson is suggesting that it is the artist's moral responsibility (which is a function of the quality of his intellect and his feeling fused in art) to be certain of the effect and value of the images he summons from the inner life. In 1974, Simpson said in the *Ohio Review:* "There is a belief that poetry must be only about the 'inner life'—anything else is not poetry. The effect of this poetry is to reduce poems to a few lines, the barest perception. I once heard someone speak of the works of one American poet as 'ghost poems,' and indeed what is going on at present in some sectors is a Ghost Dance. The cure, I think, is by means of drama and narrative to bring into poetry the feelings people have for one another. Nothing can come of the feelings they have, or say they have, for darkness and stones."

Simpson would, doubtless, argue that there is no division between the inner and outer life except for those who have gone "astray" and would argue that what poetry must do is find a direct and clear way of making this life, its Oneness, as fully visible as it was in whatever tropics we came from. He says, "People want the sights and sounds of life; they ask for life in poetry. They ask for bread, but instead they have been given stones." Putting aside the frustration and despair common to all poets, Simpson's idea of a missing sustenance in poetry is emphatic. In the final section of his book the poems are dramas of loss both witnessed by and consoled through art. They are also poems of search and of momentary joys in this world.

Simpson does not give us gratuitous harvest of bread, but he does give art's recognition of the life right under our noses, a portrait of ourselves. The plot of his collection is that ultimate search for the names of men, for realities. In the events, the actions, the momentary actors we are, what we do is to seek the ox of our spirits. We would not have it tamed exactly, but would see it and know it steadily for awhile. This search allows for a dramatic meditation on the nature of being and, implicitly, for ethical discrimination. Simpson's poems lead us to the sanctuary of the self where each one must stare at the wall, an act the Zennists call Pi-Kuan ("abandoning the false and embracing the true")—which is one of two ways of entering the Path to the Essence. The end of mature vision is surely balance, is knowing. In "The Shelling Machine" Simpson writes:

> In turn, I have changed the machine.
> No one else would have stopped to look at it—
> certainly none of the people
> who work there every day in the field.

The act of looking is the act of Pi-Kuan and everything in the world, most especially those intricate machines which are people, is the wall we must stare at. Look hard and with love, says Louis Simpson, and there is the knowing which gives us pleasure, hope, instruction, and—for the artist—images of courage.

Simpson finds the trail of the ox even in a poker game. Here is my own favorite from *Searching for the Ox,* a blessing:

THE DALED

Across the room the night city editor
has turned his face toward me
with a curious, mild stare.
Waiting for copy . . .

Later in the evening there will be a crowd
at Jack's. Discussing sports . . .
Some old codger holding forth—
what His Honor said to the Commissioner.
And there will be the usual four.

According to an ancient fable
there are thirty-six "hidden saints."
It could be the tailor, the shoemaker,
it could be a Regular Army colonel—
as long as there are thirty-six
the world will not come to an end.

Also there are the Daled—four newspapermen
who are always playing poker.
As long as this situation continues
God will hold back the final catastrophe.
"What's that? It sounds like water."
"Wait a minute," says Shapiro.
"We're here to play cards. Whose deal is it?"

"I'll see your five," says Flanagan,
"and raise it."
                    So the game goes on
from week to week. I have known them to begin
late at night when everything is silent
and to play right through till dawn.

HANK LAZER

Louis Simpson and Walt Whitman
Destroying the Teacher

With regard to recent American poetry, it is easy and fruitful to trace the influence of Walt Whitman. Particularly with the revolution in style that began in the mid-fifties with Allen Ginsberg's *Howl and Other Poems* and that continued in the early sixties with Robert Bly's *Silence in the Snowy Fields,* Whitman has been seen as a congenial poetic mentor and model for a wide range of American poets. Ginsberg, for example, was drawn to Whitman for a number of reasons: Whitman's metrics and use of the long line; Whitman's commitment to a bardic, prophetic function for poetry; Whitman's example of a national poet who can speak to (and about) all of America; Whitman's frank sexuality and homoeroticism; and Whitman's fresh use of biblical language and form. On the other hand, Bly's affinity with Whitman, though perhaps narrower than Ginsberg's, is every bit as central to Bly's own development. As Bly acknowledges in a recent essay, "one cannot imagine *The Teeth Mother* appearing without Whitman beforehand."[1] Bly seizes on the mystical and spiritual dimension in Whitman's poetry, as does Galway Kinnell, though Kinnell seems more drawn than Bly to the tangible, physical side of Whitman's poetry. The democratic impulse in Whitman, his love of individuals of all trades and classes, especially his love of the neglected and dispossessed, can be seen as a strong influence on recent poets such as Philip Levine, David Ignatow, and James Wright. And recently, in *Lucky Life* and *The Red Coal,* Whitman's long line has again been used with great success by Gerald Stern, who also makes substantial use of Whitman's catalog technique.

Walt Whitman Quarterly Review 1, no. 3 (December 1983): 1–21.

Because of the range, ambition, freedom, and magnitude of Whitman's work, as well as the attractive model of Whitman's persistence as a poet, it is to be expected that nearly every contemporary American poet of some stature will, at one time or another, bow respectfully in Walt Whitman's direction.[2] Indeed, critics delight in finding Whitman's presence everywhere (as Whitman himself had hoped and predicted at the end of "Song of Myself") until nearly each and every American poet bears some "essential" kinship to him. Harold Bloom, for example, after straining the connection between Stevens and Whitman, waxes hyperbolic by telling us that Stevens "may *not* be the culmination of Whitman's poetics either, since that begins to seem the peculiar distinction of John Ashbery."[3] The contemporary reader may begin to think that Whitman's *Leaves* is a large pinhead where *all* poetic angels live.

The relationship between Louis Simpson and Walt Whitman, however, is neither a tangential one nor a mere bow of respect. In Simpson's poetry the reader finds a complex, intelligent, skeptical playing out of affinities with and differences from Whitman's poetry. Though Simpson clearly is drawn to Whitman's work and example, Simpson does not set Whitman up as some remote, perfected poetic model. In a very recent essay, "Honoring Whitman," Simpson begins with an epigraph from "Song of Myself": "He most honors my style who learns under it how to destroy the teacher." The epigraph summarizes the outcome of Simpson's study of Whitman, but their relationship proves more complex and instructive than the epigraph might suggest. By exploring Simpson's relationship to Whitman, we can begin to see certain paradigmatic features emerge, features which are common to any contemporary poet's relationship with Whitman. As Simpson's poetry will demonstrate, to speak to Whitman is to interpret and define who and what Whitman was; to explore what an American poet is; to struggle with a major American poetic influence (as in *any* engagement with a major precursor); to explore the role of "ordinary life" in poetry; to affirm a liberation of form (*not,* however, to affirm formless poetry); to evaluate America and the American enterprise; to form a picture of an ideal poet by accepting elements of Whitman and rejecting others; and to consider the peculiarly American problem of a poet's audience and a poet's relationship to the "common man." By tracing Simpson's relationship to Whitman, or, to use Ed Folsom's term, the way that Simpson "talks back" to Whitman,[4] the shape and development of Simpson's poetry can be described. His encounter with Whitman is pivotal in Simpson's development from an Audenesque, formal, ironic poet into a writer of free verse, dramatic narratives of ordinary life. By Simpson's encounter with Whitman, I do not mean his very first reading of Whitman. Instead, I refer to Simpson's direct dialogue (in poetry and prose) with Whitman, a sustained discussion and argument which begins with Simpson's fourth book of poems, *At the End of the Open Road* (1963), and which continues, on and off, for the next twenty years, including Simpson's most recent books, *The Best Hour of the Night* (1983) and *People Live Here: Selected Poems 1949–1983*.

However, it would be inaccurate to say that Simpson's poetry required this kind of encounter with Whitman before it could begin to address and evaluate America. In *A Dream of Governors* (1959), Simpson's third book of poems, the second section is entitled "My America." Indeed, Simpson's subsequent judgments of America have not changed fundamentally from the conclusion reached in "To the Western World":

> In this America, this wilderness
> Where the axe echoes with a lonely sound,
> The generations labor to possess
> And grave by grave we civilize the ground.[5]

The vision of an America which does death's bidding receives more detailed expression in Simpson's next book, *At the End of the Open Road* (1963), but the attitude expressed is essentially the same one found in "To the Western World." The conclusion to "West," from Simpson's second book of poems, *Good News of Death and Other Poems* (1955), also demonstrates the steadiness of the poet's attitudes:

> Ranching in Bolinas, that's the life,
> If you call cattle life.
> To sit on a veranda with a glass
> And see the sprinklers watering your land
> And hear the peaches dropping from the trees
> And hear the ocean in the redwood trees,

The whales of time,
Masts of the long voyages of earth,
In whose tall branches day
Hangs like a Christmas toy.

On their red columns drowse
The eagles battered at the Western gate;
These trees have held the eagles in their state
When Rome was still a rumor in the boughs.

(GND, 173)

This critique of mellow California living eventually develops
into the beginning of "A Friend of the Family": "Once upon a
time in California / the ignorant married the inane / and they
lived happily ever after" (ADV, 53). The vision of American
civilization slipping toward its own undistinguished death recurs
directly and indirectly throughout Simpson's poetic career.

So what does change as a result of Simpson's encounter with
Whitman? Tone, style, and the actual characters of Simpson's
poetry. If we take "Orpheus in America" as representative of his
earlier poetry, we find that Simpson entangles himself in an
abstract, self-consciously literary language:

America begins antiquity.
Confronted with pure space, my Arcady
Has turned to stone.
. . . .
This gazing freedom is the basilisk.
O for a mirror!
The melancholy of the possible
Unmeasures me.

(DREAM, 21)

What must change is Simpson's tone, for the narrator's voice is
too lofty, a learned version of the know-it-all that Simpson will
later condemn in Whitman, calling Whitman "the eternal soph-
omore." Before he can give convincing consideration to the
people and objects of ordinary life, Simpson must work himself
free from the cultured Audenesque voice of American verse of

the fifties. In part, his encounter with Whitman serves as a stylistic catalyst.

As one final example of Simpson's early style, the poem "Hot Night on Water Street" illustrates the stiff style and voice that undercut his early work. Simpson, as always, comes up with his characteristically incisive, deflating observation: "Some day, when this uncertain continent / Is marble, and men ask what was the good / We lived by, dust may whisper 'Hollywood'" (DREAM, 16). In the poem the speaker, a type of Whitman traveler/wanderer, walks along Water Street, offering us a catalog of his observations. Sounding like Hawthorne's Young Goodman Brown, the speaker concludes:

> I didn't linger—sometimes when I travel
> I think I'm being followed by the Devil.
>
> At the newsstand in the lobby, a cigar
> Was talkative: "Since I've been in this town
> I've seen one likely woman, and a car
> As she was crossing Main Street, knocked her down."
> I was a stranger here myself, I said,
> And bought the *New York Times,* and went to bed.

But this poem makes us too aware of its "poetic" effects, including the rhyme scheme. We become aware of the all too literary posture of another tour "through certain half-deserted streets, / The muttering retreats / Of restless nights. . . ."

In *Poet's Choice* (1962), Simpson chooses to represent his work with the poem "Walt Whitman at Bear Mountain." He selects this particular poem, as he explains, "not because I think it is the best poem I have written, but because it marked a turning point in my work."[6] In part, Simpson has in mind the stylistic relaxation or, more accurately, the exploration of free verse, that he (and many other American poets) experienced in the early sixties. For Simpson, this turning point involves primarily style, but also a slight shift in subject matter:

What I did manage to arrive at in "Walt Whitman" was a poem that presented certain images and ideas in an almost colloquial manner, in lines whose rhythm was determined by my own habits of speech. . . . My groping toward a poetry of significant images and spoken lines enabled me to say certain things that I had not been able to say before. This poem was followed by others in which I was able to deal with material that interested me—poems about history, my own personal life, America. (COMP, 33)

The poem also marks the beginning of Simpson's direct confrontation with Whitman.

"Walt Whitman at Bear Mountain" figures prominently in *At the End of the Open Road* (1963), for which Simpson received the Pulitzer Prize. The book begins and ends with Whitman's presence and influence, the key Whitman poems being "In California," "On the Lawn at the Villa," "Walt Whitman at Bear Mountain," "Pacific Ideas—a Letter to Walt Whitman," and "Lines Written near San Francisco." The title of Simpson's book lets us know that we are getting an updating of Whitman's journey. We will learn where those who have tramped after Whitman, accepting his offer at the end of "Song of the Open Road": "Camerado, I give you my hand!" have arrived. Simpson aims to show us where Whitman's dream of American expansion ends up. The bleak vision which follows is akin to what Ed Folsom observes in Allen Ginsberg's poetry of the midfifties: "Ginsberg here sets the tone of the contemporary American dialogue with Whitman, a dialogue that involves a deep concern with the loss of the Open Road, a loss of American direction, openness, and purpose, and a concomitant loss of love" (MS, xxxxv).

Simpson's opening poem in *At the End of the Open Road,* "In California," places us at the literal end of that road, at the continent's end; the poem emphasizes fraud, trickery, and death. Simpson's version of California is closer to Thoreau's than to Whitman's. As F. O. Matthiessen observes, "Thoreau did not share Whitman's confidence in mass movements, and said that California was '3000 miles nearer to hell,' since its gold was a touchstone that had betrayed 'the rottenness, the baseness of mankind.'"[7] Simpson's poem establishes the speaker's own gloomy vision; his accurate cynicism will serve as a corrective to

Whitman's cheery "epical" optimism. But the speaker also feels a bit guilty for his gloomy vision:

> Here I am, troubling the dream coast
> With my New York face,
> Bearing among the realtors
> And tennis-players my dark preoccupation.

California is seen as a false Mecca, a fool's paradise, and Whitman is viewed as one more huckster, one more confidence man: "Lie back, Walt Whitman, / There, on the fabulous raft with the King and the Duke!" Thus, Simpson lumps Whitman together with the King and the Duke, those Twainian precursors to their mid- and late-twentieth-century brothers, the real estate agents (of Simpson's poem) and our own TV salesmen. Simpson's speaker tells Whitman,

> Lie back! We cannot bear
> The stars any more, those infinite spaces.
> Let the realtors divide the mountain,
> For they have already subdivided the valley.

At the end of the open road, the poet shows us "rectangular city blocks" planned by "the same old city-planner, death," the architect for late-twentieth-century America.

The speaker of Simpson's American poems, particularly in *At the End of the Open Road,* sniffs out the rottenness at the heart of America's muscle-flexing pride. Even before America's spiritual sickness became an international spectacle during the late sixties and early seventies, Simpson, in his anti-Whitman capacity, sensed that illness. "The Inner Part" offers Simpson's assessment of the American spirit in a characteristically concise, merciless fashion:

> When they had won the war
> And for the first time in history
> Americans were the most important people—

When the leading citizens no longer lived in their shirt sleeves,
And their wives did not scratch in public;
Just when they'd stopped saying "Gosh!"—

When their daughters seemed as sensitive
As the tip of a fly rod,
And their sons were as smooth as a V-8 engine—

Priests, examining the entrails of birds,
Found the heart misplaced, and seeds
As black as death, emitting a strange odor.

(END, 56)

Nine years later in his autobiography, *North of Jamaica,* Simpson explains his disagreement with Whitman:

I found Whitman's ideas often intolerable; celebrating progress and industry as ends in themselves was understandable in 1870, for at that time material expansion was also a spiritual experience, but in the twentieth century the message seemed out of date. The mountains had been crossed, the land had been gobbled up, and industry was turning out more goods than people could consume. Also, the democracy Whitman celebrated, the instinctive rightness of the common man, was very much in doubt. Now we were governed by the rich, and the masses were hopelessly committed to an economy based on war. It was a curious thing that a man could write great poetry and still be mistaken in his ideas.[8]

It would seem that Simpson praises the quality of Whitman's verse while rejecting outright his precursor's vision. But before I overstate (and oversimplify) the nature of Simpson's encounter with Whitman, for he does *not* merely attack and dismiss Whitman's point of view, I would like to turn to some more general remarks about influence to provide a framework for viewing the interaction between these two poets. Harold Bloom begins his study of poetic influence, *The Anxiety of Influence,* by noting that "weaker talents idealize."[9] Clearly, Simpson does not (merely) idealize Whitman. But more important, Bloom suggests that "poetic influence, or as I shall more frequently term it, poetic misprision, is necessarily the study of the life-cycle of the poet-as-poet" (ANX, 7). Such an observation rescues influence studies from becoming dry, pseudo-objective tracings of calm affinities and genial borrowings. As we shall see, Simpson's relation to Whitman is indeed based, in part, on misprision. That is, Simpson proceeds to read Whitman partially, emphasizing an aspect of Whitman's poetic vision, reacting to and against it so as to develop his own vision. Thus the study of poetic influence, as Bloom correctly asserts, is *not* a static event, but an unfolding relationship which has very much to do with the poet's (Simpson's) life cycle or development as a poet. To study Simpson's interaction with Whitman is to bear out Bloom's generality:

> We journey to abstract ourselves by fabrication. But where the fabric has already been woven, we journey to unravel. (ANX, 64–65)

In Bloom's theory of influence, the later poet, at some key moment, swerves from the earlier poet and revises or corrects the earlier poet's vision. When we consider Simpson's revision of Whitman's American prophecy, we would do well to bear in mind Bloom's warning:

> As the poets swerve downward in time, they deceive themselves into believing they are tougher-minded than their precursors. This is akin to that critical absurdity which salutes each new generation of bards as being somehow closer to the common language of ordinary men than the last was. (ANX, 69)

Clearly, there *is* a tough-minded Whitman to be found. He is not merely a cheerleader shouting for American expansion and progress while always maintaining his own sweet optimism. In *Democratic Vistas,* for example, Whitman offers the following analysis of America:

> I say we had best look our times and lands searchingly in the face, like a physician diagnosing some deep disease. Never was there, perhaps, more hollowness at heart than at present,

and here in the United States. Genuine belief seems to have left us. The underlying principles of the States are not honestly believ'd in, (for all this hectic glow, and these melodramatic screamings,) nor is humanity itself believ'd in. What penetrating eye does not everywhere see through the mask? The spectacle is appalling. We live in an atmosphere of hypocrisy throughout. . . . I say that our New World democracy, however great a success in uplifting the masses out of their sloughs, in materialistic development, products, and in a certain highly deceptive superficial popular intellectuality, is, so far, an almost complete failure in its social aspects, and in really grand religious, moral, literary, and aesthetic results.[10]

Even if we do acknowledge, as does Whitman's most recent biographer, Justin Kaplan, that Whitman "believed that America, for all its troubles, alone possessed the prerequisites for a great moral and religious civilization" and that America's "failures were transitional, growing pains,"[11] there *is* still a Whitman who sees the evil and failings of America. It is this critical, dark Whitman who often gets ignored in contemporary attacks on his views. Simpson is not alone, and indeed Bloom would claim that Simpson's actions typify "the anxiety of influence," when he "misreads" Whitman, taking a major aspect of the poet's vision and acting as if that were all Whitman had to say on the subject. After looking further at Simpson's poems in *At the End of the Open Road,* an examination of Whitman's own "Song of the Open Road" will provide further evidence of Simpson's pattern of misprision.

In "On the Lawn at the Villa," Simpson's narrator begins to feel a bit guilty for his gloomy vision. Not that he would exchange his own sarcasm for Whitman's gushy optimism; nevertheless, the narrator's irony is at times nearly too much for him to stand:

> It's complicated, being an American,
> Having the money and the bad conscience, both at the same
> time.
> Perhaps, after all, this is not the right subject for a poem.

Of course, it is the right subject for a poem; but where does this irony and acuity of observation leave the speaker? In this poem, he (and the others) are characterized as "paralyzed." At this point in Simpson's writing, Whitman seems to be an annoyance, a type: the optimistic American proclaiming the greatness of himself and the nation. As such, he is subject only to Simpson's scorn.

However, in spite of Simpson's withering ironies and deflating observations, part of Whitman's spiritual journey is a necessity for Simpson as well, even if his journey is to be, admittedly, through a bleaker world. Even in an ironic context, this stanza from "Love, My Machine" (which occurs shortly after "On the Lawn at the Villa") inherits its breadth and phrasing from Whitman:

> For every man and woman
> Is an immortal spirit
> Trapped and dazed on a star shoot.

The narrator's conclusion offers a variant of Whitman's own journey: "I am going into the night to find a world of my own."

The last three poems in *At the End of the Open Road*, "Walt Whitman at Bear Mountain," "Pacific Ideas—a Letter to Walt Whitman," and "Lines Written near San Francisco," all involve Whitman, as to let the reader know that Simpson's earlier posture of sarcasm and scorn proved an insufficient dismissal of a figure who turns out to be more compelling than the poet might wish to admit. [12]

In "Walt Whitman at Bear Mountain," Simpson addresses his question to the friendly, but ignored, statue of Whitman. But in his criticisms of Whitman, I also detect a desire on Simpson's part to find or inspire a Whitman who could speak back to him and thus, perhaps, jar the narrator out of his own gloomy vision:

> "Where are you, Walt?
> The Open Road goes to the used-car lot.
>
> "Where is the nation you promised?"

Simpson wants to drag his predecessor out to see the "real" America of the 1960s, not the idealized America of Whitman's, at times, inflated rhetoric. Simpson continues, "As for the people—see how they neglect you! / Only a poet pauses to read the inscription," and clearly that poet pauses with considerable skepticism. We should also bear in mind that these remarks are spoken to the poet who concluded the inspired introduction to the first edition of *Leaves of Grass* by stating, "The proof of a poet is that his country absorbs him as affectionately as he has absorbed it." In "On Being a Poet in America," an essay which begins with a epigraph from Whitman and which was written during the same period as his Whitman poems, Simpson extends his critique of Whitman's ideal of popular poetry:

> "To have great poets we must have great audiences too." This tag from Whitman, which adorns or used to adorn every issue of *Poetry,* is about as close to the opposite of the truth as you can get. To have great poetry all that is needed is great talent. There can be no such thing as a great audience for poetry. An audience for bad writing—yes![13]

Not only has the Whitman in Simpson's poem failed to achieve the audience he had hoped for, but the reply that Whitman makes to his question in Simpson's poem is unsatisfactory. Simpson's Whitman is a diminished Whitman, a poet whose self may no longer be universal or representative, a poet who now explains that his prophecies were in fact merely "moods." He is the huckster unmasked, which leaves Simpson alone to confront the great American ruin:

> Then all the realtors,
> Pickpockets, salesmen, and the actors performing
> Official scenarios,
> Turned a deaf ear, for they had contracted
> American dreams.

The poet wishes for a Whitman who might somehow counter his contemporary vision of an America which, as *At the End of the Open Road* began by explaining in the opening poem "In

California," does death's bidding. In the final poem of the book, "Lines Written near San Francisco," Simpson's bitter conclusion is:

> We must remain, to serve the returning sun,
>
> And to set tables for death.
> For we are the colonists of Death—
> Not, as some think, of the English.
>
> And we are preparing thrones for him to sit,
> Poems to read, and beds
> In which it may please him to rest.

Ronald Moran claims that "Walt Whitman at Bear Mountain" "is more than an engaging celebration; it is a serious indictment of the American condition and, at the same time, an exoneration of Whitman from the frequent charge that his poetry prophesies the fulfillment of the promises America held in the nineteenth century."[14] Moran correctly points out Simpson's indictment of America, but his claim for an exoneration of Whitman is mistaken. In Simpson's own essay on the poem, the poet explains,

> . . . I think that most of his prophecies have been proved wrong. It is a strange fact, when you think about it—that a poet can be great and yet be mistaken in his ideas. The Whitman who heralds an inevitable march of democracy, who praises the intelligence of the masses, is nearly always mistaken. At least, if there ever was an America like that, it no longer exists. But the Whitman who uses his own eyes and ears, who describes things, who expresses his own sly humor or pathos, is unbeatable. I tried to show the two Whitmans in my poem. I used my ideas about Whitman as a way of getting at my own ideas about America.[15]

It is Simpson's struggle with these two Whitmans that makes his encounter with Whitman a dynamic one. *At the End of the Open Road* is dominated by Simpson's attack on Whitman-as-optimist; Simpson's subsequent poetry, to a degree, recuperates Whitman by viewing him as a starting point for Simpson's own poetry of ordinary, individual lives. In *At the End of the Open Road,* a rescuing or redeeming Whitman is *not* forthcoming. Simpson hammers away at Whitman-the-mistaken-optimist, for to be joyful in modern America is to be on death's side:

> Every night, at the end of America
> We taste our wine, looking at the Pacific.
> How sad it is, the end of America!
>
> While we were waiting for the land
> They'd finished it—with gas drums
> On the hilltops, cheap housing in the valleys
>
> Where lives are mean and wretched.
> But the banks thrive and the realtors
> Rejoice—they have their America.
>
> (END, 69)

If Simpson's Whitman is at all redeemed, it is in the following acknowledgment (made near the end of "Lines Written near San Francisco"):

> Whitman was wrong about the People,
> But right about himself. The land is within.
> At the end of the open road we come to ourselves.

Perhaps why Simpson feels compelled to struggle with Whitman is precisely because Simpson's own (unstated) task is very close to Whitman's often stated (and in Simpson's opinion, failed or falsified) project: to be a national bard. But Simpson does not wish to lie about either the nation or its people, and so he must set aside one of the two Whitmans, Whitman-the-false-prophet, if he, Simpson, is to accomplish his own task.

If we return to Whitman's own "Song of the Open Road," we can locate aspects of Simpson's two Whitmans, and we can also begin to identify a further area of Simpson's critique of Whitman. The optimistic Whitman, the one attacked in *At the*

End of the Open Road, dominates this poem from the opening lines:

> Afoot and light-hearted I take to the open road,
> Healthy, free, the world before me,
> The long brown path before me leading wherever I choose.

to observations such as this:

> I think heroic deeds were all conceiv'd in the open air, and all
>   free poems also,
> I think I could stop here myself and do miracles,
> I think whatever I shall meet on the road I shall like, and
>   whoever beholds me shall like me,
> I think whoever I see must be happy.

It is this Whitman, the one who writes about "the progress of souls" and who sounds like a cheerleader at a pep rally for the spirit—"forever forward, / . . . they go toward the best—toward something great"—who remains Simpson's whipping boy. But even in as overwhelmingly cheerful a poem as "Song of the Open Road," traces of another Whitman, one nearly ignored by Simpson and many other readers, appear:

> (Still here I carry my old delicious burdens,
> I carry them, men and women, I carry them with me
>   wherever I go.
> I swear it is impossible for me to get rid of them,
> I am fill'd with them, and I will fill them in return.)

There *is* a Whitman who admits his doubts, burdens, and failings. Too often the probable occasion for Whitman's poetry is forgotten: isn't the poet of brotherhood and the crowd also the poet struggling with his own isolation and loneliness? Isn't the poet of human perfection also one who is all too acutely aware of his own failings? "Song of the Open Road" can be read as an elaborate wish spoken by a man who hopes that "Henceforth I whimper no more, postpone no more, need nothing, / Done with indoor complaints, libraries, querulous criticisms." Whitman's poems, such as "Song of the Open Road," do not enact but hope for change: "From this hour I ordain myself loos'd of limits and imaginary lines, / . . . divesting myself of the holds that would hold me."

The Whitman who receives Simpson's praise is the one "who uses his own eyes and ears," the poet who describes the world around him. In singling out this Whitman, Simpson agrees with F. O. Matthiessen's earlier assessment:

> Yet the fact is that even though Whitman did not want to be personal, but to write poems "with reference to ensemble," to make his voice that of the general bard of democracy, the evidence of the poems themselves shows that he was at his best, not when he was being sweeping, but when contemplating with delicacy and tenderness some object near at hand.[16]

In *Adventures of the Letter I* (1971), the book of poems which follows *At the End of Open Road* (and a *Selected Poems,* 1965), Simpson includes "Sacred Objects," written for Whitman on the occasion of his sesquicentennial birthday celebration in 1969. The poem states succinctly the side of Whitman which attracts Simpson:

> The light that shines through the *Leaves*
> is clear: "to form individuals."

Indeed, this formation of individuals, the particularities of an ordinary life presented at key dramatic moments, is an apt description for much of Simpson's own poetry from *Adventures of the Letter I* through *The Best Hour of the Night* (1983).

But for Simpson, Whitman's attention to individual, ordinary lives constitutes only a beginning. In "Honoring Whitman," Simpson's most recent prose assessment of Whitman, he asserts that when Whitman "looks at what he sees, he is certainly a great American poet." However, Simpson, as always, qualifies and undercuts his praise for Whitman by pointing out what his predecessor fails to accomplish:

> There are ranges of poetry that lie beyond Whitman. Of situations such as occur in people's lives he appears to have

known very little, and these are our main concerns. He is good at describing shipwrecks, which are infrequent, but does not show affection, attachments, anxieties, shades of feeling, passions . . . the life we actually have. (MS, 259–60)

In terms of Harold Bloom's theories of influence, Simpson's relationship to Whitman is of the *tessera* variety. Bloom explains that "in the *tessera,* the later poet provides what his imagination tells him would complete the otherwise 'truncated' precursor poem and poet" (ANX, 66). In exploring the origins of the word *tessera,* Bloom first quotes Jacques Lacan's translator, Anthony Wilden, then offers his own summary:

> "The *tessera* was employed in the early mystery religions where fitting together again the two halves of a broken piece of pottery was used as a means of recognition by the initiates." In this sense of a completing link, the *tessera* represents any later poet's attempt to persuade himself (and us) that the precursor's Word would be worn out if not redeemed as a newly fulfilled and enlarged word of the ephebe. (ANX, 67)

Simpson's "Sacred Objects" begins:

> I am taking part in a great experiment—
> whether writers can live peacefully in the suburbs
> and not be bored to death.
>
> As Whitman said, an American muse
> installed amid the kitchen ware.

He grasps a shard of Whitman's pottery—the portion which directs the poet's attention to ordinary life; then, Simpson completes the vessel by going much deeper than his predecessor into the stories of individual lives. The nature of Simpson's completion, as well as of his complaint about Whitman's incomplete attention to ordinary lives, can be seen in "Honoring Whitman" when Simpson describes his predecessor's failings:

> He is a stroller, an onlooker, a gazer, and has nothing to say about what goes on in the houses he is passing, or behind

office or factory windows, or in the life of a man turning a plough. He does not seem to know what people say to each other—especially what men say to women, or women to men. (MS, 260)

More and more, Simpson's own poems, as he stated in an interview which appeared in 1976, are written "in the dramatically narrative form" (COMP, 300). Simpson concludes about Whitman, "There is hardly any drama or narration in his poetry—ideas aren't realized in action" (MS, 260).

If we return to Whitman's "Song of the Open Road," we find that most of Simpson's criticisms are sustained:

> You rows of houses! you window-pierc'd facades! you roofs!
> You porches and entrances! you copings and iron guards!
> You windows whose transparent shells might expose so much!
> You doors and ascending steps! you arches!
> You gray stones of interminable pavements! you trodden crossings!
> From all that has touch'd you I believe you have imparted to yourselves, and now would impart the same secretly to me,
> From the living and the dead you have peopled your impassive surfaces, and the spirits thereof would be evident and amicable with me.

Rereading "Song of the Open Road" with Simpson's criticisms in mind, the reader finds Whitman's poem to be filled with plurals and generalizations. The poet listens to "others," he imagines himself loved by "strangers," "all seems beautiful to me," and he will scatter himself "among men and women" as he goes. Oddly enough, even the erotic moments in the poem become generalized and plural. In the seventh section, Whitman, after generalizing, does present individuals:

> What is it I interchange so suddenly with strangers?
> What with some driver as I ride on the seat by his side?
> What with some fisherman drawing his seine by the shore as I walk by and pause?

What gives me to be free to a woman's and man's good-will?
    what gives them to be free to mine?

But his specificity is momentary. Simpson's own poetic project is to complete what Whitman began. Whitman pointed to the value and importance of common lives, but Simpson's effort is not to generalize but to get *inside* those lives through individual dramatic narratives. Indeed, that inside view is the strength of Simpson's most recent work, especially in the first and third sections of *The Best Hour of the Night.*

But before we accept Simpson's criticisms of Whitman as being totally accurate, we should also keep in mind Bloom's suggestion that misreading (or partial reading) is an essential part of the dynamics of poetic influence. I cannot produce scores of counterexamples from Whitman's poetry to demonstrate that he did get inside the lives of others, for on this point there is a great degree of truth to Simpson's criticism. But in "Song of the Open Road," Whitman himself is painfully aware of the fact that he remains an outsider:

Whoever you are, come forth! or man or woman come forth!
You must not stay sleeping and dallying there in the house,
    though you built it, or though it has been built for you.

Out of the dark confinement! out from behind the screen!
It is useless to protest, I know all and expose it.

Behold through you as bad as the rest,
Through the laughter, dancing, dining, supping, of people,
Inside of dresses and ornaments, inside of those wash'd and
    trimm'd faces,
Behold a secret silent loathing and despair.

No husband, no wife, no friend, trusted to hear the confession,
Another self, a duplicate of every one, skulking and hiding it
    goes,
Formless and wordless through the streets of the cities, polite
    and bland in the parlors,
In the cars of railroads, in steamboats, in the public assembly,

Home to the houses of men and women, at the table, in the
     bedroom, everywhere,
Smartly attired, countenance smiling, form upright, death
     under the breast-bones, hell under the skull-bones,
Under the broadcloth and gloves, under the ribbons and
     artificial flowers,
Keeping fair with the customs, speaking not a syllable of itself,
Speaking of any thing else but never of itself.

If Whitman observes externals, it is, as here, to urge us to shed
those masks or to strip those surfaces away himself to expose the
soul. Those who do not travel with him, who do not "know the
universe itself as a road, as many roads, as roads for traveling
souls," are condemned to limitation, "a secret silent loathing
and despair," a life of quiet desperation. Such lives, in their
particularity, struggle, and drama, do not seem to interest Whit-
man. Bloom goes so far as to conclude that all of Whitman's
"wholly realized works" are "centered only on his isolate self,
and on Emersonian seeing, which is not far from shamanistic
practice, and has little to do with observation of externals"
(ANX, 133). In his most recent essays, Bloom tells us that Whit-
man quite simply *is* the American Sublime.[17]

It is the sublime Whitman, following closely on the heels of
the optimistic Whitman, who receives Simpson's attacks. In
"Sacred Objects," Simpson, still hoping that he and Whitman
can find a common ground, asks, "Where then shall we meet?"
But Simpson asks the question because he wants to know how
Whitman would fare in *our* world. In this world, where the
American muse is "installed amid the kitchen ware," Simpson
remarks, "and we have wonderful household appliances . . . /
now tell me about the poets."

In the development of Simpson's own poetic career, his en-
counter with Whitman in *At the End of the Open Road* is pivotal in
two ways: stylistically, and, more important, in terms of the
variety of truth-saying that will form the basis of Simpson's
writing. Simpson follows Whitman's lead in exploring the tex-
ture and variety of individual lives, but with increasing emphasis
he parts company with the mystical or sublime side of Whitman.
By this process of exclusion and rejection, Simpson clarifies the
direction of his own development. By rejecting the mystical

Whitman, Simpson also symbolically resists the sixties' fashion of "deep image" poetry. By virtue of this rejection, he parts company with poets such as Bly, Kinnell, Wright, and Merwin, each of whom continues (in a different manner) to explore the deep image for another decade. Simpson's poetry, increasingly, leaves behind the image-based mysticism of the sixties in favor of his own variety of concise narratives. To use Whitman's metaphor, Simpson's direction is a road which goes by Chekhov's house and, increasingly, away from Whitman's. In fact, the section which immediately precedes "Sacred Objects" in *Adventures of the Letter I* is entitled "Looking for Chekhov's House," and the section concludes,

> These idiots rule the world,
> Chekhov knew it, and yet
> I think he was happy, on his street.
> People live here . . . you'd be amazed.

"People live here" becomes the title for Simpson's *Selected Poems 1949–1983,* and that is his primary concern: where and how people actually live their lives. The Whitman who declares the immortality and divinity of all men and women is subject to Simpson's suspicion and, finally, rejection.

Most recently, in "Honoring Whitman," Simpson tells us,

> There is the kind of reader who, having no knowledge of religion, is always looking in books for the secret of the universe. For such a one, Whitman will be mystic, together with Kahlil Gibran and the authors of pamphlets on astrology.
>
> In so far as Whitman enthuses over "a great round wonder rolling in space" he is a rudimentary poet, the eternal sophomore enthusing over "the great ideas" and neglecting his physics lesson and his French. In so far as Whitman talks about the universe he is not worth the attention of a grown person. (MS, 258–59)

Though ultimately Simpson replaces Whitman as a mentor or guide with the more compatible figure of Chekhov, it should still be noted that Simpson *is* one of Whitman's heirs, especially in terms of subject matter and the desire to be a national bard.

Simpson refuses to idolize his benefactor, but, in his own combative way, he honors him. In fact, Simpson pays Whitman a higher honor than hero worship by doing battle with him, which is what the epigraph to "Honoring Whitman" indicates: "He most honors my style who learns under it how to destroy the teacher." Whitman, in "Song of Myself," seems to agree: "no friend of mine takes his ease in my chair."

For Simpson, friendship with Whitman requires opposition. As we have already seen, that opposition means debunking and re-forming our vision of Whitman. To draw on one final example of Simpson's ever-shifting reinterpretation of Whitman, it is useful to consider Simpson's remarks in an interview conducted in 1974:

> Now I'm not a terribly spiritual person. I'm not a mystic. In fact, I have some very cynical moods. Therefore, what is good for me is to read people who are slightly mystical and religious and deep in that way, to use some of the control for myself. It prevents me from becoming stupid, you see. I'm sure that I'm completely different from Whitman in my likes and dislikes as a man. But I love Whitman, because he explores those areas I know I should be conscious of. (COMP, 270)

Here, Simpson, as Bly, Ginsberg, and others have done, proclaims Whitman as a mystic. While Simpson declares his own difference from Whitman, he also claims, "In a way I have got to keep thinking and looking for spiritual guides" (COMP, 270). But as we shall soon find in "Searching for the Ox," Simpson thoroughly distrusts spiritual guides. The only "spirituality" palatable to Simpson is an earthly, sensual spirituality. Thus in 1981, when Simpson republishes the interview quoted above, he adds the following footnote: "Reading this six years later I cannot understand why I thought Whitman either mystical or religious. He is a naturalist throughout" (COMP, 270). Yet, a year later, in "Honoring Whitman," the mystic Whitman, "the eternal sophomore," gets lumped with Kahlil Gibran.

In 1976 in "Rolling Up," Simpson explains his objection to mysticism: "My objection to the pursuit of esoteric knowledge, shamanism and so on, is that it neglects the life right under your nose" (COMP, 313). The title poem to *Searching for the Ox* (1976) reaches a similar conclusion:

> And still, I must confess,
> I fear those *messieurs,* like a peasant
> listening to the priests talk Latin.
> They will send me off to Heaven
> when all I want is to live in the world.

"Searching for the Ox," Simpson's own spiritual journey, becomes an antispiritual story proclaiming the poet's renewed attachment to the earth. Though "Following in the Way / that 'regards sensory experience as relatively unimportant,' / and that aims to teach the follower / 'to renounce what one is attached to,'" Simpson learns the opposite:

> I find my awareness
> of the world—the cry of a bird,
> susurrus of tires, the wheezing
> of the man in the chair next to me—
> has increased.

In an interview published the same year, Simpson explains:

> Poets are very different from religious people. Religious people don't need the here and now. Their object is to get away from it and to get beyond it into mystery directly. The artist is not a religious man. He may believe in religion; he may be motivated by it largely, but in the practice of his art he cannot operate the way a saint operates. The artist must cherish this world; this is what art is made of. (COMP, 292)

In Simpson's distinction between the artist and the religious man, we can locate as well his final swerving away from Whitman's example. In a recent essay, "Reflections on Narrative Poetry," Simpson suggests that poets

> may indeed learn more about writing narrative poems from the novelist than from other poets, for in the past two hundred years it has been the novelist whose labor it was to

imitate life, while the poet prided himself on his originality, his remoteness from everyday life. (COMP, 346)

Thus, we should not be surprised to find that the primary muse or model for Simpson's *Caviare at the Funeral* (1980) is Chekhov. Indeed, in the book's central poem, "Why Do You Write About Russia?" the narrator, asked, "what are you reading now?" responds, "Chekhov." In Simpson's most recent collection of poems, *The Best Hour of the Night*,[18] while oblique references to Whitman do crop up, Simpson continues to be more attracted to European prose writers, especially Proust and Chekhov. "In Otto's Basement," however, does echo the end of "Song of Myself":

> So we endure it. This is what Jefferson
> and Lincoln had to endure,
> sitting and listening to people
> argue . . . the cost of conversion from oil to coal
> and the statement by the tree-trimming committee.
> If you want to know what freedom cost
> look for us here, under the linoleum.
>
> (BH, 66)

Simpson gauges our descent from Whitman by the difference in connotation, rhetoric, and tone between "I bequeath myself to the dirt to grow from the grass I love, / If you want me again look for me under your boot-soles" and "look for us here, under the linoleum."

If it is true that Whitman helped to turn Simpson's attention to common lives and objects, then Simpson completes the work of his predecessor by getting inside those ordinary lives. In *The Best Hour of the Night*, in poems such as "Physical Universe," "Quiet Desperation," and "The Previous Tenant," with Chekhovian coolness and clarity, Simpson takes the reader into painfully quotidian, suburban lives. And if his accomplishment represents a "surpassing" of Whitman, oddly enough, the central dilemma of Simpson's poetry, as he acknowledges indirectly in "The Champion Single Sculls" with its passing reference to "Song of Myself," remains a Whitmanian one:

Stillness, said a picture,
is not being immobile,
but a clear separation
of the self from its surroundings
while taking part (we must take part
how else are we to live?)

"Max Schmitt in a Single Scull" . . .
A river with iron bridges . . .
Schmitt is resting on his oars,
looking toward the observer,
"both in and out of the game."
Rowing! This is what I have to practice.

(BH, 58)

In writing about contemporary American life, suburban or oth-
erwise, and its attendant "quiet desperation," the observer (or
poet) will inevitably be "both in and out of the game," and
rowing, or moving precisely and gracefully across the surface, is
one approach to take. But that approach may be more "out of
the game." Another approach is Whitman's rhetoric of soli-
darity and brotherhood, a stance adopted by Pablo Neruda and
others. But Simpson remains skeptical because such rhetoric
may be merely a posture, dishonest because the proletarian bard
in contemporary America is virtually unthinkable except as a
kind of confidence man. Simpson's dilemma, as I see it, remains
the problem of the observer's relationship to the world he de-
scribes. To be "both in and out of the game" indeed requires
great practice, delicacy, and restraint, qualities which Simpson,
at present, seems to be absorbing more from Chekhov than
from Whitman.

I do not think that Simpson's combat with Whitman is
atypical of the process of poetic influence. Nor does the prepon-
derance of Simpson's criticisms and rejections of his predecessor
mean that Whitman's impact on Simpson is slight. Though
Bloom's studies of poetic influence do get out of hand—his
battles between "strong poets" verge on descriptions of tag
team wrestling—his essential point, that conflict (Blake: "In op-
position is true friendship") is crucial to the most important

instances of influence, *is* correct and is borne out by a study of Simpson's relation to Whitman. As Bloom explains:

> It does happen that one poet influences another, or more precisely, that one poet's poems influence the poems of the other, through a generosity of the spirit, even a shared generosity. But our easy idealism is out of place here. Where generosity is involved, the poets influenced are minor or weaker; the more generosity, and the more mutual it is, the poorer the poets involved. (ANX, 30).

Thus, Bloom, with approval, quotes Nietzsche: "Every talent must unfold itself in fighting" (ANX, 52). As Whitman has it, "You will hardly know who I am or what I mean, / But I shall be good health to you nevertheless, / And filter and fibre your blood." Whitman, who in poems such as "Poets to Come" foresaw his own words as but beginnings, offers health to succeeding poets not merely by positive example, but by rousing the blood and the spirit of conflict in his poetic heirs.

NOTES

1. Robert Bly, "What Whitman Did Not Give Us," in *Walt Whitman: The Measure of His Song,* ed. Jim Perlman, Ed Folsom, and Dan Campion (Minneapolis: Holy Cow! Press, 1981), 321. Since many additional references in my essay refer to essays collected in this volume, wherever possible subsequent references will be abbreviated parenthetically as MS, followed by the appropriate page number.

2. The best guide to recent reactions, salutes, arguments, and dialogues with Walt Whitman is *Walt Whitman: The Measure of His Song,* which includes poems and essays by Ginsberg, Bly, James Wright, Simpson, Ignatow, Kinnell, and others.

3. Harold Bloom, *Agon: Towards a Theory of Revisionism* (New York: Oxford University Press, 1982), 183.

4. Ed Folsom, "Talking Back to Walt Whitman: An Introduction," in *Walt Whitman: The Measure of His Song,* xxi–xxii.

5. *A Dream of Governors,* 15. Since frequent references to Louis Simpson's poetry will occur throughout my essay, the following editions and abbreviations are used: *Good News of Death and Other Poems* in *Poets of Today II* (New York: Charles Scribner's Sons, 1955), 149–95

(GND). *A Dream of Governors* (Middletown: Wesleyan University Press, 1959) (DREAM). *At the End of the Open Road* (Middletown: Wesleyan University Press, 1963) (END). *Adventures of the Letter I* (New York: Harper and Row, 1971) (ADV). *Searching for the Ox* (New York: William Morrow, 1976) (OX). *Caviare at the Funeral* (New York: Franklin Watts, 1980) (CAV).

6. *A Company of Poets* (Ann Arbor: University of Michigan Press, 1981), 32. Many of Simpson's essays, reviews, and interviews are collected in this volume. Subsequent references, wherever possible, will be abbreviated parenthetically as COMP, followed by the appropriate page number.

7. F. O. Matthiessen, *American Renaissance: Art and Expression in the Age of Emerson and Whitman* (New York: Oxford University Press, 1941), 633.

8. *North of Jamaica* (New York: Harper and Row, 1972), 222, as cited by George S. Lensing and Ronald Moran in *Four Poets of the Emotive Imagination: Robert Bly, James Wright, Louis Simpson, and William Stafford* (Baton Rouge: Louisiana State University Press, 1976), 165.

9. Harold Bloom, *The Anxiety of Influence: A Theory of Poetry* (New York: Oxford University Press, 1973), 5. Subsequent references to this book will be abbreviated as ANX, followed by the appropriate page number.

10. Walt Whitman, *Prose Works 1892,* ed. Floyd Stovall (New York: New York University Press, 1964), 2:369–70.

11. Justin Kaplan, *Walt Whitman: A Life* (New York: Simon and Schuster, 1980), 337.

12. As for the importance of these Whitman poems to Simpson's overall development, a strong, if somewhat indirect, argument can be made on the basis of Simpson's forthcoming *People Live Here: Selected Poems 1949–1983* (Brockport, N.Y.: BOA Editions) where "On the Lawn at the Villa," "Walt Whitman at Bear Mountain," "In California," "Lines Written near San Francisco," and "Sacred Objects" are all included in the selections made by the author.

13. *Company,* 37. In a more recent essay (1977), Simpson again addresses the problem of audience, but this time in relation to his own work: "This brings us to the question, 'Whom do you visualize as your reader?' It's a touchy question. I certainly don't write for people who read Rod McKuen. Nor for people who want political poetry. In fact, as far as I can see, I have few readers. On the other hand, my poems have been translated into some nine foreign languages and have been taught in schools in Africa, in Macedonia, and other places. I guess I am writing for readers in the United States in the future" (COMP, 326).

14. Ronald Moran, *Louis Simpson* (New York: Twayne, 1972), 112.

15. *Company*, 34. In an interview printed in 1979, Simpson reiterates his theory of two Whitmans present in *At the End of the Open Road:* "What I was attacking in Whitman there was one side of Whitman. There are two Whitmans as I see it. And the side I attacked was his expansionist, materialist, 1880s Gilded Age side in which Whitman was hailing the advance of the railroad, the advance of the American prosperity. That was a public Whitman used by other people and that was the side I was attacking in him and in America generally" (COMP, 328).

16. Matthiessen, *American Renaissance*, 546–47.

17. Bloom, *Agon*, 182.

18. Subsequent references to *The Best Hour of the Night* (New Haven and New York: Ticknor and Fields, 1983) will be abbreviated as BH, followed by the appropriate page number. I am grateful to Louis Simpson for sending me a manuscript copy of *Best Hour* well before the book's publication.

R. W. FLINT

Child of This World

The final test of a poet with legitimate claims to being a master of the speaking voice might be a verbatim transcription from his index of first lines. Let me turn to page 211 of *People Live Here* and see how this works for Louis Simpson.

> A bell and rattle,
> After midnight when the presses were rolling
> A guitar and drum,
> A hot summer night on Water Street—
> A light is on in my father's study.
> All he needed was fifty cents
> A man stood in the laurel tree
> And I, who used to lie with the moon,
> As birds are fitted to the boughs
> A siren sang, and Europe turned away . . .
>
> Here comes the subway grating fisher
> Here he came to a place where two creeks meet,
> *He stood still by her bed*
> He was one of the consorts of the moon,
> He woke at five and, unable
> How calm the torso of a woman
> I am taking part in a great experiment— . . .
>
> Love, my machine
> Memory rising in the steppes
> Mountains are moving, rivers
> My father in the night commanding No
> My whole life coming to this place,
> Neither on horseback nor seated,
> Now we're at sea, like the Russians . . .

Parnassus 11, no. 2 (Fall/Winter 1983–Spring/Summer 1984): 302–17.

Not bad! My strictly dispassionate transcriptions have brought forth a mysterious Webernian music. However eccentric the punctuation, however disjointed and richly allusive these verses may be, they have a definite rhythmic contour and a secure intonation. They have other common properties—"deep images" as Simpson might have called them a few years ago: the moon; sexual intimations linked to movements of large bodies like Europe, mountains, and rivers; late hours, dreams, and an air of being vaguely balked, as by fathers needing fifty cents, fathers commanding No, or by being "unable" at five in the morning. A fisher, the dictionary says, is a "somewhat foxlike marten"; that this creature should be grating subways at the crossing of two creeks only confirms the subcutaneous letch for Surrealism that this poet has often vainly tried to deny. If Simpson's first lines in straight alphabetical order fall together so fluently, what might not be achieved by the aleatoric method more rigorously applied, say by the I Ching or a blindfolded John Cage using star charts and trigonometric tables?

Kidding aside, Simpson does indeed have an unmistakable voice; a natural tessitura, or range, within which he moves easily. His might be called a high baritone of moderate volume and considerable carrying power—alert, self-aware, and carefully practiced. It moves outward with trust and affection toward its listeners, trying to enlist common sympathies, discover common rhythmic and semantic ground, pick up over- and undertones, amuse and entertain. It has a weakness for comic asides and inflections that once in a rare while runs out of control. At times it issues the most harrowing ukases in a spirit of tempered, level-headed enthusiasm that leaves the mind reeling. It has a "European" way with vowels, closer to Latin or the English classics than most American poetry of its era; vowels tend to be long or strong and to cluster: "A hot midsummer night in Water Street. . . . A light is on in my father's study. . . . He was one of the consorts of the moon. . . ." The clarity he likes comes from a confident accentual inner ear, an ear trained as much by prose as by poetry—not any prose or poetry but the sonorous periods of a Burke, Johnson, or Gibbon, the grander harmonies of an Eliot, Pound, or Yeats—which he transposes downward into sentences less obviously designed to move, persuade, or transport than those of his masters. His best effects require much cooperation from other imaginations and demonstrate much confidence, sometimes too much, in the widespread existence of that faculty.

What impresses one most throughout *People Live Here* is exactly that trust in the reader, the sense of intimately addressing a good many sorts of people.

> I am taking part in a great experiment—
> whether writers can live peacefully in the suburbs
> and not be bored to death.
>
> > (from "Sacred Objects")

> > Whatever it is, it must have
> > A stomach that can digest
> > Rubber, coal, uranium, moons, poems.
> >
> > Like the shark, it contains a shoe.
> > It must swim for miles through the desert
> > Uttering cries that are almost human.
> >
> > > ("American Poetry")

> Poetry, says Baudelaire, is melancholy:
> the more we desire, the more we shall have to grieve.
> Devour a corpse with your eyes; art consists
> in the cultivation of pain.
> Stupidity reassures you; you do not belong
> in a bourgeois establishment, it can never be your home.
> Restlessness is a sign of intelligence;
> revulsion, the flight of a soul.
>
> > (from "Peter")

> > In the kingdom of heaven
> > there is neither past nor future,
> > but thinking, which is always present:
> > > (from "Maria Roberts")

> > As a man walks he creates the road he walks on.
> > All of my life in America
> > I must have been reeling out of myself
> > this red dirt, gravel road.
> >
> > > (from "As a Man Walks")

He enjoys thinking and wants to make it contagious. He is in accord with the melancholy strain in modern Europe since the Enlightenment. His keen historical sense doesn't delude him into idealizing the past beyond the warrant of solid evidence. But the maxim one wants to dwell on most is "As a man walks he creates the road he walks on." This was a late discovery in his poetry, from a collection of 1979, but has been implicit from the outset. European or not, Simpson has always considered himself a vagrant; only in his most recent interviews has he come around to the opinion that so is everyone else. His volume in the Ann Arbor Poets on Poetry series edited by Donald Hall, *A Company of Poets,* is one of the longest and most valuable in its fearless engagement with the reigning ideas and practitioners of each of the last three decades. An amiably pugilistic tone, not unlike Norman Mailer's, is dominant, and his taste for a blunt, hearty, intimate generality is unwavering.

No poet has been more aware of the difficulties that waited for his generation of postwar poets on graduation from the fostering arms of academe (Mark Van Doren, to be specific). Once recovered from the battle fatigue of three grueling wartime years in the Army—the source of the best *old-fashioned* poems written by an American about the Second World War—he eagerly took up another kind of arms. In "Dead Horses and Live Issues" published in 1967, after admitting the tactical errors he shared with the other editors of the anthology *The New Poets of England and America* (1956), he wrote: "Repulsions held in common— that's what we find when we look at the American poets today." It was the right beginning of wisdom. He may have somewhat overlooked how the sectarian gene pool latent at all times in the U.S.A., ready to nourish the spirit of revulsion and contention, came to life in the sixties as it had just a century before. To a native-born poet the uproar may have seemed only one more seismic fission of the kind that generated countless Protestant sects during the nineteenth century. No doubt the peculiarly complex social makeup of the Jamaica of his first seventeen years somewhat blinded him to this chronic American divisiveness. At any rate, Simpson fully registered its results—no one more feelingly—and his relative obliviousness to its native sources gave his response a personal edge, a fighting anxiety, as if the whole debate had really been only about poetry and the first principles of composition.

A blend of shrewdness and healthy naïveté gives Simpson's prose an authority that several unlucky snap judgments and several labored prejudices do little to undermine. In his essay on Apollinaire one sees how wide the span can be between the two impulses:

> In one respect Apollinaire is not typical of modern times. He is full of enthusiasm. He would not have felt at home in the Waste Land of the twenties, nor would he be happy in the present circles where paranoia reigns. Apollinaire was fundamentally innocent. Under the masks—melancholy being only another mask—there is a childlike confidence in love and art. I think that as we get bored with pessimistic poetry, novels, painting and theater—and surely the creators of boredom must be beginning to bore themselves, as well as the public—Apollinaire's writings will flourish and his influence will increase. . . .

Having cited the poem "Peter" where he says that "art consists / in the cultivation of pain," I should try to square it with the above tirade against pessimistic poetry. Not the only such inconsistency in Simpson, it is nevertheless superficial. What angers him is boredom; that and not pessimism is his real nemesis, as it was for many contemporaries less willing than he to show their hand by inveighing against it.

Simpson's tonic Boswellian talent has been to pick up a number of elementary ideas and throw them at the reader in discomfiting combinations that make one think. Many critics have rapped his knuckles for asserting in several poems that the spiritual life of California is frayed, arid, and thin. This is no new idea; Nathanael West's novels are elaborate demonstrations of it. Simpson's California poems propose nothing new. They merely make a subtle comic chamber music out of ideas so strong that people expect nothing short of Straussian tone poems or Wagnerian overtures. That is, you are supposed to treat the place on its own grandiose terms, like Aldous Huxley in *After Many a Summer Dies the Swan.* Simpson's California poems are collectively inferior to his East Coast and Russian poems, no question. But they are far from despicable, a necessary terminus for his project of American colonization.

The tension between his announced fondness for "the conditions of existence" and his estimate of his adopted country has been extreme.

I believe that my attachment to the surface of things will create in the reader a greater affection for life. In American writing we have had a number of weird creations: a woman who wears a scarlet letter, a white whale, a hero who cannot make love, and so on. But it seems to me we are short of people who love their lives. Do you know the saying of Goethe? "Prophets to the right, prophets to the left . . . the child of the world in the middle." Well, I'm a child of the world. I want to write poetry for people who want to live in the world.

Hence his lifelong choice of "the dramatically narrative form." Hence, too, his steady refusal to be thought a satirist *pur sang*. On the other hand, drama requires a moral frame of goods and bads.

Three intense years in the Army taught me an awful lot about being an American. But I regret that I don't understand the high school view. So there are a lot of instinctive relations between people that I don't understand. I see a lot of things from outside. And I don't understand them quite. . . . On the other hand, as far as probing it from outside goes, and looking into America from outside, and traveling around in it, I've done more than most Americans. I mean, I've been all over America; I've spent nights in strange small towns, I've dug holes in fields, I've seen a lot of America. But there are certain instinctive things that you spend your youthful years doing that you'll never get again. And that I regret.

Indissolubly mixing lyric, comic, and dramatic narrative in the fashion Simpson chose for himself and doing so in the course of making a living in a "strange" land does suggest the fiction of Huxley and Isherwood in their American careers, suggests a helpless tinge of the didactic, the wish to reform and improve. (His opinion of Auden is another matter, too complicated to go into here.) His work exists always at the crossing of three roads; one leads from simple gusto, another from intense curiosity, a third from the memory of a boyhood tropical elysium where the habit of romantic idealization, romantic irony, came all too easily, where his badly assorted (and soon divorced) parents, a taciturn lawyer father of Scots descent and an emotional Russian-Jewish-American mother, rested in uneasy security at the top of the social heap.

In a 1961 review of William Stafford he not only showed his prescience but offered a program.

> As we read Stafford we are aware of how much has been omitted from modern American poetry only because it is not literary, or because it springs from the life of ordinary, rather than "alienated" people. . . . He actually writes about the country he is living in; all sorts of ordinary places, people and animals appear in his poems, and not as subjects of satire, but with the full weight of their own existence.

Again, the inconsistency is only apparent in his having written quite differently about himself in 1975.

> You can never be at home unless you are in the place where you were born. . . . Now I broke completely with my own birthplace. And that means that in a funny sense the rest of my life, as my wife pointed out to me, I am going to write the poems of searching and looking for guides. . . . And another reason I do that is because I believe, with Yeats, that you choose your opposite and work toward it, and that keeps you really alive: the antiself.

The seeming contradiction between these analyses shows his reluctance to apply to an admired native American the same scruples he applies to himself. What if the ordinariness in Stafford were also an antiself? But of course the difference between them is real enough and accounts for their very different careers.

The sense of coming from behind and finding something generally overlooked has, in any case, been fundamental. It accounts for a few wildly unjust opinions of other poets enshrined in *A Company of Poets,* poets he thought too well endorsed by the establishment; it may also account for abrupt switches like his early praise of James Dickey that turned to ridicule when Dickey became famous. But in a book that features admirably discriminating support of W. C. Williams, Apollinaire, Stafford, Ginsberg, Duncan, and others, the balance is distinctly positive. Dare I say that he sometimes resembles Yvor Winters in a readiness to go a long way with exotics like Ginsberg and Duncan but to pull sharply back when the shoals of irrationalism loom?

Occasionally his self-explorations beget *sententiae* of a touching obviousness: "I don't want to listen to a poet berating people for their shortcomings—for example, for not being 'politically aware' as he is. It would be better to give them some pleasure than to make them feel inferior." Now, who could argue with that? Such remarks are spasmodic salutes to the flag in the unrelenting warfare between art and dullness. One should never forget how good he could be in the ironic postgraduate lyric as written by the better fifties poets.

> Having put on new fashions, she demands
> New friends. She trades her beauty and her humor
> In anybody's eyes. If diamonds
> Were dark, they'd sparkle so. Her aura is
> The glance of scandal and the speed of rumor.
>
> One day, as I recall, when we conversed
> In kisses, it amused her to transmit
> "What hath God wrought!"—the message that was first
> Sent under the Atlantic. Nonsense, yet
> It pleases me sometimes to think of it.
>
> *Noli me tangere* was not her sign.
> Her pilgrim trembled with the softest awe.
> She was the only daughter of a line
> That sleeps in poetry and silences.
> She might have sat upon the Sphinx's paw.

Then is she simply false, and falsely fair?
(The promise she would break she never made)
I cannot say, but truly can compare,
For when the stars move like a steady fire
I think of her, and other faces fade.

That this poem should have been put under "Recapitulations" on page 164 of *People Live Here* when an equally fine, very similar rhymed lyric "The Custom of the World," published several years later, is printed on page 15 is one of those puzzling vagaries to be expected when a poet decides to arrange his work by subject and genre rather than in order of appearance. But no matter. Only very small orthographic changes have been made in the poems themselves. On the whole the book's arrangement under the headings "Songs and Lyrics," "The Fighting in Europe," "A Discovery of America," "Modern Lives," "Tales of Volhynia" and "Armidale" (poems and prose about Australia), and "Recapitulations" is entirely useful and fitting. This is poetry in which the choice of scene and subject makes a substantial difference. About two-thirds of "the war in Europe" section is from books of the fifties; the most celebrated of these, "Carentan O Carentan" and "The Bird," are in strictly rhymed, balladlike quatrains, the first close in spirit to one of his earliest enthusiasms, A. E. Housman, the second probably indebted to Heine. But two other impressive war poems, "On the Lawn at the Villa" and "On the Ledge," are from collections of 1963 and 1980 respectively.

If the war-poems section most dramatically reveals Simpson's growth in formal acumen, if the new arrangement greatly complicates any study of his stylistic evolution, the gains far outweigh the small effort of double-checking from a chronology of the poems included in the back of the book. As early as 1963 the book *At the End of the Open Road,* containing "American Poetry" already cited and the well-known "Walt Whitman at Bear Mountain," shows his emancipation from postgraduate formal constraints pretty well completed. From here forward stanza length or line groups express rational sequences, pulses of feeling, changes of scene. If American poetry was to contain "Rubber, coal, uranium, moons, poems," a shark and a shoe, surely

any one poem could also contain such seemingly disparate parts
as the following:

> Once upon a time in California
> the ignorant married the inane
> and they lived happily ever after.
> . . . .
> The dynamo howls
> but the psyche is still, like an Indian.
>
> And those who are still distending the empire
> have vanished beyond our sight.
> Far from the sense of hearing
> and touch, they are merging
> with Asia . . .
> . . . .
> "Hey Chichikov, where are you going?"
>
> "I'm off to the moon," says Chichikov.
>
> "What will you do when you get there?"
>
> "How do I know?" says Chichikov.
> (from "A Friend of the Family")

Perhaps the most useful distinction to be made would be be-
tween his more or less straightforward narratives like "Isidor"
or "Chocolates" and the lyric-narrative-discursive catchalls like
"A Friend of the Family" or "Why Do You Write About Rus-
sia?" Simpson could never, in any case, be accused of fanaticism
or rigidity. His version of "dramatic narrative" is flexible in-
deed. You might say that in Simpson form follows function as
closely as in any of the twentieth-century arts. His principal
ambition has been to encompass, simultaneously, a life, other
lives, and an evolving body of thought. That his formal skills
have evolved in step with his thought is a fortunate bonus. But
despite the scorn he eventually threw at his earliest work we can
see from what he includes in *People Live Here* that he easily held
his own with other "couth" contemporaries like Karl Shapiro,

Delmore Schwartz, Anthony Hecht, John Hollander, and John Berryman.

How successful, then, has he been in exercising the most stringent ironies and at the same time avoiding satire? And was it a reasonable ambition to begin with? Radical satire—Pope, Dryden, Voltaire, Byron—tries to draw its readers into a conspiracy of good sense and plain thinking. It depends on a high degree of spontaneous idiocy in its victims. After a long lapse of attention it rediscovers perennial strains of dullness or foolishness in the world's rulers or ruling ideas. His dramatic instincts notwithstanding, Simpson was presented with more ideas to ridicule— embodied in risibly dead language—than he was with plausible major fools. A mind as curious as his quickly grew suspicious of the press, right or left. The left, for instance, made an idiot out of Eisenhower; the right knew in its bones that Ike *wanted* for strategic reasons, half the time, to look like an idiot. It was still the century of the common man. That Stafford managed to convince Simpson that he was writing about ordinary people was more the achievement of consummate art than proof that such a breed exists. Stafford's people are ordinary by virtue of the poet's ordination of them, nothing less. That Simpson's civilized restraint while making fun of the ideas his people lived by and the language they used slips sometimes into condescension is undeniable. But the people were not rulers, not movers or shakers, so Simpson wanted to distinguish himself from a Pope or Byron. In poems dominated by thumping epigrams or aphorisms the human element sometimes failed to measure up to its possibilities. Here, from a collection of 1971, is the opening section of "Vandergast and the Girl."

> Vandergast to his neighbors—
> the grinding of a garage door
> and hiss of gravel in the driveway.

> He worked for the insurance company
> whose talisman is a phoenix
> rising in flames . . . *non omnis moriar.*
> From his desk he had a view of the street—

translucent raincoats, and umbrellas,
fluorescent plate-glass windows.
A girl knelt down, arranging
underwear on a female dummy—

sea waves and, on the gale,
Venus, these busy days,
poised in her garter-belt and stockings.

A touch of Eliot here, for sure; an echo of Rabelais in the name
Vandergast (Latin *gaster,* stomach); a tag from Horace, *non omnis
moriar;* a snatch of newspaper argot—"these busy days"—to
nail down the erotic innuendo. It's hard to see how this might
not pass for satire in the eyes of the unwary. Let's try, by way of
contrast, "American Classic" of 1980.

It's a classic American scene—
a car stopped off the road
and a man trying to repair it.

The woman who stays in the car
in the classic American scene
stares back at the freeway traffic.

They look surprised, and ashamed
to be so helpless . . .
let down in the middle of the road!

To think that their car would do this!
They look like mountain people
whose son has gone against the law.

But every night they set out food
and the robber goes skulking back to the trees.
That's how it is with the car . . .

it's theirs, they're stuck with it.
Now they know what it's like to sit
and see the world go whizzing by.

In the fume of carbon monoxide and dust
they are not such good Americans
as they thought they were.

The feeling of being left out
through no fault of your own, is common.
That's why I say, an American classic.

It seems likely that a homegrown American of Simpson's authority in this poem would not have conceived the analogy on which its force depends. Our popular notions of "mountain people," derived from *Tobacco Road,* Li'l Abner, and Snuffy Smith, would suggest a much more flexible attitude toward the law on the part of the boy's parents. To accept either scene, in the mountains or along the highway, as classic, requires an unusually strong act of distancing from the reader. The poem has a penumbra of undefined possibilities that virtually begs not to be too closely looked into. But Simpson's speed and assurance oblige one to waive one's prejudices to the extent of allowing the mountain parents their acute embarrassment at their son's compromising dependence on them, just as the car's shameful dependence on its owners, and theirs on it, produce a like effect. In both cases a code of stewardship, assumed by the poem to be deeply ingrained in American folklore, has been too rigidly, too carelessly applied. Parallels between the duties owed to children and to cars are suggested but left unexplored. The acute publicity of the car's behavior stands in the broadest contrast to the manic privacy of the son's. In no sense is it a simple or easily unravelled poem. But because it's so alive, so well written, so mysteriously assured, it is sustained by the sort of unspoken question that often lies in the background of Simpson's best work. For all the force that poetic convention and popular superstition contrive to lend it, is the dilemma the poem proposes a true dilemma? Am "I," the poet, being taken in once again? Is "America" only taking me for yet another ride? Not to detect the presence of such questions is probably to miss half of Simpson's quality.

Simpson's newest book, *The Best Hour of the Night,* takes its title from a passage whose centrality would be hard to miss. It comes eight pages along in a sixteen-page seriocomic narrative called "The Previous Tenant." It also occurs exactly halfway through the three numbered sections of a four-part book entirely given over to narratives of the same kind.

> On nights when he couldn't sleep
> he'd watch the late late show.
> In the dark night of the soul,
> says F. Scott Fitzgerald,
> it is always three in the morning.
> Hemingway says, it isn't so bad . . .
> in fact, the best hour of the night
> once you've reconciled yourself to insomnia
> and stopped worrying about your sins.
> And I say that insomnia can be
> a positive joy if you're tuned in to *Dames*
> or *Gold Diggers of 1933*.

What a witch's brew! The "I" of the passage is a writer of unlisted accomplishments who has rented a small cottage on Long Island just vacated by a doctor recently caught in adultery with a strikingly beautiful woman of Italian descent whose husband is an invalid and patient of the doctor. The narrator manages somehow to worm the essence out of this ultrafamiliar, this classic suburban idyll before the doctor makes a final appearance at the cottage to reclaim his gear, accompanied by an unidentified new helpmeet.

Though Simpson has again let down his guard in this book against the incursion of highbrow quotes or allusions, one sees in the above that those he uses are not especially subtle except in their mutual collisions. Steady readers of *Redbook* or *Cosmopolitan* would know by now what Fitzgerald had said about three o'clock in the morning. But they might not know Hemingway's reply, and if they did might well regard it as blatant nonsense. Nothing that the narrator reveals about himself in the course of the poem suggests that the Hemingway quote is anything but a piece of empty bravado. Yet it's just on doubts of this sort that the poem's success depends. The least one can say is that by making such a man his mouthpiece Simpson has added another layer of ambiguity to a tale already reeking with it. Not since some of the more recondite dramatic narratives of E. A. Robinson have apparently lucid mysteries of this kind clustered so thickly.

For a reader unacquainted with Simpson's career, coming on the book for the first time, the greatest mystery might lie in the choice of such exquisitely banal people, settings, circumstances and, above all, language, with which to celebrate the contemporary *homme moyen moyen*. This reader found the poems extremely entertaining and quite sufficiently profound. Their verbal materials have been as carefully culled and set as gems in a Tiffany tiara. But in their outward aspects they are the stuff of literature, especially the hardboiled school of the twenties and thirties, or of films and television. The poems reward the kind of attention one gives to an Ashbery, Ammons, Ignatow, or Zukofsky. But they also depend, far more vitally than the above, on an antiquarian sense of the vernacular. In which respect they may be equally esoteric and doomed to a small audience. They ask that one accept the possibility that everyone in "these spreading interconnected villages . . . the new world we are entering," as he said in an interview of 1973, is engaged in the same mortal combat with ossified locutions, trying to squeeze his or her own poetry from them against terrifying odds. In 1979 Simpson told an Australian interviewer that "It's the timidity of suburban life that is so limiting." Long ago he wrote a poem, "In the Suburbs":

> There's no way out.
> You were born to waste your life.
> You were born to this middleclass life.
>
> As others before you
> Were born to walk in procession
> To the temple, singing.

The ending is unsatisfactory. Does he mean there is a religious, temple-haunting dimension to suburbia? The John Cheever gospel? Or does he only mean that things have gone rapidly downhill, that *homo medius americanus* can but dimly understand what he has lost?

Simpson can be remorseless in a manner all his own.

Stabbed in the back by his partner.
There was blood on a green, felt-covered table
He lingered a few years, dying slowly,
moving from place to place.
At the end of a long corridor
the room in which he sat was piled with books.
A window looked across the air shaft
to a ledge where pigeons built their nests.
Here the traffic was hushed,
so that you heard the *rou* and *rou*
of the pigeons. They fluttered,
ruffled, and pecked.
The shadows of their wings
flashed across a sunlit wall.

He had been put in charge of a "cultural series"—
books with a limited audience
but "viable cultural interest."

From "Elegy for Jake," the lines are a supercooled parody of the exasperated comedies about lost intellectuals and cultural brokers once written by Mary McCarthy, Wilfred Sheed, Elizabeth Hardwick, and others with the right qualifications. About a half-dozen poets also once wrote poems in this vein, though few in number and with diminishing frequency as their careers advanced. That Simpson should be increasing his mastery of the genre, so that in 1983 he seems to be just discovering it, must mean that he senses a god-given chance to wind the whole process up. These people, these scenes—the poems say—will never come again. Then let us be as Chekhovian as we can, as remorseless as an ancient Highlander on the warpath.

Ed was in love with a cocktail waitress,
but Ed's family, and his friends,
didn't approve. So he broke it off.

He married a respectable woman
who played the piano. She played well enough
to have been a professional.

Ed's wife left him . . .
Years later, at a family gathering

Ed got drunk and made a fool of himself.
He said, "I should have married Doreen."
"Well," they said, "why didn't you?"

("Ed")

For whatever reason, perhaps to appease his own vanity, a critic
might be strongly tempted to offer a consolation prize to any
poet still willing to write like this. It's brave, it's companionable
(toward those of a certain age) and in one way or another it's
intensely literary. But for all that, reality keeps breaking in, not
only in homely details like the pigeons and the name Doreen but
in an original proportion between the leisurely and the laconic,
the hard and the soft, the sweet and the sour. A *mensch* of some
hitherto indefinable kind is out there in the wilderness, wherever
precisely that wilderness may be thought to lie, writing poems
as if everyone's life depended on it.

DAVID WOJAHN

"I Might Live Here Myself"
On Louis Simpson

By now it should be clear to everyone who cares about contemporary poetry that Louis Simpson is one of our most indispensable talents. Practically no figure of his generation is a better poet, and few are his equals. While many of his contemporaries—James Dickey, for example, or Galway Kinnell—have shown a marked decline in power during the past decade, Simpson keeps getting better and better. And yet why is it that, when I try to summon words to describe Simpson's manner, only the most harsh and negative labels seem to fit: *cynical, sarcastic, dyspeptic, misanthropic, glib?* These adjectives seem particularly appropriate in describing Simpson's most recent, narrative phase, which began with *Adventures of the Letter I* (1971), and which continues in his latest collection, *The Best Hour of the Night.* One must examine Simpson's work with care and patience before seeing that he is not, in fact, the cynic and misanthrope he may appear to be and that he has instead become (somewhat grudgingly) one of our most moral and convincingly humanitarian writers. The reason for Simpson's ambivalent stance, and also for the reader's confusion about how to judge Simpson's position, is that Simpson's major concern is one that most of his contemporaries would rather avoid confronting, the quotidian lives of suburban, middle-class America.

Simpson is, in other words, a chronicler of the "American Scene," the kind of poet that we haven't seen in some time, and unlike earlier poets who fit this category—Shapiro and Kenneth Fearing come to mind—he retains none of the Whitmanesque, gee-whiz wonder that makes even their harshest judgments of

Tar River Poetry 24, no. 1 (Fall 1984): 41–51.

society become rather tepid. Simpson doesn't care much for suburbia. As he writes in his 1976 essay "Rolling Up," "I don't like the tribe that uses supermarkets and roads." Neither does he care for what he sees as the excessive introspection of most American poets. His recent work has abandoned the hermetic image-mongering of the Surrealism that once engaged him, and though a kind of personal disclosure is essential to Simpson's technique, it is far different from the blunt urgencies of confessional poetry. Given Simpson's rejection of current literary fashion, he seems to have nowhere to go but home—to the car lots and shopping malls of suburban Long Island, where he now lives, and to the mnemonic landscape of Jamaica, where he was born and spent his childhood. Yet even at home, Simpson must be an outsider. His evocations of his childhood (his father was of Scots ancestry, his mother a Russian Jew) are singularly lacking in nostalgia, and his terse narratives about suburbia dish out their affection sparingly. As Jarrell once said of Graves, much of life comes to Simpson already sharpened into caricature, and in suburbia, of course, caricature scenes abound. Simpson loves to indulge himself in describing them. What's important about Simpson, however, and what seems to me the source of his grandeur, is that this is the *only* indulgence he allows himself. He can't resist making fun of his subjects, yet he wants to feel a tenderness for them, even though such tenderness is quite alien to his temperament. To understand Simpson, one has to see that he is a man on a quest: he's looking for something, *anything,* that is redeeming in his subjects. The task he sets for himself is sometimes, like Victorian sex, a painful duty. But if his speaker succeeds in his quest he will achieve something he has never known before—a kind of humility. The process that Simpson has undergone to prepare for this quest is amply in evidence in his two recently published collections, *People Live Here,* which includes work from his eight previous volumes, and *The Best Hour of the Night,* one of his strongest collections thus far.

Like so much poetry published in the 1940s and early 1950s, Simpson's early work is strongly influenced by Elizabethan and metaphysical poetry. One reviewer of *The Arrivistes,* his first collection, compared its poems to those of Campion. While the early work is elegant and deft, its range is limited, merely a skillful adaptation of the period style. There are a number of love lyrics in Simpson's first two books, but they are clearly about idealized figures, no more real—and far less vivid—than Herrick's imaginary Julia. The beloved of "Rough Winds Do Shake" was obviously born and deflowered in the library and exists mostly as the vehicle for some sprightly accentuals:

> She is sixteen
> > sixteen
> > > and her young lust
> Is like a thorn
> > hard thorn
> > > among the pink
> of her soft nest.
> Upon this thorn she turns, for love's incessant sake.

Yet in the numerous poems describing Simpson's experience as a combat infantryman during World War II a rather different style emerges—skeptical and terse, and within the range of its strict metrics, largely narrative in purpose. The opening of "Memories of a Lost War," from Simpson's second volume *Good News of Death* (1955), with its unadorned, deadpan description, shows the early Simpson at his best, and prefigures the tone of many of his later poems:

> The guns know what is what but underneath
> In fearful file
> We go around burst books and packs and teeth
> That seem to smile.

> The scene jags like a strip of celluloid,
> A mortar fires,
> Cinzano falls, Michelin is destroyed,
> The man of tires.

> As darkness drifts like fog in from the sea
> Somebody says
> "We're digging in." Look well, for this may be
> The last of days.

If the metaphysicals were the inspiration for many of the poems of *The Arrivistes,* then a poem such as this owes a similar debt to Hardy: the same blunt irony, the same wrenched syntax

and alteration of long and short lines. But Hardy's impact on
Simpson at this point in his career is even more important for
another reason. Like Hardy, Simpson wants his poems to tell
stories, and he seeks to tell them in the most compressed and
economical fashion. From Simpson's essays and autobiographi-
cal poems that refer to his life in the 1950s, we know that he was
also trying to write fiction during this time. But he finally came
to share Hardy's disillusionment with prose fiction as the proper
vehicle for his subjects. After publishing the novel *Riverside
Drive* in 1962, Simpson abandoned fiction altogether. Around
the same time, Simpson began to strive to change the method of
his poetry, for the forms he had been working in did not permit
a full expression of his primary impulses, didacticism and
narrative.

Simpson's method for escaping his dilemma was first to aban-
don strict metrics and to adopt for a time the neo-Surrealist
approach that during the same years was engaging poets like
Robert Bly and James Wright. On the surface, these new poems
of Simpson's look radically different from the old, incorporating
the startling imagery and dreamy introspection of Surrealism.
The opening of "There Is," from Simpson's *At the End of the
Open Road* (1963), displays a method perhaps all too familiar to
us today, a catalog of Surrealist cataloging, some Lorca here,
some Rimbaud there:

> Look! From my window there's a view
> of city streets
> where only lives as dry as tortoises
> can crawl—the Galapagos of desire.
>
> There is the day of Negroes with red hair
> and the day of the insane women on the subway;
> there is the day of the word Trieste
> and the night of the blind man with the electric guitar.

It all seems quite doctrinaire to us now, but we can imagine how
exciting writing like this must have seemed to readers twenty
years ago. Yet unlike lesser poets such as Bly, Simpson was only
a fellow traveler of the Deep Image Party and accepted the pre-
cepts of Surrealism with some reservations. Suspicious of both
the solipsism of Surrealism and its romantic amorality, he tem-

pered his use of Surrealism with a tone both ironic and discursive. In fact, as he states later in "There Is," "I have the poor man's nerve tic, irony. / I see through the illusions of the age!" He may employ the giddy pyrotechnics of Surrealism, but he is aware that they, too, are one of the age's illusions. At the conclusion of "There Is," we are meant to feel an unsettling ambivalence. We can sympathize with the speaker's anxiety and alienation, but we also feel his exasperation with his means for describing these states. He knows we know that he is stuck with warmed-over *symboliste* clichés, and this makes the poem's conclusion affecting, in a curious sort of way:

> But all night long my window
> sheds tears of light.
> I seek the word. The word is not forthcoming.
> O syllables of light . . . O dark cathedral . . .

Even in the most famous of Simpson's deep image excursions, the often anthologized "American Poetry," we can see that he is hedging his bets. Surrealism, in its purest definition, seeks to give form to the individual's unconscious desires and aspirations, but here Simpson uses Surrealism as a kind of public, didactic shorthand as the most expedient way of articulating his conflicting attitudes toward his adopted country and his own aesthetic presumptions:

> Whatever it is, it must have
> A stomach that can digest
> Rubber, coal, uranium, moons, poems.
>
> Like the shark, it contains a shoe.
> It must swim for miles through the desert
> Uttering cries that are almost human.

Throughout his career, Simpson's goal has been to find the most economical means to relate his stories and espouse his opinions. Strict forms allowed Simpson to achieve these ends in his earliest poems; Surrealism, with its abandonment of developed transitional devices and admixture of the rational and irrational, accomplished the same goals in the poems of *At the End of the Open Road.* But for a poet whose bent is discursive, Surrealism offers some difficulties. Because it achieves its effect through implication, it is precise, but indirect. It can vividly evoke, for example, states of alienation within the writer, but it is a poor vehicle for public utterance. This is why the Surrealist approach works so magnificently for Neruda in his early, introspective poems collected in *Residence on Earth,* but often becomes hollow rhetoric in the poems of his later Marxist phase. Because it is founded on the state of emotional extremity—alienation *or* transcendence—Surrealism became inadequate for Simpson's purposes by the time of his first *Selected Poems,* published in 1965. At this point, Simpson's ambition was to abandon the fierce, resentful quarrel with American society that had been the primary force behind the poems of *At the End of the Open Road.* This new approach, coming as it did during one of the most tumultuous decades in American history, was not arrived at because Simpson had suddenly decided to embrace the prefabricated mores of middle America, but because Simpson had chosen, very consciously and deliberately, to abandon one of the most hallowed tenets of modernist art—that the artist must, to a large degree, be alienated from the society in which he dwells. Instead of conceiving of himself as a solitary *poète maudit,* Simpson sought to share in the alienation felt by his peers in the suburban middle class. We see this process at work in very succinct fashion in "After Midnight," from the section of new work gathered in the 1965 *Selected Poems.* Scarcely longer than "American Poetry," its method is much different, and more convincingly visionary. While the scene is one of eerie, Hopperlike desolation, Simpson's method of description is realistic. Within the poem's twelve lines, the speaker comes to a grim revelation, one that seems to reverberate in all of Simpson's subsequent poems:

> The dark streets are deserted,
> With only a drugstore glowing
> Softly, like a sleeping body;
>
> With one white, naked bulb
> In the back, that shines
> On suicides and abortions.

Who lives in these dark houses?
I am suddenly aware
I might live here myself.

The garage man returns
And puts the change in my hand,
Counting the singles carefully.

The speaker has accepted his condition with a harrowing lucidity. He knows that he must dwell in this landscape, but also knows that he must share in the guilt for having created it. Blood is on his hands, just as it is on the hands of the suicides and abortionists mentioned in the first half of the poem, and the garage man who returns the speaker's change: there are *no* innocent bystanders. From this stance of troubled acquiescence a great many of the poems from Simpson's last twenty years have been written. This new work deals less with states of emotional extremity than with the more middle-aged (and perhaps more pressing) problem of merely coping, of living the life that the title of one of the poems in *The Best Hour of the Night* describes as "Quiet Desperation," Simpson borrowing from Thoreau. It is a state that both Simpson's speakers and the large cast of characters who have populated his recent poems must confront.

Of course, Simpson's new attitudes have significantly affected the form of his work. The new poems owe much to fictional technique in their development of character and patterns of narration, and their style, flat and unadorned, has the same telegraphic precision Simpson sought in his early work. While they make minimal use of transitions, shift point of view and person with great frequency, and are similarly liberal in their shifts of setting and time, the limpid surfaces of the poems allow for all these devices to be superbly integrated. Despite the commonplace subject matter of Simpson's recent poems, they are clearly the work of a radical poetic imagination.

"Vandergast and the Girl," from *Adventures of the Letter I,* is a good example of Simpson's mature technique. After a brief introductory section describing the poem's protagonist ("He worked for the insurance company / whose talisman is a phoenix / rising in flames"), the poem's second section, with great economy, shows Vandergast beginning an illicit affair:

                    The next day he saw her eating
                    in the restaurant where he usually ate.

                    Soon they were having lunch together
                    elsewhere.

                            She came from Dallas.
                    This was only a start, she was ambitious,
                    twenty-five and still unmarried.
                    Green eyes with silver spiricles . . .
                    red hair . . .

                            When he held the car door open
                    her legs were smooth and slender.

                    "I was wondering,"
                    she said, "when you'd get round to it,"
                    and laughed.

Like Chekhov's stories, which Simpson so greatly admires, a
passage such as this one succeeds in part because of the author's
wry combination of tenderness toward and judgment upon his
characters and in part because the style, despite its apparent
straightforwardness, is one of implication rather than directness.
In refurbishing the clichés of daily speech ("This was only a
start, she was ambitious," " 'I was wondering,' / she said,
'when you'd get round to it' ") and in his judicious use of ellip-
sis—implying a sort of conversation already so familiar to us
that we can fill the rest of it in—Simpson both winks at the
audience and gives a kind of hapless cry of foreboding. By the
end of the passage, we know full well that no good will come of
Vandergast's fling. After a section in which Vandergast relates
the events of the affair in some detail and which becomes almost
poignant in its very drabness—he buys her chocolates from
Schrafft's; they watch a soap opera together after lovemaking—
the last section of the poem functions merely as epilogue:

                    The Vandergasts are having some trouble
                    finding a buyer for their house.

When I go for a walk with Tippy
we pass the unweeded tennis court,
the empty garage, windows heavily shuttered.

Mrs. Vandergast took the children
and went back to her family.

And Vandergast moved to New Jersey
where he works for an insurance company
whose symbol is the Rock of Gibraltar—
the rest of his life laid out
with the child-support and alimony payments.

As for the girl, she vanished.

Was it worth it? Ask Vandergast.
You'd have to be Vandergast, looking through his eyes
at the house across the street, in Orange, New Jersey.
Maybe on wet days umbrellas and raincoats
set his heart thudding.

                Maybe
he talks to his pillow, and it whispers,
moving red hair.

In any case, he will soon be forty.

This sort of compassionate case study appears with great frequency in Simpson's recent work, and in "The Previous Tenant," from *The Best Hour of the Night,* we see this method applied to one of his most ambitious efforts. Nearly twenty pages long, the poem cannot be described with any brevity, but it surely ranks among Simpson's best. Adultery in the suburbs is once again the poem's nominal subject, but if "Vandergast and the Girl" reads like a short story streamlined and intensified into verse, then "The Previous Tenant," reads like a novel—a *good* novel—similarly streamlined and intensified.

Unfortunately, however, not all of Simpson's poetic forays into suburbia are as successful as these two poems. Sometimes a poem will read like Cliff's Notes for a Cheever story. And sometimes, when Simpson abandons his longish narratives for a shorter, more epigrammatic approach to the suburban land-scape, his efforts amount to little more than caricature, as in the final two stanzas of "American Classic." After watching a fam-ily stand befuddled on a roadside as they try to fix their broken-down car, Simpson writes:

> In the fume of carbon monoxide and dust
> they are not such good Americans
> as they thought they were.
>
> The feeling of being left out
> through no fault of your own, is common.
> That's why I say, an American classic.

One needn't argue with the accuracy of a poem like this; it's even funny in a brutal sort of way, but it's also too *easy*. There's an interesting passage near the end of "The Previous Tenant," in which the speaker, after seeing a vandalized statue in the public park of the bedroom community where the poem takes place, and commenting on the statue's destruction with a cheerful non-chalance, is accused by his girlfriend of being cynical:

> I said, why was it
> that when you told the truth
> people accused you of being cynical?
>
> We were on our way to having a quarrel. . . .

Even the most fanatical Simpson loyalist will have to admit that there's some truth to the woman's accusation. Simpson some-times *is* cynical, and because of the arrangement of *People Live Here*—thematic rather than chronological—we witness the cynical side of Simpson's temperament more prominently than we might otherwise see it. In Simpson's previous collections, from *Adventures of the Letter I* onward, Simpson juxtaposed his shorter, more acid poems with the longer narratives in such a way that the shorter efforts seemed less troubling, pungent in-terludes to the main business at hand. But in the poems selected in *People Live Here* we have too many of the shorter, more inconsequential poems, and they appear in a rather arbitrary arrangement. Furthermore, some of Simpson's most masterful long poems, such as "The Springs of Gadara," from *Searching for the Ox* (1975), do not appear in the new volume. By giving *People Live Here* a thematic structure, Simpson seeks to emphasize the continuity within his work, but what this structure instead does is to more harshly illuminate Simpson's limitations.

Yet one of the things that tempers our dissatisfaction with Simpson's most glib and sardonic efforts is another sort of poem which has recently concerned him and in which, throughout Simpson's last four collections, he has sought to write a verse autobiography. This sort of autobiographical approach is something most readers of poetry are quite familiar with, for it has been a dominant form in American verse ever since Lowell published *Life Studies* in 1959. But Simpson's attitude toward personal disclosure, and indeed toward the process of memory itself, is quite different from that of Lowell and the confessional poets. In Simpson we see none of Lowell's burning cathartic need to relive the most painful events of his past; we instead see a stance that is quizzical and coolly personal. In fact, many of Simpson's autobiographical poems are related by a persona named Peter, who, like Simpson, grew up in the West Indies, served in the infantry during World War II, and worked in journalism and publishing after the war. By speaking through the voice of an alter ego, Simpson frees himself from a merely documentary exploration of his past and seeks to enlarge his investigation of memory to include the realms of public, private, and even mythic history. Given the curiously international nature of Simpson's ancestry and upbringing, this goal is by no means a grandiose one. His desire for such a synthesis springs from personal necessity, as we see in a poem like "Why Do You Write About Russia?" Prompted by the speaker's recollections of his mother's Russian girlhood, its subject is Simpson's need to accept the complexities of his past:

> Once, after an illness, she was sent
> to Odessa, on the sea. There were battleships
> painted white, and ladies and gentlemen
> walking the esplanade . . . white naval uniforms
> and parasols.

These stories were told
against a background of tropical night . . .
a sea breeze stirring the flowers
that open at dusk, smelling like perfume.
The voice that spoke of freezing cold
itself was warm and comforting.

So it is with poetry: whatever numbing horrors
it may speak of, the voice itself
tells of love and infinite wonder.

Later, when I came to New York,
I used to go to my grandmother's
in Brooklyn. The names of stations
return in their order like a charm:
Franklin, Nostrand, Kingston.
And members of the family gather:
the three sisters, the one brother,
one of the cousins from Washington,
and myself . . . a "student at Columbia."
But what am I really?

Of course, as the poem progresses, this question is never really answered. As with Cavafy, whose name is evoked in the title poem of *Searching for the Ox,* Simpson can find no more solace in the past than he can in the present. He relives his personal history and tenderly mythologizes scenes from Czarist Russia not because his attitude is conventionally nostalgic, but because he acknowledges the past's inexplicable hold on him. In making sense of his past, Simpson does not seek an abiding perspective, only a sort of provisional acceptance of time as a process both ironic and cyclical. In the opening of "Working Late," Simpson recalls his attorney father laboring late through the night in his study:

He is working late on cases.
No impassioned speech! He argues from evidence,
actually pacing out and measuring,
while the fans revolving on the ceiling
winnow the true from the false.

Once he passed a brass curtain rod
through a head made out of plaster
and showed the jury the angle of fire—
where the murderer must have stood.
For years, all through my childhood,
if I opened a closet . . . bang!
There would be the dead man's head
with a black hole in the forehead.

At the conclusion of the poems, we are brought to the present,
where the poet himself is also working late:

I can see the drifting offshore lights,
black posts where the pelicans brood.

And the light that used to shine
at night in my father's study
now shines as late in mine.

What saves this poem from sentimentality is not only its evoca-
tive use of detail, but more importantly, its self-deprecating
tone. While Simpson sometimes lets his sarcasm toward his
characters weaken his studies of suburbia, here the humor is
directed toward the speaker. While Simpson's poems of mem-
ory contain all the acute narrative compression that we see in
many of his other poems, this added element of whimsy gives
the memory poems both a poignance and an associative authen-
ticity that makes them among Simpson's best. "Sway," which
recalls the speaker's unrequited love affair with a girl he once
worked with at a summer resort, ends in a kind of dreamy stasis
that's absolutely right for its subject:

She said, "When you're a famous novelist
will you write about me?"

I promised . . . and tried to keep my promise.

Recently, looking for a toolbox,
I came upon some typewritten pages,
all about her. There she is

in a canoe . . . a gust of wind
rustling the leaves along the shore.
Playing tennis, running up and down the baseline.
Down by the boathouse, listening to the orchestra
playing "Sleepy Lagoon."

Then the trouble begins, I can never think of anything
to make the characters do.
We are still sitting in the moonlight
while she finishes her cigarette.
Two people go by, talking in low voices.
A car door slams. Driving off . . .

"I suppose we ought to go,"
I say.

                    And she says, "Not yet."

It is in a passage such as this one that Simpson's goal of achieving his particular kind of humility is most finely realized, both through his careful respect for his characters and his astute particularity of detail. Though Simpson's means are modest, a steadfast adherence to revealing what Stevens's famous poem calls "the plain sense of things," Simpson seems to me as powerful and honest a poet as any writing today. He is also, surely, our most genuinely *American* poet. He is not the most likeable writer we have, nor is he our most verbally gifted or complex one, but he *is* a dependable writer, one who has carved a niche all his own and one who keeps growing in range and power. How many poets of his generation—one that includes some extremely formidable figures—can this be said about? In *People Live Here* and *The Best Hour of the Night,* we have the testament of a writer who now has every reason to call *himself* an American classic.

T. R. HUMMER

Revising the Poetry Wars

Louis Simpson's Assault
on the Poetic

> . . . very few people could live . . . with no separation between "real
> life" and the life of the mind.
>
> —Louis Simpson, "Armidale"

In a recent *Georgia Review* [(Fall 1983): 662–75], Peter Stitt
writes that Louis Simpson's *People Live Here: Selected Poems
1949–1983* "makes clear that there are three major phases to be
found in the body of Simpson's work, phases which are sepa-
rated by major changes in style, subject matter, and approach."
Simpson is certainly one of those poets (like James Wright,
Robert Penn Warren, Robert Lowell, and Elizabeth Bishop, to
name only a few other such writers of recent vintage) the study
of whose entire body of work is particularly rewarding, partly
because it exhibits drastic, unpredictable, and yet characteristic
change. Anyone who is at all familiar with Simpson's poetry
knows that there are two major shifts in his work that divide his
canon into three stylistically different parts. The first part in-
cludes Simpson's first three books: *The Arrivistes, Good News of
Death,* and *A Dream of Governors.* The second division, which is
less well defined, is transitional: it begins with *At the End of the
Open Road,* is well represented by the "New Poems" section of
Simpson's 1965 *Selected Poems,* and works itself out (or is already
over) in *Adventures of the Letter I.* Whichever phase the latter
book belongs to, the latest phase is fully under way in *Searching
for the Ox,* and clearly continues in *Caviare at the Funeral* and the
recently published *The Best Hour of the Night.* All this is a matter
of record. No one who has written on Simpson in the past few
years has failed to notice the differences: the highly traditional
and polished but often stilted early work; the far more interest-

Kenyon Review 6, no. 3 (Summer 1984): 114–23.

ing middle phase, which embodies so many of the teachings of Simpson's friend Robert Bly; and the less easily definable recent work, which is at once straightforward and aphoristic, narrative and parabolic, passionate and prosaic, mysterious and clear.

Evaluations differ, but the descriptions agree adequately. It is not my purpose to repeat them, as descriptions, any more than I have already done. Certain perhaps unanswerable questions interest me far more: what do these transitions *mean?* What do they mean to Simpson, and what do they mean to us? The generality of such questions is appalling, but it is necessary to take a stab at answering them here, because Louis Simpson seems to me perhaps the most representative poet among us— representative in that he so clearly embodies the issues with which every poet worth the name unavoidably grapples. The publication of his new selected poems *People Live Here* reveals how true this has been for Simpson in the long course of his career; the new work in *The Best Hour of the Night* demonstrates how true it continues to be.

Clearly I agree with Stitt that Simpson's work, viewed linearly, divides neatly into three distinct stylistic stages; however, I strongly disagree that *People Live Here* makes that division clear. On the contrary, Simpson has chosen to give his new book an unchronological arrangement which seems calculated to obscure that often-remarked-on developmental unfolding. Simpson explains in a headnote to the book:

> This is not the usual chronological arrangement—poems selected from the author's first book followed by poems from the second, and so on. Instead I have selected poems from all my books and placed them in groups. There is an opening section of "Songs and Lyrics"—in other sections the poems are centered around an idea. I believe that this arrangement shows the nature of my writing more clearly than has appeared up to now in separate books.

Simpson's final sentence invites us to a different kind of understanding of his body of work from the one a chronological reading yields, that linear change which Stitt, among others, is at pains to describe. Indeed, *People Live Here* seems particularly designed to undercut such description. "It follows," Simpson continues ingenuously in his headnote, "that poems in contrasting forms may stand side by side—an early poem in meter and rhyme next to a more recent poem written in free form." It also follows that, as far as Simpson is concerned, poems from one "phase" of his work can stand side by side with poems from another—not, perhaps, without tension, but certainly without contradiction—and that such a structuring should yield a different way of investigating the poems, one which is no longer concerned with the linear history of their composition, but now seeks to explain this representation (or perhaps I had better say this illusion of a representation) of the way the poems exist contemporaneously, side by side in the mind of the poet himself.

In addition to his two biographical-anecdotal books *Three on the Tower* and *A Revolution in Taste,* Louis Simpson has written a respectable amount of what (for want of a better term) I will call informal criticism—reviews and occasional essays, most of which are more or less superficial. I don't intend this as a negative observation—on the contrary, these pieces make very interesting reading. They are like the reports of a war correspondent writing from the thick of the action at the front. That's where Simpson is, and that's where he has been for years: in the trenches on the front line of the poetry wars. He was there as a child in Jamaica, reading the Georgians while the other boys played cricket; he was there at Columbia, sniping at the intellectual programmes of the academy; he was there at the end of the fifties when the feud fired up between the Redskins and the Palefaces, getting in his potshots at that mythic two-headed monster *brooksandwarren;* he served as a volunteer for a while in the camp of the new Surrealism; and later on, in another war when the alliances had changed and the issues were different, he fired a round or two at his old commanding officer, Bly. And on and on. In these conflicts, Simpson has never been a general. He is, as he says himself, a perennial dogface, a foot soldier. His policies, as he states them in his dispatches, are the rough-and-ready policies of the soldier in the trench: he consistently comes down romantically—if a little vaguely—on the side of the emotions as opposed to the intellect, and he is democratic in his leanings, but not revolutionary. Now he seems to us the scarred veteran sergeant, still in uniform, less decorated than one might expect, but ready to serve again in any general conflict.

That Simpson has not sought promotion to the officer rank is no failure and no accident. Simpson has written, ". . . I retain the dogface's suspicion of the officer class, with their abstract language and indifference to individual, human suffering." Simpson has purposely made no effort to become a major theorist because he knows perfectly well that, to the poet, critical theory is no more than a marginal skirmish in the main offensive. The poem itself is the battlefield, and the enemy is not other poets and the ideas they sometimes appear to represent; the enemy is the poet himself: his limitations, his unexamined assumptions, his blindnesses, his most basic intuitions. It is out of the war with these and other aspects of the self that poetry comes, and the only place where the battle can be joined is on the front lines, in the trenches, strategy be damned. That war is the kind Tolstoy describes in *War and Peace,* wherein the action of the battle itself is in control, not the strategies of generals. The assault takes place within the poet as he works, and it is directed at himself, at his own entrenched notions of what a poem is and is not, of what a poem can and cannot do. The image that poets have of what poetry is, its function in the world, or lack of one—the image that poets have of themselves as poets—these things are not easily arrived at, nor are they ever complete and fixed. No poet simply *decides* these things. They have to be fought for.

Speaking [in "Dogface Poetics"] of his early poems about World War II, Simpson tells us:

> Language seems to falsify physical life. . . . I wanted people to find in my poems the truth of what it had been like to be an American infantry soldier. Now I see I was writing a memorial of those years for the men I had known, who were silent. I was trying to write poems that I would not be ashamed to have them read—poems that would be, in their laconic and simple manner, tolerable to men who had seen a good deal of combat and had no illusions.

No doubt there is a strong element of revisionism in this retrospect, but it does illuminate certain aspects of Simpson's work. Knowing at least part of what Simpson had in mind helps us understand how a poet as good as he was even at the very beginning of his career could write and publish lines as bad as these:

> I must lie down at once, there is
> A hammer at my knee.
> And call it death or cowardice,
> Don't count again on me.
>
> Everything's all right, Mother,
> Everyone gets the same
> At one time or another.
> It's all in the game.
>
> (from "Carentan O Carentan")

Whatever else we might say about them, such lines would be instantly recognizable to any soldier in the trench as poetry. This is the dogface's poetic with a vengeance, something between Wilfred Owen and Kilroy. But there is another side to this coin: while the dogface would know that this was a poem, he would also know that (like most poems to most people most of the time) it was not something to be taken very seriously. If, on the other hand, the same dogface read these lines—

> For ten thousand francs
> she would let him stay the night,
> and a thousand for the concièrge.
> The maid, too, must have something.
>
> Then, finally, he would be alone with her.
> Her face a perfect oval,
> a slender neck, brown hair . . .
>
> It surprised him that a girl
> who looked delicate in her clothes
> was voluptuous when she stood naked.
>
> (from "A Bower of Roses")

—he would very likely take them seriously, but it is highly possible he would not recognize them as poetry: furthermore, if someone called them poetry, he might disbelieve it and even resent the assertion.

If we view Simpson's work linearly, we are tempted to explain the difference between the two poems I have just excerpted as dictated by direct stylistic decisions. Stitt, with Simpson's own corroboration, puts it this way:

> It was after the publication of his third book that Simpson made the first major change in his work. To bring more of his own voice into his poetry, he abandoned traditional English forms and began to write in free verse; he explains: "I had been writing poetry that was quite formal. . . . Then between 1959 and 1963 I broke all that up and tried to write poetry that would be more free, that would sound more like my own voice. . . ."

No doubt there is something perfectly true about this explanation, but I can't help thinking that it sounds too easy. It sounds as though Simpson could have made that change any time he wanted to. It should have been perfectly simple. All he had to do was use his "own voice." But if that's the case, why did it take him four years (1959–1963) to break "all that up"? Stitt's view is attractive, yielding as it does to discussion of Simpson's work in the context of the large movements of the poetry of this century: the poetry war which Pound championed, the famous "revolution in taste." And clearly that is pertinent. The problem with such an explanation is that, beyond a certain point, it loses Simpson in the pack. That line of approach only leads us to say that Simpson has done what everyone else has done, which is, to be fair, both true and untrue. The linear progression of Simpson's work bears it out; the power and unique quality of his work belies it.

The nonlinear structure of *People Live Here* suggests a more appealing angle of approach. First of all, we see right away that Simpson *has* no single "natural voice"; he has a multiplicity of voices. There is Simpson the dogface, sure enough; but there is also Simpson the "British" Jamaican, Simpson the New Yorker, Simpson the tourist, Simpson the Long Island suburbanite, Simpson the Russian Jew(!); there is Simpson the liberal, Simpson the conservative, Simpson the man on the street, Simpson the aesthete, Simpson the sophisticate, Simpson the *naïf*—the list could go on and on. At the same time, we see that every facet of Simpson's body of work reflects all the others. For instance, this stanza—

> In that so sudden summer storm they tried
> Each bed, couch, closet, carpet, car-seat, table,
> Both river banks, five fields, a mountain side,
> Covering as much ground as they were able.
>
> (from "Summer Storm")

—appeared in Simpson's first book, but it absolutely predicts the Cheeveresque tongue-in-cheek suburban "stories" of his much later work. When it stands side by side with that later work, the identity becomes immediately apparent. Furthermore, the following excerpt from *The Best Hour of the Night* courts the "poetic" as much as anything Simpson has ever written, regardless of its lack of adherence to "traditional English forms":

> . . . the winged Psyche,
> Desire, who is always wandering
> over these lawns and between these houses.
>
> (from "The Gardener")

People Live Here makes it clear not that Simpson's work is divisible into phases (though from one angle of view, of course, it is); this book makes it clear that Simpson wants us to see a different truth about his and any good poet's way of working: that there are never absolute divisions, and that no poet can ever afford to turn his back on any possibility, because just when he does, that which he has rejected or neglected will turn out to be precisely what is called for:

> Her sister, Lisa, died of typhus.
> The corpse was laid on the floor.
>
> They carried it to the cemetery
> in a box, and brought back the box.
> "We were poor—a box was worth something."
>
> (from "Typhus")

It seems to me that Simpson has been working for his whole career to reach, more and more effectively, that silent, entrenched audience he first set out to address without embarrassment. As he has grown older, though, he has come to recognize that wars are not fought only on literal battlefields—that such wars (like arguments among critics) are impressive, but they are only the fringe skirmishes of the real war that goes on constantly in the human soul. Simpson is, in a real sense, always writing about shell shock:

> He listens carefully, to get things right.
> The feud between the Andersons and the Kellys
> began with Ruth Anderson calling Mike Kelly
> a reckless driver. Finally
> the Andersons had to sell their house and move.
>
> Social life is no joke.
> It can be the only life there is.
> (from "Quiet Desperation")

In its way, this passage is the equivalent of:

> Carentan O Carentan
> Before we met with you
> We never yet had lost a man
> Or known what death could do.

Both passages mourn for casualties. The voice is different, of course. But the difference is not simply the result of a man's aesthetic desire to write a different kind of poem; it is a symptom of a vastly increased understanding and compassion. For Simpson, on the evidence of the text, to be conventional for the sake of convention is to be narrow, and to be narrow is to be unconscious, uncompassionate, inhumane. Unconventionality for its own sake leads to the same result. Only those who have been genuinely outside what most of us usually think of as either "real life" or "the life of the mind," where convention applies no more than anticonvention, see clearly; even for them, "vision" is unreliable and transient:

> It was cold, and all they gave him to wear
> was a shirt. And he had malaria.

There was continual singing of hymns—
"Nearer My God to Thee" was a favorite.
And a sound like running water . . .
it took him a while to figure it.

Weeping, coming from the cells
of the men who had been condemned.

Now here he was, back in the States,
idly picking up a magazine,
glancing through the table of contents.

Already becoming like the rest of us.
                              (from "Back in the States")

Simpson's patron saints, who include Wordsworth and Chek-
hov in addition to Whitman, bear him out; their voices are as
evident in this work from start to finish as is his "own":

"I am here," he [Whitman] answered.
"It seems you have found me out.
Yet, did I not warn you that it was Myself
I advertised? Were not my words sufficiently plain?"
. . . .
Then, vastly amused—"Why do you reproach me?
I freely confess I am wholly disreputable."
                    (from "Walt Whitman at Bear Mountain")

When he went for a walk
the shore looked as though it had been swept
with a broom. The sky was clear,
the sun was shining, and the sea was calm.

He felt that he was alone with the universe.
He, Jerry DiBello, was at one with God.
                              (from "Encounter on the 7:07")

In his practice as a poet, it is the idea of the poetic that Simp-
son assaults—other people's ideas about it, yes, but more im-
portantly his own. His new books further the frontal assault.
The "revisionary" structure of *People Live Here* is a new use of

what in another context looks like outdated material in the service of the struggle. What resonates throughout is a tension of voices, all existing, as the book presents them, in a single mind, or a single world, meeting on any edge of things where "real life" meets the life of the mind, and where both those worlds meet the unknown. The linear view of his work—which of course has its own kind of truth—depicts Simpson constantly turning his back on his past practice. Certainly there are things he has turned his back on; no doubt he will never write a poem quite like "Carentan O Carentan" again. But—as Simpson's structuring of *People Live Here* suggests—to try to leave the past behind completely would be to abandon the very thing that set him in motion in the first place: the impulse to speak to people, to real people in the real world, straight out, without embarrassment. Simpson's search has been for the means of doing that, and his great discovery seems to be that there *are* no particular means; there is only what the poet can scratch together at the moment, with his bare hands, out of the life of the language and out of a constantly altering sense of what possibilities poetry as a medium offers. There are, of course, dangers in this method, and sometimes Simpson fails in ways that more elegant and cagey writers would never allow themselves. There are times when he becomes Zennish without sufficient justification, and other times when the flatness that so often serves to further either amazement or irony seems only flat. But in the main, Simpson's greatest virtue is his willingness to chip away, with marvelous control, at the monolithic cultural notion—in the shadow of which he began his career, and on which he continues to keep a wary eye—of what a poem *is*. The answer, I suppose, that emerges from his work is that a poem is nothing in particular: it is something that works, something unpredictable.

Of course there is a linearity in the structure of this book, but it is a revised linearity. The seven sections of *People Live Here* present, in part, an unfolding awareness of humanity and of singificant human relationships. The first section, "Songs and Lyrics," brings together a selection of relatively inward-turning lyrics. Section 2, "The Fighting in Europe," contains most of the poems concerned directly with World War II, and begins to depict—despite the striking multiplicity of voices in the poems here, which range through all Simpson's linear phases—the forced social awareness which any serious consideration of war entails. The third section, "A Discovery of America," is a more stylistically uniform selection, which, as Alan Williamson has recently pointed out, "gathers together poems from the 1960s."* Many of these poems reflect, more directly than any of Simpson's other work, the influence of Robert Bly, not only in their strategies and diction but also in their particular mode of social awareness. Williamson finds these poems "displeasing," and it is true that many of them are more overt in their moral intent than Simpson usually allows himself to be. America is often directly depicted, in the Bly mode, as a spiritual disaster area. However, this section also seems to me a necessary pole of Simpson's vision. "One does not want to hate society," Simpson has written, "but society being what it is, how can one stomach it?" Simpson's placement of these poems after the war poems suggests a justification for the view he presents in this third section: section 2 concerns culturally sanctioned death by violence; section 3 presents the perhaps too familiar (but not therefore untrue) spectacle of American spiritual death by automobile and electric can opener. And section 4, "Modern Lives," is still another facet of the same phenomenon. Here American suburbanites and insurance salesmen try to resurrect themselves by acts of passion which are often self-destructive:

> Everything is a flowing,
> you have only to flow with it.
>
> If you did, you would live to regret it.
> After a while, passion would wear off
> and you would still be faced with life.
> . . . .
> The trouble with love
> is that you have to believe in it.
> Like swimming . . . you have to keep it up.
>
> And those who didn't, who remained
> on the sofa watching television,
> would live to wish that they had.
>
> (from "A River Running By")

*See Alan Williamson, "We're All in the Same Boat," in this collection.—ED.

The next two sections, "Tales of Volhynia" and "Armidale," center on Russia and Australia respectively and seem designed, in this structuring, to place the previous sections in a new perspective, as tales of exotic and peculiarly beautiful places. It may seem odd to say, but Simpson is our most accomplished poet of the exotic, and if the America he so often depicts does not seem weird and wonderful and dangerous and depraved to those of us who are accustomed to it, it is only because we *are* accustomed. Seen side by side with the poems of Russia and Australia, the poems about America take their place in a larger vision of the beautifully and perilously strange. The final section, "Recapitulations," returns us to America, but with a new aura of mysteriousness verging on the metaphysical. This structure adds up, I think, to an ever-expanding primary awareness not simply of poetry as an aesthetic mode but of the nature of the audience, a definition and redefinition carried on in virtually every poem: humanity as embattled dogface, for whom Simpson wants to write "poems that would be, in their laconic and simple manner, tolerable to men who had seen a good deal of combat and had no illusions."

If *People Live Here,* with its important structural revision of Simpson's ongoing poetry war, allows us to see his past and present work in a tense and effective suspension, *The Best Hour of the Night* plays off (perhaps) the present and the future. (This assertion is risky, I realize, but the fact that the last poem of *People Live Here* is also the first poem of *The Best Hour* gives credence to the notion that Simpson at least wants us to consider continuities.) *The Best Hour* is distinctly like Simpson's last two books in its narrative structures, its use of the rhythms of prose, and its focus on the exotic potential of the "ordinary." But Simpson is far from formulaic here; in fact, *The Best Hour* seems to me his best book yet, dense and rich. It performs, again and again, miraculously well, the thing we demand and have every right to demand of poetry: Simpson wrestles with the world for the world's own sake, to discover within it the necessary articulation, the artifice adequate to convince us of its effective truth. What makes him what I have called a representative poet is the honesty with which he reveals the contours of that struggle with the indeterminate but recognizably human voice every poet fights to claim as his own and to name by its truest possible name: without embarrassment, poetry.

THE UNWRITTEN POEM

You will never write the poem about Italy.
What Socrates said about love
is true of poetry—where is it?
Not in beautiful faces and distant scenery
but the one who writes and loves.

In your life here, on this street
where the houses from the outside
are all alike, and so are the people.
Inside, the furniture is dreadful—
floc on the walls, and huge color television.

To love and write unrequited
is the poet's fate. Here you'll need
all your ardor and ingenuity.
This is the front and these are the heroes—
a life beginning with "Hi!" and ending with "So long!"

You must rise to the sound of the alarm
and march to catch the 6:20—
watch as they ascend the station platform
and, grasping briefcases, pass beyond your gaze
and hurl themselves into the flames.

PETER STITT

Louis Simpson
In Search of the American Self

The story American literature tells is so often that of a virtuous individual, who seeks complete freedom for self-expression, pitted against a community that is at best repressive and at worst unjust, perhaps even immoral. Consider Melville's White Jacket and Billy Budd, rebels against society's sanctioned injustices. Consider his Bartleby, who in response to every entreaty from his eminently reasonable, successful, middle-American boss, says "I would prefer not to." Consider Huck Finn, who follows the promptings of his own heart, his innate sense of virtue, over what society tells him is right; "All right, then, I'll go to hell!" he says, embracing the cause of his black friend, Jim. Consider Hester Prynne, whose devotion is to passion, human emotion—to natural virtue rather than civil virtue—against the moral repression of her Puritan society.

Consider too those writers who speak more or less for themselves rather than through a character, chiefly the American transcendentalists. There is Emerson, whose counsel was to follow always your own path, no matter if it has *never* been trod before. There is Thoreau, whose independence of mind exasperated even his friend and mentor Emerson—Thoreau, who was among the first to oppose the implicit support of slavery that he found in Massachusetts, and who opposed as well that proto-Vietnam adventure, the Mexican War of 1846–48. And there is Whitman, who sang of himself only as a means of encouraging others to be more themselves: "Not I—not any one else, can travel that road for you, / You must travel it for yourself."

Reprinted from *The World's Hieroglyphic Beauty* by Peter Stitt, © 1985 the University of Georgia Press. Reprinted by permission of the University of Georgia Press.

These lists could be extended almost indefinitely—one thinks of Emily Dickinson, Isabel Archer, Edna Pontiellier, so many more. The point is clear: one of the most pervasive concerns of American literature has always been to support, promote, and encourage the individual vision, no matter how solid the opposition of the majority.

It is precisely this concern that we find at the heart of the poetry of Louis Simpson.[1] In recent years he has taken to writing narrative verse that uses many of the techniques of prose fiction. Thus we find in his work third-person protagonists who bear slight spiritual similarities to Huck Finn, Edna Pontiellier, and the others. Even at its most narrative, however, Simpson's poetry remains lyrical in its basis—and this means that the position of the individual sensibility in his work is defined most centrally by the personality of the poet himself. In his autobiography, *North of Jamaica,* Simpson gives the most important of his many definitions of poetry: "Poetry is essentially mysterious. No one has ever been able to define it. Therefore we always find ourselves coming back to the poet. As Stevens said, 'Poetry is a process of the personality of the poet.' This personality is never finished. While he is writing the poet has in mind another self, more intelligent than he. The poet is reaching out to the person that he would be, and this is the poet's style—a sense of reaching, that can never be satisfied."[2]

This sense of reaching always for a better self, which makes Simpson's individual poems so dynamic, is also what caused the profound changes that have occurred in his poetry generally since the beginning of his career. We can, in fact, identify three distinct phases within this body of work. The poems in Simpson's first three books—*The Arrivistes* (1949), *Good News of Death* (1955), and *A Dream of Governors* (1959)—are written in tight, traditional English lyric forms, forms that have the effect of dissociating the poet's sensibility from the very material he is attempting to write about. In many of these early efforts, Simpson sounds rather like the new metaphysical poets, who had their vogue in the 1940s and 1950s. The lyric "As Birds Are Fitted to the Boughs" is typical:

> As birds are fitted to the boughs
> That blossom on the tree

And whisper when the south wind blows—
So was my love to me.

And still she blossoms in my mind
And whispers softly, though
The clouds are fitted to the wind,
The wind is to the snow.[3]

However successful this poem is, there is nothing about it that is unique to the vision or voice of Louis Simpson—the subject is as conventional as the form, and we may be excused the feeling that it could have been written by almost anyone, including a poet (perhaps especially a poet) living three hundred years ago.

In fact, "As Birds Are Fitted to the Boughs" is a "poem nearly anonymous" (as John Crowe Ransom might have said of it)—its form and sentiment both seem predetermined—inherited, not from the personal experience of the author, but from literary history. In addition to poems about love, these early books also contain most of Simpson's war poems. After coming to this country from his native Jamaica in 1940, at the age of seventeen, Simpson enlisted in the United States Army, serving first in the tank corps, then in the infantry; he was among the first to go ashore at Normandy and was awarded the Bronze Star for distinguished service and the Purple Heart for his injuries. One might expect his war poems to blister with immediate, felt experience; such is not the case, however. Again, the author's personality is buried beneath the demands of a form imposed from without rather than generated from within. Thus, even in the best of these poems, we feel, not the force of the poet's experience, but the force of his mastery of traditional English lyricism. "Carentan O Carentan," for example, is a powerful war lyric; I quote stanzas from the beginning, the middle, and the end:

Trees in the old days used to stand
And shape a shady lane
Where lovers wandered hand in hand
Who came from Carentan.
. . . .
I must lie down at once, there is
A hammer at my knee.

349

And call it death or cowardice,
Don't count again on me.

Everything's all right, Mother,
Everyone gets the same
At one time or another.
It's all in the game.

I never strolled, nor ever shall,
Down such a leafy lane.
I never drank in a canal,
Nor ever shall again.
. . . .
Carentan O Carentan
Before we met with you
We never yet had lost a man
Or known what death could do.

(*PLH,* 37–38)

The lyricism is beautiful, the irony between that formal charac-
teristic and the content of the poem profound, but again the
personal voice of Louis Simpson is missing.

When Simpson agrees with Stevens that "Poetry is a process
of the personality of the poet," he is, among other things, also
agreeing with Buffon's definition, "The style is the man." As he
himself has explained, it was because he wanted to express his
own personality more directly that Simpson undertook, be-
tween the publication of his third and fourth books, to change
his style: "I had been writing poetry that was quite formal. . . .
Over the next few years, I tried to write impeccable poems,
poems you couldn't find fault with. Then between 1959 and
1963 I broke all that up and tried to write poetry that would be
more free, that would sound more like my own voice. . . . Ever
since then I've written mostly a kind of informal poetry."[4] (See
"Interview with Louis Simpson.")* In the second and third
phases of Simpson's career, then, we encounter an authentic
poetry of personality. Moreover, once he had made this impor-
tant transition, it appears that Simpson was able to look back

*In *The World's Hieroglyphic Beauty.*—ED.

and define more clearly the relationship between the missing sensibility of his early poems and the society in which that sensibility attempted to live; I will begin my larger discussion of Simpson's work with these more or less anachronistic poems, poems that, by virtue of their content, actually (though not chronologically) belong in the first phase of his career.

The middle phase of Simpson's work consists of all of the poems in his fourth book, *At the End of the Open Road* (1963), and many of those in *Adventures of the Letter I* (1971), a transitional volume. The individual portrayed in these poems feels himself seriously alienated from American society, which in his view had not only killed the American Indians but was also participating, indefensibly, in an unjust war in Vietnam. Then a curious thing happens, marking the transition from the second to the third phase of Simpson's work—through a dual interest in the work of Chekhov and in his own Jewish Russian ancestors, the sensibility of these poems recognizes his inherent kinship with the ordinary citizens of the society he had been hating. He realizes that it is not they but their leaders who are responsible for what is wrong and repressive in that society. Thus, the third phase of Simpson's work is the empathetic, even the spiritual phase—the phase in which he comes to do his most memorable and original work. It begins with the Russian poems in *Adventures of the Letter I* and continues with the poems of middle America in *Searching for the Ox* (1976), *Caviare at the Funeral* (1980), and *The Best Hour of the Night* (1983).

Before proceeding any farther, we must pause to make a crucial distinction. Although Louis Simpson writes a poetry of personality, and although the most important unifying feature of his work is the sensibility that lies at its heart, he is not a confessional poet. In fact, Simpson has been very hard on this type of poetry, which he sees as part of the "cult of sincerity" ("Interview with Louis Simpson"). Confessional poetry is personal because it takes for its subject matter the literal details of the poet's life and feelings, the truth of that life as lived in the real world; Simpson's poetry is personal because it emerges from and expresses a single, central, perceiving sensibility. Although the effect of this can be even more intimate than what the reader experiences in confessional poetry, it is achieved while the poet maintains a reticent posture with regard to the external details of his life. In fact, Simpson prefers to speak of the sensibility that inhabits his poems as a created character—based upon himself, to be sure, but made up nevertheless: "I have a very funny sense of myself in the poem—I'm not talking about me, I'm talking about how the poems make a self for me."[5] How that might come about is explained in greater detail in the afterword to Simpson's book *A Revolution in Taste,* where he gives a summary definition of what he means by a poetry of personality: "In contrast to this, what I have called the personal voice is an expression of character. And character is something made. The self that appears in the novel or poem has been constructed according to certain aesthetic principles. This version of the self is not intended to direct attention upon the author but to serve the work of art. The purpose is to create a symbolic life, a portrait of the artist that will have meaning for others and so create a sense of community, if only among a few thousand."[6]

The sensibility that unifies the poems of Louis Simpson, then, is this created "symbolic life," this "portrait of the artist"; it is a sensibility intended to express not just the personal feelings of one person but those of at least a small minority community existing within society at large. It is not until the last phase of his work, however, that Simpson's poetry will truly begin to embody this sense of community. In the first two phases we see instead a sensibility largely alienated from the society that surrounds it. As I said earlier, our understanding of the position of the Simpson sensibility in the first phase will come not so much from the poems actually written then but from later poems that comment on that phase. These poems, in fact, mostly appear together in the first section of Simpson's recent book, *People Live Here: Selected Poems, 1949–1983*—a structuring that indicates that they do indeed belong, because of their content, with the first phase.

For example, the poem "The Cradle Trap" (*PLH,* 28), originally published in *At the End of the Open Road,* seems to define the alienation of the Simpson character at almost its first moment of consciousness. The experience and feelings of the poem are those of a baby and are presented in the first two stanzas:

> A bell and rattle,
> a smell of roses,

a leather Bible,
and angry voices . . .

They say, I love you.
They shout, You must!
The light is telling
terrible stories.

The forces of society are represented by the baby's parents, who
are willing to use every means at their disposal, including both
violence and love, to impose their will upon him. In Simpson's
poems generally, as here, the depersonalizing forces of society
are associated with an unforgiving light, while darkness repre-
sents individuality and self-fulfillment. Thus, it is the darkness
that offers support and advice to the baby in the concluding
stanza of this poem:

But night at the window
whispers, Never mind.
Be true, be true
to your own strange kind.

What is presented here in embryonic form is the conflict between
the individual and the community that will dominate so much of
Simpson's poetry. Already this particular character is seen as
different from most people, one of a "strange kind." As we will
learn in later poems, this strangeness results from a commitment
not just to poetry but to a life of the mind generally.

While "The Cradle Trap" seems to set the Simpson character
against all of society and both of his parents, another poem,
"Working Late" (*PLH,* 168), indicates a potential for harmony
that we will see fully manifested in phase three. The title of the
poem refers to the speaker's father, a lawyer of precise and
methodical character—"A light is on in my father's study":

He is working late on cases.
No impassioned speech! He argues from evidence,
actually pacing out and measuring,
while the fans revolving on the ceiling
winnow the true from the false.

Within the context of the poem, the father represents society, as his association with the artificial light source indicates. That there is something of value even here, however, is implicit in the way the poem ends:

> . . . the light that used to shine
> at night in my father's study
> now shines as late in mine.

However, the real sense of kinship in the poem is felt between the speaker and his mother, who is both associated with the darkness and seen in conflict with the father:

> All the arguing in the world
> will not stay the moon.
> She has come all the way from Russia
> to gaze for a while in a mango tree
> and light the wall of a veranda,
> before resuming her interrupted journey.

The poem is autobiographical. Simpson's father was a lawyer; his mother, a passionate and restless woman of Russian ancestry, who happened to come with a dance troup to Jamaica, was courted by and married the elder Simpson, and left him some years later, when the poet was nearly grown. She functions as a sort of muse within the poem, prefiguring those human qualities that will characterize Simpson's maturest work—chiefly, the feeling of love, a sense of independence, devotion to the freedom of the self and to the creative spirit; identifying her with the moon, Simpson says: "she is still the mother of us all." For fullest expression, most of this will have to wait for phase three; until then, the sensibility that rules these poems contends instead with the negative, antagonistic feelings of betrayal expressed in "The Cradle Trap."

At the end of the first section of his new selected poems, Simpson has placed three poems that also stand together at the end of *Adventures of the Letter I*—"Trasimeno," "The Silent Piano," and "The Peat-Bog Man." The poems have much in common—each associates the light of day with a society that is somehow oppressive to the individual; each identifies as well a fugitive sense of spirituality, creativity, which is associated with the night and the moon and opposed to the forces of society. Perhaps we may take the last poem (*PLH,* 33) as representative. Seamus Heaney, that fine Ulster poet, tells many stories of the peat bogs of Ireland, which have a way of preserving anything (including human bodies) that happens to fall into them. Centuries later, peat cutters will come upon these things, perfectly preserved. The title character of Simpson's poem "was one of the consorts of the moon" who "went with the goddess in a cart": "Wherever he went there would be someone, / a few of the last of the old religion." Once this brief characterization has been given, "the moon passes behind a cloud"; we don't see the peat-bog man again until, "Fifteen centuries" later, he is dug up—

> . . .—with the rope
>
> that ends in a noose at the throat—
> a head squashed like a pumpkin.

Simpson implies that the man was executed; apparently his sensitive, religious, poetic nature came into conflict with a brutal and repressive society. At the end of the poem, Simpson associates him with the creative spirit of earth, allowing for an indirect triumph after all:

> Yet, there is delicacy in the features
> and a peaceful expression . . .
>
> that in Spring the flower comes forth
> with a music of pipes and dancing.

Because of its method, the poem seems to offer almost a blanket condemnation of how such individuals have been treated by societies throughout time. The poem is nearly allegorical, generalizing as it does from an incident that is both ancient and vague. "The Peat-Bog Man" thus reflects a quality common to most of the poems in Simpson's first three books: they do not often deal directly, personally, with the actual world inhabited at the time of composition by the poet himself. It was not until

1963, with the publication of his fourth book, *At the End of the Open Road*—significantly following the major change in style discussed above—that Simpson began to write specifically about America, where he had been living for better than twenty years.

If not a paradox, it is at least a curiosity that Louis Simpson—that native Jamaican—has become, since the beginning of the second phase of his career, the most consciously American of all contemporary American poets.[7] This is true, not just because he has come to write mostly about American life and people, but because the sensibility that informs his poems from their creative heart thinks of himself as an American—for better (phase three) or for worse (phase two). In an essay written as early as 1962, Simpson recognized that his work was moving in this direction: "I think a great deal about the country I live in; indeed, it seems an inexhaustible subject, one that has hardly been tapped. By America, I mean the infinitely complex life we have. Sometimes when I look at Main Street, I feel like a stranger looking at the via Aurelia, or the Pyramids."[8] It is interesting that James Wright commented on this aspect of Simpson's work in his own essay on Walt Whitman: "Louis Simpson's imagination is obsessed with the most painful details of current American life, which he reveals under a very powerfully developed sense of American history. . . . Mr. Simpson describes America and Americans in a vision totally free from advertising and propaganda."[9]

As mentioned earlier, the poems in phase two are the bitterest of Simpson's career. It is almost as though, rebounding from the horrors of World War II, his protagonist felt danger lurking behind every bush, a murderous stench at large in the very atmosphere. He became an idealist, venting his anger most vigorously upon the hypocrites of this world, those who profess noble, moral aims while wallowing in the mire of man's inhumanity to man. The poem "On the Lawn at the Villa" (*PLH*, 54) is set in Tuscany just after World War II, and seems to take for its theme the contrast between American innocence and European sophistication, implying that the latter is cunning, given to evil, the former a sweetness yielding only to virtue.

Though the theme of the poem seems to come from Henry James, its voice sounds more like Augie March or Studs Lonigan—a wise guy who has read Whitman. He begins the poem by commenting on his title:

> On the lawn at the villa—
> That's the way to start, eh, reader?
> We know where we stand—somewhere expensive—
> You and I *imperturbes,* as Walt would say,
> Before the diversions of wealth, you and I *engagés.*

The irony of the voice seems at this point to be directed against the hollowness, the falseness, of wealthy European society, an impression that is strengthened when the speaker introduces his companions—"a manufacturer of explosives," his wife, and "a young man named Bruno"—and goes on to justify his own presence at this little tea party. He is, he says:

> Willing to talk to these malefactors,
> The manufacturer of explosives, and so on,
> But somehow superior. By that I mean democratic.
> It's complicated, being an American,
> Having the money and the bad conscience, both at the same
>   time.

On its surface level, the poem suggests that it is people like the manufacturer of explosives who make war possible, thus perpetuating the kind of thing that destroyed "The Peat-Bog Man." The American is supposedly superior, if only because he can see the immorality inherent in this situation. However, there is another level of irony in the poem; being American is more "complicated" than it at first seems. While the speaker pretends to believe the American line, in fact he is directing his most serious criticism against it. He suggests that it is the Americans who are the greatest hypocrites in such situations. The arms maker pretends nothing; the American pretends to approve of the arms maker (no doubt for the "money" involved), meanwhile believing that he can preserve his own moral superiority through a "bad conscience." That this is a delusion is made clear through an image Simpson uses in the poem's concluding stanza:

> We were all sitting there paralyzed
> In the hot Tuscan afternoon,
> And the bodies of the machine-gun crew were draped over the
>   balcony.

Everyone in the scene, that is, ignores this very basic reality, and all are equally guilty.

Poems from this phase that are set in America are, if anything, even more bitter than "On the Lawn at the Villa." Basically, Simpson chooses to contrast the American Dream—of justice, equality, freedom, and peace—with the reality he was observing around him. Most of these poems were written during the early phase of America's involvement in the war in Vietnam, at a time when American opinion supported that involvement. In an essay first published—ironically—in William Heyen's bicentennial anthology, *American Poets in 1976*, Simpson comments on the reaction of American poets to Vietnam by speaking first of how William Wordsworth felt when his country sided with the government against the peasants during the French Revolution: "he was cut off in his affections from the people around him. It is hard to imagine a more desolate situation for a poet, and it is the situation American poets have found themselves in for some time. It would be bad enough if poets alone felt so, but what poets feel many other people are feeling too. The United States contains a large number of people who no longer like it."[10] The people who no longer like it, in fact, are those few of a "strange kind," first mentioned in "The Cradle Trap."

In a poem with the ironic title "American Dreams" (*PLH,* 79), Simpson defines the position occupied by such a person in this country 'at that time. The poem begins by contrasting the kind of dreams the Simpson protagonist would normally have with a redefined version of the American Dream:

> In dreams my life came toward me,
> my loves that were slender as gazelles.
> But America also dreams. . . .
> Dream, you are flying over Russia,
> dream, you are falling in Asia.

We are reminded that the American Dream has not been limited to the basic definition given above. The English Puritans came here originally in pursuit of religious freedom—and immediately proceeded to outlaw all religions but their own. They also saw the American Indians as the Devil's minions, and set about to eradicate them from the face of the earth. This particular aspect of the American Dream is celebrated by Simpson in yet another poem, "Indian Country," where he describes how "The white men burst in at sunrise, shooting and stabbing . . . , / the squaws running in every direction" (*PLH*, 68). Were we to view this as a kind of genocide, and were we to combine that with yet another aspect of the American Dream (the one that sees the open road leading ever westward to new horizons), then we might have found an explanation for the American bombs falling in Asia.

The second stanza of "American Dreams" expresses the feelings of the speaker through an image as violent and surreal as the one that concludes "On the Lawn at the Villa": "on a typical sunny day in California," he dreams:

> it is my house that is burning
> and my dear ones that lie in the gutter
> as the American army enters.

The feeling is one of intense alienation; the speaker is committed to the original American Dream of peace and freedom for all, while his fellow citizens seem bent on forcing the entire world to conform to their way of life. The poem concludes:

> Every day I wake far away
> from my life, in a foreign country.
> These people are speaking a strange language.
> It is strange to me
> and strange, I think, even to themselves.

The situation is strange to the speaker because he is of the minority, one of that "strange kind" that remembers the basic moral principles on which this country was founded. That the situation may have been strange as well "even to themselves"—that is, even to ordinary citizens—history has come to prove through the eventual turning of public opinion against the war in Vietnam. Thus at the time of the poem, their behavior was unnatural, an unaccustomed hypocrisy.

Another, somewhat earlier, poem on the American Dream is the famous "Walt Whitman at Bear Mountain" (*PLH*, 64–65),

originally published in *At the End of the Open Road*. It begins
with a challenge to the statue of Whitman, asking "Where is the
nation you promised?" and complaining that "The Open Road
goes to the used-car lot." Simpson refers to the degeneration of
yet another aspect of the original Dream. Our ancestors only
hoped for sufficient material goods to get by on, a chicken in
every pot; we have progressed to the point where our insatiable
hunger for wealth is scarring the countryside, polluting the air,
and dropping either a porn emporium or a pizza shack on every
village corner. Whitman is blamed because of the boundless
opportunity that he seemed to promise and because his writings
have been used by publicists and polemicists to forward just
these debased goals. Simpson goes on to imagine an answer
from Whitman, who points out that it was not the future of the
country he was prophesying, "it was Myself / I advertised"—
"I gave no prescriptions"—"I am wholly disreputable." Sud-
denly, for the speaker, "All that grave weight of America" is
"cancelled." All those who have "contracted / American
dreams"—"the realtors, / Pickpockets, salesmen"—can go
their own ways, performing their "Official scenarios"; the indi-
vidual has been freed to pursue his vision:

> . . . the man who keeps a store on a lonely road,
> And the housewife who knows she's dumb,
> And the earth, are relieved.

The answer that the speaker has found for this stage of his life is
to try to ignore what goes on around him, to cultivate his own
"Myself" in a kind of protective isolation—to live, that is, what
is described in the poem's epigraph (from Ortega y Gasset): a
"life which does not give the preference to any other life, of any
previous period, which therefore prefers its own existence."

It is in another poem, "Sacred Objects" (originally published
in *Adventures of the Letter I*), that Simpson gives a capsule version
of the general lesson learned from Whitman; he says: "The light
that shines through the *Leaves* / is clear: 'to form individuals'"
(*PLH*, 178). The attempt to be true to the singular, individual
vision of the self is the quest that entered Simpson's work once
he decided upon a personal theory of poetry. It is given eloquent

testimony in yet another poem from this period, "Summer Morning." Thinking back over fifteen years, the speaker recalls a morning spent with a woman in a hotel room, from which they watched workers across the way. The separation between him and them was more than just physical, as he now recognizes:

> I'm fifteen years older myself—
> Bad years and good.
>
> So I have spoiled my chances.
> For what? Sheer laziness,
> The thrill of an assignation,
> My life that I hold in secret.

(PLH, 90)

The tone of the poem is not one of regret but of triumph. The speaker's chances for a commercial life have been spoiled, it is true, but that is no loss; it is far preferable to have lived a life devoted to fugitive emotions, devoted to an individual vision, no matter how unpopular—a life devoted to that least commercial of all serious pursuits, poetry.[11]

Perhaps the strongest general impression one takes away from the poems written during this second phase of Simpson's career is of the alienation from society that his protagonist feels. Sometimes his attitude is bitter and sarcastic about that society; at other times he is sullen and withdrawn, almost sulking; at still other times he is strong, proud, defiant. In all cases, however, the alienation persists. Moreover, his distrust is not just of those who are obviously misguided (political leaders, pickpockets) but of common people as well—his fellow citizens, the workers in the widow across the way. *At the End of the Open Road,* source of most of these poems and Simpson's most negative book, was published in 1963. Between then and 1971, when the transitional volume *Adventures of the Letter I* was published, his work began to develop away from this attitude toward a stronger feeling of brotherly love. An indirect but telling comment on what was happening can be found in his essay "Dogface Poetics," first published in 1965:

In recent years the closemouthed, almost sullen, manner of my early poems has given way to qualities that are quite different. Like other men of the war generation, I began with middle age; youth came later. Nowadays in my poems I try to generate mystery and excitement; I have even dealt in general ideas. But I retain the dogface's suspicion of the officer class, with their abstract language and indifference to individual, human suffering. You might say that the war made me a footsoldier for the rest of my life.[12]

The difference as expressed here is slight but significant; Simpson is coming to empathize more emphatically with his fellow "footsoldiers" and their ordinary "human suffering." No longer will his protagonist feel so "cut off in his affections from the people around him"; he will not hold the citizenry at large responsible for such atrocities as the American participation in Vietnam—that rap will be pinned on those who earn it, the "officer class" generally. The most important change in Simpson's work as he moves into the third phase of his career, then, is the increased sense of empathy those poems express for other people.[13] The change in attitude—and in method of operation—on the part of the Simpson protagonist is made clear in a poem like "The Mexican Woman" (PLH, 103), originally published in Caviare at the Funeral. In the first section of this poem, the speaker is panhandled by an old man who claims to have been "in Mexico with Black Jack Pershing":

> He lived with a Mexican woman.
> Then he followed her, and was wise.
>
> "Baby," he said, "you're a two-timer,
> I'm wise to you and the lieutenant."

The second section tells the reaction of the speaker to this chance encounter; "the old man's tale still haunts me," he begins:

> I know what it's like to serve
> in Mexico with Black Jack Pershing.
>
> And to walk in the dust and heat . . .
> for I can see her hurrying

to the clay wall where they meet,
and I shall be wise to her and the lieutenant.

Through the use of his imagination, the speaker is able to be-
come the old man, able to experience a portion of his life. The
poem is curiously both objective and subjective; objective be-
cause of the interest in the life and concerns of a character other
than the speaker, but subjective in that it is also his story, the
story of his imagination.

In its use of a narrative structure and reliance on significant
details that illuminate action, character, and meaning, this poem
resembles prose fiction.[14] Simpson is the author of one novel,
Riverside Drive, published in 1962, and has recently talked about
writing another. In fact—if such things can be judged by what
the protagonist of his poems says—it would appear that as a
young man Simpson may have aspired more to writing fiction
than poetry. For example, the speaker in "Sway" remembers a
summer spent courting the already engaged girl whose nick-
name gives the poem its title: "Sway was beautiful. My heart
went out to her"; "I told her of my ambition: / to write novels
conveying the excitement / of life" (*PLH,* 108). In another
poem, "The Man She Loved," the speaker remembers how, as a
young student at Columbia, he would visit his relatives in
Brooklyn on Sundays and spend at least part of the afternoon
indulging in youthful, charmingly egotistical fantasies:

> Little did they know as they spoke
> that one day they would be immortal
> in a novel that commanded the sweep
> of Tolstoy, a magnificent creation
> that would bring within its compass
> offices in Manhattan and jungles
> of the Amazon. A grasp of psychology
> and sense of the passing of time
> that can only be compared to,
> without exaggerating, Proust.
>
> (*PLH,* 105)

And yet, despite this ambition, despite his skill at manipulat-
ing narrative, detail, and imagery, Simpson did not become a

good novelist. In fact, it is in the poem "Sway" that he himself gives what is probably the best critique of *Riverside Drive,* as of his talent as a fiction writer generally. During that summer long ago, the girl has asked:

> . . . "When you're a famous novelist
> will you write about me?"

> I promised . . . and tried to keep my promise.

Years later the speaker comes upon the resulting pages in an old box; the images are touching, the buildup to action promising, but: "Then the trouble begins. I can never think of anything / to make the characters do" (*PLH,* 110). The failure occurs in the area of plot—the individual scenes of *Riverside Drive* are pointed and affecting, excellent at conveying mood, but they never add up to a cohesive overall statement. In short, Simpson's fiction embodies all the qualities that would be needed should one wish to write a narrative kind of lyric poetry—which is precisely the choice he ultimately made. In an essay published in 1976, he explains in hypothetical terms the use to which such a poetry would put narrative: "As it deals with life, this poetry will frequently be in the form of a narrative. Not a mere relation of external events, but a narrative of significant actions. The poet will aim to convey states of feeling. In our time poets have stayed away from narrative because it has often been merely descriptive—there has been too much dead tissue. But this can be avoided if the poet reveals a situation with no more than a few words, and concentrates on the feeling."[15]

Narrative is used in Simpson's best poems, then, not to channel action toward an exciting climax but to organize images and relatively minor incidents toward some revelation of personality and feeling. Because this poetry is more or less static in terms of external action, imagery is of considerable importance in the achievement of its effects. Simpson, in fact, considers himself a kind of latter-day Imagist poet, which makes his definition of the goal of Imagist writing important here: "There is a time lag, therefore a separation, between thought and experience. The more elaborate the comparison, as in Milton's epic similes, the harder it is to 'feel' the thought. An imagist poem, on the other hand, concentrates on giving you the experience—handing over sensations bodily, as Hulme said. Imagist writing aims to make you feel, rather than to tell you what feeling is like."[16] In Simpson's use of imagery there is something of the idea behind Eliot's objective correlative: if the image is properly prepared for and invested with appropriate suggestions, it should call up in the reader the same emotions it evokes in the author or in the character he is writing about.

Most often, the feelings that are expressed in the poems of phase 3 are again those of the Simpson protagonist, the sensibility that has always been at the heart of his work. However, because of the greater degree of empathy that informs this phase, we find poems as well that are spoken by characters who are obviously different from this one; also, there are poems written from the third-person point of view, in which Simpson imagines from the outside and sympathetically presents the feelings of another. Simpson is, in short, actively following advice he gave indirectly to Robert Lowell in a review written in 1977: "He ought to try getting inside the skin of a few people who aren't like himself."[17] Perhaps the most astonishing thing about Simpson's recent work is just how different the people he writes about are—not just from the sensibility that inhabits his work, but from the characters who appear in contemporary American poetry generally. In fact, without the example of Simpson, we might not be able to tell just how special, how atypical, that cast of characters generally is.

Most contemporary poets, of course, write primarily about their own personalities; Simpson is no exception to this rule. When we get beyond this level, what we generally find is characters who are very much like the poets—sensitive, intelligent, well educated, of refined taste in food, music, literature, what have you. When we go beyond the poet as character in the poems of Simpson's phase 3, by contrast, what we find are the *ordinary* citizens of America—not college professors and orchestra conductors, not manual laborers and nuclear protestors, but middle-class burghers; people who shop in shopping centers rather than in boutiques; people who watch "Love Boat" rather than "Masterpiece Theatre"; people who worry about their mortgages, their false teeth, their teenage children when they don't come home on time. Simpson's goal is to write, not about an unusual and privileged way of life, but about the life most real people are living in this country today. As he said in his address to the Jewish Book Council in 1981: "At the present time American poetry has very little to say about the world we live in. The American poet is content to have a style that sets him apart, to produce a unique sound, to create unusual images. But in my poems I have been attempting to explore ordinary, everyday life with the aim of showing that it can be deep, that though the life itself may not be poetic and, in fact, can be banal and sordid, yet it is the stuff of poetry, and the kind of poetry I believe to be most important—that which shows our common humanity."[18]

"Quiet Desperation" (*BHN*, 15–17), which appears in Simpson's most recent individual book of poems, *The Best Hour of the Night* (1983), is written from the third-person point of view and concerns a single day in the life of an unnamed citizen of suburbia. The poem begins while this man is doing errands, probably on a Saturday afternoon:

> At the post office he sees Joe McInnes.
> Joe says, "We're having some people over.
> It'll be informal. Come as you are."

When our hero arrives home, he finds his wife preparing dinner, "an experiment":

> He relays Joe's invitation.
> "No," she says, "not on your life.
> Muriel McInnes is no friend of mine."

> It appears that she told Muriel
> that the Goldins live above their means,
> and Muriel told Mary Goldin.

> He listens carefully, to get things right.
> The feud between the Andersons and the Kellys
> began with Ruth Anderson calling Mike Kelly
> a reckless driver. Finally
> the Andersons had to sell their house and move.

> Social life is no joke.
> It can be the only life there is.

At first reading, a passage like this sounds very much like prose. One thing that makes it poetry is the understatement, the restraint and precision, of the writing. The lines are mostly end-stopped, and many of them consist of single sentences; there is nothing here of the easy flow prose normally has. There is also no extravagance in the images and incidents; again, everything is kept to a careful and pointed minimum. Finally, as is characteristic of lyric poetry to a far greater degree than of prose, the passage depends for its coherence less on its details than on the sensibility that perceives and reflects on these details. The plainness of language is typical of Simpson in this phase; like Wordsworth (and others) before him, he wishes to write his poems essentially out of the mouths of his ordinary characters; as he has said in an essay: "In my attempts to write narrative poetry I have used the rhythms of speech. I bear in mind what it would be like to say the poem aloud to someone else. This helps me to form the lines. At the same time it eliminates confusion—I have to make my ideas clear. I eliminate words out of books, affected language, jargon of any kind."[19]

In the second section of the poem, the protagonist goes into the living room where his son is watching a movie on television: "the battle of Iwo Jima / is in progress." He watches for a moment; the Americans are pinned down by machine-gun fire; a man falls; "Sergeant Stryker / picks up the charge and starts running." He watches until the pillbox is destroyed by Stryker, then gets up and goes out: "He's seen the movie. Stryker gets killed / just as they're raising the flag." This man is restless and dissatisfied, and as the third section of the poem begins, we learn what he is feeling:

> A feeling of pressure . . .
> There is something that needs to be done
> immediately.
>
> But there is nothing,
> only himself. His life is passing,
> and afterwards there will be eternity,
> silence, and infinite space.
>
> He thinks, "Firewood!"—
> and goes to the basement . . .

After cutting several logs into the proper size, arranging them carefully by the fireplace—but still restless, still feeling the pressure—he thinks of "The dog! / He will take the dog for a walk."

It is autumn and the trees are turning yellow; approaching "the cove," he admires the blue water and the swans. The poem ends:

> But when you come closer
> the rocks above the shore are littered
> with daggers of broken glass
> where the boys sat on summer nights
> and broke beer bottles afterwards.
>
> And the beach is littered, with cans,
> containers, heaps of garbage,
> newspaper wadded against the sea-wall.
> Someone has even dumped a mattress . . .
> a definite success!
> Some daring guy, some Stryker
> in the pickup speeding away.
>
> He cannot bear the sun
> going over and going down . . .
> the trees and houses vanishing
> in quiet every day.

The story of an ordinary mid-life crisis perhaps, but told with sympathy and from the inside of the man who is suffering through it. He feels his age when he looks at his son, when he remembers how long ago it was that he first saw the movie; he feels the futility of his life in the encounters with his wife and Joe McInnes, the emptiness of human contact. All around him are images of mortality—the death of Stryker, the firewood, the yellow leaves on the trees—culminating in the image of the setting sun, how everything is "vanishing" into "eternity /silence, and infinite space."

"Quiet Desperation" establishes a common ground of ordinary human feelings where the guiding sensibility of Simpson's poems and his middle-class protagonist can meet to share what they have in common. There are many poems like this in the third phase of Simpson's work, poems that express, on the part of that sensibility, an authentic degree of empathy for humankind generally. However, there are also many poems in this phase that express something that may seem contrary to this—the continuing recognition by the Simpson sensibility of a difference between himself and most other people. It is not the feelings themselves that make him different, nor their quality and depth; rather, it is the degree to which these feelings are speculated upon and understood. This realization does not lessen the empathy felt by the protagonist, but it does reinforce his sense of isolation, of an ultimate and irremediable aloneness.

"Encounter on the 7:07," also from *The Best Hour of the Night* (8–12), is spoken from the first-person point of view and puts the Simpson speaker in contact with a man something like the central character of "Quiet Desperation." Again, the poem is long, in this case organized into six sections. The speaker is riding a commuter train when "a man of about forty, with a suntan" gets on and sits next to him. The man's doctor had advised a vacation, so he had gone to Florida. Meanwhile, on the train itself there is a "car card advertising / 'Virginia Slims'":

> The man sitting next to me,
> whose name is Jerry—Jerry DiBello—
> observes that he doesn't smoke cigarettes,
> he smokes cigars. "Look at Winston Churchill.
>
> He smoked cigars every day of his life,
> and he lived to be over eighty."

An ordinary guy who likes to talk—the advertisement provides enough of an excuse for this personal comment.

Later he says that "His family used to own a restaurant," that his father had come "from Genoa / as a seaman, and jumped ship," got a job washing dishes, and "Ten years later / he owned the restaurant." Jerry goes on to say that he sells cars, etc.,

> But I'm not listening—I'm on deck,
> looking at the lights of the harbor.
> A sea wind fans my cheek.

> I hear the waves chuckling
> against the side of the ship.

The passage illustrates that same empathy, that same imaginative absorption into the skin of another character, that we saw in "The Mexican Woman."[20]

The thematic heart of this poem comes in its fifth section; the speaker says that he had brought along a copy of *Ulysses* to read on the train and begins by giving D. H. Lawrence's opinion of the book:

> "An *olla putrida* . . .
> old fags and cabbage-stumps of quotations,"
> said Lawrence. Drawing a circle about himself
> and Frieda . . . building an ark,
> envisioning the Flood.
>
> But the Flood may be long coming.
> In the meantime there is life
> every day, and Ennui.
>
> Ever since the middle class
> and money have ruled our world
> we have been desolate.
> . . . .
> A feeling of being alone
> and separate from the world . . .
> "alienation" psychiatrists call it.
> Religion would say, this turning away
> from life is the life of the soul.
>
> This is why Joyce is such a great writer:
> he shows a life of fried bread
> and dripping "like a boghole,"
> an art that rises out of life
> and flies toward the sun,
>
> transfiguring as it flies
> the reality.

The problem that the sensibility of Simpson's poems faces is that the society of which he is a part is so much more superficial in its interests than he is; it is committed to money, to the everyday problems of work, but ignores the depths of human emotion, the life of the soul. Lawrence provides no answer, because he went to the opposite extreme; he wrote of the depths but ignored the superficial realities of life. Thus, it is left to James Joyce to be the literary hero of this poem, the one who could write about both things at the same time, transfiguring reality while flying it toward the sun. This is precisely the goal that the speaker of "The Man She Loved" had wanted to express to his relatives:

> . . . how could he explain what it meant to be a writer . . .
> a world that was entirely different,
> and yet it would include the sofa
> and the smell of chicken cooking.
>
> (PLH, 105)

The alienation of Simpson's protagonist results precisely from his devotion to the things that are unseen by the middle class generally—a full range of genuine emotions, the life of the soul. In the final section of "Encounter on the 7:07," we are returned to Jerry DiBello, who had encountered a hurricane during his stay in Florida; "For days afterwards they were still finding bodies":

> When he went for a walk
> the shore looked as though it had been swept
> with a broom. The sky was clear,
> the sun was shining, and the sea was calm.
>
> He felt that he was alone with the universe.
> He, Jerry DiBello, was at one with God.

Although a casual reader might not at first think so, these lines are neither satirical nor sarcastic; they give a straightforward, even sympathetic, rendering of the feelings this automobile salesman had when confronted with a vision of the ultimate. We must remember that he only went on this trip because of a doctor's orders, thus bringing with him a newly discovered awareness of his own mortality. As the poem ends, the speaker recognizes both his difference from DiBello and the human bond that they share.

Reactions to poems like these vary, but a common one is the assumption that Simpson is being satirical.[21] In the interview that follows, Simpson described both the original response to his poem "The Beaded Pear" and his motivation:

> The poem is meant to be absolutely descriptive of the kind of domestic life we actually live in this country today. When the poem first came out—in the Long Island newspaper *Newsday*—it upset a lot of people. I got hate mail from people who thought I was being devastatingly sarcastic. But I don't see it that way. There is an element of ridicule in the poem, but it is directed at the culture which fosters these kinds of values, not at the people themselves. No—mostly it is a purely descriptive poem, an attempt at absolutely dead-on, accurate truth. There is even a touch of pathos at the end.

This attitude is given further amplication in yet another comment in the same interview: "Now this may be romantic, but I feel that the ordinary people are pretty decent, even though their attitudes may not be mine. I don't feel that they're at all contemptible. I mean the people you meet in a shoestore or pub or shopping mall. I have always felt that there is a lot of poetry in those people."

And yet those crucial differences between the Simpson protagonist and the average middle-class citizen remain. It is the expression of these differences that makes some readers think such poems are satirical. The tone of these poems is an extremely delicate one and results from the understatement and restraint that is built into their form. Simpson is attempting to balance very different opinions of two nearly identical things— his empathy for the people and his contempt for the values by which they sometimes live their lives. How delicate this tone is, how hard for some readers to understand, is indicated by the following, rather remarkably misguided, judgment: "Louis

Simpson's work now suggests too much comfort: emotional, physical, intellectual. He has stopped struggling, it seems, for words, for rhythms, for his own deepest self. His is a middle-class, middle-brow poetry, the major value of which is to steer other poets from the same course, and to raise some questions about poets joining an Establishment, whether it be one of social class, national or literary identification."[22]

How far Louis Simpson is from joining the middle-class "Establishment" is apparent in another new poem, the longest of his career. "The Previous Tenant" (*BHN*, 21–36) consists of ten sections and deals once again with the conflict between society and the individual. It is spoken from the first-person point of view by the Simpson sensibility and is primarily concerned with the story of his alienation from the suburban community in which he lives—ironically named Point Mercy. The speaker's awareness of his own alienation is brought to the surface through the story of Dr. Hugh McNeil, whose illicit love affair makes him the enemy of the forces of decency in the town. The speaker is renting a cottage—

> Thoreau, who recommends sleeping in the box
> railroad workers keep their tools in,
> would have found this house commodious.

—that contains several cartons of goods left behind by the previous tenant, McNeil; he learns McNeil's story from his landlord, from some letters he finds, and from community gossip.

Probably the most important "character" in the poem is the collective force that acts as antagonist to both these men—the society itself. At first McNeil and his family are welcomed with open arms to the community; he is an ideal citizen,

> . . . one of the fathers on Saturday
> dashing about. He drove a green Land Rover
> as though he were always on safari
> with the children and an Irish setter.

An early and very mild conflict involving him helps to define the community. He speaks at a village meeting in favor of "retaining / the Latin teacher at the high school"; despite his arguments, the community votes instead to

> . . . remodel the gymnasium.
> McNeil accepted defeat gracefully.
> That was one of the things they liked about him.

In a summary comment, Simpson speaks ironically for the community, which is able to find a silver lining in this incident:

> Contrary to what people say
> about the suburbs, they appreciate culture.
> Hugh McNeil was an example . . .
> doing the shopping, going to the club,
> a man in no way different from themselves,
> husband and family man
> and good neighbor, who nevertheless spoke Latin.

The passage reflects the "thinking" of Helen Knox, president of the Garden Club and the character whom Simpson uses as spokesperson for Point Mercy. She has a rare ability:

> She knew how to put what they were feeling
> into words. This was why
> she was president—elected not once
> or twice . . . this was her third term in office.

Like her highly cultured community, Helen Knox is anti-Semitic and a racist. Thus, when McNeil begins his adulterous affair with Irene Davis, whose maiden name was the Italian Cristiano, Helen says:

> "I met her once" . . .
> "Harry introduced her to me
> at the bank. A dark woman . . .
> I think, a touch of the tar brush."

Things start to get out of hand—McNeil appears one day with "broken ribs, black eyes, / and a missing tooth," claiming that he was mugged. A service-station attendant comments:

> "He was never mugged.
> It was Irene Davis's brothers,
> the Cristianos. They had him beat up."

> He knew about gangsters. They would beat up a guy
> to warn him. The next time it was curtains.

Helen Knox leads a delegation that calls on the chief of staff at the hospital to demand McNeil's dismissal. Dr. Abrahams replies that "McNeil's private life / . . . / had nothing to do with his work"; "they were fortunate / to have a surgeon of Hugh McNeil's caliber." Helen Knox sums up the feelings of the entire Garden Club:

> "What can you expect?" . . .
> "It was bad enough letting them in,
> but to make one chief of staff!"

Eventually, McNeil is divorced and moves into the cottage now occupied by the speaker; he breaks up with Irene, begins seeing her again, breaks up again. Finally he comes back to pick up his things, "accompanied by a young woman / wearing jeans and a sweater":

> It appeared he was back on the track
> once more, after his derailment.
> With a woman of the right kind at his side
> to give him a nudge. "Say thanks!"

It is at this point in the poem that the story of the speaker's own conflict with the society of Point Mercy comes to the fore. He is eating lunch with his friend Maggie at the Colony Inn when he sees Irene Davis for the first time:

> They said she was dark. What they hadn't said
> was that the darkness, jet-black hair,
> was set off by a skin like snow,
> like moonlight in a dark field glimmering.

In the final section of the poem, a minor incident causes an argument between the speaker and Maggie. A gazebo has been vandalized, and Maggie defends the youth of Point Mercy: "I'm sure . . . it wasn't anyone / from around here." The speaker replies that "You don't have to go into New York City" to find "vandals," "thieves," and "illiterates." His attack on the community convinces Maggie that the speaker is "cynical," a disease that infects his whole "attitude":

> "Like what you said in the restaurant
> about Hugh McNeil and the Davis woman
> being better than the rest of us."

Then she becomes "really angry":

> "I know, you prefer vulgar people.
> Anyone who tries to be decent and respectable
> is either a hypocrite or a fool."

Certainly the speaker does hate hypocrisy, but the real basis for this disagreement is his admiration for people who are true to their emotions, whatever the cost in social respectability or status. This is the same attitude that made the speaker of "Summer Morning" "spoil his chances," for "The thrill of an assignation, / My life that I hold in secret." In the eyes of society, conformity is more important than self-fulfillment, complimentary fictions more comfortable than the truth about themselves. Thus, despite the affection that he has learned to feel for individuals, the Simpson protagonist still can never have more than an uneasy alliance with American society at large. His sensibility is that of the young poet "Peter," as defined in the poem of that title originally published in *Caviare at the Funeral:*

> Stupidity reassures you; you do not belong
> in a bourgeois establishment, it can never be your home.
> Restlessness is a sign of intelligence;
> revulsion, the flight of a soul.

> (*PLH,* 169)

At the end of *The Best Hour of the Night,* Simpson has placed an ars poetica devoted to the plight of the poet who chooses to

live and work in suburbia. Entitled "The Unwritten Poem"
(*BHN*, 69), it begins by asking where poetry is to be found;
"Not in beautiful faces and distant scenery," he answers, but:

> In your life here, on this street
> where the houses from the outside
> are all alike, and so are the people.
> Inside, the furniture is dreadful—
> floc on the walls, and huge color television.

However much he may dislike the details of this way of life, its
tastelessness, the absence of emotion, the poet still must also
love the people he writes about; as Pound said fifty years ago,
unless poetry is based upon affectionate feelings, it will inevita-
bly corrode and die from the inside out. Simpson knows, how-
ever, that his feelings will never be reciprocated by the commu-
nity: "To love and write unrequited / is the poet's fate." The
poem ends with a vision of the soullessness of American life, as
the poet watches the morning commuters, "grasping brief-
cases," as they "pass beyond your gaze / and hurl themselves
into the flames." They are like the dead souls of Eliot's "Waste
Land," seen crossing London Bridge every morning. It is, then,
finally the soullessness of American life that places the individual
in Simpson's poems at odds with this society.

The fugitive-agrarian poets—John Crowe Ransom, Robert
Penn Warren, Allen Tate—used to say that, because the South
lost the Civil War, southerners were more in touch with the
humble realities of life, with its tragic potentialities, than north-
erners. It is when he looks at American life as a whole that
Simpson finds the emptiness that the earlier poets found in the
North. Americans have been too successful, too insulated from
want and deprivation.

"The Inner Part," for example—a one-sentence poem first
published in *At the End of the Open Road*—makes this point in a
striking fashion:

> When they had won the war
> And for the first time in history
> Americans were the most important people—

When the leading citizens no longer lived in their shirt sleeves,
And their wives did not scratch in public;
Just when they'd stopped saying "Gosh!"—

When their daughters seemed as sensitive
As the tip of a fly rod,
And their sons were as smooth as a V-8 engine—

Priests, examining the entrails of birds,
Found the heart misplaced, and seeds
As black as death, emitting a strange odor.

(*PLH*, 72)

It is because of this moral emptiness, this lack of tragic experience, this absence of failure, in America that Simpson turned for the subject matter of many of his poems to Russia, home of his and his mother's ancestors. There he found a people who had suffered, a people who knew the full range of indignities life has to offer those who haven't won every battle.

The poem "Why Do You Write About Russia?" (*PLH*, 137–40) draws essentially this contrast between the two nations. It begins with the speaker sitting in his suburban American home, remembering how his mother used to tell him, a child in Jamaica, stories about the old country, "of freezing cold," wolves, and Cossacks. The poem is meditative; as he looks out of his window, the speaker contrasts the dreamlike stories he remembers with the life that now surrounds him:

> This too is like a dream, the way we live
> with our cars and power-mowers . . .
> a life that shuns emotion
> and the violence that goes with it,
> the object being to live quietly
> and bring up children to be happy.

Because it exists in the absence of all other emotions, the speaker feels that such happiness can only be a delusion; this is a crazy way to bring up children. Thus dissatisfied with the life that surrounds him, he asks himself, "What then do I want?":

        A life in which there are depths
        beyond happiness. As one of my friends,
        Grigoryev, says, "Two things
        constantly cry out in creation,
        the sea and man's soul."

Grigoryev is an imaginary friend, whom the speaker has created
to tell him stories about the old country, identified later as "the
same far place the soul comes from."
    The poem ends with an indirect definition of Russia that indi-
cates what the speaker feels he has inherited from his ancestry:

        When I think about Russia
        it's not that area of the earth's surface
        . . . .
        It's a sound, such as you hear
        in a sea breaking along a shore.

        My people came from Russia,
        bringing with them nothing
        but that sound.

It is that crying out, that longing, that loneliness, that hunger of
the unfulfilled soul, that defines the sensibility of the poet and
makes poetry what it is.
    When pushed to an ultimate extreme, such an intense lone-
liness of the soul reflects a religious or a spiritual longing, and in
the poems of Louis Simpson there is indeed posited a rela-
tionship between the poetic sensibility and the religious sen-
sibility. "Baruch" (*PLH,* 134–36) is one of his best and most
characteristic poems; through the stories of two other charac-
ters, Russian ancestors of the nineteenth century, it leads up to a
central revelation about its speaker, the Simpson character we
have been following throughout this essay. The first section of
the poem deals with the title character:

        There is an old folk saying:
        "He wishes to study the Torah
        but he has a wife and family."

> Baruch had a sincere love of learning
> but he owned a dress-hat factory.

When the factory burns down one night, Baruch takes this as a sign from God to "give myself to the Word." He has only begun his studies, however, when death takes him: "For in Israel it is also written, / 'Prophecy is too great a thing for Baruch.'"

The second section tells of

> . . . Cousin Deborah
> who, they said, had read everything . . .
> The question was, which would she marry,
> Tolstoy or Lermontov or Pushkin?

Her family makes the choice and marries her off to a timber merchant from Kiev; when they are locked in the bedroom after the ceremony, she cries and screams all night long:

> As soon as it was daylight, Brodsky—
> that was his name—drove back to Kiev
> like a man pursued. . . .

The third section is reflective and personal; the Simpson protagonist is traveling late at night:

> The love of literature goes with us.
>
> On a train approaching midnight
> everyone else has climbed into his sarcophagus
> except four men playing cards.
> There is nothing better than poker—
> not for the stakes but the companionship,
> trying to outsmart one another.
> Taking just one card . . .
>
> I am sitting next to the window,
> looking at the lights on the prairie
> clicking by. From time to time

two or three will come together
then go wandering off again.

Then I see a face, pale and unearthly,
that is flitting along with the train,
passing over the fields and rooftops,
and I hear a voice out of the past:
"He wishes to study the Torah."

All three characters feel the tension that exists between the world of physical reality and the world of the spirit or the imagination. Though he at first thinks otherwise, Baruch belongs in the shadowless world of everyday reality. Cousin Deborah suffers from no such delusion; she exists entirely at the opposite pole. It is left for the Simpson protagonist to live in both worlds at once, to love the physical and to venerate something spiritual at one and the same time.

Louis Simpson is by no means an overtly religious poet; and yet among the poems in the third phase of his career, the phase that locates the poet so firmly in the American suburbs, are several that quest for something spiritual: "I feel that I have two directions I must follow—one leads to this straightforward kind of poem about ordinary life as it really looks and smells, and the other leads to a poetry which is altogether more imagistic and more mysterious" ("Interview with Louis Simpson").[23] Insofar as this thinking is based upon traditional religious ideas, it grows out of Simpson's studies of Zen Buddhism, about which he has said:

Buddhism teaches that your physical existence and your mental existence are one thing; in the West, we tend automatically to split them apart, as in the Christian idea of the body and the soul. I prefer the medieval idea—they had a term for the body which recognized it as the form for the soul, which I take to mean that the body is the outward garment of the soul. Whitman says that too, that there is no split between the body and the soul. And this is what the Buddhists say also. This way of thinking leads to a poetry that is very physical in its orientation, a poetry that concentrates on ordinary life. ("Interview with Louis Simpson")[24]

Simpson's most ambitious poem of a more "mysterious" sort—based very loosely on the ox-herding cartoon series by the Zen master—is "Searching for the Ox" (*PLH*, 183–87). The poem consists of a "free-floating series of associations," all of which help express one idea. Section 2 speaks of those who wish to manipulate the world through an abstract understanding of it—"engineers from IBM," for example. Their success at sending a rocket toward the moon is very impressive, the speaker says, but

> . . . still, I must confess,
> I fear those *messieurs,* like a peasant
> listening to the priests talk Latin.
> They will send me off to Heaven
> when all I want is to live in the world.

Similarly, when he learns the practice of Zen meditation in section 5 and tries to follow "in the Way / that 'regards sensory experience as relatively unimportant,'" the speaker finds instead that "I am far more aware / of the present, sensory life." The poem ends with a central understanding that sends the Simpson protagonist back to where he started:

> There is only earth:
> in winter laden with snow,
> in summer covered with leaves.

Simpson can, at times, sound almost like a mystic when discussing this aspect of his work; the poem "Adam Yankev," for example, asserts: "Around us / things want to be understood" (*PLH*, 124)—and in the afterword to *People Live Here,* he says: "I have always felt that there is a power and intelligence in things. I felt it as a boy when I watched the sun setting from the top of a mountain and rode a bicycle in the lanes on Kingston and walked along the shore, listening to the sea. I felt that power when I first saw Manhattan rise out of the Atlantic, the towers a poet describes as 'moody water-loving giants.'"[25]

However, just as he is probably the most consciously American of the poets treated in this book, Simpson is also the most pragmatic of them. Simpson's orientation, even at its most religious, is not otherworldly; for him, the ultimate meaning of the world, of the earth, is to be found in "the things of this world" themselves and not in abstract ideas about them. In the poem "The Foggy Lane" (*PLH*, 182), Simpson's speaker encounters in succession three abstractionists: the first extols poets who deal only in a world of dreams; the second is a radical who wants "to live in a pure world"; the third is a salesman who thinks an insurance policy can protect one from harm. In the final stanza, the speaker replies to them all:

> Walking in the foggy lane
> I try to keep my attention fixed
> on the uneven, muddy surface . . .
> the pools made by the rain,
> and wheel-ruts, and wet leaves,
> and the rustling of small animals.

What we see here is not just a theory of poetry but a philosophy of how the world should be understood and dealt with; it is real, it is uncertain, it is beautiful, and it deserves our complete attention.

NOTES

1. The theme of the individual's sense of alienation from society has been noticed by other of Simpson's critics. C. B. Cox, for example, writes: "Always something of an alien, his criticisms reflect personal dissatisfaction because he can never completely associate his own cosmopolitan literary inheritance with the brash and expansive landscapes of America. For him, the real search is not for new lands, but for one's true identity and the meaning of one's death" ("The Poetry of Louis Simpson," *Critical Quarterly* 8 [1966]: 77 [included in this collection]). Karl Malkoff has expressed much the same notion using slightly different terms: "Simpson has reconstructed the romantic myth of the conflict between innocence and experience, between the infinite possibilities of childhood and the narrow confines of adulthood, between romantic optimism and existential despair" (*Crowell's Handbook of Contemporary American Poetry* [New York: Thomas Y. Crowell, 1973], 297).

2. Louis Simpson, *North of Jamaica* (New York: Harper and Row, 1972), 199.

3. Simpson, "As Birds Are Fitted to the Boughs," in *People Live Here: Selected Poems, 1949–1983* (Brockport, N.Y.: BOA Editions, 1983), 14. Subsequent quotations from this volume will be documented parenthetically within the text, using the abbreviation *PLH*. The other abbreviation that will be used is *BHN*, for Simpson's *The Best Hour of the Night* (New Haven and New York: Ticknor and Fields, 1983).

4. Many critics have commented on the change in Simpson's style. In fact, as early as 1958, before the change had occurred, Robert Bly was already calling for it: "the specter appears of a war between content and form, with the form acting so as to render the content innocuous, or as a sort of protective camouflage to conceal exactly how revolutionary the content is. . . . he should avoid his fault, which is a tendency in form to do what has already been done. He should search for a form as fresh as his content" ("The Work of Louis Simpson," *Fifties*, no. 1 [1958]: 25 [included in this collection]). As for the change itself, Ronald Moran (in the only full-length critical study yet devoted to Simpson's work) ascribed it to Simpson's 1959 "move to California [that] marked the beginning of a significant stylistic change in which the conventions gave way to the freedom inherent in colloquial expression and in meterless lines" (*Louis Simpson* [New York: Twayne, 1972], 59). While William H. Roberson has taken note of the connection between the change in style and an increase in personal subject matter—"The increased flexibility of the poetry also marked a movement away from the impersonal toward a more personal quality" (*Louis Simpson: A Reference Guide* [Boston: G. K. Hall, 1980], x)—Richard Howard has explained the connection more fully: "*At the End of the Open Road* appeared to jettison all the scrimshaw-work which had been such a typical and such a reassuring aspect of Simpson's verse. . . . The poet [came to rely] more on *personality*, his own awareness of his voice . . . as a mortar to hold his lines together, dispensing him from certain evidences, certain cartilages in his text" (*Alone with America: Essays on the Art of Poetry in the United States since 1950* [New York: Atheneum, 1969], 465–66 [included in this collection]). The new style itself has been accurately characterized by Duane Locke: "In *Open Road*, the style loosens, the lines become uneven, and the movement of the natural voice and phrasal breaks replaces preconceived measurement. The imagery tends toward inwardness, and the result is a more phenomenal poetry, one in which the subjective imagination transforms by its own operations the objective into what constitutes genuine reality" ("New Directions in Poetry," *dust* 1 [1964]: 68–69 [included in this collection]).

5. Simpson, "Capturing the World as It Is: An Interview with Wayne Dodd and Stanley Plumly," in his *A Company of Poets* (Ann Arbor: University of Michigan Press, 1981), 225.

6. Simpson, *A Revolution in Taste: Studies of Dylan Thomas, Allen Ginsberg, Sylvia Plath, and Robert Lowell* (New York: Macmillan, 1978), 169–70. That the created Simpson protagonist has an inevitably subjective basis is made clear by Yohma Gray, who wrote in 1963 that Simpson's "point of view is more subjective than objective; the reader is aware of the intrusion of the poet's private, inner life in the poems rather than the insertion of an invented character from whom the poet is detached. He does not demonstrate what Keats called 'negative capability,' or what has been more recently called aesthetic distance. Although he sometimes writes in the third person, the reader senses a subjective 'I' in the poem" ("The Poetry of Louis Simpson," in *Poets in Progress,* ed. Edward Hungerford [Evanston: Northwestern University Press, 1967], 229 [included in this collection]).

7. Several critics have noticed Simpson's preoccupation with an American subject matter. Writing in 1965, James Dickey commented: "His *Selected Poems* shows Louis Simpson working, at first tentatively and then with increasing conviction, toward his own version of a national, an American poetry. . . . He demonstrates that the best service an American poet can do his country is to see it all: not just the promise, not just the loss and the 'betrayal of the American ideal,' the Whitmanian ideal—although nobody sees this last more penetratingly than Simpson does—but the whole 'complex fate,' the difficult and agonizing *meaning* of being an American, of living as an American at the time in which one chances to live" (*From Babel to Byzantium: Poets and Poetry Now* [New York: Farrar, Straus and Giroux, 1968], 195–96 [included in this collection]).

8. Simpson, "Walt Whitman at Bear Mountain," in *A Company of Poets,* 34.

9. James Wright, "The Delicacy of Walt Whitman," in *Collected Prose* (Ann Arbor: University of Michigan Press, 1983), 19.

10. Simpson, "Rolling Up," in *A Company of Poets,* 314.

11. Another opinion on this poem (one with which I obviously disagree) is expressed by Ronald Moran: "The last line, 'My life that I hold in secret,' is actually a lament for the speaker's inability to feel—for his inability now to become involved with any degree of commitment with a woman" (*Louis Simpson,* 104). This interpretation is repeated almost verbatim in a book that Moran later wrote with George S. Lensing: "'Summer Morning' . . . ends with the line, 'My life that I hold in secret.' This is the speaker's lament for his own inability to feel

any degree of commitment with a woman now" (*Four Poets and the Emotive Imagination: Robert Bly, James Wright, Louis Simpson, and William Stafford* [Baton Rouge: Louisiana State University Press, 1976], 157).

12. Simpson, "Dogface Poetics," in *A Company of Poets*, 17.

13. It is interesting that Robert Bly should have pointed out, as early as 1958, this same quality in Simpson's early poems: "The poet's strength is great love of humanity . . ." ("The Work of Louis Simpson," 25). Early reviewers were more likely to see Simpson as misanthropic than humane.

14. Speaking specifically of the poems in *Searching for the Ox* (1976), Dave Smith noted that Simpson "has come to a certain unfashionable narrative base, to a poetry that unabashedly employs the devices of prose fiction" ("A Child of the World," *American Poetry Review* 8, no. 1 [1979]: 11 [included in this collection]).

15. Simpson, "Rolling Up," 316.

16. Simpson, *Three on the Tower: The Lives and Works of Ezra Pound, T. S. Eliot, and William Carlos Williams* (New York: William Morrow, 1975), 35.

17. Simpson, "Lowell's Indissoluble Bride," in *A Company of Poets*, 199.

18. Simpson, "To the Jewish Book Council" (unpublished address, May 3, 1981), ms. p. 3.

19. Simpson, "Rolling Up," 316.

20. On the role of personality in Simpson's poems, Dave Smith has commented: "Like Whitman, he contains many selves who go adventuring within the letter I" ("A Child of the World," 12).

21. Indeed, a common reaction to much of Simpson's poetry has been that it is satirical. Certainly there is a bitter edge to many of the anti-America poems of phase 2; however, as Robert Bly pointed out in the passage quoted above, in general it is Simpson's humanistic impulse that is dominant. Thus, when Karl Malkoff writes, of "Hot Night on Water Street," that "It is a satire of small-town America" (*Crowell's Handbook*, 295), it seems to me that he is wrong. The poem instead intends to present the feelings of loneliness experienced by its speaker.

22. Nikki Stiller, "Shopping for Identity: Louis Simpson's Poetry," *Midstream*, December 1976, 66.

23. Writing in 1966, C. B. Cox was already able to see Simpson moving toward mystery: "In his most recent work his rhythms have become more free, less tied to iambic norms, and he makes increasing use of mysterious imagery whose total effect is beyond rational appraisal" ("The Poetry of Louis Simpson," 83).

24. The best critical discussion of the spiritual dimension in Simpson's recent work is that by Dave Smith in *American Poetry Review*,

where he suggests: "Simpson would, doubtless, argue that there is no division between inner and outer life except for those who have gone 'astray' and . . . that what poetry must do is find a direct and clear way of making this life, its Oneness, as fully visible as it was in whatever tropics we came from" ("A Child of the World," 14).

25. Simpson, "The Sound of Words for Their Own Sake—an Afterword," in *People Live Here,* 203.

MICHAEL MILBURN

Louis Simpson, Poet

While Cheever and Updike, Carver and Beattie were claiming
portions of the American vernacular landscape in fiction, a qui-
eter but no less artistic appropriation was being undertaken in
the world of poetry. Its genius was Louis Simpson, whose po-
etic voice has achieved the kind of perfect pitch which is the
result of both talent and years of hard labor with words. Simp-
son seems to shed all signs of trial and struggle as he writes. Like
the most intimate conversations, his poems are casual structures
of sound and feeling, born in the throat and surviving in the ear.
We are less able to say why they mean so much than that they do
and are impossible to improve. Simpson has always told the
stories of our lives, but in his recent poems he has mastered a
way of speaking indistinguishable from our own. It's fruitless to
imitate him, and any explanations for his embodiment of the
elusive dream/nightmare of suburbia must defer in the end to
the magic of his style and voice. Simpson's characters can go
through the motions—taking out the garbage, having affairs,
riding the commuter rails—with the best of our recent prose
heroes, but these poems are the songs playing inside their heads,
as quiet and humble and unbearable as their lives.

Erato 1 (Summer 1986): 1–2.

Index

"Adam Yankev," 89

Adventures of the Letter I, 7–8; review by Terry Eagleton, 87–88; review by Ian Hamilton, 83–84; review by Grevel Lindop, 85–86; review by Dave Smith, 89–90

"Advice to the English" (essay), 156

"Aegean," 218

"After Midnight," 81, 325–26

"Against the Age," 226

Air With Armed Men, 8, 131. See also *North of Jamaica*

"Alain Alain," 248

Alienation, 167, 168, 351, 361; in "In California," 189–90; in "The Cradle Trap," 352–53; and Surrealism, 325

America: concern with, 233–35, 242–44, 356; poems about, 199, 252; theme in *Five American Poets*, 72; theme in *Selected Poems*, 73–74. *See also* individual poems and books

"American Classic," 144, 160, 169, 314–15, 329

American dream, 59–60, 236

"American Dreams," 358–59

American identity: meaning for Simpson, 75–76; struggle toward, 308–9; theme in *Adventures of the Letter I*, 83

"American in the Thieves' Market, An," 48

American life in *Caviare at the Funeral*, 142

"American Peasant, An," 86

"American Poetry," 55, 60, 78, 80; applied to Simpson's poems, 143, 145; most famous deep image poem, 324

American poets, attempts to define, 75

"American Preludes," 81, 219

Angel in the gate, explanation of, 239

Antiself, 309

Anti-Semitism in Pound, Eliot, and Williams, 107, 115

Apollinaire, Guillaume, 105

"Apollinaire! The Perfect Romantic" (essay), 307

"Armidale," 153–54, 345

"Arm in Arm," 177–78, 248

Arrivistes, The, 2, 5; review by Randall Jarrell, 27; review by Gerard Previn Meyer, 25–26

Arrowsmith, William, reviewing *Good News of Death and Other Poems*, 31–33

"As Birds Are Fitted to the Boughs," 33, 73, 348–49

"Ash and the Oak, The," 248

At the End of the Open Road, 5; attempts to define America, 55–56, 66; concern with America, 57–58, 61; review by Thom Gunn, 54–56; review by Duane Locke, 63–65; review by Thomas McGrath, 57–60; review by Ronald Moran, 66–67; review by William Stafford, 61–62

Auden, W. H., influence on American poetry, 125–26

Audience, description of, 260

Australia, 153–54

Autobiography of Simpson. *See* Simpson, Louis

"Back in the States," 169

"Ballad of the Beery Boys," 185

"Baruch," 118, 254–55, 379–81

"Basic Blues," 144

"Battle, The," 40, 175

"Beaded Pear, The," 139, 142, 145, 148–50, 151; comments by Simpson, 372

Berchtesgaden, 94, 163

Best Hour of the Night, The, 13–14; review by Richard Tillinghast, 158–61; review by Alan Williamson, 162–65; source and meaning of title, 315–16

"Big Dream, Little Dream," 272

"Birch," 54, 183, 198

"Bird, The," 43, 47, 195, 246, 251

Bloom, Harold, 19, 282–83, 291, 293, 294, 300

Bly, Robert, 17–18, 258–59, 261

"Boarder, The," 198, 132, 233; imagery in, 183–84

Boatwright, James, reviewing *North of Jamaica,* 97–100

Bogan, Louise, reviewing *The New Poets of England and America,* 36–38

"Bower of Roses, A," 144–45, 151

Breslin, Paul, reviewing *Caviare at the Funeral,* 137–40

Buddhism, Simpson's comments on, 381; Zen, in "Searching for the Ox," 267, 269–74

California, 58–59, 235

"Carentan O Carentan," 39, 70–71, 80–81, 194; criticized, 338; lack of personal voice in, 349–50; praised, 166, 247–48

"Caviare at the Funeral," 142, 144

Caviare at the Funeral, 12–13; review by Paul Breslin, 137–40; review by Douglas Dunn, 143–46; review by Peter Makuck, 147–55; review by G. E. Murray, 141–42

"Champion Single Sculls, The," 298–99

Character of the Poet, The, 14; review by Richard Silberg, 170

Characters in poems, 365

Chekhov, Anton, 90, 124, 295, 298, 351

"Chimneys," 267

"Chocolates," 142, 144

Ciardi, John, reviewing *Good News of Death and Other Poems,* 30

"Cliff Road," 267

"Climate of Paradise, The," 90

Colonial life in *North of Jamaica,* 103

Common life, 22

Company of Poets, A, 13, 306; review by William Scammell, 156–57

Confessional poetry, 330, 351–52

"Confessions of an American Poet" (essay), 196–97

Connolly, Cyril, reviewing *North of Jamaica,* 91–93

Conrad, Joseph, 263

Content and form. *See* Form and content

Content of poems, general, 178. *See also* Themes

"Côte d'Azur," 43, 64

Cox, C. B., 16; reviewing *Searching for the Ox,* 124

"Cradle Trap, The," 65, 352–53

"Custom of the World, The," 43, 45

"Daled, The," 274

Davison, Peter, reviewing *A Dream of Governors,* 45–46

"Dead Horses and Live Issues" (essay), 306

Deep image, 64, 70, 71, 195–96, 323. *See also* Bly, Robert; Phenomenalism

Dembo, L. S., reviewing *Three on the Tower,* 110–11

Deutsch, Babette, 2

Dialectic, literary, 178

Dickey, James, 258–59; reviewing *Selected Poems,* 75–76

Diction. *See* Language

"Dinner at the Sea-View Inn," 263–64

"Discovery of America, A" (Section 3, *People Live Here*), 164, 344

"Dogface Poetics" (essay), 337, 361–62

"Donkey Named Hannibal, A," 256–57

"Doubting," 86, 90

Dramatic narrative, 312. *See also* Narrative poetry

Dramatic verse, 33

"Dream in the Woods of Virginia, A," 55

Dream of Governors, A, 4; review by Peter Davison, 45–46; review by Thom Gunn, 39–41; review by Anthony Hecht, 42–44; review by Daniel Hoffman, 47–49

Duncan, Robert, 157

Dunn, Douglas, reviewing *Caviare at the Funeral,* 143–46

Eagleton, Terry, reviewing *Adventures of the Letter I,* 87–88

"Early in the Morning," 190–91, 217

"Ed," 319

"Elegy for Jake," 318

"Eleventh Commandment, The," 160

Eliot, T. S., 106, 107–9, 110–11, 113–15

Elitism in Pound, Eliot, and Williams, 108

Emotive imagination, 120

Empathy, 362

"Encounter on the 7:07," 369–72

Engle, Paul, reviewing *The New Poets of England and America,* 34–35

Experience of the poem, 133

"Fighting in Europe, The" (Section 2, *People Live Here*), 343–44

Five American Poets: review by Martin Seymour-Smith, 68; review in the *Times Literary Supplement,* 69–72

"Flight to Cytherea, The," 47, 68

Flint, R. W., 19

"Foggy Lane, The," 87, 383

Folsom, Ed, 277

Form: flexibility of, 62; loosening of, 65, 70, 71–72; traditional, classification of poems, 174; traditional, in *The New Poets of England and America,* 36–37; traditional, used in new ways, 195

Form and content: conflict of, 246–47, 249, 251, 253; harmony of, 31–33

Free verse, 54

"Friend of the Family, A," 85, 90, 278, 312

"Frogs," 182–83

Frontiers, 66

Front line in poetry wars and life, 336

Frost, Robert, 36, 132, 133

Gasset. *See* Ortega y Gasset

Ginsberg, Allen, 126, 128, 135, 156; parody of, 92; and William Carlos Williams, 133

"Good News of Death," 200, 216–17, 248–49

Good News of Death and Other Poems, 2; complexity of, 33; other poets in volume, 3; review by William Arrowsmith, 31–33; review by John Ciardi, 30

"Goodnight, The," 45–46, 226

Gray, Yohma, 15–16

"Green Shepherd, The," 39, 43, 47, 63, 188, 222–23

Grigoryev, Apollon, 97–98, 99

Gunn, Thom, 234; reviewing *A Dream of Governors,* 39–41; reviewing *At the End of the Open Road,* 54–56

Hall, Donald, 3, 234–35, 258–59; reviewing *Selected Poems,* 73–74

Hallucination, 39–41, 193–94, 198, 249–50

Hamilton, Ian, reviewing *Adventures of the Letter I,* 83–84

Hardy, Thomas, 322–23

Heaney, Seamus, reviewing *Selected Poems,* 80–82

Hecht, Anthony, reviewing *A Dream of Governors,* 42–44

Hemingway, Ernest, 263

"Heroes, The," 187–88

Heroic couplets, 32

History, literary, 112, 195

Hoffman, Daniel, reviewing *A Dream of Governors*, 47–49
Hoffman, Theodore, 176
"Honoring Whitman" (essay), 276, 290, 291–92, 295, 296
"Hot Night on Water Street," 39, 64, 150, 180, 279
"Hour of Feeling, The," 169, 266
Howard, Richard, 16–17
Hummer, T. R., 20
Humor, 27, 142; in "Sway," 332–33
Hutchens, John K., reviewing *Riverside Drive*, 50–51

"Ice Cube Maker, The," 145
"I Dreamed That In a City Dark as Paris," 39, 40–41, 48–49, 187, 193
Imagery, 364–65; in *At the End of the Open Road*, 64–65; in "The Boarder," 183–84; in *Five American Poets*, 69, 70, 71, 72; in *Good News of Death*, 30
Imagination, 73, 74, 80
Imagism, 112–13, 114–15, 364–65
"In California," 58, 68, 159; attitude toward the American dream, 235, 236–37, 244; failure of the American dream, 189–90; pessimism, 280–81; technique, 71, 72
"Indian Country," 90, 169
Individualism in American literature, 347–48
Inner life, 64–65, 270–73
"Inner Part, The," 58, 67, 169, 181, 281–82, 377–78
"In the Suburbs," 67, 74, 317
Introduction to Poetry, An, 1–2, 14–15
"Invitation to a Quiet Life," 177, 184–85
Inwardness, 60. *See also* Inner life
Irony, 32, 33, 177
"Isidor," 85
"Islanders," 31, 32–33, 179, 221

James, Henry, 82
Jamaica, 120, 122
"Jamaica," 178–79
James Hogg: A Critical Study, 1

Jarrell, Randall, reviewing *The Arrivistes*, 27
Jewish consciousness, 103–4
Johnson, Samuel, 126, 136
"John the Baptist," 30, 55
Joyce, James, 97, 370–71

Kalstone, David, 127, 129–30
Kaplan, Justin, 284

Lacan, Jacques, 291
"Lady Sings, The," 176–77
"Laertes in Paris," 212
Landscape, 219
"Landscape with Barns," 233
Language: in *Adventures of the Letter I*, 84, 87, 88; like actual human speech, 261; plainness of, in "Quiet Desperation," 367; Simpson's approach to, 263; transparent, 14, 151, 170
"Laurel Tree, The," 73
Lawrence, D. H., 370–71
Lindop, Grevel, reviewing *Adventures of the Letter I*, 85–86
"Lines Written Near San Francisco," 66, 153, 169, 235, 287, 288; death and the true self, 191–92, 199, 200–201; meaning discussed, 237–38; structure and imagery, 242–44; transcending nationality, 55–56
Lingeman, Richard D., reviewing *Three on the Tower*, 106–9
"Little Colored Flags," 140, 159
Lives of the Poets, 126, 136
Locke, Duane, reviewing *At the End of the Open Road*, 63–65
Long Island, 120, 122
"Lorenzo," 265
Louis Simpson: A Reference Guide, 2
"Love, My Machine," 285
Love poems, 33, 45–46, 188–89
"Lover's Ghost, The," 48, 68
"Love, That Wears the Moonlight Out," 33
Lowell, Robert, 126, 129–30; and confessional poetry, 330; style in *Life Studies*, 136

"Luminous Night," 198
Lyric poetry, 80, 173, 174–75

McDowell, Robert, 13
McGrath, Thomas: reviewing *At the End of the Open Road,* 57–60
Makuck, Peter, reviewing *Caviare at the Funeral,* 147–55
"Man She Loved, The," 142, 143–44, 363
"Maria Roberts," 154, 169
"Marriage of Pocahontas, The," 55, 62, 67
Matthiessen, F. O., 280, 290
"Memories of a Lost War," 218, 248, 322
Metaphor, use of: in "Birch," 183; in "Frogs," 182–83; in "Jamaica," 178–79; in "Orpheus in the Underworld," 40
"Mexican Woman, The," 163, 362–63
Meyer, Gerard Previn, reviewing *The Arrivistes,* 25–26
"Middleaged Man, The," 257
Milburn, Michael, 21, 389
"Mississippi," 220, 233
"Modern Lives" (Section 4, *People Live Here*), 344
Moran, Ronald, 17, 287; reviewing *At the End of the Open Road,* 66–67
"Morning Light, The," 54
Mortality in "Quiet Desperation," 368
"Moving the Walls," 59, 67; quoted in full and discussed, 201–7
Murray, G. E., reviewing *Caviare at the Funeral,* 141–42
"Music in Venice," 180–81
"My Father in the Night Commanding No," 62, 68, 135, 158; restlessness in, 55; technique and tone, 196–98
Mysticism, 382

Narrative poetry, 45, 89, 122, 364; value of, 272–73

Narrator, 146. *See also* Persona; Voice
Nature, 154, 198
Nepo, Mark, reviewing *Three on the Tower,* 112–16
Neruda, Pablo, 325
"New Lots," 139, 140, 154
New Poets of England and America, The, 3; review by Louise Bogan, 36–38; review by Paul Engle, 34–35
"Night in Odessa, A," 85
North of Jamaica: prose, 102; review by James Boatwright, 97–100; review by Cyril Connolly, 91–93; review by Anthony Rudolf, 101–5; review by Webster Schott, 94–96

"Old Soldier," 39
"On Being a Poet in America" (essay), 286
"On the Eve," 90
"On the Lawn at the Villa," 65, 67, 284–85; morality in, 356–58
"On the Ledge," 162, 166
Ordinary life as poetic material, 366
Ordinary people as characters in poems, 365
"Orpheus in America," 278
"Orpheus in the Underworld," 39, 40, 199–200
Ortega y Gasset, 199
"Over at the Baroque Ryehouse," 185

"Pacific Ideas—A Letter to Walt Whitman," 67, 235, 239–42, 244
Pack, Robert, 3
Paulin, Tom, reviewing *A Revolution in Taste,* 131–36
"Peat-Bog Man, The," 354–55
People Live Here: Selected Poems 1949–1983, 13–14, 303–4; arrangement of the poems, 162, 311, 329–30, 335–36; structure discussed, 339–40, 342–45; review by M. L. Rosenthal, 166–69; review by Richard Tillinghast, 158–61; review by Alan Williamson, 162–65

Perception, heightening of, through the poems, 181–82, 186–87

Persona: Peter, 262–63; in *Searching for the Ox*, 117, 118. *See also* Voice

Phenomenalism, 5, 14, 64–65. *See also* Deep image

"Physical Universe," 165

Plath, Sylvia, 126, 129, 134–35

Plumly, Stanley, reviewing *Searching for the Ox*, 120–23

Poems: identification of three phases, 348, 350–51; phase one, 348–50; phase two, 350, 356, 358, 361; phase three, 350, 362, 365, 369, 381

Poet as artist, identity and responsibility of, 265–67

Poetics, 157, 158, 195–96; summary of Simpson's development, 321–33

Poetry: Simpson defining, 348; sources of, 132

"Port Jefferson," 268

Portrait of the Artist as a Young Man, A, 97

Pound, Ezra, 106–9, 110–11, 113–15

Pragmatism, 382–83

"Previous Tenant, The," 160–61, 316–17, 328–29, 373–76

Proust, Marcel, 50, 52–53

"Psyche of Riverside Drive, The," 264–65

"Quiet Desperation," 169, 366–68

Reader, 117, 305; engagement of, 61–62, 267

"'Recapitulations" (Section 7, *People Live Here*), 345

"Redwoods, The," 59, 81

"Reflections on Narrative Poetry" (essay), 297–98

"Resistance," 28

"Return, The," 218–19

Revolution in Taste, A, 11–12; review by Tom Paulin, 131–36; review by Paul Zweig, 125–30; Simpson's approach to literary biogra-

phy/criticism in, 126–27, 128, 134; title discussed, 125, 126

Rhetoric, 31–33. *See also* Language; Technique

Rhyme, 31–33, 138. *See also* Technique

Rhythm, 102, 121. *See also* Technique

"Riders Held Back, The," 55

Rimbaud, Arthur, 26

"River Running By, A," 145, 151, 152, 169

Riverside Drive, 4–5, 209, 363–64; review by John K. Hutchens, 50–51; review by Dick Wickenden, 52–53

Roberson, William, 2

"Rolling Up" (essay), 296, 321

"Room and Board," 176, 185

Rosenthal, M. L., 136, 258, 259; reviewing *People Live Here*, 166–69

"Rough Winds Do Shake," 45, 185, 195, 247, 322

Rudolf, Anthony, reviewing *North of Jamaica*, 101–5

"Runner, The," 39, 45, 48, 193, 249–51

Russia, 138–39, 351

"Sacred Objects," 86, 90, 290, 291, 360

"Sanctuaries, The," 257, 267–68

Satire, 313, 371–72

Scammell, William, reviewing *A Company of Poets*, 156–57

Schott, Webster, reviewing *North of Jamaica*, 94–96

"Searching for the Ox," 118–19, 122–23, 297, 382; and Zen Buddhism, 269–74

Searching for the Ox, 10–11; review by C. B. Cox, 124; review by Stanley Plumly, 120–23; review by Peter Stitt, 117–19

Selected Poems, 6–7; review by James Dickey, 75–76; review by Donald Hall, 73–74; review by Seamus

Heaney, 80–82; review by Karl Shapiro, 77–79

Sensibility, 369, 371, 377, 379; personal voice engaging the reader, 351–52, 354; wisdom, 163, 164

Seymour-Smith, Martin, reviewing *Five American Poets*, 68

Shapiro, Karl, reviewing *Selected Poems*, 77–79

"Shelling Machine, The," 273

Silberg, Richard, reviewing *The Character of the Poet*, 170

"Silent Generation, The," 47

"Silent Lover, The," 188–89

"Silent Piano, The," 354–55

Simpson, Aston (Father), 94

Simpson, Louis: autobiography in *Riverside Drive*, 52; biography of, 174; on becoming a poet, 102–3; colonial childhood, in *North of Jamaica*, 103; postwar breakdown, 98–99

Smith, Dave, 18; reviewing *Adventures of the Letter I*, 89–90

"Song," 33

"Songs and Lyrics" (Section 1, *People Live Here*), 343

"Son of the Romanovs, A," 85

Spirituality, 381

Stafford, William, 120, 234, 309, 313; reviewing *At the End of the Open Road*, 61–62

Stanza, formal, 30. *See also* Form; Technique

Statement poem, 67

"Stevenson Poster, The," 254, 256, 266

Stitt, Peter, 20–21, 334, 335, 339; reviewing *Searching for the Ox*, 117–19

"Story About Chicken Soup, A," 144, 163–64, 167, 184

Storytelling in free verse, 145, 161. *See also* Narrative poetry

Structure, nonlinear, in *People Live Here*, 339–40, 342–45

Style: in *Adventures of the Letter I*, 83;

change of, 60, 63–65, 350–51; in *Riverside Drive*, 52

Subjects, range of, 47–48, 251

Suburban life, 74, 160, 161, 164

"Summer Morning," 361

"Summer Storm," 45

Surrealism, 73, 164, 323–25

Suzuki, D. T., 269, 270

"Sway," 144, 162, 169, 332–33, 363, 364

Symbolism: of light and darkness in "The Cradle Trap," 352–53; in "The Silent Piano," 354–55; in "Working Late," 353–54

"Tales of Volhynia" (Section 5, *People Live Here*), 345

Technique, 83, 85, 86, 207, 326–28

Themes, 340–41, 343–45; boredom, 147, 148, 153; death, 64, 200; distraction, 150, 153; love, 50; restlessness, 147, 148, 152. *See also* America; World War II

"There Is," 323, 324

"Things," 73, 74, 207–8

Thomas, Dylan, 126, 127–28, 132–33

Three on the Tower, 9–10; biography serving literature, 113; review by L. S. Dembo, 110–11; review by Richard D. Lingeman, 106–9; review by Mark Nepo, 112–16; title explained, 110–11; tone, non-academic, 107

Tillinghast, Richard, reviewing *The Best Hour of the Night* and *People Live Here*, 158–61

"Tom Pringle," 39

Tone: compared to Randall Jarrell's, 76; in narrative poems of ordinary life, 372–73; in *North of Jamaica*, 97

"Tonight the Famous Psychiatrist," 196

Total poetry defined by Simpson, 260–61

"To the Western World," 70, 81, 233, 277

Tradition: in *Good News of Death,* 31,
33; in *A Dream of Governors,* 45
"Trasimeno," 354–55
Travel as journey motif, 237
"Tree Seat, The," 257
Trilling, Lionel, 101
"Troika, The," 65, 198
"True Weather for Women, The," 31
"Typhus," 142, 162
Tytell, John, 128–29

"Ulysses and the Sirens," 31, 218
Unconscious, 253–54, 255–57
"Unfinished Life," 151, 153, 155
"Unwritten Poem, The," 346, 376–
77

"Vagrants, The," 27, 28
"Vandergast and the Girl," 313–14,
326–28
Van Doren, Mark, 128, 221
"Venice in the Tropics," 121, 262–
63
Vietnam War, Simpson citing
Wordsworth in reference to, 358
Villon, François, 26
Voice: in *North of Jamaica,* 97–98;
personal, as an expression of char-
acter, 352; poetic, 159; range, 304–
5, 339–40, 342–43
Volhynia, 89

"Walt Whitman at Bear Mountain,"
59, 66, 81, 161, 162, 167–68; con-
fronting America through Whit-
man, 285–86, 287; cultivation of
the Self, 360; effect on Simpson's
style, 235; flexibility of tone, 73,
74; meaning discussed, 238–39;
technique discussed, 71–72; a
touchstone, 62; turning point in
Simpson's work, 279–80; and
Whitman as key to understanding
America and the self, 237, 244
War poems, 70–71, 163–64, 247–48;
in *A Dream of Governors,* 47, 48–

49; hallucination in, 193–94; mes-
sage in, 187. *See also* World War II
Waste Land, The, 108–9
"West," 233, 277–78
Whitman, Walt, 235–36, 237, 240–
42; sought in *Adventures of the Let-
ter I,* 90; as "blood brother," 82;
influence on American poets, 275–
76; and Simpson compared regard-
ing form and content, 246; "Song
of the Open Road," 288–90, 292–
94; theories of Harold Bloom on,
276–300
"Why Do You Write About Rus-
sia?," 142, 147, 330–31; loneliness
and the search for real feeling,
378–79
Wickenden, Dick, reviewing *River-
side Drive,* 52–53
Williams, William Carlos, 106–9,
110–11, 113; and Allen Ginsberg,
133; and anti-Semitism, 115–16
Williamson, Alan, reviewing *The
Best Hour of the Night* and *People
Live Here,* 162–65
Wojahn, David, 19–20
"Woman Too Well Remembered,
A," 310–11
Wordsworth, William, 124, 260,
261
"Working Late," 148, 168; use of
autobiography, 331–32; language
and technique, 137–38; poet's sen-
sibility, 353–54
Works, poetical, three major phases
of, 334–35, 348
World War II, 193–94; best poems
about, 42; clearly identified, 248;
in *North of Jamaica,* 92; in *Riverside
Drive,* 51. *See also* War poems
Wright, James, 120, 258–59, 260,
261, 356

Zen Buddhism. *See* Buddhism
Zweig, Paul, reviewing *A Revolution
in Taste,* 125–30

POETS ON POETRY   Donald Hall, General Editor

Poets on Poetry collects critical books by contemporary poets,
gathering together the articles, interviews, and book reviews
by which they have articulated the poetics of a new generation.

Goatfoot Milktongue Twinbird
Donald Hall

Walking Down the Stairs
Galway Kinnell

Writing the Australian Crawl
William Stafford

Trying to Explain
Donald Davie

To Make a Prairie
Maxine Kumin

Toward a New Poetry
Diane Wakoski

Talking All Morning
Robert Bly

Pot Shots at Poetry
Robert Francis

Open Between Us
David Ignatow

The Old Poetries and the New
Richard Kostelanetz

A Company of Poets
Louis Simpson

Don't Ask
Philip Levine

Living Off the Country
John Haines

Parti-Colored Blocks for a Quilt
Marge Piercy

The Weather for Poetry
Donald Hall

Collected Prose
James Wright

Old Snow Just Melting
Marvin Bell

Writing Like a Woman
Alicia Ostriker

A Ballet for the Ear
John Logan

Effluences from the Sacred Caves
Hayden Carruth

Collected Prose
Robert Hayden

Platonic Scripts
Donald Justice

A Local Habitation
John Frederick Nims

No Evil Star
Anne Sexton

The Uncertain Certainty
Charles Simic

You Must Revise Your Life
William Stafford

A Concert of Tenses
Tess Gallagher